BUDDHA AND CHRIST

STUDIES
IN THE HISTORY OF RELIGIONS

(*NUMEN* BOOKSERIES)

EDITED BY

H.G. KIPPENBERG • E.T. LAWSON

VOLUME LX

BUDDHA AND CHRIST

Nativity Stories and Indian Traditions

BY

ZACHARIAS P. THUNDY

E.J. BRILL
LEIDEN • NEW YORK • KÖLN
1993

The paper in this book meets the guidelines for permanence and durability of the
Committee on Production Guidelines for Book Longevity of the Council on Library
Resources.

ISSN 0169-8834
ISBN 90 04 09741 4

© *Copyright 1993 by E.J. Brill, Leiden, The Netherlands*

*All rights reserved. No part of this publication may be reproduced, translated, stored in
a retrieval system, or transmitted in any form or by any means, electronic,
mechanical, photocopying, recording or otherwise, without prior written
permission of the publisher.*

*Authorization to photocopy items for internal or personal
use is granted by E.J. Brill provided that
the appropriate fees are paid directly to Copyright
Clearance Center, 27 Congress Street, SALEM MA
01970, USA. Fees are subject to change.*

PRINTED IN THE NETHERLANDS

It [Europe's acquaintance with Sanskrit and the culture of India] has added a new period to our historical consciousness, and revived the recollections of our childhood, which seemed to have vanished forever....We all come from the East....Everybody ought to feel that he is going to his "old home" full of memories, if only he can read them.

—Max Müller, *India—What Can It Teach Us?*

The West is passing through a new Renaissance due to the sudden entry into its consciousness of a whole new world of ideas, shapes, and fancies. Even as its consciousness was enlarged in the period of the Renaissance by the revelation of the classical culture of Greece and Rome, there is a sudden growth of the spirit today effected by the new inheritance of Asia with which India is linked up. For the first time in the history of mankind, the consciousness of the unity of the world has dawned on us. Whether we like it or not, East and West have come together and can no more part.

—S. Radhakrishnan, *Eastern Religions and Western Thought*

All literature has always been a borrowing. It starts with Homer. What do you think Ariosto was doing, or Cervantes? I would say that this continual intertextuality is the principal characteristic of literature. The difference is that now the game has become intentional, has been discovered, whereas before it was covered over.

—Umberto Eco, From the *Newsweek* Interview, 1989

TABLE OF CONTENTS

Preface ix
Prolegomenon 1
Chapter One: Method 18
    A. Comparative Literature 18
    B. Deconstruction 20
    C. New Historicism 26
    D. Intertextuality 29
    E. Literary Relationship 44
Chapter Two: Historical and Literary Chronology 53
    A. History and Faith 53
        1. The Historical Buddha 53
        2. The Historical Christ 56
    B. Literary Chronology 58
        1. Buddhist 58
        2. Christian 65
Chapter Three: Buddhist and Christian Infancy Parallels 75
    A. Priority of the Mahayana Traditions 75
    B. Buddist and Christian Infancy Parallels 79
Chapter Four: Infancy Gospels and Other Sources 129
    A. Hebrew and Greek Sources 130
    B. Biographical Theory 151
Chapter Five: Indian Subtext and Context 156
    A. Orientalism 156
    B. Jesus Movements 161
        1. Ethnos 162
        2. Ethos 163
        3. Ethics 163
    C. Context: Confrontation and Self-Definition 164
Chapter Six: Gnosticism, The New Testament, and India 174
    A. Gnosticism 175
    B. Gnosticism and the Christian Scriptures 184
    C. Gnosticism and Indian Thought 190
Chapter Seven: India and the West in Antiquity 212
    A. India and the Old Testament 212
    B. India and the Greek World: Before Alexander 217
    C. India and the Greek World: After Alexander 223
        1. More Knowledge About India 226
        2. Bactria 227
        3. The Indian Gymnosophists 229

TABLE OF CONTENTS

        4. Buddhism in Central Asia 233
    D. Indians in the Greco-Roman World 237
        1. Indians in the West 242
        2. The Therapeutae 244
    E. Western Travellers in India 250
        1. Non-Christian Witnesses 250
        2. Christian Witnesses 252
    F. India's Debt to the Greeks 256
    G. Evidence of Fables 253
    H. Conclusion 264
Epilegomenon: Pre-Text and Pretext 268
Abbreviations 277
Bibliography 278
Index 291

PREFACE

Many years ago, when Darwin's theory of evolution was perceived as a threat to the biblical doctrine of creation, the gentle wife of an Anglican bishop told her husband: "My dear, I hope Darwin is wrong about evolution. Even if Darwin is right about evolution, let us pretend that we know nothing about it at all." Today most Christian theologians think that it is unwise to bury one's head ostrich-like in the sands of ignorance; they readily admit that there is no contradiction between creationism and evolutionism, between science and religion. They are right: evolution has not eroded the intrinsic value of the Christian teaching on creation, and science has not displaced religion. In spite of this kind of optimism, some Christian apologists vehemently object to the search of biblical sources in Oriental religions for fear that it would challenge the superiority and uniqueness of the Christian religion.

First of all, Christianity is in no way superior to other religions just as one language is not superior to another language. Secondly, Christianity itself is an Oriental religion in its origins, like Judaism, Zoroastrianism, Hinduism, Buddhism, and Islam. Thirdly, every religion has its own uniqueness and value for its followers even if outsiders brand that religion as superstitious or inferior. Just as each language is useful, beautiful and good for the users of that language, so also each religion is useful, beautiful, and good for the followers of that religion. A case in point is the Christian belief in the resurrection of Jesus: No Christian thinks it absurd to believe in the resurrection of Jesus even if others vilify this article of Christian faith as superstitious. Fourthly, there is no substance in the apprehension that the value of the Christian religion would erode; for instance, even if it were proven "historically" that Jesus Christ had never risen from the dead and that the idea of the resurrection is only a literary motif derived from Buddhist scriptures—in spite of St. Paul's assertion that if Christ had not risen from the dead the Christian's faith would be in vain—, most Christians would not give up their faith in Jesus and their Christian affiliations. Similarly, if the New Testament writers are proven to have written under Buddhist influence, the essential nature of the Christian religion will not change in the least. On the contrary, Christians' respect for other religious traditions will increase and Christians will be inspired to give up their superiority complex, to identify themselves more closely with Jesus who was "meek and humble of heart," and to work more closely with the members of other religions toward understanding and solving problems of local, national, and global dimensions. Men and women can contribute immensely to an intellectual dialogue of religions and eventually to international collaboration, as interfaith dialogue groups do at present.

Though as an academic I am interested in intellectual exercises and critical responses that are often designed to ruffle feathers and make waves in tea cups, I sincerely hope that this study will lead *ad superiora*, to better relations among religions by bringing East and West closer together.

In the final analysis, the study of the influence of Buddhism and Hinduism on Christianity will help us understand both religious traditions better. It is like saying that when we understand others we understand ourselves. Indeed, an unbiased attempt at understanding other religious traditions like Hinduism and Buddhism will lead to a more profound self-knowledge for Christians especially of the West.

I wish to thank Northern Michigan University, its former president Dr. James Appleberry, its former vice-president Dr. John F. Kuhn, former dean Donald Heikkinen, and the English Department head Dr. Leonard Heldreth for granting me a paid sabbatical leave during the preparation of the manuscript of this book. I did most of my writing while at the University of Notre Dame which granted me Visiting Fellow's privileges during the year 1988-89. I am grateful to the University of Notre Dame, its Provost Dr. Timothy O'Mara, and all my friends and colleagues both at Northern Michigan University and the University of Notre Dame for their camaraderie and fellowship. I also want to thank Michelle Williams of Manpower Agency of Marquette for preparing the final copy of the manuscript. Last but not least, I am always very appreciative of my wife Gina Marie and sons Zachary Joe and Antonio, who were very helpful and understanding during the period of the preparation of this book.

Marquette, Michigan　　　　　　　　　　　　　　　　　　Z. P. T.
September 1992

PROLEGOMENON

BUDDHA AND CHRIST

The phenomenon of Christian-Buddhist affinities has intrigued Westerners from the sixteenth century, the age of exploration and expansion. European missionaries who visited Asia were disturbed by the similarities they had discovered between Christianity and Buddhism. They found striking resemblances between the life-stories of Gautama Buddha and of Jesus Christ, between the teachings of these Masters, between the doctrines of Christianity and Buddhism, and between the practices of both. In the nineteenth century, with the advent of "Higher Criticism," Christian scholars began to study other religions scientifically and to speculate boldly on the genetic relationship among religious doctrines and practices. The thesis that Christianity might be influenced by other sources such as Greek and Indian, besides the Hebrew Bible, became academically respectable, though apologetically untenable. Today not only Christian scholars but also Christian fundamentalist preachers admit without much reticence that early Christianity was influenced by Hellenistic ideologies like neo-Platonism. But they are very reluctant to talk about, let alone admit, Christianity's indebtedness to Oriental religions like Hinduism and Buddhism.

The first break in this entrenched critical position came with the bold theory propounded by the German philosopher Arthur Schopenhauer (1788-1860). He argued with some passion that Jesus was influenced by Buddha. According to him, Jesus derived his teaching from Egyptian priests who were influenced by the Indians. After comparing the Christian Bible with the Buddhist Scriptures, he concluded that Jesus' ethical teachings and the Christian notion of incarnation are Indian in their origins. Schopenhauer writes:

> The New Testament...must be in some way traceable to an Indian source: its ethical system, its ascetic view of morality, its pessimism, and its Avatar, are all thoroughly Indian. It is its morality which places it in a position of such emphatic and essential antagonism to the Old Testament, so that the story of the Fall is the only possible point of connection between the two. For when the Indian doctrine was imported into the land of promise, two very different things had to be combined: on the one hand the consciousness of the corruption and misery of the world, its need of deliverance and salvation through an Avatar, together with a morality based on self-denial and repentance; on the other hand the Jewish doctrine of Monotheism, with its corollary of

that "all things are very good".... And the task succeeded as far as it could, as far, that is, as it was possible to combine two such heterogeneous and antagonistic creeds....The Christian faith [is]...sprung from the wisdom of India.[1]

Later scholars took up this challenge of Christian-Buddhist relationship seriously. The Sanskritist, Émile Burnouf, argued in favor of the influence of Vedic religion on the rise of Christianity. The Dutch scholar, Ernst de Bunsen, was another proponent of the position of Buddhist influence on the New Testament;[2] his thesis was that foreign Jews introduced into Israel and among the Essenes the concept of the Angel-Messiah from Buddhism. He made an elaborate attempt to trace almost every dogma of Christianity to a Buddhist source.

In 1882 Rudolf Seydel argued for Buddhist influence in the New Testament from the *Lalitavistara*, especially in the infancy gospels.[3] Seydel believed that he was able to establish a Buddhist literary source for the gospels from fifty-one parallels, for which he was praised by admirers and damned by detractors.

Unfortunately he tried to prove more than the evidence was capable of sustaining.

Another Dutch theologian, G.A.van den Bergh van Eysinga, took the side of Buddhist influence, like Seydel, but based his case only on six parallels, wherein the medium of influence was claimed to be oral, rather than written, for both the canonical and non-canonical gospels.[4] Otto Pfeiderer agreed that Luke's infancy gospel must have been influenced by the Buddhist legends since Buddhism was one of the religions synthesized into early Christianity.[5]

Arthur Lillie, while a civil servant in India, became fascinated by the Indian religions and wrote two books on the relationship between Buddhism and early Christianity;[6] Lillie was so convinced by the parallels of virginal conception by Mary and Maya, the annunciation by the angels, the star in the east, the tree that bends

---

[1] Arthur Schopenhauer, *The Essential Schopenhauer* (London, 1962), 24.
[2] Ernst de Bunsen, *The Angel-Messiah of Buddhists, Essenes, and Christians* (London, 1880).
[3] Rudolf Seydel, *Das Evangelium von Jesu in seinen Verhältnissen zu Buddha* (Leipzig, 1882).
[4] Van den Berg van Eysinga, *Indische Einflüsse auf evangelische Erzählungen* (Göttingen, 1909).
[55] Otto Pfeiderer, *Das Christusbild des urchristlichen Glaubens in religionsgeschichtlicher Beleuchtung* (Berlin, 1903).
[6] Arthur Lillie, *Buddhism in Christianity* (London, 1887) and *India in Primitive Christianity* (London, 1909).

down to aid the mother, and the old sage who predicts the child's future that he argued that early Christianity was heavily influenced by Buddhism.

In the first decade of this century, the American scholar Albert J. Edmunds published his two-volume work in comparative religion[7], in which he brought together a large number of parallels from Buddhist scriptures and the New Testament with the purpose of fostering mutual understanding between both religions, after repeatedly asserting that the loan problem was only incidental. He wrote:

> I believe myself that Buddhism and Christianity, whether historically connected or not, are two parts of one great spiritual movement—one cosmic upheaval of the human soul, which burst open a crater in India five hundred years before Christ and a second and greater one in Palestine at the Christian Advent. Whether the lava which the twain ejected ever met in early times or not is of little moment: it came from the same fount of fire. And now, over the whole planet, the two have assuredly met, and the shaping of the religion of the future lies largely in their hands.[8]

Edmunds' continued research gradually convinced him that the Buddhist-Christian parallels were more than coincidental. In later articles he made a case for the influence of Buddhism on Christianity in several parts of Luke's infancy narrative, in the story of the Good Thief, in the story of the temptation of Jesus and in John 7:38 and John 12: 34 (II:97). Edmunds suggested in a study: "My general attitude toward the Buddhist-Christian problem is this: Each religion is independent in the main, but the younger one arose in such a hotbed of eclecticism that it probably borrowed a few legends and ideas from the older, which was quite accessible to it."[9]

Ernst Windisch, who published the brilliant analytical work, *Mara und Buddha*,[10] first suggested the possibility of a remote influence, but later in the chapter on "Comparative Science" in his book on Buddha's birth[11], in spite of calling attention to similarities in the literary form of the earliest Buddhist and Christian tradition, changed his position somewhat: "We should not let the

---

[7] Albert J. Edmunds, *Buddhist and Christian Gospels Now First Compared from the Originals* (Philadelphia, 1902).
[8] Edmunds, II: 71-72.
[9] Cited by Richard Garbe, *India and Christendom* (La Salle, 1959), 19.
[10] ErnestWindisch, *Mara und Buddha* (Leipzig, 1895).
[11] Windisch, *Buddhas Geburt und die Lehre von der Seelenwanderung* (Leipzig, 1908).

parallels between Buddhism and Christianity escape us, but the word 'parallels' must be understood in its proper sense as lines that do not touch or intersect."[12]

In his earlier writings Richard Garbe refused to accept Buddhist influences on Christian Gospels purely on scholarly grounds. But in his major work, *Indien und das Christentum* (1914), which is available in the English translation *India and Christendom*, reversed his former position and admitted the strong possibility of Buddhist influence on several New Testament passages and apocryphal gospels. He writes:

> After years of deliberation, during which certain striking agreements in the new Testament and early Buddhist sources appeared to me less and less in the light of pure coincidence, and under the influence of criticisms of my position by A. J. Edmunds in the *Monist* which I gladly acknowledge, I have changed my conviction. I now believe a somewhat different conclusion is to be drawn from that dissimilarity in the position of the canonical and apocryphal books and I would like to formulate it as follows: Whereas a *direct* Buddhist influence is unmistakable in the apocryphal gospels, only an *indirect* reflection glimmers through the canonical writings, and then merely in a few stories that are of Buddhist origin but lost their specifically Buddhist character in passing from mouth to mouth outside the realm of Buddhist expansion and finally became assimilated to the Christian genius. Of course we cannot expect agreement in every particular, although many scholars make this a condition for the acceptance of an external connection between the narratives. It is also true...that we are considering different phases of Buddhism, an older phase for the canonical and a later one for the apocryphal gospels. In this view I approach more closely to the standpoint of Van den Bergh and Edmunds.[13]

Opponents were quick to point out that writers like Seydel and Lillie were unscholarly, unscientific, and unhistorical in their methodology since they paid little attention to dates, schools of thought, geography, and textual criticism. One critic, E. Washburn Hopkins, in his "Christ in India"[14], after thoroughly investigating the problem of parallels, finally concluded that Christianity rather influenced the Indian epics and Indian religions. A second scholar, the Catholic Louis de la Vallée-Poussin, a brilliant Sanskritist, rejected the position of Edmunds and denied any sort of

---

[12] See Garbe, 19.
[13] Garbe, 21-22.
[14] Washburn Hopkins, *India Old and New* (New York, 1901).

Buddhist influence on the canonical gospels[15] and in a later article even denied the obvious Indian influence on the apocryphal gospels, on the Catholic legends of saints, and also on Christian worship.[16] What is remarkable about de la Vallée-Poussin's position is that he gives a theological answer to a literary problem by stating that similarities between the Christian Bible and the Buddhist scriptures are the natural outcome of the divine preestablished harmony between revelation and reason, whose ultimate source is the same God. He writes:

> We do not, in fact, find anything Buddhist or Buddhist like in the old Christian tradition. The parallels of which Seydel, van Eysinga, or Edmunds have made so much—losing all self-control to the point of believing in actual translation of Buddhist Pali Texts in St. Luke—are interesting, but they do not betray the actual presence of any specifically Buddhist theme. With regard to the question of the influence of Christianity on Old India and Buddhism, I think that this is not probable. Chronology forbids the hypothesis of an influence on Early Buddhism (Hinayana). But the dogmatic relations between some aspects of Mahayana and Christianity are certainly worthy of remark, and show the "preestablished harmony" between Revelation and human needs; they can and, to my opinion, must be explained by independent evolutions.[17]

De La Vallé Poussin is not entirely wrong. Indeed, for many of the resemblances between religions, causes other than borrowing can be assigned. As S. Radhakrishnan points out,

> If religion is the natural outcome of the human mind, it would be strange if we did not find coincidences. The highest type of self-sacrifice exalted in both may be regarded as common to all lands and ages. The hopes and fears of men, their desires and aspirations, are the same on the banks of the Ganges as on the shores of the Lake of Galilee. If the same examples and modes of illustration are employed, it may be because they are both members of an agricultural society. Possibly some of the incidents, stories, and sayings were common tales of a widespread folklore. If both taught in parables, it is because it is the easiest form of teaching for simple men.[18]

However, as Radhakrishnan continues, "it is not easy to account for the illustration of two careers with the same legends and embel-

---

[15] "Le Buddhisme et les Evangiles canoniques," *Révue Biblique*, 15 (1906): 353-381.
[16] *RSPT*, 6 (1912): 595-97.
[17] "Buddhism," in E. C. Messenger, ed., *Studies in Comparative Religion* (London, n.d.), I: 29-30.
[18] *India and Western Religious Thought* (Oxford, 1940), 184-85.

lishments. They cannot be traced to natural evolution."[19] According to him, the real reason that Western scholars appeal to natural evolution to explain the similarities found between Christ and Buddha is that "those who are trained in European culture, find it irksome, if not distasteful, to admit the debt of Christian religion to non-Christian sources, especially Hindu and Buddhist."[20] And they are tempted, as Max Müller points out, "to suppose that that the Buddhist stories were borrowed from our Christian sources and not *vice versa*. But here the consciousness of the scholar comes in. Some of these stories are found in the Hinayana Buddhist canon and date, therefore, before the Christian era."[21]

What is very interesting and remarkable about all these scholarly discussions on the relationship between Christian and Buddhist Scriptures is that they came to an abrupt end during World War I. Since then there had been no concerted or serious attempts at scholarly dialogues except for a few unchallenged studies. In 1927 Dwight Goddard argued strongly for Budhhist influence on early Christianity on the basis of the Buddhist nature of Jesus' teaching and life style; the medium for this influence, according to him, was the Essene community. He writes: "Only Buddhism accounts for the early dominant characteristic of economic and ethical practices of loving self-control, kindness, and communism. If Christians should be proud of anything, they should be proud of their Essene origin."[22]

In the same year Edward J. Thomas published a historical study, in which he expressed his serious reservations about any direct influence of Buddhism on the gospels for lack of scholarly consensus, on account of inadequate evidence, and due to his misunderstood view of the canonical gospels as historical documents dating from the first century and recording events exactly as they had happened.[23] It is important to add that most Christian scholars of today do not share Thomas's view of the historicity of the gospels. They are willing to admit that the gospels were not completed and published in their present form at the earliest before the middle of the second century and that the gospels are not records of the *ipsis-*

---

[19] Radhakrishnan, 185.
[20] Ibid.
[21] *Last Essays*, 1 st series (London, 1901), 289.
[22] *Was Jesus Influenced by Buddhism? A Comparative Study of the Lives and Thoughts of Gautama and Jesus* (Thetford, Vt, 1927), 116.
[23] *Life of Buddha as Legend and History* (London, 1927).

sima verba et facta (the exact words and deeds) of Jesus. Thomas writes:

> The validity of these parallels in furnishing evidence for the incorporation of Buddhist legends in the Gospels has sometimes been judged merely by the amount of resemblance to be found between them, and the different conclusions drawn show how very subjective are the results. But there are two considerations that might lead to firmer ground. Firstly, whether there is enough reason to think that Buddhist legends can have reached Palestine in the first century A.D....The possibility of the transmission of legends cannot be denied, but the particular way in which it may have taken place has never been shown....The second point raises the question of Biblical criticism. The Gospel stories all belong to the first century A.D. They were all written down at a time when a living tradition and memory of the events may have existed. For one school this tradition did exist. The story of the Samaritan woman or the choosing of the disciples was told because there really was a Samaritan woman and disciples who had been fishermen. In this case we are dealing with historical events, so that any resemblances to the legend of Buddha are merely accidental curiosities.... If scholars could come to an agreement on what instances are 'cogent parallels' or cases of borrowing, we should then have the data of a problem for the historians to decide. But so far this hope is illusory.[24]

It is true that liberal Protestant scholars enjoyed and exercised greater freedom of thought and expression than Catholic writers in their discussions of the influence of Buddhism on Christianity. As a matter of fact, Catholic scholars were less daring and rather inhibited. They were afraid of censorship and persecution. So they tended to be circumspect and prudent by acting sceptical, vacillating, and ambiguous toward the issue of Buddhist influence on Christianity. A striking example of this phenomenon is the eminent Catholic historian and theologian Henri de Lubac, who was reprimanded, silenced, and censored by the Vatican. Fear of Vatican authorities led him to make the following overly cautious statement in his comparative study of the three bodies of Buddha and Origen's views on the docetic body of Jesus:

> In general, the problem of the Indian contribution to the formation of Neo-platonism remains an open issue; the existence of a Buddhist colony in greater Alexandria is not a fabricated story. At least it seems that the Alexandrians were less misinformed of Buddhist matters than the other inhabitants of the rest of the Empire. Some borrowings from Buddhism have often been suggested, not always without some likelihood, in many

---

[24] Thomas, 246-247.

Christian apocrypha, in the Jewish-Christian literature, and by the Gnostics, especially Basilides.[25]

After Vatican II, however, Catholic scholars became more open to the idea of studying Eastern influences on their religion, as the life and writings of Thomas Merton show. Yet, reticence and fear of offending the authorities at the Vatican seem to characterize Catholic thinking on the issue, and it is best exemplified in the words of J. Edgar Bruns who has published two books on the influence of Buddhism on the Gospel of John.[26] Though he has proposed earlier that John's Christology and theology are Buddhist (Mahayana) because the Buddhist maintains that the all-knowledge of the Buddha has come forth from the perfection of Wisdom, in the end he writes: "I am merely suggesting, once more, that some of the mystery surrounding the gospel and its community may perhaps be sought in its (hypothetical) contact with the teaching and tradition of that other great missionary religion farther to the East but no stranger to the heterogeneous society of the Hellenistic West."[27]

The late S. Radhakrishnan, who was at home both in Eastern religions and Western thought, emerged during the forties and fifties of this century as the most prominent scholar in the field of the history of religions. In his comparative studies of Eastern and Western religions,[28] he reviewed many of the parallels and concluded:

> Whether historically connected or not, they are the twin expressions of one great spiritual movement. The verbal parallels and ideal similarities reveal the impressive unity of religious aspiration. Buddha and Jesus

---

[25] "Têxtes Alexandrines et Bouddhiques," *Récherches de Science Réligieuse* 27 (1937): 337-338:
La question générale d'un facteur indien dans la formation du néo-platonisme demeure ouverte; l'existence d'une colonie bouddhique dans la grand Aléxandrie n'est pas décidément controuvée, et tout au moins il semble que les Alexandrins aient été un peu moins mal renseignés sur les choses bouddhiques que les habitants de beaucoup d'autres régions de l'Empire; des emprunts au bouddhisme ont été maintes fois signalés, non toujours sans vraisemblance, dans plusieurs apocryphes chrétiens, dans la littérature judéo-chrétienne, ou chez des gnostiques, surtout chez Basilide.

[26] *The Art and Thought of John* (New York, 1969), *The Christian Buddhism of St. John* (New York, 1971).

[27] "Ananda: The fourth evangelist's model for 'disciple whom Jesus loved'?" *Studies in Religion /Sciences Religieuses* 3 (1973), 240.

[28] *Eastern Religions and Western Thought* (London, 1940).

are the earlier and later Hindu and Jewish representatives of the same upheaval of the human soul.[29]

Radhakrishnan's suggestion that the Buddhist concepts and teachings may have infiltrated the circle of the evangelists, who mistook them for the words of Jesus was developed by Roy C. Amore.[30] Amore argues as a historian of religion that the Q-source used in the synoptic gospels could very well be a Buddhist work. He writes:

> The Buddhistic passages may have come into the New Testament tradition with the Q-source. This approach is suggested by the fact that almost the whole of Luke's version of the Sermon on the Mount, a part of Q, has Buddhist parallels. Furthermore, several others of the parallel passages...come from the Q-source. Let us consider whether Q is in part a Buddhist source—whether in part "Q is B."[31]

In the concluding chapter of his book Amore suggests the hypothesis that "Jesus drew upon Buddhist as well as Jewish concepts and images in presenting his own teaching, which was not identical with traditional Judaism or Buddhism. By this means the Buddhist ideal of nonviolence, the concept of treasures in heaven, the quest for a pure mind, and other Buddhist teachings came into the Christian tradition."[32]

In this study, I work within the tradition described above and borrow many of the findings of scholars like van den Bergh, Garbe, Edmunds, Radhakrishnan, Amore, and others. But I go beyond their work. I discuss the problem of the relationship between early Christianity and Buddhism by looking at the scriptures of these religions primarily as literary works; so my book is an exercise primarily in literary criticism or comparative literature rather than in comparative religion or theology. By no means do I argue in this study that Jesus was a Buddhist or that he was necessarily in contact with Buddhism and its scriptures. Of course, Jesus, being a seeker of wisdom, could have heard about Buddha and studied Buddhism, as it had been suggested before:

> There can be hardly any doubt that Jesus of Nazareth, whose doctrines in their most essential parts are identical with those of the Buddha, must have been a disciples of Buddhist Mendicants from the age of twelve to thirty, a space totally unaccounted for by the Gospels, and that under

---

[29] Radhakrishnan, 186.
[30] *Two Masters: One Message* (Abingdon, 1978).
[31] Amore, 138-139.
[32] Amore, 185.

their guidance he must have attained Arahatship. Later on He returned to his native country to preach the doctrine to his people.[33]

In this book I look at Jesus not as a certain historically identifiable person who extensively borrowed Buddhist/Hindu views and concepts; I look only at the literary portrayal of Jesus' person, of his deeds, and of his words as found in the canonical and non-canonical scriptures of early Christianity. I concentrate mostly on similarities found in the early Christian writings and Buddhist-Hindu scriptures and look for possible connection between these two literary traditions. Wish we could connect!

The history of Western colonialism seems to have given ample support to Kipling's fear: "For East is East and West is West, and never the twain shall meet." During the last five centuries of colonial expansion, the colonial powers were not interested in understanding the natives, their religions, and their ideologies. They were rather driven by crass materialism which sought to exploit the colonies without much opposition from the Christian moral code. This attitude is echoed in Kipling's doggerel:

Ship me somewhere East of Suez,
Where the best is like the worst,
Where there aren't no ten commandments,
And a man can raise a thirst.

Those of us who have lived with Europeans in India and the West during the colonial period and after know that most of them as a rule carry the "White Man's Burden" (Kipling) and the conception of the Orientals as "lesser breeds without the law" (Macaulay); like colonial masters everywhere, they were not accustomed to consider the Easterners as their equals. As Radhakrishnan's observation cited earlier points out, in general, Western scholars, though fascinated by Eastern wisdom, have always found it hard to admit that the West could ever have borrowed anything of worth from the East or the East was ever equal or superior to the West in their cultural accomplishments.

This "critical" myopia or misguided elitism is called "Eurocentrism," which describes a provincial outlook that focuses overwhelmingly on European and Western culture while giving short shrift to Asia, Africa and Latin America. Eurocentrism is best exampled in the dogma that Columbus "discovered" America as if

---

[33] Subbhadra Bhikshu, *A Buddhist Catechism*, 80; cited by T. Sterling Berry, *Christianity and Buddhism: A Comparison and Contrast* (London, 1890), 221.

there had been no other people on the continent. One reason for the growth of Eurocentrism is probably that most Europeans share the Hegelian view of the East, which combines the Romantic glorification of the East's antiquity with the rejection of the relevance of it for the present. Like most Christians, Hegel believed in the so-called "Christian" view of the irreversible direction of history. He could not glorify origins and early stages. According to him, the spirit of world history progresses to greater richness and complexity. What has been in the beginning cannot be richer and more perfect, and the more perfect stage of European achievement has displaced the accomplishments of the East. For Hegel the paradigmatic encounter between two peoples or ideologies is a duel to death. It is because they are "self-infinitizing" beings. They develop fantasies of omnipotence. What happens when one omnipotence meets another? Two omnipotences cannot occupy the same psychic space at the same time. Therefore, there is a duel to the death of one or the other![34] Such is the confrontation between the earlier system of Oriental India and the later system of Western Christianity! Since India's tradition belongs to the past, it cannot teach the West. Martin Bernal suggests that there was even a deliberate attempt by eighteenth- and nineteenth-century "Romantics and racists" to erase African, Asian, and Near Eastern roots of Greek and Roman civilization.[35] Many Westerners, in fact, believed in this Hegelian dialecic and went on to ridicule Eastern religions and tried to impose Christianity and Western culture on the East. Mahatma Gandhi writes in his *Autobiography*:

> He [Gandhi's father] had, besides, Musulman and Parsi friends, who would talk to him about their own faiths, and he would listen to them always with respect, and often with interest....Only Christianity was at the time an exception. I developed a sort of dislike for it. And for a reason. In those days Christian missionaries used to stand in a corner near the high school and hold forth, pouring abuse on Hindus and their gods. I could not endure this. I must have stood there to hear them once only, but that was enough to dissuade me from repeating the experiment. About the same time I heard of a well-known Hindu having been converted to Christianity. It was the talk of the town that, when he was

---

[34] For Hegel's view on India, see Hegel, *The History of Philosophy* (New York, 1955) I:125-48. See also Wilhelm Halbfass, *ndia and Europe: An Essay in Understanding* (Albany, 1988), 84-90. For more on Hegel, consult Daniel Bell, *The End of Ideologies* (Cambridge, Ma., 1987) and Richard Bernstein, "Undermining Capitalism," New York Times, February 7, 1989, p. 14.

[35] See Joseph Berger, "Ibn Batuta and Sitar: Challenging Columbus and Piano in Schools," *New York Times*, April 12, 1989, p. 1.

baptized, he had to eat beef and drink liquor, that he also had to change his clothes, and that henceforth he began to go about in European costume including a hat. These things got on my nerves. Surely, I thought, a religion that compelled one to eat beef, drink liquor, and change one's clothes did not deserve the name. I also heard that the new convert had already begun abusing the religion of his ancestors, their customs and their country. All these things created in me a dislike for Christianity."[36]

World War II spelled the beginning of the end of Hegelian triumphalism and of Western colonialism. Subsequently, there took place a significant change of attitudes in the West, especially in the sixties. For instance, the recent dialogues between Christians and Buddhists, —besides all the other cultural, political, and commercial ties between the East and West—show that Kipling's fear that East and West might never meet is slowly changing into mutual trust, at long last. East and West have not only begun to communicate like equals but also have started to live side by side with a give-and-take attitude. Both sides have even reached the point that neither can survive without the other: Japan, for instance, cannot guarantee its own national security without Western help; the economy of the U. S. could easily go into a recession or even depression if ever Japan were to abandon the U. S. Indeed, the world has ceased to be divided into East and West. The idea of the global village is slowly turning into reality.

Actually, this current development is only a return to the pristine state of the East and West which were once one; that is, there was no profound and unbridgeable cultural and political differentiation between the East and the West until the collapse of the Roman empire and the rise of Islam. That earlier stage of human history reminds us of the beginning of the world according to the Hebrew biblical tradition. First God created the hermaphrodite Adam from whom Eve was later separated; since then Adam and Eve had been seeking each other. Plato developed a similar idea in the metaphor of the mythical species of man-woman who were cut in half by Zeus on account of their defiance of the gods. After the vivisection, each half sought after its mate frantically and asked for nothing better than to be rolled into one. So much so, they began to die of hunger and general inertia since neither would do anything without the other. As the race was dying out, Zeus felt so sorry for them that he moved their privates round to the front and made them propagate. If a man should chance upon a woman, conception

---

[36] Homer A. Jack, *The Gandhi Reader* (Bloomington, 1956), 16.

would take place. If the male should conjugate with male, he might at least obtain such satisfaction as would allow him to turn his attention to the everyday affairs of life without being procreative. Plato concludes: "So you see, gentlemen, how far back we can trace our innate love for one another and how this love is always trying to re-integrate our former nature, to make two into one, and bridge the gulf between one human being and another."[37]

My study reaffirms the same mythological tradition with regard to the significance of contemporary East-West relations and Buddhist-Christian dialogues. I suggest that these dialogues are not only archetypally significant but historically relevant with regard to the origins of the Christian scriptures and the textual community of the Christians because Christianity is also a religion of the book or a community shaped by its sacred scriptures. That is, Christianity grew up in the neo-Platonic, Hellenistic, Gnostic cultural and literary milieu which was influenced by Indian—Buddhist and Hindu—thought. Christianity's relationship to Indian thought is very similar to its relationship to Jewish and Hellenistic culture. Jesus' followers associated themselves very closely with the Jewish community and its religion before they went their separate ways. Even after its separation from Judaism, Christianity was closely linked to the Hellenistic religion before it declared its independence from Hellenism without relinquishing many of its Hellenistic features. Coming closer to our own times, the beginnings of Christianity can be compared to the origin of Protestantism which declared its individuality in the sixteenth century without giving up many medieval Catholic features even though it reinterpreted several Catholic doctrines differently than its Roman Catholic counterpart.

Presently, during dialogues and comparative studies, different religions are returning to their origins, like the bisected humans of Plato's *Symposium*: Either they discover nothing really new because of "religious endogamy"—Christians associating with Christians and Buddhists with Buddhists in splendid isolation—and "religious narcissism"—Catholics associating themselves only with Catholics and the Vajrayana Buddhists dealing only with Vajrayana Buddhists—and thus languish in futile embrace; or they engender something new or make new discoveries in self-understanding out of these exogamous religious encounters. For example,

---

[37] *Symposium*, 190-191.

until the sixties Catholics had always thought that the Protestant doctrine of Justification was worlds apart from the Catholic teaching of the same; however, Hans Küng's study revealed that the Protestant and Catholic teachings of Justification are almost identical.[38] Up until the eighties Catholics were told that the Anglican Orders were invalid, but a recent joint study of the issue both by the Anglicans and Catholics has arrived at the consensus that the Anglican Orders are valid. Similarly, historicized comparative Christian-Buddhist studies done in the Gnostic milieu, for example, could reveal the genetic relationship between many Christian and Buddhist teachings so that several New Testament passages could be clarified and better understood in their historical context.

Let me give a few tantalizing illustrations of the last point. Take for instance the saying of Jesus: "In the case of those who will not receive you nor hear your words: going forth out of their house or city, shake off the dust from your feet. Amen, I say to you, it shall be more tolerable for the land of Sodom and Gomorrah in the day of Judgment than for that city" (Matthew 10: 14-15). What is puzzling in this passage is that the second verse goes counter to the forgiving spirit of Jesus. If Jesus uttered the first verse, Matthew gave his interpretation in the following verse by deconstructing the words of Jesus. Matthew 10:14 makes better sense if it is interpreted against the saying of Buddha, under the assumption that the gospel writer was familiar with the Buddhist tradition: "The dust on the feet of good men is better than a mountain of gold. That dust decreases sorrow; that mountain increases it"—found in the *Surupa Jataka*-story. The Buddhist text implies that the ministry of Buddha and his disciples benefits mankind even if they do not provide the poor with money. In the same way the disciples of Jesus should work among people who are not apparently receptive of their teachings and whom they cannot feed with food obtained from the multiplication of loaves. So the true intent of Jesus in Matthew 10: 14 would be that the disciples should work even among people who do not receive them with open arms. Such an interpretation would do justice to Jesus' much-acclaimed teaching: "Love your enemies." Likewise, the beatitude "Blest are the pure of heart, or rather the single-minded, for they shall see God (Mt. 5: 8) is best understood in the Buddhist-Hindu concept of meditation-concentration-yoga which

---

[38] *Justification: The Doctrine of Karl Barth and a Catholic Reflection* (New York, 1964).

leads to an intellectual gnosis or mystical experience of God. Or, take this passage from Asvaghosha's sermons:

> Come, now, I will use a comparison to illustrate this argument. It is like a grain of corn; when all concomitant circumstances are in suitable relation, then the blade is produced; but in truth it is not this grain which produces the blade, for the grain dies (in the ground); the new blade grows and increases, but the old grain perishes; because it dies the blade lives, the two cannot be separated. So it is Buddha speaks with respect to the future body.[39]

It is in the light of this passage, I submit, that John 12:23-25 should be understood and explicated:

> The hour has come for the Son of Man to be glorified. I tell you the truth, unless a kernel of wheat falls to the ground and dies, it remains only a single seed. But if it dies, it produces many seeds. The man who loves his life will lose it, while the man who hates his life in this world will keep it for eternal life.

The following passage from Asvaghosha is also fascinating: "Have you not rather heard what Thathagata says in the Sutra (where he bids his followers) not to despise the little child called 'Snake-fire'? So neither should we despise the young Shamis."[40] Certainly, Luke 18:15-17 that follows reminds us of Asvaghosha:

> People were bringing babies to Jesus to have him touch them. When the disciples saw this, they rebuked them. But Jesus called the children to him and said, "Let the little children come to me, and do not despise them for the kingdom of God belongs to such as these.[41]

Edward Conze refers to an interesting verbal parallel found in the Revelation of John (second century A.D.) and the Buddhist *Perfection of Wisdom (Prajnaparamita)*(dating from the first century B.C.) Conze writes:

Revelation (5:1) refers to a book "closely sealed" with seven seals, and likewise the *Perfection of Wisdom* is called a book "sealed with seven seals." It is shown to a Bodhisattva by the name of "Ever-weeping" (*Sadaprarudita*) and St. John "weeps bitterly" (5:4) because he sees no one worthy to open the book and to break its seals. This can be done by the Lamb alone, slaughtered in sacrifice (5:9). In the same way, chaps 30 and 31 of the Mahayana

---

[39] Samuel Beal, *Buddhist Literature in China* (New York, 1884), 119; cited by Sterling Berry, 227.
[40] Beal, 228.
[41] Ibid.

book describe in detail how Everweeping slaughtered himself in sacrifice, and how he thereby became worthy of the Perfection of Wisdom.[42]

There are many such passages in the New Testament which are begging to be reinterpreted in their "original"—I realize, of course, that *original* is a misleading term in modern historicist criticism—or rather in the Oriental context.

At this point Samuel Beal's commentary on Asvaghosha's sermons is interesting. He writes:

> Altogether, having translated the Buddhacharita throughout, and also the greater portion of Asvaghosha's Sermons, I am impressed with the conviction that Christian teaching had reached his ears at the time when Asvaghosha was in Parthia, or at any rate in Bactria (viz., about A.D.70), and that he was influenced by it so far as to introduce into Buddhism the changes we find beginning to take shape at this period. The doctrine of a universal salvation, and of Buddha's incarnation by the descent of the Spirit, and by a power of Bodhi, or wisdom, by which we are made sons or disciples—these and other non-Buddhist ideas found in Asvaghosha's writings, convince me that there was such an intercommunication at this time between East and West as shaped the later school of Buddhism into a pseudo-Christian form; and this accounts very much for some other inexplicable similarities.[43]

I have a historical difficulty with this line of interpretation. There is no reliable evidence to claim that the gospels were composed in their present form before the middle of the second century A.D. Further, if Asvaghosha was active as a preacher and writer in the middle of the first century, as Beal indicates, it is more than likely that the Christian gospels were shaped by the much older Buddhist tradition than vice versa. Further, the so-called non-Buddhist ideas that Beal mentions are only non-Theravada doctrines; they are, on the other hand, genuine Mahayana ideas which were formulated at the latest as early as the first century B.C.

In this context, a study like mine is thought-provocative and important for the textual history of the New Testament.

Let me conclude this section by recalling an interesting observation that Thucydides makes in his great *History* and a comment that a modern scholar makes on it, which are both relevant to the very heart of textual criticism and the nature of textual history.

---

[42] Edward Conze, "Mahayana Buddhism," in *Thirty Years of Buddhist Studies* (Columbia, S.C., 1968), 49.

[43] Beal, xiv; cited by Sterling Berry, 227-28.

Thucydides begins the summary of his narrative of the plague at Athens:

> Such was the nature of the calamity which now fell on the Athenians; death raging within the city and devastation without. Among other things which they remembered in their distress was, very naturally, the following verse, which the old men said had been uttered long ago: "A Dorian war shall come and with it death." A dispute arose whether dearth and not death (*limos* or *loimos*) had not been the word in the verse; but at the present juncture it was of course decided in favour of the latter; for the people made their recollection fit in with their sufferings. I fancy, however, that if another Dorian war should ever afterwards come upon us, and a dearth should happen to accompany it, the verse will probably be read accordingly.[44]

Jerome McGann comments on this anecdote:

> The scholarship in this commentary does not lie in the recording of a textual dispute, and it clearly has nothing at all to do with adjudicating between the two received readings of the line, nor even with explaining what each version means. Thucydides' mordant eye is not directed toward the "original version" of the line but toward the versions produced by later "editors" and interpreters; and his interest lies in the meaning of scholarship and criticism rather than in the meaning of that line of ancient verse.[45]

---

[44] Thucydides, *The History of the Peloponnesian War*, ed. and trans. Sir Richard Livingstone (Oxford, 1960), 122 (book 2, sec. 54).
[45] *Textual Criticism and Literary Interpretation*, (Chicago, 1985), 199.

CHAPTER ONE

METHOD

My enterprise in this book is an exercise in comparative literature; everything else, like the historical and religious dimensions of this work, is secondary to my purpose in this study. Therefore, it is important to underscore the parameters of the type of literary criticism employed in this book. This study of Christian and Buddhist literary texts is characterized by five foci: Comparative Literature, Deconstructionism, New Historicism, Intertextuality, and Literary Relationship.

These terms may make some readers object that the twentieth-century research in matters like intertextuality and deconstruction and the New Testament of the first century make strange bedfellows because of their unfamiliar positions at the opposite ends of the chronological spectrum. On the contrary, the above-mentioned poetic principles were practiced consistently in all the literary genres from time immemorial because all literary discourse is born of a process of textual assimilation which employs deconstruction and intertextuality. This process was known as *Midrash* in biblical times, as *translatio studii* during the Middle Ages, as *imitatio-emulatio* during the Renaissance, and as *plagiarism* in the twentieth century. More on this later.

A. *Comparative Literature*

Comparative literature is the study of literature beyond the confines of one particular culture; it is the study of the relationship between one literature and another (other) literature(s) and the comparison of literature with other spheres of human expression such as arts, social sciences, physical sciences, religions, and so on. In this book I compare the early Christian literature of the New Testament and the apocryphal gospels with the Buddhist tradition found in the Mahayana and Theravada scriptures.

To justify my approach, the following clarifications are in order. One school of comparative studies—call it the Historical School—limits its scope in favor of problems which can be solved on the basis of factual evidence which is well documented. This school is represented by such leading French scholars as Fernand Baldensperger, Jean-Marie Carré, Paul Hazard, Paul Van

Tieghten, Henri Roddier, Marcel Betaillon, M. F. Guyard, and others.[1] The members of this school distrust studies which "merely" compare and point out analogues and contrasts. They warn against influence studies as being too hazy and uncertain. They urge that comparatists concentrate on questions of the reception of one particular author, one single idea, intermediaries, foreign travel and attitudes toward a given country or author in a given period. Carré and Guyard look askance at vast syntheses of literatures like European literature as superficial and simplistic. Indeed, this positivistic approach is justifiable to a certain extent because the seekers of influence studies really need encyclopedic knowledge in order to compare vast literatures. Lacking such knowledge and time needed to acquire such wisdom, they do not and cannot satisfactorily answer questions such as the following: What was retained and what was rejected? Why and how was the material absorbed? How successfully was the material integrated?

The preoccupation with locating and proving influences can become so time-consuming that it may overlook the more important question of literary interpretation and evaluation of different authors/works like Homer and Virgil, *Beowulf* and *Aeneid* , Balzac and Dickens, *Moby Dick* and *Faust*, Luke and Virgil, Thomas Mann and André Gide, Shakespeare and Chaucer and so on. Further, we need syntheses and comparisons of different syntheses, cultures, literatures, and religions to escape and to avoid eternal fragmentation and isolation. We cannot afford to play it safe by saying, "We must wait till all the data is in." All the data will never be in, we know. Indeed, cautionism is good, but perfectionism is illusory; interminable waiting or procrastination is neurotic, and sometimes bold action is the sign of creativity, not necessarily of temerity and presumption.

The Germans make a valuable distinction between *Untersuchung* and *Darstellung*, between original research and presentation in a new light of known facts in a usable—not necessarily infallible— form. Most people know that original, utterly profound, seminal scholarship is a *rara avis* like a Michelangelo, Newton, Mendel, Darwin, Einstein, Kalidasa, or Shakespeare. But many of us can now and then make a contribution to the vast configuration of human knowledge by pulling together tentative insights and some

---

[1] See "Comparative Literature: Its Definition and Function," in *Comparative Literature: Method and Perspective* ., eds. Newton P. Stallknecht and Horst Frenz (Carbondale, 1971), 1-58.

results achieved by the research of different scholars in different disciplines.

Consequently, in view of the limitations of the first school, there has arisen a more inclusive concept—let us call it the New School—in comparative literature. This new concept emphasizes the *functional* rather than the stringent theoretical aspects. The practitioners of this concept, also like their French counterparts, seek a more comprehensive understanding of literature as a whole by extending the investigation of literature across geographical and generical barriers. This can be done best by relating several literatures to each other and by relating literature to artistic and ideological fields.

The New School of comparative literature shares the same methodology as other literary disciplines. It is the same scientific law of gathering, selecting, and interpreting evidence that applies here as elsewhere. In principle, comparative literature, like all literature, admits different methods of approach for pragmatic reasons. If one scholar's method yields results persuasive to other scholars, it is then appropriate in that person's field of study. The temptation has always been to lay down rules, guidelines, and recommendations. However, strict application especially of antiquated rules stifles imagination and initiative in scholarship, which has always been full of surprises. It is this element of surprise that I like to offer in my study by introducing the parameters of Deconstructionism, New Historicism, and Intertextuality to my attempt of comparing Christian and Buddhist scriptures.

B. *Deconstruction*

The word deconstruction in the context is misleading. It suggests the violent demolition of the helpless text. It suggests the mirage of a child who takes apart its father's watch beyond the hope of repair. However, far from reducing the text to detached fragments, deconstruction inevitably restores the text again in a form different from the text it destructs. It does again as it undoes.

The deconstructionists believe in the power of the critic over the text. They are not overawed by the critics of the past or inhibited by their own previous interpretation of the text; they do not believe that conformity to the past and consistency in their own previous works extended over a significant period of time are necessarily virtues. They are not afraid of rejecting the past and of dismantling themselves. They do not believe that they are part of a movement that goes deeper and closer to a definitive interpretation of the text, reaching the finality of infallibility, for it inhibits one insight into becoming the still point, the firm resting place. What deconstructionism does is resist the totalitarian tendencies of received criticism; it resists even its own tendency to be the final word on a text; it puts its own claims and discoveries into question. The deconstructionist reading of a text is plainly and clearly a refusal to admit that there is one single obvious or univocal reading of a given text.

The text has an equivocal richness which one single type of reading can totally exhaust. This is due to the fact that one text embeds other texts by a cunning assimilation. Thus, meaning remains in an intertextual sphere. New, hitherto undiscovered meanings emerge when embedded texts are revealed. It is like the overturning of the conviction of a suspect with the introduction of new evidence. The newly discovered evidence would point to a new directional meaning for the text without necessarily identifying the exact meaning.[2] Deconstructionism accomplishes its task with the hermeneutics of suspicion; for, while texts restore, they also deceive; hence reader beware. Robert Scholes writes: "Texts are places where power and weakness become visible and discussable, where learning and ignorance manifest themselves, where the structures that enable and constrains our thoughts and actions become palpable."[3] Deconstructionists suggest a pluralistic theory of interpretation that affirms, on the one hand, that texts are meaningful and, on the other hand, establishes a critical distance from the text in the form of a hermeneutics of suspicion. The reason for this stance is that, on account of the excess or richness of meaning, there is no single definitive interpretation of a text. In this sense the literary text is like a freely performed action of an individual human being or like the individual itself. As the old adage goes, the individual is ineffable, simply because of the various possibilities implied in the interpretation of the human action as well as because of the unfathomable richness of the individual. As for the text, in the words of Gadamer, "insofar as we understand at all, we understand differently (from the the original

---

[2] See J. Hillis Miller, "The Critic as Host," in *Deconstruction and Criticism*, ed. Harold Bloom et al. (New York, 1979), 217-254

[3] *Textual Power* (New Haven, 1985), ix.

author).'"[4] Contrary to popular misconceptions, the deconstructionist theory, for example, of Gadamer as interpreted by David Tracy encourages genuine creativity and lays down criteria of adequacy not only in social sciences and literary criticism but also in religion.[5]

As Tracy points out in his article, creativity is a categorical imperative in religious studies because the religious phenomenon is cognitively so ambiguous that it has yielded over the centuries numerous interpretations. To recognize the reality of radical pluralism in religious interpretations, it is enough to read the contemporary works in religious studies or attend one session of one of the major conferences in the field. This radical pluralism is revealed also by the fact that major religions recognize today that there are different ways of being religious in different religions. Yet the same cognitive ambiguity can also yield negatively extreme forms of irrationality, obscurantism, and mystification. This religious plurality is the result of the hermeneutics of suspicion. Tracy writes:

> All the great hermeneutics of suspicion (Marxian, Freudian, Nietzchean) remain relevant methods of interpretation. Each develops a critical theory (psycho-analytic theory, ideology critique, genealogical method) to inform its hermeneutics of suspicion. These critical theories are employed to spot and emancipate the repressed, unconscious distortions that are also operative in the classic religious texts and in their history of effects through the classic religious traditions. Not only is this need for hermeneutics of suspicion along with a hermeneutics of retrieval allowed by this general interpretation theory, it is also...demanded by the nature of the religious phenomenon itself...Bultmann is correct, on purely hermeneutical grounds, to insist that the prophetic-eschatological strand of Christianity (and not merely the problematic of modernity) demands the demythologizing of Christianity by Christianity. At the heart of any prophetic tradition is a profound hermeneutics of suspicion toward all religious expressions as possibly idolatrous. At the heart of every prophetic tradition is an opening and a demand for any critical theory that helps to uncover repressed illusions—including the repressed illusions (not mere errors) of sexism, racism, classism, and so forth that are also operative in the Jewish and Christian religious classics.[6]

Though religious creativity is desirable and laudable, it should not become a totally arbitrary or subjective reading of the text; it should have methodological (historicist, for example, in our case)

---

[4] See Hans-Georg Gadamer, *Truth and Method* (New York, 1975), 91-119
[5] "Creativity in the Interpretation of Religion: The Question of Radical Pluralism" *New Literary History* 15 (1983-84): 289-309.
[6] Tracy, 306-307.

controls to prevent serious, anachronistic misunderstandings of ancient texts. Therefore, I follow three steps in my comparative enterprise of the texts of Christianity and Buddhism.

The first stage: Realizing that the interpreter looks at the text anew with all his/her preundersanding, I enter this interpretation of the New Testament in the light of my renewed interest in the Buddhist traditions. Let me point out that I was brought up as an Indian Catholic with academic training in the Christian and biblical tradition which was supplemented by a cursory study of the Indian religions. I was taught to believe that the Catholic religion was the only true religion and that the Bible was totally inspired by God with very little human input in it. Then I came to study in greater depth the religions of Buddhism and Hinduism, to teach Oriental or Western religions to students at the university, and to interact with the followers of these religions in greater proximity. During this period of study, teaching, contact, and reflection, I gradually began to appreciate the religions of Hinduism and Buddhism in a new light: I realized that these religions with their own ancient traditions are as great, if not greater, as Christianity in liturgy, theology, morality, mythology, and symbology and that they deserved comparison. As I undertook the comparative study of the Christian and Indian traditions, I became aware of the works of Western scholars in the same area. When many minds are independently involved in the same research, I realized, they cannot be entirely off the right track and target. Obviously they are asking the right questions at the least, even if they are not arriving at the same answers; it is like listening to St. Augustine again: "O God, thou hast created us to tend toward thee (*Fecisti nos ad te, Domine*)." Like my colleagues in the field, I, too, was dissatisfied with the traditional understanding of the relationship of Christianity and the Indian religions. Again, to quote Augustine, "Our hearts are restless (*Inquietum est cor nostrum*)", and to paraphrase him, "until we find the right answers." For Augustine, religion is fundamentally a problem of heart and love; my comparative study is also a labor of love, but of an intellectual sort, which keeps scholarship and religion separate by deepening the understanding and appreciation of both religions for the doer and the reader.

The second stage: On the objective level, the text claims and captures the attention of the interpreter to the extent that the text unsettles and provokes the preunderstanding of the interpreter. Let me cite two examples: the story of the Christian saints Barlaam and Josaphat and the story of Gautama Buddha, the former being a hagiographical and unhistorical adaptation of the latter, and the Buddhist doctrine of the three bodies of Buddha—*nirmanakaya, dharmakaya,* and *sambhogakaya* vis-à-vis the thinking of Origen on the docetic body of Christ. The Catholic scholars de la vallée-Poussin and Henri de Lubac were puzzled and provoked by these two examples. Both these scholars are willing to admit, against traditional teaching, that "the story of the Catholic saints, Barlaam and Josaphat is clearly a re-cast of the legend of the Bodhisatva."[7] These scholars, however, are unwilling to admit any more influence of Buddhism on Christianity. They would rather play it safe. De la Vallée-Poussin writes: "The 'prudent' scholar when he reads in the Apocryphal Books of Egypt the story of the Divine Child led to the school and better acquainted with the lesson than the master himself—a story to be found in the Lalitavistara—will promptly say that parallel themes (a divine child) cannot but give birth to parallel details."[8] Subjectivity seems to influence the work of the religious historian in this case, as de La Vallée-Poussin himself admits: "The problems of influence and borrowing are difficult, and the historian, despite his efforts to be critical, is likely to follow his congenital tendency. There are scholars who believe, from the point of view of scientific method, that Palestine must be explained by Palestine, India by India."[9] Nonetheless, the text unsettles the interpreter, for the scholar is willing to look at the problem that vexes him and others even though he is unwilling to do any bold thinking for fear of ecclesiastical censure, which is still true in the case of many Catholic scholars.[10]

The Third Stage: the interpreter uses Gadamer's model of the "game" of conversation between the interpreter and the text.[11] Tracy writes:

> The model of conversation is not imposed upon our actual experience of interpretation as some new de jure method, norm, or rule. Rather, the phenomenon of the conversation aptly describes anyone's de facto experience of interpreting any classic text. To understand how this is the case, first consider the more general phenomenon of the game itself

---

[7] De la Vallée-Poussin, *Comparative Religion* , 28; De Lubac, *La Rencontre du Bouddhisme et de l'occident* (Paris, 1952), 28-29.
[8] Poussin, 28.
[9] Ibid.
[10] See de Lubac, "Textes Alexandrins et Bouddhiques," *Recherches de Science Religieuse* 27 (1937): 336-351.
[11] Gadamer, 91 ff., 325 ff.

before describing the specific game of conversation. The key to any game is not the self-consciousness of the players in the game but rather the release of self-consciousness into consciousness of the to-and-fro, back-and-forth movement which constitutes the game. The attitude of the players of any game is a phenomenon dependent above all upon this natural back-and-forth movement of the game itself. When we really play any game, it is not so much we who are playing as it is the game which plays us. For if we cannot release ourselves to the back-and-forth movement of the game, then we cannot play. But if we can play, then we experience ourselves as caught up in the movement of the game itself. We realize that our usual self-consciousness cannot be the key to playing. Rather, we may even find, however temporarily, a new sense of a self given in, by, and through our actual playing, our release to the to-and-fro movements of the game.[12]

Let us face it: interpretation, as Gadamer insists correctly, is a game and conversation, which can take the form of debate, gossip, confrontation, or the logic of question and answer. In interpretation we allow the text to make us ask questions and try to answer them; we cannot interpret if we stop asking questions.

My present study is not a debate either with the text or with the other interpreters in the false hope of achieving ultimate control over the meaning of the text in the heat of a confrontational debate. It is more than gossip, which is frivolous in nature and is a way of whiling away time. My interpretational effort is serious in intent: it asks vexing questions and seeks enlightening answers, and thus engages in an authentic conversation with the text. This mutual interaction or dialogue between the text and me the interpreter is a process of discovering meaning. What is important in this enterprise is the process of dialogue, not so much the finality of the end product. It is a search, in which I, the interpreter, gain myself by losing myself, for in questioning not only do I toy with my prior certainties but also allow my preconceptions and previous interpretations of the text to disintegrate like the proverbial grain of wheat, which when it dies produces abundant fruit. Tracy concludes:

> We attempt primarily to gain ourselves by losing ourselves in the logic of questioning the subject matter disclosed by the text. Interpretation is inevitably creative. The meaning of the text does not lie "behind" it (in the mind of the author, the original social setting, the original audience) nor even "in" the text itself. Rather, the meaning of the text lies *in front of* the text—in the now shared question, the now common subject matter of both text and interpreter. We do not seek simply to repeat, to reproduce the original meaning of the text in order to understand its

---

[12] Tracy, 296-297.

(and now our) questions. Rather, creativity must be involved as we seek to mediate, translate, interpret its meaning—the meaning in front of the text—into our own horizon. We seek...to fuse the horizon (the horizon of meaning in front of the text) with our own horizon. More basically, we seek to converse with the subject matter found and expressed in the classic text. We seek, in sum, to interpret in order to understand.[13]

C. *New Historicism*

Contemporary literary criticism is characterized by the phenomenon of new historicism. Jean Howard writes in a recent issue of Shakespeare Quarterly 35 (1984):

> A common criticism of the New Criticism, of structuralism, and—in some readings—of deconstruction is that each is fundamentally indifferent to history: to the local context of literary production and to the social space occupied by the literary text in a particular culture. But suddenly indifference to history has been replaced by avid interest. Renaissance journals are full of essays placing the works of Milton, Donne, and Spenser in historical context! Some of the work represents a clear flight from the theoretical debates of the last fifteen years. It assumes a positivist notion of history as the realm of objective fact which literature simply reflects and it arrests the play of textual indeterminacy by gounding the "meaning" of literature in this extrinsic world of fact.[14]

The new historical criticism attempts to do two things: one, put the text back into the context from which it was generated; two, recognize the limitation of all interpretations *qua* historical.

Let me start with the second point. The art of understanding and interpreting involves the task of discussing meaning in terms that are not native to the original speech or text. That is easy to understand. Jesus spoke probably most of his life in Aramaic, but Jesus' disciples discussed his meaning to a different audience in Greek, Latin, Hebrew, and other non-Semitic languages. Likewise, we discuss Christianity and Buddhism in languages that are different from Pali, Sanskrit, Aramaic, and Greek, and we use categories and conceptions that are in our view equivalent, though not native, to the original texts. When we look at the various interpretations given the Christian and Buddhist texts, we find that no single interpretation has exhausted the meanings of the texts during their life that spans perhaps two thousand years; they have, however, brought into bold relief different aspects of the

---

[13] Tracy, 298.
[14] *Shakespeare Quarterly*, 35 (1984). 236.

meaning of the texts.[15] Thus all these various interpretations, even the most outlandish ones, contribute to understanding; that is, two different interpretations are not necessarily self-contradictory in method and content; they can often be complementary.

The fact that different interpretations are at least in partial agreement reminds us of the old nostrum that every age must reinterpret the great works of the past—we practice this imperative categorically when we we reread the classics and teach them in schools and colleges. We teachers and writers earn our place under the sun by reinterpreting, not just by reading classic texts aloud either in the church/temple or the classroom. We reinterpret because we find new sorts of significance and new strands of meaning relevant to our particular cultural contexts. Thus, the interpreter takes into account the language, interest, and concerns of his audience. For instance, the missionary-scholar of the past compared the Christian scriptures with Buddhist writings, emphasized differences, and then denied any Buddhist influence on the Christian religion. He could possibly not do otherwise, for he was only trying to convert Buddhists to Christianity rather than change his own religion. Today's Christian scholar, on the other hand, is not trying to proselytize but rather is trying to understand Buddhists in an attempt at promoting good will and improving mutual relations. This example shows that the textual interpretations of both eras are historically controlled: not only is historicity a given fact, but different in both instances.

The new historicism—it should not be identified exclusively with the Marxist criticism of Louis Althusser and Frederick Jameson or with the leftist criticism of Frank Lentricchia and Edward Said—recognizes a variety of competing centers in the complex cultural environment. Negatively speaking, the historicist is not a New Critic: "He does not conceive of the text as an iconic object whose meaning is perfectly contained within its own formal structure. Yet for him historical research has the effect of conferring autonomy and fixity upon the text."[16] Another articulate spokesman of the new movement, Jerome McGann, writes:

> Historical criticism tries to define what is most peculiar and distinctive in specific poetical works. Moreover, in specifying these unique features and sets of relationships, it transcends the concept of the-poem-as-verbal-object to reveal the poem as a special sort of communication

---

[15] E. D. Hirsch, *Validity in Interpretation* (New Haven, 1976), 128-134.
[16] Stephen Greenblatt, "Introduction" to *The Form of Power and the Power of Forms in the Renaissance Genre* 15 (Norman, 1982), 4-5.

event. This new understanding of poems takes place precisely because the critical act, occurring in a self-conscious present, can turn to look upon poems created in the past not as fixed objects but as the locus of certain past human experiences. ... In this way does a historical criticism define poetry not as a formal structure or immediate event but as a continuing human process.[17]

Again, negatively speaking, the new historicist differs from the earlier historicist who tended to be monological; that is, he was concerned with discovering a single historical vision. For instance, there are scholars who would still view the New Testament exclusively as a Jewish document, as a product of Palestinian Jewish history, exclusive of the various sects and segments of the surrounding Hellenistic world. They would try to interpret the New Testament entirely by referring it to the Old Testament. This kind of historical vision, presumed to be internally consistent and coherent, can protect the reader from the conflicts of interpretations and serve as a stable point of reference. On the contrary, the new historicism, like deconstructionism, shakes the firm ground of criticism and literature; it questions the methodological assumptions of itself as well as of others. The new historicist holds the mirror up to other centers of historical realities. In the present case, I hold that the books of the Christian New Testament were composed in a cultural milieu which was shaped not only by the scribes, pharisees, Sadducees, the Jewish high priests of the Sanhedrin, the rabbis, the Old Testament, and Hellenized Christians but also by Gnostic Christians and even Buddhist Christians.

True, the history of the Mediterranean culture of the first century, in which Christianity grew up and in which the Christian Scriptures were formed, is the history of all its religious and political ideologies and of all its products, the New Testament being just one such product. We are forced to make an artificial distinction among these various cultural texts and then demonstrate how the New Testament books were influenced by the Old Testament texts and concepts, forming a seamless discourse.

Such an attempt in reality is only a partial one, the new historicist recognizes, for there exist other cultural texts as terms of comparison for the New Testament texts and ideas. Thus, the new historicist, without denying the partial achievement of earlier historical studies, would like to include other centers of political

---

[17] "The Text, the Poem, and the Problem of Historical Method," in *Literary Theories in Praxis*, ed., Shirley F. Staton (Philadelphia, 1987), 212.

and religious power and reaffirms with all the past practitioners of the art of literary criticism that texts do not exist without contexts and that it is the complex contexts that allow us to determine the facts of the text and create subtexts, or interpretation.

D. *Intertextuality*

There are two related skills or aspects to textual competence: reading and interpretation. Reading is understanding the text, and it is based not only on the knowledge of the language in which the text was written but also on the other codes or subtexts that the author used and on the historical context in which the text was composed. The ideal reader can process the text effortlessly, depending upon the complexity of the text, by constructing a whole world from a few indications. When the reader experiences difficulty with the words and the meanings of the text or when he suspects that the text has a concealed meaning, he turns to interpretation. It is like the difference between the reading of a parable and interpreting it for its meaning. In both reading and interpreting its meaning, the subtexts and the reader-interpreter's awareness play a very significant role.

Though we had known all this before, in the past a good many of us were content to limit, partly due to circumstances, the study of the historical contexts and subtexts of the New Testament to Jewish history and the Old Testament to the exclusion of Greek history, Greek classics, commercial history, Gnosticism, Hinduism, Buddhism, and so on. In this section, I would like to define and amplify the notion of intertextuality and look closely at the role subtexts and the author of a text play in the composition of a text.

Intertextuality is "the act of writing by which a text emerges as a product of prior texts."[18] Roland Barthes reminds us that texts that make up another text are often anonymous and untraceable.[19] Julia Kristeva who defines intertextuality as the trans-position of one or several system(s) of signs into another[20] admits that at times the prior text (subtext, source, or model) can be identified. In this

---

[18] Mary E. Barnard, "Garcilago's Poetics of Subversion and the Orpheus Tapestry," *PMLA* 102 (1987): 316. See also Roland Barthes, *S/Z* (Paris, 1974); Julia Kristeva, *La Révolution de langage poétique* (Paris, 1974): J, Kristeva, *Semeiotiké: Recherches pour une semianalyse* (Paris, 1969); Jonathan Culler, "Presupposition and Intertextuality," in *The Pursuit of Signs: Semiotics, Literature and Deconstruction* (Ithaca, 1981), 100-118.

[19] Barthes, *S/Z*.

[20] *Revolution*, 59.

study, following Kristeva's lead, I argue that only at times can we identify exactly the Buddhist sources of the New Testament even though the Christian writers have made extensive use of the Buddhist tradition, primarily in an indirect Gnostic version.

Matthew Arnold once said that every critic should try and possess one great literature, at least besides his own; and the more unlike his own the better. In fact, Arnold took pains to master Indian classics besides Greek, Roman, and Hebrew classics! If this is the law of criticism, it is all the more so the law for creative imagination today as in the past. It is important to remember that all acknowledged poets our time—Eliot, Stevens, Lowell, Rilke, Pasternak, Yeats, Joyce, and so on—are learned poets. For instance, Ezra Pound—though his learning has often been shown to be superficial and wrong-headed—tried to read or "misread" Chinese and Japanese literatures, Homer, Sappho, Propertius, Catullus, and Old English. Pound's ecumenical interests moved from the Victorian poetry of Browning and the Pre-Raphaelites to Provençal and Italian medieval writers. Even though he is called a "translation poet," Pound was concerned with seeking out and enlarging the tradition. His Cantos were designed as a contribution to world literature, a meeting of waters. The Cantos open with reference to the *Odyssey* and the *Poema de mio Cid* and soon reaches "the pines at Takasago," "Ecbatan, of plotted streets," and the beginnings of civilization in Mesopotamia and Egypt in Canto V. And, as a result, many of Pound's allusions, as in the case of T. S. Eliot, are lost on the reader.[21] Eliot shared the same ecumenical views as Pound did. According to Eliot, the poet should write "not merely with his own generation in his bones, but with a feeling that the whole of the literature of Europe from Homer and within it the whole of the literature of his own country has a simultaneous existence and composes a simultaneous order."[22]

Indeed, no single literature or single text stands complete by itself. Behind any literature a larger tradition becomes visible because it participates in a culture with shared assumptions. The interpreter of a text, therefore, should be aware of the cultural codes and subtexts that lie behind the ancient texts as well.

The abundant use of obvious Old Testament passages and allusions by the the New Testament writers like Matthew, Luke, and John indicates that their writing is a form of intertextuality,

---

[21] Henry Gifford, *Comparative Literature* (London, 1969), 1-6.
[22] "Tradition and Individual Talent," in *Selected Essays* (New York, 1950), 4.

the act of writing by which a text emerges as a product of the imitation and emulation of prior texts. What Terence Cave says apropos the Renaissance theory of imitation is applicable to all literature:

> Imitation theory...recognizes the extent to which the production of any discourse is conditioned by pre-existing instances of discourse; the writer is always a rewriter, the problem then being to differentiate and authenticate the rewriting. This is executed not by the addition of something wholly new, but by the dismembering and reconstruction of what has already been written.[23]

Writers who incorporate subtexts into their own text do not just copy the subtext verbatim and acknowledge their indebtedness to their sources. Rather, they dismember the sources, adapt and transform these fragments, reconstruct them, and in the process create their own text. The appropriation of the sources (*imitatio*) involves elements of emulation (*aemulatio*), a correction of models to excel them, surpass them, and even establish victory over them. The ancients often compared this process of emulation to bees gathering pollen from flowers and converting it into honey. So imitations do not necessarily indicate, as Pushkin points out, "intellectual poverty," but they may show "a noble trust in one's own strength, the hope of discovering new worlds, following in the footsteps of a genius, or a feeling in its humility even more elevated, the desire to master one's model and give it a second life."[24]

The author of the Gospel of Matthew uses different metaphors for the process of imitation-emulation: "Do not pour new wine in old bottles"(9: 16-17); "Every scribe instructed in the kingdom of heaven is like a man who brings forth out of his treasure new things and old" (13: 52). John, the traditional author of the Fourth Gospel, uses the metaphor of metamorphosis to this process in the miracle story of Jesus turning water into wine (ch. 2); in the story of the healing of the man born blind (ch. 9), emulation consists in a new way of seeing things and in making others see things in this new way.

Since emulation seeks victory, it is revisionary and corrective; it implies the criticism of the subtext. In the language of the contemporary literary theory of Harold Bloom, "the revisionist

---

[23] *The Cornucopian Text: Problems of Writing in the French Renaissance* (Oxford, 1979), 76.
[24] Cited by J. T. Shaw, "Literary Indebtedness and Comparative Literary Studies," in Stallknecht and Horst-Frenz, 89.

poet strives to see again, so as to esteem and estimate differently, so as then to aim correctively."[25] Bloom's revisionist poets correct their precursors in order to win a victory, seeking to seem self-begotten!

The gospel writers seem to have had similar concerns and the same purpose. As imitators of the Old Testament models, they show great erudition in the Old Testament and explicitly use the Old Testament. Luke even admits to his use of subtexts other than the Old Testament:

> Many have undertaken to set forth in order a narrative of the things that have been accomplished among us just as they have delivered them to us, who from the beginning were eye-witnesses and ministers of the word. It seemed good to me also...to write to you in order, most excellent Theophilus, that thou mayest know the truth of those words in which thou hast been instructed (1: 1-4).

And the purpose of the gospel writers was power, not only over the subtexts but also over the minds of their readers and hearers: "These were written that you may believe that Jesus is the Christ and that believing you may have life in his name" (John 20:31).

There are hundreds of direct references to and quotations from the Old Testament in the canonical gospels, the Acts, the Epistles, and the apocryphal gospels. Sometimes they quote verbatim from many books of the Old Testament; other times the New Testament writers use the Old Testament without directly referring to them and by deliberately altering and transforming them. They are, in fact, following the rhetorical conventions of imitation and emulation. In biblical criticism, some scholars call this deconstructionist method *midrash*.

The word *midrash* occurs only twice in the Old Testament, where it appears as the title of literary works.[26] In Qumran literature, the word means "juridical investigation, study, interpretation, and exposition."[27] In rabbinical literature, *midrash* means the study of the Bible in general, but more particularly a commentary or explanation of a homiletic nature for purposes of edification. *Midrash* also means a specific corpus of literature within the Jewish oral tradition as well as a literary genre and a type of biblical exegesis. Addison Wright classifies midrashim under three headings: exegetical midrashim, homiletic

---

[25] *Map of Misreading* (New York, 1975), 4.
[26] 2 Chronicles 13: 22 and 24: 27.
[27] Addison Wright, *Midrash* (New York, 1967), 38-39

midrashim, and narrative midrashim.[28] In exegetical midrashic works like *Bereshit Rabbah* and *Midrash Tehillim*, the rabbis provide long and short explanations of successive passages of the Bible with running commentaries and with references to other scriptural passages; in these rabbinic writings, the text is always and invariabley set apart from the exegesis. Homiletic midrashim give interpretive material of select scriptural passages in the form of homilies. Narrative midrashim are "Bible rewritten," as Geza Vermes puts it[29]; they are, like *Sefer hayashar, Pirke de Eleazar*, and *Midrash Wayyissa'u*, "completely rewritten biblical narrative embellished with legends and non-biblical traditions."[30]

Realizing the different meanings given to *midrash* from "anything but the plain meaning of Scripture," to "everything said about Scripture" or particular verses of Scripture, Gary G. Porton gives the following simple definition:

> Midrash [is] a type of literature, oral or written, which stands in direct relationship to a fixed, canonical text, considered to be the authoritative and the revealed word of God by the midrashist [the one who makes the midrash] and his audience, and in which this canonical text is explicitly cited or clearly alluded to.[31]

Though a reflection on the sacred text, narrative midrash is also an imaginative reconstruction of the scene and episode narrated. It is creative historiography or the fictionalizing of history to make the meaning of a person or scene or law relevant to the present. As Addison Wright points out, though the rabbis' "primary aim was to make the Bible relevant, to make the Bible come alive and serve as a source of spiritual nourishment, refreshment and stimulation,...some times...the midrashim are...attempts by the rabbis to justify or confirm their concepts, ideas, and teachings and to find for them a biblical foundation."[32]

The midrashic method seems to have taken a different twist at the hands of Christian writers of the books of the New Testament. Instead of defining events in the light of the Old Testament, they

---

[28] Wright, 52.
[29] See *Scripture and Tradition in Judaism* (Leiden, 1961), 67-95
[30] Wright, 58-59.
[31] Gary G. Porton, "Defining Midrash," in *The Study of Ancient Judaism*, ed. Jacob Neusner (New York, 1981), I: 62. See Jacob Neusner, "The Word and the World: Midrash, Literature, and Theology," *Religious Studies and Theology*, 7 (1987): 48-55; Neusner, *Midrash and Literature: The Primacy of Documentary Discourse* (Lanham, 1987); Neusner, *Midrash in Context: Exegesis in Formative Judaism* (Atlanta, 1988); Geoffrey Hartman and Sanford Buddick, eds., *Literature and Midrash* (New Haven, 1986)
[32] Wright, 65.

redefine the Old Testament in the light of their understanding of Jesus. René Laurentin puts it thus:

> Midrash is in fact turned around by the coming of Christ, inasmuch as in him Scripture is unexpectedly fulfilled and also yields a new and hidden meaning, the meaning of words as well as their symbolic reality. Christ is the rock in the desert (1 Cor 10:14), the manna, the bread of life (Jn 6), the paschal lamb (Jn 19:36), the Temple (Jn 2:19), and the cornerstone (1 Pt 2:6). Mary becomes the Ark of the Covenant (Lk 1:35 and Ex 40:35; Lk 1:39-56 and 2 Sm 6) and the eschatological Daughter of Zion (Lk 1: 28-32 and Zep 3).[33]

A close look at the first two chapters of Luke reveals extensive use of revisionism. So the gospel midrash is not the traditional Jewish midrash of the rabbis who tried to make the Hebrew scriptures relevant to the needs of the present. On the other hand, the gospel writers attempt to make the Jesus of the present relevant to the Old Testament or meaningful to the Jewish believers . What we find, therefore, in the exegesis of the New Testament writers is deconstructionist midrash, which can be seen by a close look at the parallels given below.

Luke 1:31-33	2 Samuel 7: 12-16
And behold, you will conceive in your womb and bear a son, and you shall call his name Jesus. He will be great, and will be called the son of the Most High and the Lord God will give him the throne of his father David. He will reign forever over the house of Jacob and of his kingdom there shall be no end.	I will raise up your offspring after you, who shall come forth from your body, and I will establish...his kingdom. I will be his father, and he shall be my son. Your throne shall be established forever. Your house and your kingdom shall be made sure forever before me.

---

[33] *The Truth of Christmas*, (Petersham, 1986), 91; according to John L. McKenzie, *Dictionary of the Bible* (Milwaukee, 1965), 574-76, there are numerous examples of Midrash in the Old Testament and in the New Testament, particularly in the birth stories of Jesus told by Matthew and Luke. Of course, it should be emphasized that the Gospel of Matthew is not a midrash, but it contains much midrash.

Luke 1:26-35
The angel Gabriel was sent...to a virgin....Behold you will conceive in your womb and you shall have a son and you shall call his name Jesus.

Luke 1:10-11
And all the multitude of the people was praying without, at the hour of incense. And there appeared to him an angel of the Lord, standing on the right side of the altar of incense.

Luke 1:12
And Zachariah seeing him, was troubled, and fear fell upon him.

Luke 1:19
And the angel answering, said to him: I am Gabriel, who stand before God; I am sent to speak to you and to bring you these good news.

Isaiah 7:14
Behold a young lady [virgin (LXX)] shall conceive and bear a son and shall call his name God-with-us.

Isaiah 9:6-7
A son is given to us...upon the throne of David, and over his kingdom forever, peace with no end.

Isaiah 11:2
The Spirit of the Lord shall rest upon him.

Isaiah 12:6
For great in your midst is the Holy One of Israel.

Daniel 9:21
As I was yet speaking in prayer, behold the man Gabriel, whom I had seen in the vision at the beginning, flying swiftly touched me at the time of the evening sacrifice.

Daniel 10:12
And he said to me: Fear not, Daniel.

Daniel 10:11
Daniel,...I am sent now to thee.

Luke 1:35
And the Holy One to be born of you shall be called the son of God.

Luke: 2:4, 6-7
Joseph also went up from Galilee to Judea to the city of David which is called Bethlehem.
While they were there, the time came for her to be delivered. And she gave birth to her first-born son.

Luke 1:17,76
And he will go before him in the spirit and power of Elijah.... The prophet of the Most High for you will go before the Lord to prepare his ways.

Luke 1:28-33
Rejoice, full of grace, The Lord is with you! Do not fear, Mary....And behold, you will conceive in your womb and bear a son, and you shall call him Lord, Savior. And he will reign.

Luke 1:35
The power of the Most high will overshadow you; therefore, the child to be born will be called holy, the son of God.

Daniel 9:24
The saint of saints may be anointed.

Micah 5:2-3
But you, O Bethlehem Ephrathah, from you shall come forth for me one who is to be ruler in Israel. Therefore he shall give them up until the time when she who is in travail has brought forth.

Malachi 3:1
Behold, I send my messenger to prepare the way before me, and the Lord whom you seem will suddenly come to his Temple; the messenger of the covenant in whom you delight.

Zephaniah 3:14-17
Sing aloud, O daughter of Zion; shout, O Israel! Rejoice, O daughter of Jerusalem. The king of Israel, the Lord, is with you. ... Do not fear, O Zion. ... The Lord, your God, is in your midst a warrior who saves. ... The King of Israel, the Lord, is with you.

Exodus 40:34-35
The cloud overshadowed the meeting tent and the glory of the Lord filled the tabernacle.

Luke 1:39	2 Samuel 6:2
In those days Mary arose and went ... into the hill country to a city of Judah.	David arose and went ... from Baale—Judah to bring up from there the Ark of God.
Luke 1:43	**2 Samuel 6:9**
And why is this granted to me that the mother of my Lord should come to me?	How can the Ark of the Lord come to me [enter my house]!
Luke 1:56	**2 Samuel 6:11**
Mary remained with her [Elizabeth] about three months.	The Ark of the Lord remained in the house of Obededom three months.

The parallel passages given above shows that Luke obviously used several books of the Old Testament. He did not just copy indiscriminately passages from the Old Testament, but rather he judiciously used words, phrases, sentences, and motifs to advance his views on the person and the details of the life of Jesus. He made Jesus appear as fulfilling the prophecies and promises of the Old Testament, thus reducing the Old Testament figures and events to the status of shadows in relation to the reality of Jesus. What the rabbis and Jews considered as primary reality the gospel writers considered as secondary to the reality of Jesus. This way the gospel writers took apart the Old Testament texts and the Old Covenant and constructed a new text (the gospels) and the New Covenant, which in their view followed the old order but surpassed, supplanted, and supplemented the old texts and the old order. Luke and the other Christian writers of the gospels thus imitated and emulated the Old Testament models by creating their own testament which would later be canonized as the New Testament. Ever since the Christians were excommunicated by the Pharisees or had left the Jewish church voluntarily, they had been trying to show that the new order or the new dispensation in Jesus Christ and the Church was superior to the old order and the old dispensation.

Not only did Luke and the other evangelists show similarities between Jesus and his Old Testament antetypes but also the superiority of Jesus over the same Old Testament figures: "I assure you that there is something greater than Solomon here" (Mt 12:42, Lk 11:31); "I tell you there is something here greater than Jonah"

(Mt 12:41, Lk 11:32). According to the Fourth Evangelist, Jesus is greater than Abraham:

> "Abraham is dead and the prophets are dead. Do you claim to be greater than our father Abraham, do you?"... "Your father Abraham rejoiced to think that he would see my day; he saw it and he was glad." The Jews said, "You are not fifty yet, and you have seen Abraham!" Jesus replied, "In all truth I tell you, before Abraham ever was, I am"(8:53-58).

Though in the transfiguration scene Moses and Elijah appeared and conversed with Jesus, the Apostles were instructed to listen to Jesus, not to Moses the founder of the Jewish religion nor to Elijah the popular Jewish prophet: "This is my son, my chosen one. Listen to him" (Lk 9:35).

Though the New Testament writers deconstructed the Old Testament, they did so respectfully. The reverence shown by the New Testament writers to the Old Testament of antiquity is quite transparent : they quoted passages from the Old Testament with the greatest reverence and looked upon the Old Testament as the Word of God. As a rule, when they directly quoted a passage from the Old Testament, they identified their source. They did not want to appear totally as self-begotten—artists have a tendency to parade themselves as creating out of nothing—in this case; simply they could not, for the Jewish audience of the gospels were all so familiar with all the books of the Old Testament that they could easily detect plagiarism and impersonation. On the contrary, in their use of non-biblical sources, the New Testament writers do not acknowledge their sources. Luke, who occasionally only identifies his Old Testament sources, does not even mention by name any of the many narratives of Jesus he used in composing his gospel (Lk 1: 1-4). Obviously, identifying their non-biblical sources did not fit in with the plan and purpose of their writing the gospels; however, using these sources did fit in with their plan. One wonders why. The answer is fairly simple.The argument goes like this. A religious literary work is generally considered to be a product of divine inspiration. Since Jesus is divine, his teachings are God-begotten. John is explicit on this point: "He who comes from above is above all others; he who is of the earth is earthly himself and speaks in an earthly way. He who comes from heaven bears witness to the things he has seen and heard.... He whom God has sent speaks God's own words.... Anyone who believes in the Son has eternal life" (3:31-35). Indeed, the gospel writers have recorded "the signs Jesus had worked in the sight of his disciples" (Jn 20:30) and "dealt with everything Jesus had done and taught from the beginning"

(Acts 1:1). The implicit argument goes like this: Jesus is the Son of God and speaks the Word of God; the gospels that repeat the words of Jesus and records his deeds are also the Word of God. Since the Old Testament also is the Word of God, it is all right for the Gospel writers to quote the Old Testament. But the gospel writers disallow Jesus any ties with other rival literary and religious traditions, for he alone is the Logos, and, being divine, he is not in need of other logoi which are not necessarily of divine inspiration. In the light of this type of argumentation, it is easy to see why the final redactors of the gospels refrained from identifying passages belonging to alien religious writings.

In this respect the gospel writers are no different from Homer who invokes the gods at the beginning of the *Iliad*, and occasionally thereafter as reminders. "Tell me now, you Muses, who have your homes on Mount Olympus. For you, who are goddesses, are there, and you know all things, and we have heard only the rumor of it and know nothing" (*Iliad*, 2: 484-486). The text contains truths for Homer because the gods tell the story. Likewise, the gospel texts are true because they are the word of God recorded by hearers and eyewitnesses. Further, the foundation of the truth is God himself, and the believers, by associating themselves with these eyewitnesses, gain fellowship with them and through them with God himself:

> That which was from the beginning, which we have heard, which we have seen with our eyes, which we have looked upon, and our hands have handled, this we proclaim concerning the word of life. For the life was manifested; and we have seen and do bear witness, and declare unto you the life eternal, which was with the Father, and has appeared to us. That which we have seen and have heard we declare unto you that you also may have fellowship with us and fellowship may be with the Father and with his son Jesus Christ (1 John 1:1-3).

This fellowship of faith or truth of the gospels is something all believers of the Christian communities share whether they are aware of it or not. By the fact they are Christians they have the faith, and no one can take it away from them unless they deliberately abjure it. It is like having a citizenship, which one acquires usually by birth .

In this perspective, belonging to a religion or church is not necessarily a matter of personal decision and choice; it is most often a result of birth. And for the member of a religion, the truth of the religious text is seldom *adaequatio rei et intellectus* (conformity of the mind with an objective reality); it is a lived experience (*adaequatio vitae et religionis*). The truth of a religious text is the lived experience of the community and individuals who created the text; it is, therefore, not necessarily a conformity between the text and history (*adaequatio litterarum cum historia*). This means that some facts of the gospels may be true in the historical sense, and some others may not be, historically speaking. Actually it is unimportant whether the facts of the gospels and other religious texts are historically true and historically verifiable or not. In fact, none of the facts recorded in the gospels is historically verifiable from external evidence. It means that the religious truth of the Christian gospels like the religious truths of Hinduism, for instance, are existential rather than referential; that is, history is not central to any religion, even to the so-called historical religion of Christianity.

As the believers and others read the religious texts, they are handling not a religious text *qua* religious text because there is no room for impersonal analysis and demythification on the religious level. Rather, then they are reading a religious text *qua* literary text. In the critical analysis of the religious text all the rules of literary criticism apply. The critic would agree with Plato (*Republic* X) that literature has no truth or that it is not concerned with truth as truth, and he would prefer to look at the text *qua* text: its genre, sources, forms of discourse, historical contexts, borrowing, influences, method of composition, rhetorical devices, logical structure, philosophical assumptions, and so on. The literary critic engages in all these activities not as a believer from within the code of faith, but as an observer from without. As a believer, the inquirer can look at these texts and discover new truths for life, but as a literary critic he/she can look at the very same texts and discover new meanings and new dimensions and new insights, which are not necessarily useful for the person's life as a believer but nonetheless useful for scholarly work toward appreciating the texts as literature. In other words, the meaning of a literary text is different from the religious truth of the very same text. New research and new readings can reveal new meanings in the text, and the textual critic raises and tries to answer Collingwood's historicist question: "What does it mean?" It is a fact that sometimes literary interpretations have been incorporated into the understanding of religious texts, which phenomenon has often created heresies and political factions and divisions within religious communities; the cause of this is that people do not often keep religious and literary activities separate and they unwittingly confuse meaning, which is constantly subject to change due to different interpretations, with truth, which is unchanging and which is reflected primarily in faith and cult. In other words, *fides quaerens intellectum* (faith seeking understanding) is a temptation that is to be overcome rather than succumbed to; one does not overcome this temptation by yielding to it but rather by keeping the realms of faith and inquiry separate.

Further, if we can keep the realms of faith and inquiry, religion and the study of religion, the theological study of religious texts and the literary study thereof separate and divisible, then the study of religion will not be problematic at all and will not smack of secularizing of the sacred. Edward Gibbon gives us the classic formulation of this problem and its solution:

> The theologian may indulge in the pleasing task of describing Religion as she descended from Heaven, arrayed in her native purity. A more melancholy duty is imposed on the historian. He must discover the inevitable mixture of error and corruption which she contracted in a long residence upon earth, among a weak and degenerate race of beings....Our curiosity is naturally prompted to inquire by what means the Christian faith obtained so remarkable a victory over the established religions of the earth. To this inquiry, an obvious but satisfactory answer may be returned; that it was owing to the convincing evidence of the doctrine itself, and to the ruling providence of its great Author. But, as truth and reason seldom find so favourable a reception in the world, and as the wisdom of Providence frequently condescends to use the passions of the human heart, and the general circumstances of mankind, as instruments to execute its purpose; we may still be permitted, though with becoming submission, to ask not indeed what were the first, but what were the secondary causes of the rapid growth of the Christian church.[34]

One more important observation on intertextuality is in place at this juncture; it is about the role of what is left out in a text. Kinesics and linguistics remind us that what is left unsaid, like body language and suprasegmental phonemes (tone, stress, and juncture), is often as important as what is said in human discourse. Similarly, what is left out of a text could become as crucial as what is left in the text toward the understanding of the text. Both in speech and writing the audience/reader is asked to read between lines to seek missing links, to supply motives, to ask questions, to recognize irony, and to readjust interpretations on the basis of what is not explicitly stated in words. It is like defining presence by

---

[34] Edward Gibbon, *The Decline and Fall of the Roman Empire*, ch 15; cited by Richard F. Gombrich, *Theravada Buddhism* (London: Routledge, 1988)., 5-6.

absence.[35] St. Augustine's famous definition of darkness as the absence of light is relevant here. We can talk about absence-presence because they are not totally antithetical or contradictory; they are only partially opposing; they are only contraries, to use logical distinctions. That is, contraries can partially co-exist within the same entity at the same time, unlike contradictories which cannot be true simultaneously. For example, there can be some darkness while there is at the same time some light. Similarly, the proverbial Christ and Apollo, Athens and Jerusalem, Ingeld and Christ, Buddha and Christ are not necessarily antithetical realities.

All this implies that there is nothing inherently contradictory for the New Testament writers to have used Buddhist ideas in expounding Christian doctrines; they could have used dimensions of Buddha in their portrayal of Christ so much so a Buddhist Christ, like a Socratic Christ or a Mosaic Messiah or a Christian Buddha or a Christian Mani or a Buddhist Mani or a Hindu American or an American Indian, is not a contradiction in terms. We know that the Christian Saint Josaphat of the seventh century is none other than the Christianized version of the Bodhisatva. Likewise, the central Asian Christian documents preserved in the Syrian Sogdian, Turkic, and Chinese documents of the thirteenth and fourteenth centuries show the Asian Christians' "attempt to express their faith in Buddhist terms, almost to the point of losing their own identity, yet they always remain aware of the core of their faith."[36] Klimkeit also refers to the attempt of the Chinese Nestorian Christians to formulate their Christian faith in Buddhist terms.[37] In the "Jesus-Messiah-Sutra" (Hsu-t'ing Messias-Sutra) "hsu-po (Jehova), who is Lord of heaven," is first described in terms taken from Mahayana. Thus it says: "The Lord of Heaven is is incessantly going around all over the world, is constantly present everywhere. ...On account of this, every man existing in this world only obtains life and continues his existence by the strength of the Lord of Heaven."[38]

---

[35] See Beth Rigel Daugherty, "Virginia Woolf's Use of Distance as Patriarchal Control of Women, Death, and Character,"Diss. Rice University, 1982; S. L. Clark and J. M. Wasserman, "The Heart in *Troilus and Criseyde* ," *Chaucer Review* , 18 (1984): 316-328; S. L. Clark, "Said and Unsaid, Male and Female ..." *Proceedings of the PMR Conference* 11(Villanova, 1986): 51-70.

[36] Hans-J. Klimkeit, "Christian-Buddhist Encounter in Medieval Central Asia," in *The Cross and the Lotus* , ed. G. W. Houston (Delhi, 1985), 14.

[37] Klimkeit, 18.

[38] P. Y. Saeki, *The Nestorian Documents and Relics in China* (Tokyo, 1951), 125.

A similar situation obtains in the New Testament. While the presence of the Old Testament in the New Testament is abundantly clear from explicit references "left in," the absence of the Old Testament is also equally clear from the Old Testament references "left out" of passages which carry traces of the Old Testament. For instance, as I have mentioned above, in the infancy narratives Luke has used Daniel and 1 Samuel even though he makes no explicit references to those books of the Old Testament. So their absence is noticeable in the text even though they are not physically present there with the signs of their exact identification. This is the way the Buddhist-Hindu texts are present in the New Testament: by their absence. The Buddhist texts have not been explicitly cited as such by Luke or Matthew in their gospels. But there are too many traces of these Indian traditions in the gospels to be ignored by a serious reader.

Is this practice plagiarism, one may ask. It is plagiarism, all right in a sense, that is, in the modern sense,.because it is artistic adaptation (some read it: theft! Great writers steal and bad writers imitate, as T. S. Eliot would put it) of the words and ideas of another without crediting the source or presenting as new and original an idea derived from an existing source. Apart from plagiarism's modern pejorative connotation, all great writers of the past have consistently borrowed truths wherever they could find them and used them in their own works as their own either intentionally or unintentionally. But they changed their source material considerably. Erica Jong, a modern writer, describes this phenomenon in her novels as follows:

> I would say that the chapter on the husband [in *The Fear of Flying*] who goes mad is probably the most autobiographical thing I wrote. But like all things a writer writes about, it's so transformed and condensed and metamorphosed into something else that I can no longer rembember what actually happened....Most first novels use the materials of the author's life. Sometimes they're disguised. Perhaps the author went to Barnard and says Vassar in the book. Nearly every first novel is autobiographical, and years later you cannot remember anymore the things you change.[39]

When ancient writers "plagiarized" the mythological traditions of other nations, they did not deliberately try to deceive by uttering falsehoods; they only tried to communicate truths, which unfortunately are always admixtured with falsehoods because of the imperfect nature of the human language and human

---

[39] Jacquelyn Denalli, "Trade Secrets," *USAIR* April, 1989, p. 88.

understanding. It is in this sense that Hesiod's Olympian Muses tell him: "We know to tell many lies that sound like truth,/but we know to sing reality, when we will" (*Theogony*). That is, no human discourse is the whole truth or wholly original. T. S. Eliot recognizes this built-in limitation of all art:

> Between the idea
> And the reality
> Between the motion
> And the act
> Falls the shadow.[40]

In passing, Hesiod's Muses themselves decided to borrow a few things, like the animal fable, succession of divine rulers, and the Myth of Ages from Mesopotamian, Egyptian, Jewish, Persian, and Indian sources! [41]

Many Western Christians are unduly disturbed when it is suggested that the gospel writers may have borrowed literary motifs from the East. The reason for this discomfort is not only that they confuse divine inspiration with creative originality but also place a premium on the sancity of private property or copyright. Such an indisposition is uncalled for. Religious people keep divine inspiration and human authorship separate and remember that Western culture itself has prized originality in creative arts only beginning the eighteenth century and legislated it in the twentieth century. Of course, no one wants art or literature to be nothing but an imitation of older and better works. What is important is not originality in itself, but the way it may be combined with creative imagination. What is needed is innovation and revitalization. This we have in abudance in the gospels, especially when they interpret the Hebrew and Oriental traditions in the light of their theology of Jesus.

E. *Literary Relationship*

The history of religions and literary texts shows that the interpretation of the texts has varied from the beginning. This is obvious from the number of different denominations in Judaism,

---

[40] "Hollow Men" (1928).
[41] See M. L. West, trans. *Hesiod: Theogony and Works and Days* (Oxford, 1988), xi-xvii.

Hinduism, Christianity, Buddhism, and Islam which have created themselves on the bases of different interpretations they have given to their sacred scriptures. At the root of this diversity stands, first of all, the fact that religions are unwilling to distinguish between religious texts and their literary interpretations. Secondly, a healthy scepticism has always been part of the practice of literary interpretation.

Deconstructive scepticism, which characterizes modern post-Modern Criticism, post-Aristotelianism, and post-Structuralism, holds the view that the language of written discourse—both of the text and its interpretations, the text itself being an interpretation of previous texts—is inherently unreliable. No matter how hard a text may try to sustain the illusion of unity, coherence, meaning, and truth, the text is so prone to disunity, incoherence, and incomplete truth that it helps the reader only with incomplete meaning and even contains errors. For the modern sceptic, reading becomes deconstruction, a process of discovering the sources of error or incompleteness of the meaning of a text or its interpretation. Indeed, the great texts, or their authors, knew their own incoherence. Hesiod, the first poet of the Western tradition, was explicitly conscious of this problem. He says that his own inspiring Muses, as mentioned above, have told him that they can say many true and false things. And, as Gadamer tells us, "what is true and what is false in such a context seems to be hopelessly entangled and inseparable."[42]

This incoherence of the the text is both subjective and objective. It is subjective in the sense that the author himself has intentionally put the ambiguity in the text, as the Muses have done in the case of Hesiod. Clearly, we will never be able to unearth all the intentional ambiguities of the text. Objectively, the ambiguity is due to the presence of unidentified subtexts hidden in the text. Often research and interpretation can reveal the presence of these subtexts and open up new interpretations of the text. This is accomplished through the study of literary indebtedness and historical scholarship.

The study of literary influences has always enjoyed a pre-eminent place as an important branch of literary criticism within particular literatures and especially in comparative literature. In biblical scholarship, the study of the influence of the Old

---

[42] "The Eminent Text and Its Truth," *The Bulletin of the Midwest Modern Language Association* 13 (1980), 4.

Testament on the New Testament writers is just as popular as the study of the influence of the Bible on English writers like Chaucer and Shakespeare. Though that is the case, some critics feel that to suggest an author's literary debts diminishes his/her originality. But they often forget that originality is not necessarily always innovation. It is not the great masters who are ashamed to admit the influence of other masters on their thoughts and life. Mahatma Gandhi was always willing to acknowledge the indebtedness of his philosophy of non-violence to Jesus' Sermon on the Mount, just as Martin Luther King, Jr. used to point out to Gandhi's influence on his own thought. It is the disciples who, most often out of jealousy, are unwilling to admit that their masters were influenced by other masters especially since the disciples of the respective masters are at loggerheads with each other. That is, indeed, the case between rabbinic Judaism and the Jesus movements, between Christianity and Islam, and between Christianity and Buddhism-Hinduism. No wonder then that the disciples of Jesus who wrote the gospels are unwilling to admit the presence of Buddhist and Gnostic ideas in the teachings of Jesus!

Even though the gospel writers use unacknowledged Buddhist and other subtexts, they do not appear to be doing so; this is because these writers make their subtexts as their own original text. Their writings are thus an account also of the moving power, effectiveness, and genuineness of their own creative work. As Shaw reminds us, "The original author is not necessarily the innovator or the most inventive, but rather the one who succeeds in making all his own, in subordinating what he takes from others to the next complex of his own artistic work."[43]

Direct interrelationships between literatures can come about through the popularity of one author or authors of one country in another. This is especially true if the author's works were written in a language understood in a particular country. For example, American books and movies can be directly read and seen by the English in Britain and vice versa. Often, however, it is through translations that a Russian writer like Dostoevsky is read in English-speaking countries.

It is important to note that translators more or less adapt and modernize the translated work to the tastes and needs of their audiences. Very often in the past, translation of a work was made not from the original but from other translations. Even today a

---

[43] Shaw, 86.

Hindi writer translates Solzhenitsyn from the English translation of the Russian original. Then again the English bibles of Bishop Challoner and Ronald Knox are translations from the Latin Vulgate of St. Jerome, which itself is a translation from the Hebrew and Greek originals. Even the New Testament authors, even though they presumably could read the Hebrew Bible, quoted from the Greek Septuagint rather than from the original Hebrew and Aramaic texts of the Old Testament! Certainly the same new Testament authors will not accuse me of the crime of using the English translations of the Buddhist and Hindu scriptures written originally in Sanskrit and Pali; they will be no less guilty of the same crime that I could be accused of. The old theory of translation as redaction has allowed a great deal of freedom of excision, addition, and paraphrase. Modern biblical scholarship has shown how true this is in the redaction of the synoptic gospels.

Fidelity of a translation to the original text will appear to vanish when the transmission is made orally. One fact is beyond cavil: even today much teaching in any literate society is accomplished orally at home and in the educational institutions. In all teaching and instruction, faithfulness to the tradition is the most valued of all qualities. That is the reason why every society keeps a careful eye on the qualities of the instructors and the content of their instruction. In the oral-aural culture the tale-teller or the singer of the epics was/is expected transmit it as he has heard it without making significant alterations; if he did unauthorized alterations, he would be caught by the knowledgeable audience anyway. The recitation of tales, songs, laws, and sermons, of course, required a prodigious memory. It is a well-known fact that priests and folk singers in India preserved religious texts and the long epics of *Ramayana* and *Mahabharata* for centuries by reciting them from memory. Even today not only Indian singers but also Yugoslavian and African singers can recite epic poems as long as the *Iliad* and the *Odyssey* in their entirety from memory. They can quote long lists of facts, figures, speeches, quotations, poems, and so on almost verbatim. This is even true today of preachers, teachers, and writers. What I am trying to say is that the writers of the gospels could have easily remembered numerous passages of the Buddhist tradition even if they had heard it only in Greek or Aramaic and even if they had not read the Buddhist Scriptures in the original. By the same token the Buddhist scriptural tradition written down at a later period bears close resemblance and fidelity to its preliterary ancestors, just as the Christian gospels probably record many of the *ipsissima verba* of Jesus. However, it is also a commonplace occurrence that a long story is often greatly reduced in size and then reconstructed during its retelling.[44] Gadamer points to some of the built-in constraints of imitation-translation:

> Artists are at the mercy of a new kind of seduction: the seduction of copying, to which we affix the pejorative inflection "imitation." Certainly copying and faithful succession (for example in the form of the generational succession of masters, students, and grand-students) could be seen as all cultures' constantly renewing law of life. But wherever this law operated as a matter of course, it provided freedom for the most individual self-expression. Set against this, imitation (like its opposite: affected originality) is really, as Plato characterized art, "thrice removed from the truth." Imitative constraints prevail most blatantly in the case of literary translation: constrictions of verse form, rime, and content force the translator, whether voluntarily or not, to the mere imitation of poetic models found in his own language.[45]

Very often what happens in literary influences is not that the later writer copies, imitates, or translates entire poems, stories, or sermons. It is rather the writer borrows materials or methods or helps himself selectively to aphorisms, images, figures of speech, motifs, or plots. For instance, the gospel writers borrowed the rabbinic method of midrash. Similarly, they borrowed elements of the trial of Socrates from Plato to portray Jesus as a second Socrates. As for presenting the journeys of Paul, Luke used the plot of the *Odyssey* and the *Aeneid* by making Paul travel to almost all the places Odysseus and Aeneas visited, even by shipwrecking him in Malta as Odysseus was in Calypso's Ogygia (Malta) and by ending Paul's journey in Italy as Aeneas' travel took him there. Such borrowings are allusions pointing more or less clearly to literary texts.

We must, therefore, distinguish different sources in the case of borrowing. For instance, part of the material used in the infancy narratives of Matthew and Luke have come from Indian sources, while some other parts from Jewish and Greek sources; further, in the use of their sources the gospel writers might even have employed the Jewish literary method, the so-called *midrash*, besides other Hellenistic hagiographical conventions.

Today, when many ecumenists study Christian and Buddhist traditions, they just juxtapose similarities and differences without

---

[44] Stith Thompson, "Literature for the Unlettered," in Stallknecht and Horst-Frenz, 201-217.
[45] "The Eminent Text," 9.

demonstrating any direct or indirect relationship to each other. They do so under the assumption that the parallels may be produced by different religious traditions on their own. In this sense one may compare Dickens and Gogol, Christ and Buddha, *Dhammapada* and *Bhagavadgita*. While studying parallels in this sense, the critic should nevertheless consider the possibility of direct and indirect relationships, which is what I do in this book, besides giving parallels as such. We can argue that an author can be considered to have been influenced by a foreign author "when something from without can be demonstrated to have produced upon him and/or his artistic works an effect his native literary tradition and personal development do not explain."[46] Further, influence should not be confined to a few individual details or images or borrowings or sources. It should be pervasive.

In the case of the New Testament writer, if at all they had been influenced by the Indian tradition, it should be shown that a large number of the New Testament ideas and descriptive details were not inherited from their native Jewish-Hellenistic tradition or developed by the individual authors themselves. On the one hand, we know very little about the education of the New Testament writers to conclude anything definitive about their evangelical preparation and other literary accomplishments. Though traditionally the Apostles and the authors of the gospels are considered to be illiterate, their works, on the contrary, show great education and erudition. There is every reason to believe that many of the main ideas found in the gospels like the notions of incarnation, human condition, non-violence, ethical conduct, gnosis, salvation, heaven, hell, and so on are not at all native to the Jewish-Hellenistic tradition. Since that is the case, these elements of the gospels must have come from elsewhere.

It must also be shown that the New Testament writers were ready and willing to be influenced by sources other than their native ones. As in the parable of the sower and the seed, only those seeds that have fallen on good soil will yield an abundant harvest. Often literary influence is fruitful at the radical change of the direction of a particular religious movement or during social or political upheavals. For instance, the modern Indian literary tradition was extensively influenced by British writers during the British occupation and by Marxist ideology during the Indian struggle for independence. Similarly, Christianity came under the

---

[46] Shaw, 91.

influence of non-Jewish literary traditions and unjewish ideologies during the Hellenistic times and especially during the second half of the first century, when Christians were excommunicated by the rabbinic establishment and when they were frowned upon by the Roman world as uncivilized and unsophisticated. It is quite understandable that at this juncture the Christian writers must have turned to esoteric ideologies and kindred communities for literary inspiration. It is, however, not easy to document these influences by the mentions, quotations, diaries, and written testimonies of contemporaries, and the internally certified evidence of the New Testament writers' reading of Indian literature as in the case of modern writers. Alas, such evidences are lacking not only for the New Testament writers but also for most ancient and medieval writers.

It is, therefore, unrealistic in the case of the ancients writers, like the authors of the gospels, to demand documentary evidences of direct influence from the Indian tradition simply because of the paucity of extant manuscripts dating from the first and second centuries. The best we can do in a situation like this is to seek evidences of indirect influence. Of course, the situation is different in the case of writers from the eighteenth century on simply because of the abundance of written sources preserved since then. For instance, du Perron translated and introduced Indian classics into Europe. Many eighteenth-century and and nineteenth-century European writers, like Schopenhauer and Goethe, were influenced indirectly by Indian thought popularized in the West by du Perron and missionaries and travelers to the East. The same is true of American writers like Emerson, Thoreau, and Whitman who were influenced indirectly by Indian religious thought through the translations of Sir William Jones and the English publications of the Royal Asiatic Society. In a similar way, I suggest that the New Testament writers were influenced indirectly by Indian thought through their contact with Gnosticism, which was extensively influenced by Indian thought and Indian religions. On account of such indirect influence and on account of the unavailability of Indian classics in Greek translations, it is often difficult to provide extensive verbal parallels, especially of long parallel passages from Christian and Buddhist scriptures.

Indeed, a few verbal parallels between Christian and Buddhist scriptures do come by; it is all the more so with parallel ideas, which are numerous in the scriptures of both religions. In this context, an idea may be roughly defined as a theme or topic we may reflect upon. There are general or more inclusive ideas that most people are concerned with, as opposed to esoteric ideas which are discussed by specialized groups like nuclear physicists, computer scientists, and so on. Outstanding among general ideas is the idea of human nature itself—the perfectibility of man, the depravity of man, and the dignity of man. In the religious context there are also the concepts of God, salvation, grace, sin, providence, merit, afterlife, and so on. Very likely, such a discussion will also involve the recognition that these ideas may belong to some school of thought or an "ism," that is, a complex of ideas occurring together that warrant identification. It is in this sense that I talk about the Gnosticism or Buddhism of the gospel writers in this book.

Since these days we recognize that ideas to have a history, we will naturally look for reciprocal influence and continuity of thought and expression among different communities. However, tracing the flow of ideas from one culture to another and their transformation require extensive research in the fields of philosophy, religion, arts, and sciences. Such a vast research is beyond the scope of the present work though I have integrated in this book studies done by other scholars.

In discussing ideas one important *caveat* is in order. Ideas are not units, in some way comparable to coins, that are passed intact from one culture to another. Rather, ideas are chameleon-like or protean in their life and behavior. For instance, Marxism as an ideology has different expressions in Russia, China, India, Poland, and so on; so also capitalism is not understood in the same sense in America, China, or Russia. Similarly, the idea of the Church is different in different Christian denominations. In short, ideas are interpreted when passed on from one individual to another, from one culture to another. Ideas are neither entirely objective nor entirely subjective; they are intersubjective; their existence is not permanent; they are becoming or they are in a state of flux all the time. Even when ideas like the avatar are found in both Buddhism and Christianity, they are never understood in the same way in both traditions.[47] The old Scholastic adage is relevant to this discussion: "Id quod recipitur ad modum recipientis recipitur" (Whatever is received is received according to the predisposition of the receiver). No culture will receive all the ideas of another culture; in receiving the recipient selects and interprets. Though the notion of unit-ideas is necessary in mathematics and the physical sciences, in philosophy and

---

[47] Geoffrey Parrinder, *Avatar and Incarnation* (New York, 1982).

religion we should avoid the concept and view ideas rather as "tendencies," "inclinations," or "dispositions of thought and feeling."[48]

Indeed, in passing from author to author, from culture to culture, or from religion to religion, ideas undergo significant changes through restatement, reinterpretation, and transformation. Any biblical scholar will admit that the monotheistic Jewish ideas of the Transcendent God has undergone almost a radical shift both in the teaching of Jesus and that of the early Church which formulated the notion of one God in three persons. Therefore, a comparative study of ideas must always recognize the phenomenon of shift and change in ideas, and readers should see such a study as a commentary upon this process. All this does not mean that we should seek and find historical continuity and actual influence whenever and wherever we find analogies and parallels. For instance, when Oswald Spengler identifies ancient Stoicism with modern Socialism or when he calls Cromwell, Muhammad, and Pythagoras contemporaries, he is not suggesting that they were historically influenced. These intuited analogies could open up new paths of investigation, however. Such was the case of the study of Buddha-Christ parallels in the nineteenth century. But during the last seventy years or so, we have come to recognize that these Christ-Buddha parallels are more than mere independent analogues and speculations. Today they belong to history and the subject of serious investigation and dialogue.

Since my study is primarily in comparative literature, I cannot altogether ignore the historical connection of literary relationship. So I will raise also the historical issue and suggest my answer to the historical question.

---

[48] See Newton P. Stallknecht, "Ideas and Literature," in Stallknecht and Horst-Frenz, 152.

CHAPTER TWO

HISTORICAL AND LITERARY CHRONOLOGY

The traditional distinction between the Buddha/Jesus of history and the Buddha/Jesus of faith is very useful in a literary study of this kind. If this study were a theological work, my exclusive emphasis would be on the Christ and Buddha of faith. On the other hand, if this book were a historical work, my total attention would be on the Christ and Buddha of history. Since this is a literary study, I combine both approaches as the literary texts, which are an amalgam of both, do it. As a literary work, this study does not presume that the entire infancy narratives as given in the Buddhist and Christian scriptures are historical in the modern sense of history that the events narrated took place exactly as they had happened. Regrettably, some Christian theologians, unlike Buddhist scholars, confuse history and truth and claim that theology is history in its modern sense that the theological events took place exactly as they were narrated.

Since all the infancy narrative material cannot be historically verified from contemporary documents, there is no compelling reason to regard this material as historical in the modern sense; however, I do not say that they are totally fictional either. That would be far from the truth, which is also derived not only from documentary evidence but also from reliable folk traditions. While some infancy data are historical, the others are products of fertile theological imagination and of folkloric development. So it is important to distinguish between biographical and hagiographical chronologies with regard to the persons of Buddha and Jesus and the literary traditions about them.

A. *History and Faith*

1.*The Historical Buddha*

Buddha, the founder of Buddhism, was born c. 568 B.C. as the son of Sudhodana of the Gautama clan of the Sakya tribe. Buddha's own name was Siddhartha, and his mother was Mayadevi of the Lichchavi clan. Since Buddha was the subject of numerous legends and because the earliest Buddhist chronicles were written two hundred years after the events, it is impossible to write a historical biography of the Master based on written documents. The following details of his life gleaned from different traditions—from the Chronicles of Sri Lanka (*Dipavamsa* and *Mahavamsa*) and Sarvastivadin *avadanas*—stand out as important in the Master's life and may be accepted as more or less historical.

Queen Maya died when the child was one week old, and Siddhartha was raised by his mother's sister, Mahaprajapati (Gotami). At the age of nineteen, the prince married his cousin Yasodhara, daughter of Dandapani, and lived a very happy life with her. About eight years after his marriage, a son (Rahula) was born to him.

One night, six days after his son's birth, the young Siddhartha awoke suddenly, "like a man who has been told that his house is on fire," left the palace with his charioteer and rode off into the night in search of peace of mind and enlightenment. He was twenty-nine at the time. He became successively a disciple to the leading religious masters of his time; for six years he lived a life of extreme penance and asceticism; he lived on seeds and herbs and for a time even on dung; he slept in burial grounds with rotten corpses. But enlightenment eluded him.

One day the famished and the barely conscious ascetic accepted the hospitality of the beautiful Sujata, who refreshed him by serving him a hearty meal, which gave him a new lease of life. When his fellow ascetics found out that he had betrayed them by breaking fast, they deserted him. Next, Siddhartha went to Budhgaya, near the banks of the Nairanjana, where he sat under a pipal tree to meditate and resolved to stay there until enlightenment came to him.

After seven weeks of meditation, on the full moon day in the month of Vaisakha in the year 533 B.C., as he sat engrossed in meditation, suddenly with the vision of endless births and rebirths, enlightenment on the self-realized means of escaping the endless cycle of rebirth dawned on him. From then on, Siddhartha was honored as Buddha, the enlightened one.

He proceeded to Varanasi and preached his first sermon, the *Dharma-chakra-parivartana* ("setting in motion the Wheel of Law") in the deer park at Sarnath. As his band of disciples increased in number, he traveled from city to to city and preached the new doctrine in the common language of the people in the form of Socratic questioning, parables, formulas, and sermons. Though he rejected miracles and philosophy, his disciples attributed to him many miracles and sophisticated philosophies.

Buddha was basically a preacher of fundamental ethics which he developed to help human beings save themselves from the cycle of endless births. He taught the Four Noble Truths (*chatvari arya satyani*), which relate to suffering, its cause, and the method of release from suffering: (1) Suffering (*dukkha*) is part and parcel of life. He said in his famous Fire Sermon: "All things are on fire—with the fire of passion and hatred and of infatuation with birth, parting, sickness, old age, death, sorrow, lamentation, misery, grief, and despair; with all these they are on fire." (2) The cause of suffering, leading to rebirths, is desire (*iccha*) or craving (*tanha/trishna*): the thirst for existence, experience, immortality, pleasures, possessions, and power. (3) Release from desire can be achieved only by abandoning desire, by destroying the selfish ego, and by detachment from the things of this world. (4) The only way one can achieve release from the cycle of becoming is by avoiding the extreme of attachment to the world and its pleasures and excessive self-mortification or asceticism. The mean between the two extremes is called the Middle Path (*Madhyama pratipad*). One follows the Middle Path by following the precepts called the Eightfold Path (*Ashtanga-marga*), which leads to wisdom, peace, knowledge, enlightenment, and final liberation. The eightfold rules are right views, right aspirations, right speech, right conduct, right livelihood, right effort, right mindfulness, and right meditation. The person practicing the eightfold path will reach the state of the saint (*arhat*) and his final beatitude called *nirvana*.

The famous followers of Buddha were Ananda, his cousin and intimate disciple, Kasyapa, the most learned of his disciples, the rich youth Yasa, the king Bimbisara, the barber Upali, and the courtesan Ambapali. Buddha had his enemies, too. The most important one was his cousin Devadatta who made several attempts on his life, once by throwing a huge rock at him. Though Devadatta was finally converted on his death, he had to spend some time in hell to atone for his sins, according to Buddhist tradition.

Buddha founded the order (*sangha*) which consisted of *sravaka* (listeners or lay people), *upasaka* (lay disciples), *bhikshu* (religious mendicants), *Bhiskshuni* (nuns), and *sramana* (ascetics).

The Master died—of food poisoning after he had eaten of pork and mushrooms at the house of a poor smith called Chanda—under a sal tree at Kushinagara about the age of eighty and entered into *parinirvana* (final extinction). Seven days after his death, the body was cremated, and later stupas were erected over the places where his ashes were buried.[1]

2. The Historical Christ

Although there is an abundance of information about Jesus Christ in the New Testament, there are historical difficulties in interpreting and evaluating them because there was very little written about Jesus in the first century after his death. Tacitus (*Annales* 15.44) said that Christians were named after a Christus who had been condemned to death by Pontius Pilate. Pliny the Younger (*Epistola* 10.69) mentioned that the Christians sang hymns to a certain Christus as to a God. The Jewish Josephus, a contemporary of Tacitus makes references to Jesus in his *Antiquities* (18.63 and 20.9), where he talks about James, "the brother of Jesus, the alleged Christ." In 112 A.D., the younger Pliny, who was the Roman governor of Bithynia in Asia Minor, wrote a letter to Emperor Trajan asking for advice as to how he should handle the Christians (*Epistola* 10.96). From the middle of the second century, there is an abundance of testimonies from non-Christian writers about Christians.

These non-biblical testimonies confirm with the Christian gospels that Jesus was a historical person. Everything else that we know of Jesus has been derived from the New Testament, especially the four canonical gospels and the apocrypha. According to the gospel testimonies, Jesus was born in Judea during the reign of Herod the Great, c. 4 B.C. He is identified in the later gospel traditions with the village of Nazareth, located in lower Galilee; since there is no reference in earlier testimonies to the existence of a village called Nazareth, it is possible that the village itself was named after Jesus who was called "the Nazorean" or teacher. Hardly anything is known about the first thirty years of his life.

At the age of twenty-nine Jesus left home and went into the wilderness in search of enlightenment. There he fasted and prayed for over a month and fought against the temptations of Satan just as Buddha fought against the temptations of Mara. At long last, during his baptism from the hands of his cousin John, Jesus received

---

[1] See A. K. Coomaraswamy, *Buddha and the Gospel of Buddhism* (New York, 1916); C. A.. F. Rhys Davids, *Gotama the Man* (London, 1928); A Foucher, *La Vie du Bouddha d'après les Textes et les Monuments de l'Inde* (Paris, 1949); E. J. Thomas, *The Life of Buddha as Legend and History* (New York, 1927).

enlightenment and became a wandering preacher throughout the land of Palestine.

His followers proclaimed him the Messiah, the awaited Davidic king, who would restore Israel and prepare the way for the full manifestation of God's reign among His people. He preached the dawn of a new age, the arrival of the kingdom of God in his famous Sermon on the Mount. There he analyzed the human condition and proposed the eight beatitudes for obtaining entry into the Kingdom of God. In the sermons he preached, he appears to be a teacher of interpersonal morality. In this respect, Jesus resembles Buddha, who too was a teacher of morality rather than a professional theologian.

Jesus' intentions as a peaceful messiah—the gospel portrayal of him—were too far removed from the attractive militant messiah of popular expectation even for his own followers to understand. Jesus preached the coming of the Kingdom of God and went about making disciples. It seems that his public ministry of healing and preaching lasted about three years. However, when his preaching and the activities of some of his followers challenged the authority of the social, political, and religious establishment, his enemies used his alleged messianic—divine and royal—claims to prosecute him for blasphemy and treason.

Finally, his enemies had him arrested and put him on trial before the Roman Procurator Pontius Pilate for whom *messiah* probably had only one meaning: a military rebel against Rome. Earlier, according to the canonical gospels, Jesus was convicted by the Jewish court of Sanhedrin of blasphemy, a charge that was no crime under the Roman law. However, Pilate took the messianic claim literally and seriously and pronounced Jesus guilty of treason against Caesar and had him executed. Jesus' death took place probably in 30 A.D.[2] It is interesting to note here that according to a

---

[2] Christian E. Hauer and William A. Young, *An Introduction to the Bible: A Journey into Three Worlds* (Englewood Cliffs, 1986); Howard Kee, *Understanding the the New Testament* (Englewood Cliffs, 1983); John Hayes, *Introduction to the Bible* (Philadelphia, 1971); Günther Bornkamm, *Jesus of Nazareth* (New York, 196); Norman Perrin, *Rediscovering the Teaching of Jesus* (New York, 1967). As for the historicity of the infancy narrative of Matthew , Georg Soares Prabhu writes: "One might , in fact, query the usefulness or even the legitimacy of asking such historical questions of narratives which, quite obviously, are not intended as history; and whose historicity is largely irrelevant to the point they intend to make. It is now a commonplace of NT exegesis that Mt's Infancy Narrative is a *theological* prologue to the Gospel" (*The Formula Quotations in the Infancy Narrative of Matthew* (Rome, 1976), 299.

very early (c. end of the first century) Christian account, The Gospel of Peter, Jesus was condemned to death by King Herod!

B. *Literary Chronology*

1. *Buddhist*

There is reason to believe that even while Buddha was alive many of his disciples considered him as a divine being. He was called *Bhagavat* ("the Lord"), *Jina* ("Conqueror"), *Tathagata* ("the one who has come the same way"), *Sugata* ("well gone"), *Mahapurusha* ("the great person'), and so on. Once the brahman Dona seeing the Master sitting at the foot of a tree and noticing the mysterious marks on Buddha's feet, asked him: "Are you a god (*deva*)? And the Lord answered: "I am not." "Are you a celestial being (*gandharva*)?" "I am not." "Are you a spiritual apparition (*Yaksha*)"? "I am not." "Are you a man?" "I am not." Buddha spoke to the brahman: "O brahman, truly I was a god, a celestial being, a spiritual apparition, a man, as long as I had not purged myself of fluxes. Brahmin, just as a lotus or a water-lily born of the water...remains unstained by the water, even so, brahmin, being born of the world...I remain unstained by the world. Therefore, brahmin, consider me as the enlightened one."[3]

Very early in the history of Buddhism we find the Buddhist act of faith in the three jewels: "I take refuge in Buddha; I take refuge in the Teaching (*dharma*); I take refuge in the Church (*sangha*)." For the average believer Buddha is the greatest of divinities; even the educated Buddhist of the Thearvada persuasion, when he places flowers at the feet of the statue of Buddha, in the privacy of the faith of his heart venerates Buddha not merely as a teacher of the truth, but as a deity.

It is this faith in the divinity of Buddha that is reflected in the birth stories of the Master. The birth stories celebrate not the Buddha of history but the Buddha of faith; so they are as old as faith in Buddha. As the faith in the divinity of Buddha gradually developed, so did rise the stories of the supernatural origin and birth of the Master.

The Buddha stories are found in the Buddhist canonical literature which contains not only the word of the Lord

---

[3] *Anguttara Nikaya* 2.37-38.

(*Buddhavacana*) but also much that is not in any sense the utterance of the Master. Many of the discourses are attributed to the disciples. In the two oldest collections of discourses, the *Digha* and the *Majjhima*, there are over twenty discourses attributed to the disciples.

Originally the discourses of Buddha and legends about him were recited and handed down from memory, because writing at that time was used customarily not for study and discourse but for business and commerce. We know of the traditional reciters of religious doctrines like the *sutradharas*, and, in addition, of two schools that applied themselves to learning different sections of the Buddhist canon and reciting them, the *Dighabhanakas* ("reciters of the Digha") and *Majjhimabhanakas* ("reciters of the Majjhima").[4]

The First Council (*Mahasamgiti*—"chanting or reciting together") was convened at Rajagrha immediately after the *parinirvana* (death of Buddha). This Council of 500 *arhants* (perfected ones) was convened by Mahakasyapa for the recital of the Dharma by Ananda and the Vinaya by Upali. According to some schools, Kasyapa recited the Abhidharma, the third part of the Tripitaka (the Pali Buddhist Canon) at the Council. There is general agreement among different Buddhist traditions that at the Council of the Sthaviravadins (Theravadins) at Rajagrha the *arhants* worked systematically through everything Buddha was remembered to have said and that they produced an agreed upon-canon of texts embodying it.[5] Kern writes about the accomplishments of the First Council:

> If we are asked how much we have to believe of the canonical accounts of the first Council, we are in good conscience bound to acknowledge that the only really historical fact is thus that the Council of the Sthaviras at Rajagrha is recognized by all Buddhists. It is by no means incredible that the disciples after the death of the founder of their sect came together to come to an agreement concerning the principal points of the creed and of the discipline.[6]

The Second Council was held at Vesali a century after Buddha's death (386 or 376 B.C.). It was attended by 12, 000 monks, according

---

[4] Edward J. Thomas, *The History of Buddhist Thought* (London, 1933), 265.
[5] Thomas, 28; A. K Warder, *Indian Buddhism* (Delhi, 1980), 201.
[6] H. Kern, *Manual of Indian Buddhism* (Delhi, 1974), 10.

to the *Mahavamsa*. At the Council they made a collection of the Teaching of the Dharma. The *Mahavamsa* writes:

> At that time the thera Revata, in order to hold a council, that the true faith might long endure, chose seven hundred out of all that troop of bhikkhus; those chosen were arahants endowed with the four special sciences, understandings of meanings, and so forth, knowing the tripitaka. All these theras met in the Valikarama protected by Kalasoka, under the leadership of the thera Revata, and compiled the dhamma. Since they accepted the dhamma already established in time past and proclaimed afterward, they completed their work in eight months."[7]

The dissident monks, belonging to the Mahasanghika school, convened their own Council, which they called the Great Council (*mahasamgiti*), according to a statement in the *Dipavamsa*.[8] They charged that the Vesali Council changed the order of the discourses, introducing spurious ones, rejecting certain works, and changing the grammar. There they altered the *Tripitaka* canon to suit their own needs and added new texts. It was at this Council that the Mahasamghika school and the later Mahayana traditions began to assert themselves. This school viewed Buddha as a being of quite a different nature, far above other human beings or not really a human being at all.[9]

Around this time, the Buddhist monks popularized the teachings and religion of Buddha among the masses by means of edifying stories and legends added to the *Ksudraka Agama* and in some cases to the *Vinaya*. The beginning of the composition of the *Jataka* stories belongs probably to this period, though a few *Jataka* poems belong to about 400 B.C.[10]

The Third Council of Pataliputra (247 B.C.), during the reign of Asoka, was instrumental in the establishment of the current Buddhist canon whose general arrangement was fixed then and there. According to the *Mahavamsa* (V: 275-280),

> The elder (Tissa) from the numerous assembly chose a thousand monks, learned, possessing the six higher knowledges, knowing the three Pitakas, versed in analysis, to form the Council of the Doctrine. With these in the Park of Asoka he formed the Council of the true Doctrine. Just as the elder Mahakassapa and the elder Yasa had held a Dhamma-

---

[7] Wilhelm Geiger, trans. *The Mahavamsa* (London, 1980), 24-25.
[8] Thomas, 31; Warder, 211.
[9] Warder, 218.
[10] Warder, 218.

council, so did the elder Tissa hold it. And in the meeting of the Council he spoke the work of *Kathavatthu* for the refutation of other sects. So under the protection of King Asoka this Dhamma-council was completed by the thousand monks in nine months.[11]

Internal evidence suggests that the Tripitaka must have been written at least before the Third Council since no mention is made of the Third Council in the canonical works though there are references in it to the First and Second Councils. Evidently the canon as it has come down to us was closed after the Second Council and before the Third Council.[12]

Much of the canon came to be written down especially after the Third Council in the third century with more additions and deletions. During the reign of Asoka the Mahasamghika school produced a new offshoot, the Lokottaravada (the Transcendent) School, which claimed that Buddha was a transcendent being even before he attained *nirvana;* some claimed that he became a transcendent being only after his renunciation while others believed that he was a transcendent being already at his birth—the ultimate result of it was the paving of the way to the transcendentalist views of the Mahayana on the nature of Buddha. It was the Lokottaravadins who produced the unorthodox *Vinaya* text of the *Mahavastu*. In this book they collected all the traditions concerning the biography of Buddha, including a good many *jataka* stories.[13]

By the end of the third century B.C., the Sarvastivadins, another school of Buddhism, were instrumental in the creation of a poetic biography of Buddha, the *Lalitavistara*, which was later appropriated and further elaborated upon by the Mahayana writers. Meanwhile the Dharmaguptaka school produced another biography, the *Sakyamunibuddhacarita* or *Abhinishkramanasutra* and the Sthaviravadins included the *Nidanakatha* in their commentary on the *Jataka*. Much later the Mulasarvastivadins produced a biography more complete than all the preceding ones and included it in the enlarged *Vinaya* canon.[14]

---

[11] Thomas, 34

[12] S. Radhakrishnan, *The Dhammapada* (Madras, 1977), 2.

[13] Warder, 271: "The text of the *Mahavastu* as now extant may be the work of several centuries of gradual elaboration of doctrine. It states that even the body of the Buddha is not of this world, is transcendental and his actions, though seemingly those usual among men, are done merely for the sake of convention, not through actual need." See also J. J. Jones, *The Mahavastu* (London, 1973), I: 11.

[14] Warder, 225-287.

What is important about all these biographies is that they all agree with one another in all essential episodes, though they differ extensively, like the Christian gospels themselves, in their actual texts. This means that the fundamental points of the legend or the hagiography of Buddha belonging to popular Buddhism was well known and believed in by the end of the third century B.C. Evidence for this position comes from the bas-reliefs at the archaeological sites of Sanchi, Bharhat, and Budhgaya, which depict the leading episodes in the life of Buddha. Mitra argues:

> At the time [of Asoka] a great many of the Avadanas and Jatakas were well known, and believed to be authentic....All the leading facts in connection with the life of the Reformer were then well known and accepted as unquestioned truths, and repeatedly represented in bas-reliefs at Sanchi, Bharahat, and Buddha Gaya; and in the face of them it is extremely difficult to believe that there was no biography of the founder recorded at the time, and that nothing was done in that line until two centuries later. It appears to me extremely inconsistent to assume that records in stone, literal and pictorial, preceded writing in books by two centuries of more, or even that they are synchronous. Had the early Buddhists been generally unlettered people, who neglected to preserve their scriptures, the case would have been different; but seeing that the founder of the religion did not himself write any book, and that the very first things his followers did immediately after his death was to reduce to writing the sayings of their teacher, and to classify them under different heads, it would be quite unwarrantable to suppose that a life of the saint was not thought of until several centuries afterwards.[15]

The other great Mahayana biography of Buddha, the *Buddhacarita* written in Sanskrit and attributed to Asvaghosha took shape between 150 and 100 B.C. before the reign of Kanishka.[16] There is another legendary biography of Buddha which is used in this study. It is also of the Avadana type and exists only in Chinese; it has been translated by Samuel Beal under the title, *The Romantic Legend of Sakya Buddha*.[17] It is constructed from the Pali Vinaya material ; its Chinese title *Fo-Pan-hing-tsi-ching* seems to indicate, according to one author, that it is a translation of a non-

---

[15] Rajendralala Mitra, *The Lalitavistara* (Calcutta,1877), 50.
[16] E. H. Johnston, *The Buddhacarita* (Delhi, 1984), xvii. See also Samuel Beal, *Texts from the Buddhist Canon* (San Francisco, 1977), 8-9. According to Fleet, Kanishka was a predecessor of Kadphises I and Kadphises II and was the founder of the Vikrama-samvat era of 58 B.C. Other historians do not favor this chronology; some ascribe Kanishka to the first century A.D., while others to the third century. See R. C. Majumdar, *The History and Culture of the Indian People*, Vol. I (Bombay, 1968), 144-147.
[17] *The Romantic Legend* (London, 1875).

extant Sanskrit work *Buddha-purva-carya-sangraha-sutra* ("sutra of the collection of the previous life of Buddha"),[18] which also in its original dates from the first century B.C., though Beal is of the opinion that the work is a Chinese translation of the non-extant *Abhinishkramana Sutra* by Jnanakuta, a Buddhist monk from North India. Beal writes about the date of the composition of the *Romantic Legend*:

> We know from the "Chinese Encyclopedia," *Kai-yuen-shi-kiau-mu-lu*, that the *Fo-pen-hing* was translated into Chinese from Sanskrit, by a priest called Chu-fa-lan, so early as the eleventh year of the reign of Wing-ping (*Ming-ti*), of the Han dynasty, i.e., 69 or 70 A.D. We may therefore safely suppose that the original work was in circulation for some time previous to this date.[19]

A great deal of literary activity toward the redaction of the lives of Buddha after the time of Asoka took place during the reign of the Kushana (Turkish) Emperor Kanishka (40 B.C.)[20], who was a patron of Buddhism and of the Sarvastivada School. What is remarkable about all the Hinayana and Mahayana hagiographies of Buddha is that since there is general agreement among them on most episodes in the life of the Master and since this consensus is supported by evidence provided by the stone sculptures which depict these episodes, we must conclude that the literary tradition goes back to the third century B.C. at the latest.[21]

The Asokan rock edicts provide some epigraphical evidence for the existence of written Buddhist scriptures in the third century B.C. For instance, the Kalinga Separate Edict, addressed to officials, tells them to follow the "Middle Path"—a Buddhist term—by avoiding such vices as jealousy, cruelty, and laziness.[22] The Kalsi Edict RE IX is more important in this regard. Asoka says:

> People perform various ceremonies. In troubles, marriages of sons and daughters, birth of children, departures from home—on these and other occasions people perform many different ceremonies. But in such cases mothers and wives perform numerous and diverse petty and worthless ceremonies. Now ceremonies should certainly be performed. But these

---

[18] Thomas, *The History of Buddhist Thought*, 281.

[19] Samuel Beal, *The Romantic Legend of Sakya Buddha*, 18; Samuel Beal, *Texts from the Buddhist Canon* (San Francisco, 1977), 8.75), vi.

[20] Samuel Beal, *Texts from the Buddhist Canon* (San Francisco, 1977), 8.75), vi.

[21] Warder, 349. In this study I use also the oldest hagiographies of Buddha preserved in the Hinayana canon, the *Mahapadana Sutta* and the *Accharyabhutadamma Sutta* along with the *Nidanakatha*.

[22] Richard F. Gombrich, *Theravada Buddhism* (London, 1988), 130.

bear little fruit. That, however, is productive of great fruit which is connected with Dharma. Herein are these: Proper treatment of slaves and employees, reverence to teachers, restraint of violence towards living creatures and liberality to Brahman and Sramana ascetics. These and such others are called *Dharma-mangalas*.[23]

The idea of this edict was suggested by the *Mahamangala Sutta*, found in the *Sutta Nipata*, and *Sigalovada Suttanta* ("Advice to Sigala"), found in the *Digha Nikaya* (ii.4) In the former, among the best *mangalas*, Buddha refers to "waiting on father and mother, protecting child and wife, giving alms, looking after relatives, patience, and pleasant speech, intercourse with samanas, and so forth."[24] In the latter, Buddha says that the master should minister to his servants and employees in five ways: "by assigning them work according to their strength, by supplying them with food and wages, by tending them in sickness, by sharing with them unusual delicacies, by granting them leave at times."[25] It should be be pointed out here that two words used here *dhamma-dana* and *dhammanuggaha* occur in the *Itivattuka*. Here the verbal and conceptual resemblances are so close to suggest the availability of Buddhist texts to Asoka at the time the edicts were written.[26] In the last chapter I shall show that the Therapeutae of Alexandria, who had books, were most likely Buddhist monks, which would suggest that the Buddhists had been using books in the first century B.C. outside India.

We also have the documentary testimony from the Chronicles of Ceylon that during the time of King Vattagamani Abbhaya (c.88-76 B.C.) the monks of Sri Lanka assembled and had the three Pali Pitakas with their commentary written in books officially.[27] Yuan Chwang's seventh-century testimony that the Tripitaka was written down at the end of the First Council under the orders of Kasyapa as well as the fourth-century testimony of the Sri Lankan Chronicles that the Buddhist Theravada monks had assembled the canon already in the fourth century B.C. are similar to the Christian testimony of Eusebius of Caesarea of the fourth century about the composition of the Christian gospels: if the Christian

---

[23] R. K. Mukerjee, *Asoka*, 153-155.
[24] Mukerjee, 153.
[25] Mukerjee, 154.
[26] Gombrich, 130.
[27] *Deepavamsa*, ed. and tr. H. Oldenberg (London, 1879): xx. 20-21; *Mahavamsa*, ed, G. Turnour (Colombo,1837): xxxiii. 100-101; Thomas, *The Life of Buddha*, 251.

Eusebius is credible, then the Buddhist *Mahavamsa* (459-477 A.D.) is also credible and *vice versa* since we do not possess manuscripts dating to the time during which the Christian gospels and the Buddhist scriptures were put into writing. As for Buddhism, most of its ancient literature was destroyed by the Muslim invaders when they swept through India with sword and fire, especially in the thirteenth century A.D. The invaders sought out and destroyed all the great Buddhist libraries so much so that many of the canonical texts of the Theravada tradition are preserved only in Sri Lanka, Burma, Cambodia, and Thailand; several Mahayana books are preserved only in Nepal; however, there are large collections of translations of the original corpus of the Mahayana texts in Chinese and Tibetan.

2. Christian

There is sufficient reason to believe that while Jesus was alive many of his followers not only considered him as a teacher but also believed in his supernatural powers and even divinity. Besides being proclaimed throughout the gospels as a miracle worker, Jesus was considered as the royal Messiah by many of his followers: the inscription Pilate had affixed to the cross indicated the charge for which he died; both Josephus and Tacitus affirm this as the cause of Jesus' death. That Jesus' followers thought he was the Davidic/divine messiah can be inferred from his answer to the High Priest in Mark 14:62, in the stories of his triumphal entry into Jerusalem, and of the cleansing of the Temple (Mt.21:1-7; Lk.19-:28-46) as well as in the transfiguration vision (Mk.9:2-8; Mt.17:1-8). Jesus was also called the *Son of Man*, Jesus' own favorite self-reference in the gospels; this title meant more than a euphemism for the first person pronoun. In the apocalyptic sense already present in the Book of Enoch, the term meant someone who would return in glory to judge the earth and establish the Kingdom. In the New Testament, especially in the earliest records of the epistles of Paul, Jesus is addressed as Lord (*kurios*), the title of the savior deity in some of the Hellenistic mystery cults. This transcendent view of Jesus is well articulated in a passage in the Gospel of Matthew:

> When Jesus came to the region of Caesarea Philippi, he asked his disciples, "who do people say the Son of Man is?" They replied, "Some say John the Baptist; others say Elijah; and still others, Jeremiah or one of the prophets." "But what about you?" he asked. "Who do you say I am?" Simon Peter answered, "You are the Christ, the Son of the living

God." Jesus replied, "Blessed are you, Simon son of Jonah, for this was not revealed to you by man, but by my Father in heaven" (Mt.16:13-17).

Just as in Buddhism, it is the same faith in the founder that dictates the attitude of the believers towards the antiquity and authenticity of the canonical scriptures of Christianity. In Buddhism the tendency is to push the date of the composition of the scriptures to the First Council which took place immediately after the death of Buddha. In Christianity, too, the tendency is to attribute the date of the gospel of Mark to 68 A.D. to account for the internal evidence of the prophecy of Jesus on the destruction of Jerusalem which took place in 70 A.D. Historical scholarship, however, views the literary composition of the Buddhist scriptures to have taken place only in the third century B.C.; similarly, textual scholarship places the date of the composition of the gospels to a later date.

It is not out of place to point out here that no single autograph of any book of the New Testament nor an autograph copy of even a single verse of any of the books of the New Testament is extant today. In the light of the extreme credulity placed on the historical nature of the Christian religion, it is surprising why the early Christians did not make scrolls of the words and deeds of Jesus to be read in their liturgical gatherings after the fashion of the Jews who were already in possession of written scriptures at that time, as recorded in the New Testament itself (Luke 4:17). If the earliest Christians considered the written text terribly important, they could, of course, continue to use the Old Testament as they were wont to do in the Jewish synagogues. It seems that during the first two centuries the Christians did not really think that the preservation and transmission of the words of Jesus in canonically written form was all that important. The truth of this statement becomes clear when we compare the ancient manuscripts of the New Testament and discover the many discrepancies among themselves. In the words of Raymond Collins,

> No two ancient manuscripts of the New Testament agree in every respect. When any two of these manuscripts are compared, it is found that they differ in several respects and in several places. Indeed, uniformity of text had to await the invention of the printing press in the fifteenth century. Prior to that time, manuscripts were hand-copied and

were subject to the inevitability of human error as well as to the occasional caprice of a scribe's whim or erudition.[28]

Fathers of the Church like Origen (ca.185-254) and Augustine (354-430) were well aware of this situation. In the seventeenth century John Mill (1645-1707) was able to identify some 30,000 variant readings in the manuscripts available to him. Today the number of variants amount to 200,000.[29] Such a large number of textual variations seem to indicate that the Christian churches knew that they did not possess the *ipsissima verba* of Jesus and that they did not strive for textual fidelity from the very beginning.

The complete copies of the New Testament (Codex Sinaiticus and Codex Vaticanus) that have survived were written in the fourth century. However, beginning the second century, a few sayings ascribed to Jesus, some of which bear even close verbal resemblances to their counterparts in the gospels, have found their way in the writings of Christian writers like Clement of Alexandria, Justin Martyr, Ignatius of Antioch, Polycarp, the author of *Didache*, Tatian, Papias, and others. The fourth-century historian Eusebius of Caesarea refers to Clement of Rome (c. 96), Ignatius (c. 35-107), and Papias (60-130). In his *Ecclesiastical History* (A.D. 312) Eusebius cites Papias as follows:

> This also the presbyter used to say, "When Mark became Peter's interpreter, he wrote down accurately, although not in order, all that he remembers of what was said or done by the Lord. For he had not heard the Lord nor followed Him, but later, as I have said, he did Peter, who made his teaching fit his needs without, as it were, making any arrangement of the Lord's oracles, so that Mark made no mistake in thus writing some things down as he remembered them. For to one thing he gave careful attention, to omit nothing of what he heard and to falsify nothing in this." Now this has been related by Papias regarding Mark, and regarding Matthew he has spoken as follows: "Now Matthew collected the oracles in the Hebrew language, and each one interpreted them as he was able."[30]

Eusebius also cites Polycarp of Smyrna (c. 69-155), whose Epistle to the Philippians has survived. It contains citations of 1 John 4:3

---

[28] Raymond F. Collins, *Introduction to the New Testament* (New York, 1987),75-76.
[29] Collins, 77.
[30] Eusebius, *Ecclesiastical History* III, 39, 15-16; cited by Raymond Collins, 18.

and an exact citation of Matthew 13:14-15, besides several references to the Pauline epistles.[31]

Ignatius of Antioch, who is best known for his seven letters, cites passages which seem to indicate that he was conversant with the gospels, especially John, Matthew, and perhaps Luke. His Letter to the Ephesians 5:1 talks about the Eucharist as "bread of God" (John 6:51-58) and Smyrna 1:1 notes that Jesus was baptized by John so that all righteousness might be fulfilled by him (Matthew 3:15). Scholars dispute, however, as to whether Ignatius knew the written gospels or the oral traditions.[32]

In a letter written about 96 A.D. in the name of the church of Rome to the church of Corinth, Clement writes:

> Let us do what is written...especially remembering the words of the Lord Jesus, which he spoke when he was teaching gentleness and patience....Be merciful, so that you may obtain mercy; forgive, so that it may be forgiven you; as you do, thus it will be done to you; as you give, thus it will be given to you; as you judge, thus you will be judged; as you are kind, thus kindness will be shown you; with the measure you measure, by it will be measured to you."[33]

Indeed, this text echoes the words of Jesus found in Matthew 5:7; 6:14-15; 7:1-2,12; Luke 6:31, 36-38, though by no means is it an exact citation of the gospel text. The so-called Second Epistle of Clement, whose origin is unknown, also makes about five allusions to the words of Jesus found in Luke 10:3; 12:4-5; and Matthew 9:13.

Probably, *Didache*, a late first-century or early second-century document, is the first text that gives the closest parallels to the sayings of Jesus found in the written gospels. The Didachist writes:

> Bless those who persecute you, and pray for your enemies; fast for those who persecute you. For what credit is it if you love those who love? Do not the gentiles do the same? But as for you, love those who hate you, and you will have no enemy"(1:3)....Do not reprove one another in wrath, but in peace, as you have it in the gospel, and let no one speak to anyone who wrongs his neighbor, nor let that one be heard among you until he repents. But perform your prayers and alms and all your actions as you have it in the gospel of the Lord (15:3-4).[34]

No doubt, these words recall Matthew 5:44-47; 7:12; Luke 6:31-33; Matthew 5:22-26; 18:15-35. It is possible that the Didachist

---

[31] Collins, 19.
[32] Collins, 18.
[33] 1 Clement 13; cited by Collins, 15-16.
[34] Collins, 17.

might have had a written gospel in front of him when he wrote his work; however, since the citations are not verbatim, it is more likely that he was relying only on oral traditions.[35]

The studies of John Knox and Hans von Campenhausen tell us that the four-gospel canon merged only in the second half of the second century as a reaction to Marcion's (d. c. 160) Bible. Tatian's (d. c. 160) *Diatesseron,* which is essentially a harmony of Mark, Matthew, Luke, and John, indicates that by the end of the second century there existed the four canonical gospels. According to Jerome's testimony, Bishop Theophilus of Antioch (late second century) also compiled a similar gospel harmony.[36] It was Ireneus of Lyons (c. 130-200) who first acknowledged the New Testament as we know it today, both in theory and practice. For him there are only four genuine gospels: "These four gospels possess such a degree of certainty, that even the heretics themselves testify to them, and every apostate strives to maintain his own teaching with their assistance"[37] Ireneus' position did not, however, win universal approval within the larger church for a long time. For instance, in the African church, Tertullian (c. 160-225) relegated Luke to a lesser status; Gaius, an early-third-century Roman presbyter, even ascribed John and Revelation to the Gnostic Cerinthus, suggesting that these were not orthodox works. According to Epiphanius'(315-413) testimony, some Christians refused to accept Johannine writings as canonical as late as the fourth century.[38]

My purpose in bringing together these early Christian testimonies of the first, second, and third centuries is to suggest that the Christian gospels were not necessarily written in the first century and immediately thereafter accepted as canonical by the universal church. All available historical evidence rather shows that the redaction of the gospels and the creation of the New Testament canon took several centuries before the New Testament as we know it today reached its present form.

Indeed, in many ways the problems of the textual transmission of the New Testament are not different from those encountered in Buddhism. For instance, parallel texts of the gospels were often assimilated to each other; corrections were made, as in Mark 6:5

---

[35] Collins, 17.
[36] Collins, 22-23.
[37] *Adversus Haereses* III. 11.7: cited by Collins, 24.
[38] Collins, 25-26.

that Jesus was not able perform miracles in Nazareth; a number of additions were made to the original text. Even after the second century, other traditions were still added to the gospels such as the passage of the laborer on the Sabbath in Luke 6:5 and the pericope about Jesus and the adulteress found after John 7:52. So there is no reason to believe that the gospels in their canonical form were written before 70 A.D.; probably the gospels appeared more or less in their canonical form only in the first half of the second century or even later, as mentioned earlier.[39] To repeat: manuscript evidence shows that in early Christianity the canonical gospels did not enjoy any unique position, nor is there evidence to suggest that they were written before the apocryphal gospels. As Koester points out, among the surviving fragments of these gospels one finds a somewhat even split between canonical and apocryphal gospels up to about the year 200.[40]

Most modern biblical scholars recognize the role of oral tradition in the formation of the Christian gospels. During the time between the death of Jesus and the actual composition of the Gospel of Mark, Christian communities handed down orally the sayings of Jesus, stories about him, parables of Jesus, miracle stories, and passion narratives during liturgical, apologetic, catechetical, and missionary meetings and made collections of them. In the next stage evangelists made use of these diverse collections to form their gospels. In spite of the evidence to the contrary, most Christian scholars still tend to hold the following time scheme for the composition of the canonical gospels: Mark was written about the year 70; fifteen to twenty years later, Luke and Matthew undertook a revision of Mark; in addition, each had access to special collections of the sayings of Jesus and materials, known as Q, for their infancy narratives. The Gospel of John was composed toward the end of the first century.[41] Needless to mention that the above-given early dates for the composition of the gospels are rather very tentative in view of the fact that there is very little internal or external evidence to definitively prove them. The reason for

---

[39] Helmut Koester, *History and Literature of Early Christianity* (Philadelphia, 1980), 14-50.
[40] Helmut Koester, "Apocryphal and Canonical Gospels," *Harvard Theological Review* 73 (1980), 105-130. Dominic Crossan, *The Cross That Spoke* (New York, 1988), xi.
[41] Joseph Fitzmyer, *A Christological Catechism: New Testament Answers* (New York, 1982); Daniel J. Harrington, *Interpreting the New Testament* (Wilmington, 1979); Howard Kee, *Understanding the New Testament* (Englewood Cliffs, 1983).

arguing for an early date (68 A.D.) for the Gospel of Mark is that its author indicates that the destruction of Jerusalem is either imminent or has just taken place (13:2;14); however, the earliest tradition that refers this gospel to the authorship of Mark can be traced approximately only to 150 A.D. The earliest witness to the Gospel of Matthew is Ignatius of Antioch in Syria about 110 A.D.; the oldest tradition to the Gospel according to Luke comes only from 200 A.D.; the earliest evidence for the Gospel of John comes from a papyrus fragment of several verses of the gospel (18:31-33, 37-38) found in Egypt and dated by scholars to the first half of the second century. In short, in spite of the paucity of evidence, Christian scholars, exactly like the Buddhist scholars, tend to stretch the authorship of their scriptures as far back as they can, even to the immediate disciples of Jesus: the Christians attribute their canonical gospels to Matthew, Mark, and John; the Buddhists ascribe their canonical scriptures of the Tripitaka to Ananda, Kasyapa, and Yassa. Such a position is not totally untenable, even though it is not historically verifiable. Since the faith of a community is as reliable as written evidence for its traditions, I can readily accept the theory that the gospels originated in the first century at least in their oral forms. Hindus and Buddhists do not find this Christian position unacceptable at all. However, I expect that Christian scholars extend the same courtesy and apply the same criteria in adjudging the antiquity of the Hindu and Buddhist scriptures.

Besides the four canonical gospels, there are a number of non-canonical or apocryphal gospels, representative of the diversity of the schools of thought found in early Christianity. These writings also claim to preserve the memories of Jesus and the apostles. Most of this literature, though written down probably only in the second century and later, followed the same stages of redaction which involved oral transmission and literary collection, which the canonical gospels underwent. The recent discovery at Nag Hammadi of many apocryphal documents has reemphasized the role of the non-canonical gospels toward the understanding of Christian origins, especially of the theological diversity of the early Christian communities. For some of these apocryphal works, especially for the Gospel of Thomas, a first-century date can by no means be excluded.[42] Among the apocryphal works used in this study, the prominent ones are the Protoevangelion of James, the Infancy Gospel of Thomas, the Infancy Gospel of Matthew, and the Gospel of Mary.[43]

Briefly noted: Neither Buddhism nor Christianity possesses any copies of their respective scriptures from the century in which they are claimed to have been composed. If the Christian claim that the gospels were written by Matthew, Luke, Mark, and John in the first century is true, it is to be noted that it is based on tradition and on written testimonies from the second and third centuries reported often in the fourth century or later. So also the Buddhist claim that their scriptures were written at the First or Second Council is based only on oral traditions and on later written testimonies. If both religions rest their case on internal evidence, then we can readily agree that that the Christian gospels were written during the latter part of the first century and the Buddhist scriptures as early as the fourth century B.C. If there are some manuscript evidences from gospel fragments dating from the second century A.D. for the Christian gospels, then the Buddhists have iconographical and epigraphical evidence for their claims, dating from the third century B.C. for the antiquity of their canonical scriptures as well as for several of their non-canonical works. All in all, we must concede that the Buddhist religious traditions—both in their oral and literary versions—are much anterior to the Christian traditions in their oral as well as literary forms. To put the argument in another form: Christian scholars have never been able to show definitively that the canonical gospels have come down to us in their present form before 200 A.D. and that the Buddhist scriptures were written only after the Buddhists had come in contact with Christianity. On the contrary, all evidence points to the thesis that the Buddhist religious traditions are much older than the Christian religious traditions both in their oral and written forms; further, priority of the transmission of religious

---

[42] Stevan L. Davies, *The Gospel of Thomas and Christian Wisdom* (New York, 1983); Helmut Koester and James M. Robinson, *Traajectories Through Early Christianity* (Philadelphia, 1971); Helmut Koester and Thomas O. Lambdin, "The Gospel of Thomas," in James M. Robinson, ed. *The Nag Hammadi Library in English* (San Francisco, 1977), 117-13 .

[43] E. Hennecke and W. Schneelmelcher, eds. *New Testament Apocrypha*. 2 vols. Philadelphia, 1963; M. R. James, *The Apocryphal New Testament* (Oxford, 1924); James M. Robinson, *The Nag Hammadi Liberary in English* (San Francisco, 1977).

traditions lies in their oral forms rather than in their literary expressions. So contact between the Christian religion and the Buddhist religion took place primarily through oral and indirect contact rather than through the medium of written scriptures. In a study like this we have recourse only to written scriptures in our attempt to reconstruct the oral past of historical contacts.

Another important common trait that these two religions share is that they were made up of diverse groups right from the beginning. For instance, there were numerous Buddhist schools of thought in existence already in the second century B.C. with their own versions of the Buddha-legend and Buddha-words; likewise, different early Christian communities had their own versions of the Jesus-legends and Jesus-logia as can be seen from a comparative study of the canonical and apocryphal gospels. In other words, the early Christian communities were very diverse, not only ethnically but also theologically, and the Christian canon was not established until after the second century. There is one major difference between Christian and Buddhist scriptures, however. It is that the Buddhist religious traditions have come down to our times in large collections of books, compared to the sparse data contained in the Christian gospels and the apocrypha. The upshot of all this is that the Christian writers may have used traditions belonging to various Buddhist schools of thought and that the Christian acquaintance of the Buddhist religion was most likely and most often indirect through hearsay and intermediaries rather than through a careful study of the Buddhist scriptures written in Pali, Sanskrit, Greek, or Aramaic. One cannot, however, entirely rule out the possibility that Aramaic and Greek were totally unknown in India and that Indians could not have translated Sanskrit and Pali works into Greek and Sanskrit, since Aramaic inscriptions have been found at the Buddhist university center of Taxila and Greek inscriptions in northwest India, dating from the third century B.C.[44] Of course, Greek was spoken in the Hellenistic kingdom of Bactria since the invasion of India by Alexander.

---

[44] More about this later in the book. At least I must point out that India is mentioned in the phrase "from India [Hebrew *hodu* , the Indus Valley] to Ethiopia" in Esther 1:1 and 8:9 as the eastern boundary of the Persian empire under Ahasuerus (fifth century B.C.). In I Macc. 6:37 a reference is made to the "Indian drivers" of each of the war elephants of Antiochus (second century B.C).

In the following pages I shall identify the various common motifs found in the Christian and Buddhist infancy gospels with appropriate commentaries wherever they are applicable.

CHAPTER THREE

BUDDHIST AND CHRISTIAN INFANCY PARALLELS

Two of the four gospels, Matthew and Luke, begin their narratives with the stories of the conception, birth, and childhood of Jesus; they devote two chapters to cover this material; the Lucan narrative is twice as long as the Matthean. Strictly speaking, the phrase "infancy narrative" is inaccurate, because the canonical gospels contain only depiction of short scenes as opposed to the accepted meaning of *narrative* which is "an organized historical, biographical, or fictional account of events; however, the phrase "infancy narrative" is customary in English as a translation of the German *Kindheitsgeschichte,* when the phrase is applied to the canonical gospels attributed to Matthew and Luke. On my part, as in French I prefer to use the expression "infancy gospels" simply because I use also the apocryphal infancy gospels like those of Pseudo-Matthew, Thomas, and James. I shall show in this chapter that many Buddhist and Hindu subtexts are embedded in the texture of these infancy gospels, which would naturally raise the problem of the literary relationship between Christian gospels and Indian religious traditions.

A. *Priority of the Mahayana Traditions*

One objection most Western scholars raise against any prospective comparative study of the Christian gospels and Buddhist scriptures is that it is a historical error to compare the earlier Christian gospels with the later Mahayana texts from which most of the material given below is taken. In the case of similarities between Christian and Indian themes, they would say that the Indians borrowed Christian ideas in their oral form through the Indians' familiarity with the Greek language. The latest example of this kind of argumentation one finds in Duncan Derrett's study.[1] In one single sweep of the hand he would make all Buddhist scriptures arise from Christian influences transmitted

---

[1] J. Duncan Derrett, "Greece and India: the Milindapanha, the Alexander-romance and the Gospels," ZRGG 19 (1967), 33-63.

orally in India, while he is willing to admit that due to a reverse process Buddhist stories found their way into the apocryphal gospels. But he is unwilling to admit that during the the same period Indian ideas could have found their way into the canonical gospels because as literature they are older than the written books of Buddhism. All such disguised historicism shows in general a prejudicial refusal to face squarely the hypothesis of possible Indian influences on the Christian gospels. Derrett gives himself away when he says what follows:

> The substantial and challenging works of ...van Eysinga and of Garbe remain unanswered, for the church has no material with which to answer them. If in the words of Professor Caird no New Testament teacher would give Indian claims any "credence for a minute" it is...because their minds are not prepared to approach the subject. The key to the whole thing lies in *priority*. Everyone knows that Buddhist missions were operating in the Middle East two centuries before Christ. The sculptures at Barhut and Sanchi, which are certainly B.C., depict tales of the life of the Buddha. The Buddhist canon was settled in various synods which took place...centuries before Christ.[2]

Derrett would deny all this evidence on grounds mentioned above and on the shaky basis of his own unproven hypothesis that the *Milindapanha*, a non-canonical Buddhist work, which contains many similarities to the New Testament cannot have been composed before 50 A.D. and not after 150 A.D., which theory does not in any way prove that the Buddhist work was based on the Christian gospels which were composed after 50 A.D.! What we need in a comparative study like this is a willing suspension of disbelief.

On the issue of priorities: Firstly, the Christian scriptures in the form in which they have come down to us go back only to the third century, as mentioned before, even though they may have been composed orally and in written fragments in the second century and that the Mahayana form of Buddhism was already in existence in the first century B.C. Edward Conze writes on the origin and development of the Mahayana movement and their literature:

> The Mahayana developed in two stages: first in an unsystematic form, which went on between 100 BC and AD 500, and then, after AD 150, in a systematized philosophical form, which led to two distinct schools, the Madhyamikas and the Yogacarins....About 100 BC a number of Buddhists felt that the existing statements of the doctrine had become

---

[2] Derrett, 37.

stale and useless. In the conviction that the Dharma requires even new re-formulations so as to meet the needs of new ages, new populations and new social circumstances, they set out to produce a new literature. The creation of this literature is one of the most magnificent outbursts of creative energy known to human history and it was sustained for about four to five centuries. Repetition alone, they believed, could not sustain a living religion. Unless counterbalanced by constant innovation, it will become fossilized and lose its life-giving qualities.[3]

Secondly, the Mahayana scriptures, though in their present form were probably edited only in the first century B.C., in their oral and earlier written forms go back to the second century B.C. and before, for the beginnings of Mahayana movement in Buddhism should further be traced to the beginning of the third century B.C., since the movement itself claims to have been founded by Buddha himself, though at first limited to a select group of Buddha's disciples. There are references in the Mahayana *sutras* themselves as to their being known in the South after the *Parinirvana*.[4] They claim that the Mahayana Sutras were codified by an assembly of Bodhisatvas on the mythical mountain of Vimalasambhava and that the texts were miraculously preserved for five centuries and stored away in the subterranean palaces of the Nagas, or with the king of the Gandharvas, or the king of the Gods. Then, as Nagarjuna puts it, five hundred years after Buddha's *parinirvana*, when the *dharma* was in danger of decay, these treasures were unearthed and revealed to revivify the religion.[5]

The origin of the Mahayana movement, which teaches the broad path of salvation that all sentient beings possess Buddha nature and hence are capable of attaining enlightenment, has its starting point among the Mahasanghikas who set forth their ideas after the Second Great Council of Vesali (383 B.C.). The Mahasanghikas were less strict in interpreting the disciplinary rules, less exclusive with regard to the possibilities of the householders and women attaining Buddhahood, and were more willing to consider as authentic later additions to the scriptures. In fact, such a liberal attitude was obviously only a natural extension of the basic religious attitude of the Hindus among whom Buddhism developed and of the foreign nation of the Greeks in Bactria among whom the new movement seems to have found a home. Edward Conze writes:

---

[3] *A Short History of Buddhism* (London, 1980), 44.
[4] *Astasahasrikaprajnparamita;* Warder, 352.
[5] Conze, 46.

> By placing all the emphasis on the supernatural, or supramundane, qualities of the Buddha, in which he differed from all other men, they [the Mahasanghikas] led the believer away from the fortuitous historical circumstances of his appearance. Some Mahasanghikas even went so far as to maintain that Shakyamuni had been no more than a magical creation who, on behalf of the Supramundane Buddha, had preached the Dharma. If the Buddha existed only about 500 BC, then he could teach only at that time, and the body of his teachings would have to be completed at his death. If, however, the true Buddha exists at all times, then there is no reason, why he should not at all times find instruments to do his teaching. A free and unfettered development of the doctrine was thus assured, and innovations, even if untraceable in the existing body of Scriptures, could be justified as revelations of the real principle of Buddhahood.[6]

The Mahayanists co-existed with the members of the Old Wisdom School or the Hinayanists, whom the Mahayanists referred to as *The Disciples and Pratyekabuddhas*. They even lived together in the same monastries, adhering to the same Vinaya rules. As I-tsing (c.700) reports:

> The adherents of the Mahayana and Hinayana both practice the same Vinaya, recognize the same five categories of faults, are attached to the same four truths. Those who worship the Bodhisattvas and who read the Mahayana sutras get the name of Mahyanists; those who do not are Hinayanists.[7]

There was not only great tolerance of sects among themselves but also mutual borrowing and interaction among them. As Conze says, "a certain amount of Mahayana teaching was tacitly absorbed [by the Hinayanists]."[8] The Mahayanists based their own literary traditions on the Hinayana scriptures, which were composed first. In other words, during the period of the formation of the Christian religious scriptures and even before, both the Hinayana and Mahyana teachings were available to inquisitive persons. That is the reason why I include both the Hinayana and Mahayana texts in this study, though I am more inclined to lean towards the view that the Mahayana doctrines are closer in letter and spirit to the Christian religious traditions. This is because the Mahayana version of Buddhism was the one that was exported outside India after the first missionary thrust of Asoka in the third century failed to make any great impact. Besides, in spirit the Mahayana

---

[6] Edward Conze, *Buddhism* (Oxford, 1951), 120-21.
[7] Conze, *Buddhism*, 122.
[8] Conze, 122.

is closer to the Christian religion than the Hinayana. The Mahayana made Buddha divine and surrounded him with angels and other spiritual beings; it argued that Buddha had two sets of teachings: a simple one for the uninitiated and the esoteric other for the elect; it emphasized salvation by faith unlike the Hinayana which stressed salvation by works; it placed the law of compassion above the law of karma; while the Hinayana ideal was the *arhat*, who strives after his own slavation,the Mahayana unheld the *bodhisatva* idea of the savior who is concerned with the slavation of others.

Further, since there is no reason to believe that the Jewish-Christian gospel writers used any one particular version of the Buddha-story from beginning to end from a literary text, but rather at random and selectively from oral traditions, and since the core tradition of the various Indian birth stories permeate the entire infancy gospel narratives, I shall try to show all the significant parallels from a topical rather than from a linear approach.

B. *Buddist and Christian Infancy Parallels*

1. *Pre-existence*

1.1 *Buddha*

The idea that gods descend from heaven to earth is common to many ancient religions including Judaism whose Garden-of-Eden story says that God walked in the garden in the cool of the night. In this and other accounts, gods visit humans in some sort of a spiritual body. But in Buddhism and Hinduism there is the powerful belief that God visits mankind in a human body. Some Buddhists thought that Gautama Buddha was not a god; however, the most common faith of the Buddhists is that Buddha had preexisted as a divine being in the Tushita heaven with other gods. According to the *Mahapadana Suttanta*, the Exalted One (Buddha) discussed the subject of his former lives with his disciples:

> "Now is the time, O Exalted One,...to give us a religious discourse on the subject of former lives."..."It is now ninety-one aeons ago, brethren, since Vipassin, the Exalted One, Arahant, Buddha Supreme, arose in the world. It is now thirty-one aeons ago, that Sikhi, the Exalted

One,...arose in the world....It is in this auspicious aeon, brethren, that now I, an Arahant, Buddha Supreme, have arisen in the world."[9]

When Boddhisatva was born, he said, "Now then I have arrived at my last birth; no more shall I enter into the womb to be born; now shall I accomplish the end of my being, and become Buddha."[10]

1.2 *Jesus*

The fundamental faith of the Jesus movement enshrined in all the gospels and the apocrypha is that Jesus is the Son of God who became man. For instance, the Gospel of John begins with this profession of faith: " In the beginning was the Word, the Word was with God, and the Word was God.... The Word became man and dwelt among us" (1:1-4). Like Buddha, according to the Johannine tradition, Jesus discussed his pre-existence with his audience: "Before Abraham I was" (John 8:57). Peter's confession at Caesarea Philippi (Matt. 16:16ff) to Jesus' question, "Who do you think I am?" is the clearest answer we find in the synoptics as to the divine origin of Jesus: "You are the Christ, the Son of the Living God."

It is important to note that there are many incarnations of Buddha or Vishnu in the Indian tradition; the reason for this is that at the end of each aeon (*kalpa*) a savior appears on earth; the more the aeons, the more the savior-figures. The *Mahapadana Suttanta* gives details of six previous Buddhas; the *Buddhavamsa* extends the knowledge to twenty-four Buddhas; the *Mahavastu* gives the names of more than one hundred Buddhas. In all these stories it is the same divine being being born in different ages. The gospels and the Christian tradition talk about only one incarnation because they talk about only a single aeon! Obviously, the gospel writers reject the Indian theory of reincarnation and the cyclical view of history! Christian writers seem to telescope the entire duration into the present aeon, which is the first and the last. Buddhists view the present aeon as the last one in the sense that the last Buddha has already appeared in the person of Gautama Siddhartha. However, in both religious traditions there is some uncertainty as to the finality of Sakyamuni and Jesus; Buddhism talks also about Buddha Maitryea who is yet to come, while the Christians talk about a Paraclete—he is usually identified with

---

[9] *Dialogues of the Buddha,* translation of *Dighanikaya,* T. W. & C.A.F. Rhys Davids (London, 1971), 5.
[10] Samuel Beal, The Romantic Legend of Sakya Buddha (Delhi, 1985), 44.

the Holy Ghost in theology—who is to come; traditional Christian theology talks just about the second coming of Jesus at the end of the present aeon which will be followed by the establishment of a new heaven and a new earth (Revelations 21-22).

2. Royal origin and genealogy

2.1 Buddha

All the versions recognize the royal lineage of Buddha. The belief that Buddha is born in a noble family is given in the *Jatakas*, according to which, Buddha makes this statement:

> "The Buddhas are never born into a family of the peasant caste, or the servile caste; but into one of the warrior caste, or of the Brahman caste, whichever at the time is higher in public estimation. The warrior caste is now the higher in public estimation. I will be born into a warrior family, and king Suddhodana shall be my father....The mother of a Buddha is never a wanton, nor a drunkard, but is one who has fulfilled the perfections through a hundred thousand cycles, and has kept the five precepts unbroken from the day of her birth. Now this queen Maha-Maya is such a one; and she shall be my mother."[11]

Several versions of the life of Buddha, like the Chinese version of the *Abhinishrkramanasutra*,[12] contains a genealogy of kings related to Buddha belonging to the present aeon (*bhadra kalpa*). The *Dighanikaya* (I:113) speaks of Buddha's lineage on his father's side and mother's side for seven generations. In most traditions, Gautama Buddha is the son of King Sudhodana and Queen Maya. Rudolf Seydel has a chapter on the genealogies of Buddha and Christ. The portion he cites has a strong analogy with the Christian lists:

> King mahasammata had a son named Roja, whose son was Vararoja, whose son was Kalyana, whose son Varakalyana, whose son was Mandhatar, whose son was Varamandhatar, whose son was Uposatha, whose son was Kara, whose son was Upakara, whose son was Maghadeva.[13]

2.2 Jesus

According to the gospel traditions of Matthew and Luke, Jesus is a member of the royal family of David. Matthew opens his gospel with the genealogy of Jesus (1:1-16) and traces it to Abraham: "The

---

[11] H.C. Warren, *Buddhism in Translation* (New York, 1963), 41.
[12] Samuel Beal, *The Romantic Legend of Sakya Buddha*, 16-23.
[13] R. Seydel, *Das Evangelium von Jesu* (Leipzig, 1882), 106; cited by Arthur Lillie, *Buddhism in Christendom* (London, 1887), 10.

birth record of Jesus Christ, son of David, son of Abraham: Abraham was the father of Isaac; Isaac was the father of Jacob...Jacob was the father of Joseph, the husband of Mary; of her was begotten Jesus, called the Christ." However, the Fourth Gospel never uses the title of Son of David, and it is possible that John 7:42 shows ignorance of Jesus' Davidic origins: "Doesn't Scripture say that the Messiah, being of David's family, is to come from Bethlehem, the village where David lived?"; here some people in Jerusalem object against Jesus, citing his Galilean origins. Also, since the genealogies of Matthew and Luke do not agree and since there is no guarantee of their historical value, scholars have been expressing increasing scepticism as to the historical worth of the gospel claim that Jesus was a Davidid. Biblical scholars —Bultmann, Heitmüller, Goguel, Conzelmann, and Burger—explain Jesus' descent from David as a theologoumenon, i.e., as the historicizing of what was originally a theological statement.[14] In a sense, Matthew and Luke displaced the Sinaitic Messiah with the Davidic Messiah. Thus they adopted Paul's position that the Jewish Christians were exempted from the law of Moses since faith in Jesus, the son of David, enables the Christian to experience grace without the observance of the *mitzvot*.[15]

Obviously, the purpose of Matthew is to connect Jesus not only with the royal Davidic family but also with Israel, not only as children of Jacob but also as children of Abraham. Luke, on the other hand, traces the genealogy of Jesus all the way to Adam. Luke's purpose probably is to indicate that Jesus is the savior not only of the children of Israel but also of all mankind. Another purpose of Matthew in the genealogy section is to refute the slanderous accusation that Jesus was of illegitimate birth. Apparently the slander was very old since it is alluded to in John: "We are not born of fornication" (8:41). One version of the slander was that Jesus was born of a Roman soldier named Pantheras and Mary, who had been divorced from her husband after having been found an adulteress; according to Origen, Celsus (c.170-180) knew this story.[16] Of course, a biased comparison of the Buddhist-Christian texts could suggest that the Christian writer Judaized

---

[14] See Raymond Brown, *The Birth of the Messiah* (New York, 1977), 505-512.
[15] J. C. Rylaarsdan, "Jewish-Christian Relationship: The Two Covenants and the Dilemmas of Christology," *JES* 9 (1972): 249-270.
[16] Origen, *Contra Celsum* I.28,32,33,39; see S. Krauss, *Das Leben Jesu nach jüdischen Quellen* (Berlin, 1902), 181-194.

the Buddhist idea of the royal genealogy of Buddha and applied it to the case of Jesus especially since the Davidic origins of Jesus is historically unreliable. On my part, I find this parallel, like all the parallels that follow, interesting and intriguing enough to record.

3. Universal Salvation

3.1 *Buddha*

One outstanding feature of Buddhism, as opposed to Hinduism, is its concern for the salvation of the entire human race and its missionary zeal in spreading the reign of *dharma* throughout the whole world. In fact, as early as the third century B.C., Emperor Asoka sent missionaries to the different nations of the mediterranean world in order to convert them to Buddhism. That Ashoka was very serious about his missionary intentions can be inferred from the fact that he published at least one of his edicts (the Kandahar Edict) in both Greek and Aramaic, two languages of the non-Indians. The Rock Edict XIII of Asoka claims to have accomplished the conversion of non-Indian nations:

> *Dharma-vijaya*, moral conquest, is considered by His Sacred Majesty the principal conquest. And this has been repeatedly won by His Sacred Majesty both here (in his dominions) and among all the frontier peoples even to the extent of six hundred yojanas where (are) the Yona king, Antiochos by name, and, beyond that Antiochos, the four kings named Ptolemy, Antigonos, Magas and Alexander; below the Cholas, Pandyas, as far as Tamraparni.[17]

The missionary dimension of Buddhism is found also in the canonical Vinaya-texts:

> At that time there were sixty-one Arahats in the world. And the Lord said unto the monks: "I am delivered, O monks, from all fetters, human and divine. Ye, O monks, be on your journey, for the weal and the welfare of much people, out of compassion for the world, and for the wealth and weal and the welfare of angels and mortals.[18]

As for the idea of universal salvation, which is anticipated in the famous phrase of the *Suttanipata* that Buddha was born "for the weal and welfare of mankind" (*manussaloke hitasukhataya*), is also found in the Inroduction to the *Jatakas* (I:47), where the gods

---

[17] R. Mookerji, *Asoka* (Delhi, 1972), 165-66.
[18] *Sacred Books of the East*, 13:112; cited by A. J. Edmunds, *Buddhist and Christian Gospels*, 225.

address the Future Buddha: "Sir, it was not to acquire the glory of a Sakka, or of a Mara, or of a Brahma, or of a Universal Monarch, that you fulfilled the Ten Perfections; but it was to gain omniscience in order to save the world, that you fulfilled them."[19]

This universalistic and missionary attitude is more pronounced in Mahayana Buddhism than in Theravada Buddhism. The ideal Buddhist monk of the Mahayana tradition is expected to instruct his disciples in their languages as Buddha did during his earthly life in the vernacular instead of Sanskrit. As for Buddha's pedagogical practice, his *upayakausalya* (skill in means) enabled him to speak all languages or to speak a "transcendental" language which the listeners could understand in their own mother tongues.[20] It is this Buddhist concept of glossalalia that was picked up by the author of the Acts of the Apostles in his narrative of the Pentecost (Acts 2: 1-13).[21]

3.2 *Jesus*

Jesus' missionary charge to his disciples after his resurrection is well known: "Go ye, therefore, and make disciples of all the nations...teaching them to observe all things whatsoever I commanded you" (Mt. 18:19). This notion of universal salvation to be brought about by the Christians is anticipated in the birth narrative, where the angels announce, as in the Aramaic version of the New Testament: "Glory to God in the heights. Peace on earth. Good hope to mankind" (Luke 2: 14).

Indeed, this universalist view of Christ's relevance for mankind, which is not precisely a dominant Jewish concept, is in perfect agreement with the Buddhist view that Budddha became incarnate for the salvation of the entire human race.

4. *Virginal Conception—virginitas ante partum*

4.1 *Buddha*

Virginal conception or *virginitas ante partum*, in the physical sense, means that the divine child is conceived in the mother's womb without the agency of a male progenitor, that the divine child discends directly into the mother's womb, and that she should not have had any children before. The canonical account of the miraculous conception of Buddha is given in the Discourse on

---

[19] Warren, 40-41.
[20] E. Lamotte, *Histoire du Bouddhisme indien* (Louvain, 1958), 607 ff; Halbfass, 188)
[21] See also Acts 10: 46, 11: 15, 19: 6; I Cor. 12-14; Mark 16: 17.

the Wondrous and Marvelous Events (*Acchariyabhuta-dhammasutta*), in which Ananda, the favorite disciple, recites to Buddha the events of conception and birth. This is reported as an inspired statement because Ananda states that he heard them from the Lord:

> Face to face, reverend one, have I heard from the Lord, face to face have I received: being mindful and conscious, Ananda, the Bodhisatta was born in a Tushita heaven....This I remember as a wondrous and marvelous thing of the Lord.... Throughout his full span of life the Boddhisatta stayed in the Tushita body. Mindful and conscious, the Boddhisatta descending from the Tushita body entered the womb of his mother. When the Bodhisatta descending from the Tushita body entered the womb of his mother, then in the world with its gods, Maras, and Brahmas, among the creatures with ascetics, brahmins, gods, and men, appears a boundless great splendor surpassing the divine majesty of the gods. And in the spaces between the worlds, gloomy, open, dark, of darkness and obscurity, where too this and sun so mighty and majestic are unable to shine, even there a boundless great splendor appears surpassing the divine majesty of the gods. And the beings that have been reborn there perceive one another by that splendor, and think, "Surely, sirs, there are other beings that have been reborn here. "And this universe of ten thousand worlds shakes and trembles and quakes, and a boundless great splendor appears in the world surpassing the divine majesty of the gods....When the Bodhisatta has entered his mother, the Bodhisatta's mother is in possession of the five senses, and is surrounded and endowed with the five senses (III: 120-121).

Anando, when the future Buddha is descending into his mother's womb, she is pure from sexuality, has abstained from taking life, from theft, from evil conduct in lusts, from lying, and from all kinds of wine and strong drink, which are a cause of irreligion.[22]

She abided in penances like a hermit, always performing penances along with her consort. Having obtained the sanction of the king, she had not entertained carnal wishes for thirty-two months. In whatever place she sat...there dazzled her celestial nature, resplendent by her attachment to virtuous actions. There was not a god, nor a demon, nor a mortal, who could cast his glance on her with carnal desire. All of them, throwing aside all evil motive, and endowed with honorable sentiments, looked on her as a mother, or a daughter....Like unto her, there was none to be seen worthy of the venerable being, or one more fully endowed with good qualities, or compassion,--that mother is Maya (*Lalitavistara*, iii).[23]

---

[22] *Majjhimanikaya*, cited by A. J. Edmunds, 173.
[23] Mitra, 46.

4.2 Jesus

> In the sixth month the angel Gabriel was sent from God to a city of Galilee known as Nazareth, to a virgin betrothed to a man of the House of David whose name was Joseph, and the virgin's name was Mary. He came and addressed her thus: "Hail, O favored one, the Lord is with you." Now she was startled at what he said and wondered what such a greeting might mean. But the angel said to her: "Do not be afraid, Mary, for you have found favor with God. And behold, you will conceive in your womb and give birth to a son, and you will call his name Jesus. He will be great and will be called Son of the Most High. And the Lord God will give him the throne of his father David; and he will be king over the House of Jacob forever, and there will be no end to his kingdom." However, Mary said to the angel, "How can this be since I do not know man?" The angel responded: "The Holy Spirit will come upon you, and power from the Most High will overshadow you. Therefore, the child to be born will be called holy—Son of God. And behold, your relative Elizabeth, despite her old age, has also conceived a son; indeed, this is the sixth month for a woman who was deemed barren. Nothing said by God can be impossible." Mary answered, "Behold the handmaid of the Lord. Let it happen to me according to your word." Then the angel went away, leaving her (Luke 1:26-38).

Strictly speaking, according to the Buddhist and Christian scriptures, both Maya and Mary conceive their children without male intercourse and they had no children before the conception of the divine child, and that is all what is meant by *virginitas ante partum* in the physical sense. However, later tendency in both religions has been to claim that these women were so chaste and pure that they never had any carnal relations and carnal desires at all. For instance, in the *Lalitavistara*, one of the requirements of the mother of the Bodhisatva is that, besides being full of merit and virtue, she should not yet have had a child at the time of the descent of the Bodhisatva into her womb. The Buddhist tradition does not explicitly state that Queen Maya has never had any sexual relations with Sudhodana as in the Christian tradition; both traditions are clear on the point that the child is not the result of the union of the husband and wife. In both traditions, virginity is understood primarily in its religious sense that the virgin is morally and spiritually perfect or untouched by sin *ante partum, in partu*, and *post partum*.

Ironically, the earliest clearest testimony to the virginity of Buddha's mother before his birth comes from a Christian source, St. Jerome (A.D.340-420). Since Jovinian has rashly asserted that virginity is a state no higher than that of marriage, Jerome tries to show that virginity was esteemed by the pagan by referring to stories of virgin birth among the pagans. One of his examples is that of Buddha: "Apud gymnosophistas Indiae, quasi per manus huius opinionis auctoritas traditur, quod Buddam principem dogmatis eorum e latere suo virgo generarit."[24] Obviously, the details of the story of Buddha were known in the Christian West in the fourth century.[25]

5. Dream Vision

5.1 Buddha

According to the best known legends of Buddha, he is conceived virginally when his mother Maya has the vision of a white elephant which enters her womb. This narrative is given in the *Nidanakatha*:

> At that time in the city of Kapilavatthu the festival of the full moon day of the month Asalha (June-July) had been proclaimed, and many people celebrated it. Queen Maya from the seventh day before full moon celebrated the festival without intoxicants and with abundance of garlands and perfumes. Rising early on the seventh day she bathed in scented water, and bestowed a great gift of 400,000 pieces as alms. Fully adorned she ate of choice food, took upon herself the uposatha vows, entered her adorned state bed-chamber, lay down on the bed, and falling asleep dreamt this dream: the four great kings, it seemed, raised her together with the bed, and taking her to the Himalayas set her on the Mansila tableland of sixty leagues beneath a great sal-tree, seven leagues high, and stood on one side. Then their queens came and took her to the Anotatta Lake, bathed her to remove human stain, robed her in heavenly clothing, anointed her with perfumes, and bedecked her with divine flowers. Not far from away is a silver mountain, and thereon a golden mansion. There they prepared a divine bed with its head to the east, and laid her upon it. Now the Bodhisatta became a white elephant. Not far from there is a golden mountain, and going there he descended from it, alighted on the silver mountain, approaching it from the direction of the north. In his trunk, which was like a silver rope, he held a white lotus, then trumpeting he entered the golden mansion, made a rightwise circle three times round his mother's bed, smote her right side and appeared to enter her womb. Thus when the moon was in the lunar mansion Uttarasalha, he received a new existence. The next day the queen awoke and told her dream to the king. The king summoned sixty-four eminent brahmins, showed them honor, and satisfied them with excellent food and other presents. Then when they were satisfied with these pleasures, he caused the dream to be told, and asked what would happen. The brahmins said,"Be not anxious, O king, the queen has

---

[24] *Adversus Haereses* 1.42; PL 23:273.
[25] See E. Senart, "Essai sur la légende de Bouddha, son caractere et ses origins," *Journal Asiatique*, April-May, 1874, p. 384.

conceived, a male not a female, and thou shalt have a son, and if he dwells in a house he will become a king, a universal monarch.[26]

5.2 Jesus

Now, as for Christ, his birth took place in this way. His mother Mary had been betrothed to Joseph; but before they began to live together, it was found that she was with child—through the Holy Spirit. Her husband Joseph was an upright man, but unwilling to expose her to public disgrace; and so he resolved to divorce her quietly. Now, as he was considering this, behold, an angel of the Lord appeared to him in a dream, saying, "Joseph, son of David, do not be afraid to take Mary your wife into your home, for the child begotten in her is through the Holy Spirit. She will give birth to a son; and you will call his name Jesus, for he will save his people from their sins." All this took place to fulfill what the Lord had spoken by the prophet who said, "Behold, the virgin will be with child and will give birth to a son, and they will call his name Emmanuel. So Joseph got up from sleep and did as the angel of the Lord had commanded him. He took his wife home, but he had no sexual relations with her before she gave birth to a son. And he called his name Jesus (Matthew 1:18-25).

6. White Elephant vs. White Dove

In the Buddhist tradition, it is in the form of a white elephant that the Bodhisatva enters the womb of his mother. Interestingly, this idea is preserved in a Christian apocryphal work where the metaphor of the white elephant is changed into that of a white dove. The Ethiopic *History of Hanna* describes birth of Mary as follows:

He appeared unto her that day in a vision of the night, in the form of a White Bird which came down from heaven. Now this Bird had its being in the days of old, for it overshadowed the Cherubim of glory; and there was the hand of a man beneath the wing thereof, and held in it the cord of life. Now this was the Spirit of Life, in the form of a White Bird, and it took up its abode in the person of Hanna, and became incarnate in her womb, at the time when the Pearl went forth from the loins of Joachim, and when, according to the ordinance of carnal union Hanna received the Pearl, which was the Body of our Lady Mary.[27]

It is interesting to note that even the canonical gospels do not refrain from presenting the Holy spirit as a white dove. For instance, Luke 3:22 reads: "And the Holy Spirit discended upon him

---

[26] Edward J. Thomas, *The Life of Buddha as Legend and History* (New York, 1927), 31-32.
[27] E. A. Wallis Budge, *The Legends of Our Lady Mary the Perpetual Virgin and Her Mother Hanna* (London, 1933), 19.

in bodily for, as a dove, and a voice came from heaven, "Thou art my beloved Son; with thee I am well pleased." (Matt 3:16-17; Mark 1:10-11). The Gospel of the Ebionites has the following interesting passage:

> After the people were baptized, Jesus also came and was baptized by John. And as he came up from the water, the heavens were opened, and he saw the Holy Spirit descending in the form of a dove and entering into him. And a voice from heaven said, "Thou art my beloved Son; with thee I am well pleased." And again, "Today I have begotten thee." And immediately a great light shone around the place; and John seeing it, said to him, "Who are you, Lord?" And again a voice from heaven said to him, "This is my beloved Son, with whom I am well pleased." Then John, falling down before him, said, "I beseech you, Lord, baptize me!" But he forbade him, saying, "Let it be so; for thus it is fitting to fulfil all things."[28]

These passages seem to suggest that Jesus had a second miraculous conception as a divine person in his baptism as well. What is more important is the presence of the White Dove in this passage and the reference to begetting as in the case of Buddha and Mary.

7. Annunciation to the Husband

7.1 Buddha

Immediately after the miraculous conception, Maya Devi sent messengers to the king expressing her desire to see him. According to the *Lalitavistara* (vi):

> The king was agitated with delight by the message, and, rising from his noble seat, proceeded...to the Asoka grove; but he could not enter it. Near the entrance he felt himself very heavy....Now, the Devas of the class Suddhavasakayika (pure in body and dwelling) assuming semi-developed forms, came under the sky, and addressed the king Suddhodana in a Gatha: "O king, the noble Bodhisattva, full of the merits of religious observances and penances, and adored of the three thousand regions, the possessor of friendliness and benevolence, the sanctified in pure knowledge, renouncing the mansion of Tushita, has acknowledged sonship to you by entering the womb of Maya. Join your ten nails, bend down your head, and enter the grove, O king, with a humbled, devout mind." The king did so, and beholding Maya in her greatness, said, "Dear one, what may I do for your gratification?"[29]

---

[28] See Epiphanius, *Against Heresies*, XXX.13.7-8.
[29] Mitra, 95.

7.2 Jesus

> His mother Mary had been betrothed to Joseph; but before they began to live together, it was found that she was with child—through the Holy Spirit. Her husband Joseph was an upright man, but unwilling to expose her to public disgrace; and so he resolved to divorce her quietly. Now, as he was considering this, behold, an angel of the Lord appeared to him in a dream, saying, "Joseph, son of David, do not be afraid to take Mary your wife into your home, for the child begotten in her is through the Holy Spirit. She will give birth to a son; and you will call his name Jesus, for he will save his people from their sins." ...So Joseph got up from sleep and did as the angel of the Lord had commanded him. He took his wife home (Matthew 1:18-25).

Though the annunciation in Luke is made by the angel to Mary, in Matthew the annunciation is made to Joseph, as in the Buddhist tradition, where King Suddhodana is the recipient of the annunciation. In both narratives, the husbands are in turmoil; they receive a heavenly message; they are asked to accept the new situation of the pregnancy of their wives; and they accept it wholeheartedly.

It should be emphasized again that the fundamental fact that is common to both the Buddhist and Gospel narratives here is the datum of virginal conception of the Masters without the medium of a human father. The consent of the mother for impregnation is implied in Luke's account and the *Accharya*-account. Dream-motif and supernatural agents are found in Matthew and the *Nidanakatha*; the supernatural beings' role is creating confidence in the recipients of visions in both narratives: the four great heavenly kings are present to ward off demons in case they tried to frighten the mother of Buddha; in the Lucan narrative the angel says to Mary: "Be not afraid." In fact, interpretation of the vision is found both in Luke and the *Nidanakatha*.

8. Turmoil at Birth

In the *Buddhacarita* (27-28) by Asvaghosha, there is a reference to King Sudhodana being disturbed at the birth of Buddha, as in the case of King Herod at the birth of Jesus, though the contexts of both episodes are quite different:

> When the Guru [Teacher] was born for the salvation of all creatures, the world became exceedingly peaceful, as though, being in a state of disorder, it had obtained a ruler. Kamadeva (god of love) alone did not rejoice. On seeing the miraculous birth of his son, the king, steadfast

though he was, was much disturbed, and from his affection a double stream of tears flowed, born of delight and apprehension.[30]

Now, after the birth of Jesus in Bethlehem of Judea in the days of Herod the king, behold, magi from the East came to Jerusalem asking, "Where is the newborn King of the Jews? For we have seen his star at its rising and have come to pay him homage." When King Herod heard this, he was troubled, and so was all Jerusalem with him. Assembling all the chief priests and scribes of the people, he inquired of them where the Messiah was to be born. "In Bethlehem of Judea," they told him (Matthew 3:1-5).

The motif of the summoning of priests and wise men is found in Matthew as well as in the Buddhist story. Of course, the Old Testament provides several instances of the summoning of wise men to interpret dreams as in the case of the Pharaoh and King Nebuchadnezzar; however, what is striking here is the association of the wise men and the birth of the saviors.

9. Masters in Mothers' Wombs

9.1 Buddha

From the time the Future Buddha was thus conceived, four angels with swords in their hands kept guard, to ward off all harm from both the Future Buddha and the Future Buddha's mother. No lustful thought sprang up in the mind of the Future Buddha's mother; having reached the pinnacle of good fortune and of glory, she felt comfortable and well, and experienced no exhaustion of body. And within her womb she could distinguish the Future Buddha, like a white thread passed through a transparent jewel. And whereas a womb that has been occupied by a Future Buddha is like the shrine of a temple, and can never be occupied or used again, therefore it was that the mother of the Future Buddha died when he was seven days old, and was reborn in the Tushita heaven.[31]

Whenever she [Mayadevi] looked towards her right side she beheld the Bodhisatva in her womb, even as a person beholds his own face in an untarnished mirror. Seeing him, she became satisfied, excited, affected, delighted, and soothed in mind with affection (*Lalitavistara*, vi).[32]

There are also several special circumstances that distinguish the conception, gestation, and birth of the Boddhisatva. He always remains on the right side of his mother, without movement; such movement, from right to left, gives constant pain and anxiety

---

[30] E. H. Johnston, *Buddhacarita* (Delhi, 1984), II: 7.
[31] *Nidanakatha*, H. C. Warren, *Buddhism in Translation* (New York,1963): 45-46.
[32] Mitra, 107-08.

to the mother. But the Boddhisatva remains ever at rest whether the mother rise, or sit, or sleep.[33]

9.2 *Jesus*

> At that time Mary got ready and hurried to a town in hill country of Judah, where she entered Zechariah's home and greeted Elizabeth. When Elizabeth heard Mary's greeting, the baby leaped in her womb; Elizabeth was filled with the Holy Spirit... She exclaimed: "Blessed are you among women, and blessed is the child you will bear! But why am I so favored that the mother of my Lord should come to me? As soon as the sound of your greeting reached my ears, the baby in my womb leaped for joy" (Luke 1:39-44).

In the Ethiopic Apocryphal text of *The Narrative of the Virgin Mary as Told by Herself to Timothy, Patriarch of Alexandria*, the child to be born appears as a gem within the expectant mother as in *Lalitavistara*. It is Mary who is speaking:

> And from that time my heart became strong. And I reckoned nine months His time, like all women. And when I returned from her I did not know the appearance of his coming until my pearl shone brightly by his good pleasure, and became lighted up throughout, and I saw the splendor of His light and heard His voice.[34]

What is important to note here is that the Masters, being fully formed, are divine from the start and that some persons are able to recognize them even while they are hidden in the wombs of their mothers; this is because the child in the womb is visible to a select few, like to Elizabeth in the case of Jesus and to the gods and angels in the case of Buddha. Rhys Davids has pointed out the interesting fact that certain medieval frescoes represent Christ as visible when in his mother's womb.[35]

10. *Virgin Birth—virginitas in partu*

10.1 *Buddha*

> Queen Mahamaya bearing the Bodhisatta for ten months like oil in a bowl, when her time was come, desired to go to her relatives' house, and addressed king Suddhodana, "I wish, O king, to go to Devadaha, the city of my family." The king approved, and caused the road from Kapilavattu to Devadaha to be made smooth and adorned with vessels filled with plantains, flags, and banners, and seating her in a golden palanquin

---

[33] Beal, 41.
[34] E. A. Wallis Budge, *Legends of Our Lady Mary The Perpetual Virgin and Her Mother Hanna* (London, 1933), 82.
[35] *Buddhist Birth Stories* (London, n.d), 65.

borne by a thousand courtiers sent her with a great retinue. Between the two cities and belonging to the inhabitants of both is a pleasure grove of sal-trees named the Lumbini grove. At that time from the roots to the tips of the branches it was one mass of flowers, and from within the branches and flowers hosts of bees of the five colors and various flocks of birds sport, singing sweetly. When the queen saw it, a desire to sport in the grove arose. The courtiers brought the queen and entered the grove. She went to the foot of a great sal tree, and desired to seize a branch. Thereupon she was shaken with the throes of birth. So the multitude set up a curtain for her and retired. Holding the branch and even while standing she was delivered. At that moment the four pure-minded Mahabrahmas came with a golden net, and therewith receiving the Bodhisatta set him before his mother, and said, "Rejoice, O queen, a mighty son has been born to thee." And as other beings when born come forth stained with impure matter, not so the Bodhisatta. But the Bodhisatta like a Preacher of the Doctrine descending from the seat of Doctrine, like a man descending stairs, stretched out his two hands and feet, and standing unsoiled and unstained by any impurity,...descended from his mother.[36]

Deluded persons will not be able to understand that the body of men of noble deeds is not produced in a mass of excrement and urine; that of such beings the descent from the womb is perfectly pure. It is from his mercy to created beings that the Bodhisattva, abiding in the womb, takes his birth on the region of the mortals. Remaining as a Deva he cannot set the wheel of religion in motion(*Lalitavistara*, vii).[37]

A woman [probably a midwife] announces the miraculous birth of Buddha to Mahanama: "Great minister, pray listen to me well; the circumstances attending the birth of the child were very wonderful! Our queen, Maya, standing upright on the ground, the child came forth of her right side; there was no rent in her bosom, or side, or loins [38]

The *Buddhacarita* also states clearly that the birth of Buddha was a virginal one: "Then as soon as Pushya became propitious, from the side of the queen, who was hallowed by her vows, a son was born for the weal of the world, without her suffering either pain or illness. As was the birth of Aurva from the thigh, of Prthu from the hand, of Mandhatr, the peer of Indra, from the head, of Kakshivat from the armpit, one such wise was his birth.(I: 9-10).[39]

---

[36] *Nidanakatha*, Thomas, 32-33.
[37] Mitra, 127.
[38] Beal, 47.
[39] E. H. Johnston, II: 3.

10.2 Jesus

> All this took place to fulfill what the Lord had said through the prophet: "The virgin will be with child and will give birth to a son, and they will call him Immanuel." (Matthew 1:22).

> And the midwife went out from the cave, and Salome met her. And the midwife said to her, Salome, Salome, I will tell you a most surprising thing which I saw. A Virgin hath brought forth, which is a thing contrary to nature. To which Salome replied, As the Lord my God liveth, unless I receive particular proof of this matter, I will not believe that a virgin hath brought forth. Then Salome went in, and the midwife said, Mary shew thyself, for a great controversy is risen concerning thee. And Salome received satisfaction. But her hand was withered, and groaned bitterly .. Salome...went to the child, and said, I will touch him. And she proposed to worship him, for she said, This is a great king which is born in Israel. And straightway Salome was cured (Protoevangelion 14:14-28).

> He [Joseph] ordered the midwife to go to [Mary] and she stood before her. For hours Mary permitted herself to be watched, then the midwife cried with a loud voice and said, "Lord, great God, have mercy, because never has this been heard, nor seen, nor even dreamed of, until now, that the breasts should be full of milk and a male child, after birth, should make his mother known to be a virgin. There was no offering of blood in the birth, no pain occurred in the parturition. A virgin conceived, a virgin has given birth and after she gave birth, she remained a virgin.[40] (A Latin Infancy Gospel, 69).

> In those days Caesar Augustus issued a decree that a census should be taken of the entire Roman world. This was the first census that took place while Quirinius was governor of Syria. And everyone went to his own town to register. So Joseph also went up from the town of Nazareth in Galilee to Judea, to Bethlehem the town of David, because he belonged to the house and line of David. He went there to register with Mary, who was pledged to be married to him and was expecting a child. While they were there, the time came for the baby to be born, and she gave birth to her firstborn, a son. She wrapped him in cloths and placed him in a manger, because there was no room for them in the inn (Luke 2:1-7).

Both *Lalitavistara* (109) and *Abhinishkramanasutra* (Beal, 47) say that the Bodhisatva came from his mother's right side, and take care to add that her right side was uninjured—Jerome knew this story and referred to it in his *Adversus Jovinianum*, 1, 26. The canonical gospel narratives, however, refrain from giving physical and graphical details of the birthing of Jesus. Though they do not

---

[40] *Documents for the Study of the Gospels*, eds. David R. Cartlidge and David L. Dungan, (Philadelphia,1988), 105.

even suggest the idea of *virginitas in partu*, except perhaps Matthew, later Christian tradition is nearly unanimous about Jesus' virginal birth.

11. *Virginity —post partum*

11.1 *Buddha*

> After the birth of the Bodhisatva, his mother's flank became unbroken and scarless; as it was before so it became after (*Lalitavistara*, vii).[41]

> King Sudhodana, forsaking all worldly affairs, and the society of even pure women, and adopting the life a *Brahmachari*, engaged himself in religious work, even as if he had retired to a grove of penance (*Lalitavistara*,vi).[42]

11.2 *Jesus*

> When Joseph woke up, he did what the angel of the Lord had commanded him and took Mary home as his wife. But he had no union with her until she gave birth to a son. (Matthew 1:24-25)

Mary is a virgin *post partum*, according to Catholic tradition, which tradition perfectly accords with the Buddhist tradition with the difference that Mary does not die soon after after giving birth to Jesus; in fact, she outlives Jesus. On the contrary, Queen Maya dies seven days after the birth of her son, because the mothers of Bodhisatvas should die immediately after giving birth in order to have their virginal purity preserved. At death, Maya is taken into Tushita heaven; according to Catholic tradition, Mary is also taken into heaven at her dormition, which comes only after she has performed a role in the life of Jesus and his disciples.

As for the Christian tradition of the perpetual virginity of Mary, it is a development from the second century. The earliest witness to this tradition is the *Protoevangelion* of James. Here the author describes Mary's miraculous origin, her saintly childhood and upbringing in the Temple, and her marriage to the aged widower Joseph, who, of course, has no intention of making the "virgin of the Lord" his sexual partner. The author also extols the miraculous continuance of Mary's virginity even after the birth of Jesus. Later Christian tradition picked up this trend of thought and proclaimed the perpetual virginity of Mary. Jesus' brothers, who

---

[41] Mitra, 134.
[42] Mitra, 108.

are mentioned in the gospels, become Jesus' stepbrothers from Joseph's first marriage. According to Hans Van Campenhausen,

> Unfortunately it cannot be determined more precisely where this writing comes from. The only thing that seems certain is that it cannot have originated in Jewish Christian circles; nor, however, can it be asserted that it was subjected, in its fantasy and asceticism, to "gnostic" or any other heretical "influence."[43]

Maybe it is time that Christian scholars looked in the Buddhist tradition for the source of the idea of the perpetual virginity of Mary!

12. *Righteous Fosterfather*

12.1 *Buddha*

> Sudhodana was the noblest among all the royal personages; he was of imperial family, and absolutely pure in his body. He was rich, thriving, calm, august, good, and virtuous (*Lalitavistara*, iii).[44]

12.2 *Jesus*

> Joseph, her husband, was an upright man (Matthew 1:19).

13. *Manger, Taxes, Holy Innocents, and Exile*

Some other details surrounding the birth of Jesus in both Matthew's and Luke's narratives seem to have been derived from another Indian birth story, the story of the birth of Krishna, who is the most celebrated deity of the Hindu pantheon and is also regarded as the eighth incarnation of Vishnu who assumed the form of Krishna in order to destroy the tyrant Kamsa. Though the earliest Buddhist works do not narrate the events connected with the birth of Krishna, *Jataka* 454 contains a brief narrative of Krishna. We find the following reference to Krishna in the Chinese version of the "plowing match" found in the *Abhinishkramanasutra*: "Then the Rishis, looking downwards, beheld the prince underneath the tree, sitting with his legs crossed...Then the Rishis began to consider—"Who can this be?" "Is it Brahma, Lord of the world?—or is it Krishna Deva, Lord of the Kama Loka?"[45] *Lalitavistara* (ii) also refers to Krishna: "Who can

---

[43] Hans Van Campenhausen, *The Virgin Birth in the Theology of the Ancient Church* (Naperville,1984), 54.
[44] Mitra, 45.
[45] Beal, 75.

this seated one be? Is he...Krishna the valiant?...His beauty is greater than that of Vaisravana...Is he the image of Krishna?"[46] "By the fourth century before Christ, the cult of Vasudeva was well established. In the Buddhist work, *Niddesa* (fourth century B.C.) included in the Pali canon, the writer refers to the worshippers of Vasudeva and Baladeva among others."[47]

13.1 *Krishna*

Krishna, the leader of the Yadava tribe and the son of Devaki is mentioned in the pre-Buddhist *Chandogya Upanishad* as a knower of the Brahman and as the pupil of Ghora Angirasa (III.17.6). He is celebrated as a warrior and religious teacher in the *Mahabharata* completed probably in the third century B.C.. In that epic, Krishna is represented both as an historical inidvidual and as an incarnation, though there are also indications there that Krishna's supremacy was not accepted without a challenge. The pre-Christian *Ghata Jataka* establishes the connection with the cowherds since, according to this story, Krishna spent his childhood among the gopas.[48] In support of this claim it should be pointed out that Megasthenes, who lived as the ambassador of Seleukos Nikator at the Indian court of Pataliputra from 302 to 288 B.C., recognizes in his accounts Krishna as an avatar of Vishnu under the name of Heracles by the side of Dionysos. Megasthenes states that the Indian Herakles was worshipped by the Saurasenoi (Surasenas) in whose land are two great cities Methora (Mathura) and Kleisbora (Krishnapura). Heliodorus, the Greek Bhagavata from Taxila, calls Vasudeva, devadeva (god of gods) in the Besnagar inscription (180 B.C.). The Nanaghat inscription, which belongs to the first century before the Christian era, mentions Vasudeva among the deities invoked in the opening verse.[49] Krishna's life is narrated in *Harivamsa*, which is an appendix to the *Mahabharata*, in the *Vishnupurana*, and in the *Bhagavatapurana*. As for Kirshna's presence and function in the

---

[46] Mitra, 191.
[47] S. Radhakrishnan, *The Bhagavadgita* (New York: Harper, 1973), 29.
[48] Bimanbehari Majumdar, *Krishna in History and Legend* (Calcutta, 1969), 58.
[49] See S. Radhakrishnan, *The Bhagavadgita*, 28-29; Richard Garbe, *India and Christendom* (La Salle, 1959), 206-207. Scholars for the most part identify Herakles and Dionysus with Krishna and Shiva; however, Allan Dahlquist, *Megasthenes and Indian Religion* (Stockholm, 1962), final chapter, thinks Herakles is Indra, while Dionysos is a non-Aryan deity of the Indian hill peoples.

pre-Christian *Bhagavadgita*, where Kirshna manifests himself to Arjuna as an avatar of Vishnu, Franklin Edgerton says:

> We know nothing of the process by which he (Krishna) attained divine honors nor of his earlier history as a God, before the Bhagavad-Gita, which is probably the earliest work presented to us in which he appears as such. In this work he has all the attributes of a full-fledged monotheistic deity, and at the same time, as we shall see, the attributes of the Upanishadic Absolute.[50]

Garbe rejects the view that it was Christianity which gave Hinduism the impetus for developing the cult of Krishna:

> In the second century before Christ not only the powerful hero Krishna but also the child Krishna already played a significant role in Brahmanic India; and indeed the *divine child* ...Krishna had already been worshiped as God as early as the sixth century before Christ. The divine child Krishna accordingly does not appear in India about 500 A.D ...but was known there at least seven hundred years earlier, and even in his special relation to pastoral life. Therefore, his veneration is of genuinely Indianorigin. [51]

Since the Krishna-texts as given in *Harivamsa* and the *puranas* are long, I shall give a short summary of the relevant matter affecting the infancy gospels of Jesus:

In the city of Mathura there reigned a wicked king, Kamsa. Sage Narada told him that he would meet death at the hands of the eighth son of Devaki and Vasudeva. The king's servants kept a careful watch on Devaki, and six of her children were put to death as soon as they were born. Legend has it that that at the moment that Vasudeva impregnated Devaki, Vishnu plucked a white hair from his body and caused it to enter Devaki's womb, and that in the fullness of time the fair-complexioned Balarama was born. The seventh son, Baladeva—a precursor who grew up with Krishna, like John the Baptist— was transferred by Nidra, the goddess of

---

[50] *The Bhagavadgita*, 30; cited by Majumdar, 54-55; see also Jean Sedlar, *India and the Greek World*, 188: "The *Bhagavadgita*. does treat Krishna as a deity (indeed his divine status is essential to the piece); and the Gita *may be* pre-Christian. Chronology is crucial to the argument here; and unfortunately the chronology is vague. The date of the Gita is generally given as between the 2nd century B.C. and 2nd century A.D.– obviously no very precise estimate. The poem has certain passages in common with some of the middle Upanishads, especially Isha, Katha, Mundaka, and Svetashvatara, and must be regarded as belonging to the same general period as they. But even the latest date ordinarily accepted for the Gita--the 2nd century A.D.–seems too early to justify any reasonable hypothesis of Christian influence upon it." Radhakrishnan assigns a fifth-century (B.C.) date to the *Gita* (14).
[51] Garbe, 217.

sleep, who took the child before his birth into the womb of Rohini, another wife of Vasudeva. When Vasudeva impregnated Devaki again, Vishnu plucked a black hair which also entered Devaki's womb so that the dark-colored Krishna was born. Kamsa at that time had Vasudeva and his wife in prison and in chains to prevent their escape; suddenly the chains fell off. Vasudeva took the eighth son, Krishna, as soon as he was born, in the dead of the night, when all the guards had been put to sleep by Yoganidra, to the household of Nanda and Yasoda, the cowherds in Braj across the Yamuna, and exchanged him for their daughter who was born at the same time in a barn filled with shepherds and shepherdesses. Nanda and his pregnant wife Yasoda had actually come to Braj to pay taxes to Kamsa; they did not discover the actions of Vasudeva. Meanwhile Kamsa's soldiers reported to the king about the birth of the girl, and Kamsa came and seized the child and hurled her against a rock. By a series of miracles the child Krishna escaped the general massacre of infants ordered by Kamsa. Krishna grew up with his brother Balarama who was entrusted by Vasudeva to the care of Nanda as a herdman's son, tending his flocks.[52] In a forthcoming study I shall show the close resemblances between Krishna and the Christ of the Gospel of John, which presents Christ as a good shepherd with his religion of love—a trait shared by Krishna himself.

13.2 *Jesus*

> When the Magi had gone, an angel of the Lord appeared to Joseph in a dream. "Get up," he said, "take the child and his mother and escape to Egypt. Stay there until I tell you, for Herod is going to search for the child to kill him." So he got up, took the child and his mother during the night and left for Egypt, where he stayed until the death of Herod. And so was fulfilled what the Lord had said through the prophet: "Out of Egypt I called my son." When Herod realized, he had been outwitted by the Magi, he was furious, and he gave orders to kill all the boys in Bethlehem and its vicinity who were two years and under, in accordance with the time he had learned from the Magi (Matthew 2:13-16).

> And it came to pass, that there went forth a decree from Emperor Augustus that all the Jews should be taxed, who were of Bethlehem of Judea. And Joseph said, I will take care that my children be taxed; but

---

[52] The Mathura museum has a fragmentary relief of the second or third century A.D., depicting Vasudeva with the new-born Krishna in his hand crossing the Yamuna, obviously with the view of taking him to the house of Nanda and Yasoda; see ASIAR, 1925-26, pp. 183-194; referred to by B. Majumdar, 59-60.

what shall I do with this young woman? To have her taxed as my wife I am ashamed; and if I tax her as my daughter, all Israel knows she is not my daughter (Protoevangelion 12:1-3).

The similarities between the Krishna-Jesus stories are obvious. For instance, both infants are born in mangers or rather in the homes of cowherds/shepherds; both infants are born when their parents go to pay taxes (go to register to vote); both infants escape the murderous wrath of tyrants who massacre innocent children; both go into exile. The most obvious difference is that Krishna's conception and birth are not virginal. The reason is that virginal conception is not very important in Hinduism, just as Judaism does not place any importance on virginal conception.

14. *Angels and Others at Birth*

14.1 *Buddha*

Now at the time of the birth of Bodhisatva in Lumbini, when the supernatural light appeared and the earth shook, then the Rishis and the Devas, who dwelt on earth, exclaimed with great joy, "This day Buddha is born, for the good of men, to dispel the darkness of their ignorance." Then the four heavenly kings took up the strain, and said, "Now because Bodhisatva is born to give joy and bring peace to the world, therefore is there this brightness." Then the Gods of the thirty-three Heavens took up the burthen of the strain.[53]

When...the Bodhisatta was issuing from his mother's womb, then an illimitable glorious radiance, surpassing even the Deva-majesty of Devas, appeared in the world with its Devas, its Maras, its Brahmas, among the generations with recluses and brahmans, Devas, and men. And even in those spaces between the worlds, gloomy, baseless, regions of blackness plunged in blackness, where the moon and the sun, powerful and majestic though they be, cannot make their light prevail—even there there appeared the illimitable glorious radiance, surpassing even the Deva-majesty of Devas.[54]

14.2 *Jesus*

And there were shepherds living out in the fields nearby, keeping watch over their flocks at night. An angel of the Lord appeared to them, and the glory of the Lord shone around them, and they were terrified. But the angel said to them, "Do not be afraid. I bring you good news of great joy that will be for all the people. Today in the town of David a Savior has been born to you; he is Christ the Lord. This will be a sign to you: You will find a baby wrapped in cloths and lying in a manger." Suddenly a

---

[53] Beal, 55-56.
[54] *Acchariyabhuta-dhammasutta*, 123.

great company of heavenly host appeared with the angel, praising God and saying, "Glory to God in the highest; on earth peace to men on whom his favor rests." When the angels had left them and gone into heaven, the shepherds said to one another, "Let us go to Bethlehem and see this thing that has happened, which the Lord has told us about." So they hurried off and found Mary and Joseph, and the baby, who was lying in the manger....The shepherds returned, glorifying and praising God for all the things they had heard and seen, which were just as they had been told (Luke 2:8-20).

15. *Earthquakes and the Redemption of the Dead from Hell*

15.1 *Buddha*

When the Bodhisatta was issuing from his mother's womb, then an illimitable glorious radiance, surpassing even the Deva-majesty of Devas, appeared in the world with its Devas, its Maras, its Brahmas, among the generations with recluses and brahmans, Devas, and men. And even in those spaces between the worlds, gloomy, baseless, regions of blackness plunged in blackness, where the moon and the sun, powerful and majestic though they be, cannot make their light prevail—even there there appeared the illimitable glorious radiance, surpassing even the Deva-majesty of Devas. And those beings who had uprisen there recognized one another by means of this radiance, and they thought: "Indeed there are other beings who are uprising here." And this ten-thousand-world-system quaked, trembled, and shook, and there appeared there the illimitable glorious radiance surpassing even the Deva-majesty of the Devas. I regard this too as a wonder. [55]

15.2 Jesus

And when Jesus had cried out again in a loud voice, he gave up his spirit. At that moment the curtain of the temple was torn in two from top to bottom. The earth shook and the rocks split. The tombs broke open and the bodies of many holy people who had died were raised to life. They came out of the tombs, and after Jesus' resurrection they went into the holy city and appeared to many people (Matthew 27:50-51).

The difference between the Buddhist and Christian perception of earthquakes and the rising of the dead is that for the Buddhists these marvels take place already at the birth of the Savior; for the Christians these miracles happen only at the death of Jesus. According to Christian theology, Christ achieves salvation primarily through his death and resurrection; the Buddhists see the birth of Buddha rather than his death as the real salvific event.

---

[55] *Acchariyabhutadhammasutta*, 123-124.

16. Harrowing of Hell

16.1 Buddha

The entire life of Buddha was also a battle with Mara, the Devil. From the beginning to the end, Buddha fought and won all his battles without at any time falling into the temptation of Mara. At his birth, a heavenly light permeated the dark recesses of Hell and enlightened the dwellers of the netherworld. Later, according to the *Lalitavistara*, "Mara, the wicked one, followed close behind the Bodhisatva, as he was practising austerities for six years, seeking and pursuing an entrance, and at no time succeeding in finding any. And finding none he departed gloomy and sorrowful."[56] In the Buddhist legend of *Karandavyuha*, the merciful Bodhisatva Avalokitesvara descended into the terrible hell of Avici in order merely by his appearance to free the condemned from their agony, to transform hell into a joyful place; the apalling heat changes to agreeable coolness; the kettle in which millions of the damned are boiling becomes a lotus pond; in the world of the pretas (the departed souls), which he also visits, he comforts these hungry and thirsty hosts with food and drink. He is the one who decided to remain a Bodhisatva (Buddha to be) until such time as he has secured deliverance for all mankind.[57] In the *Abhinishkramanasutra*, it is a Deva who descends into Hell to redeem the prisoners:

> Then again there was a certain Deva called "Fleet-goer," who, with rapid flight, went down to all the hells, and cried out with a loud voice, "All ye wretched ones! understand now that Bodhisatva is incarnated; quickly, then, pray ye and vow with all your might, that ye may be born on earth." Then the wretched inmates, having heard this cry, as many of them as in ages gone by had acquired any merit, but for some consequent act of sin had been born in hell,--these, I say, regarding one another, saw plainly their appearance changing, and their bodies becoming bright and beautiful; and so their minds received great joy; and when they heard the voices of the fleet-goer and all the angels singing on earth, they were delivered from hell; and such as had acquired previous merit were born on earth, in the immediate neighborhood of Kapilavastu.[58]

> He advanced seven steps downwards and said: "I shall destory Mara and his army; I shall shower on hell the rain of the cloud of the great religion, and blow out the fire of the nether regions, so that they may be restored to happiness."...The sufferings of those who dwelt in Avici

---

[56] Thomas, 72.
[57] Garbe, 76.
[58] Beal, 40.

and other hells were suppressed at the time. The brute creation were free from the pain of devouring each other, and the dwellers in the region of Yama suffered not from hunger, thirst, and the like (*Lalitavistara*, vii).[59]

16.2 Jesus

Jesus' descent into hell, which is part of the Apostles Creed, is the subject matter of the Gospel of Nicodemus:

> The mighty Lord appeared in form of a man, and enlightened those places which had ever before been in darkness, and broke asunder the fetters which before could not be broken; and with his invincible power visited those who sat in the deep darkness....Then the King of Glory trampling upon death, seized the prince of hell, deprived him of all his power, and took our earthly father Adam with him to his glory....Then the Lord stretching forth his hand, made the sign of the cross upon Adam, and upon all his saints. And taking hold of Adam by his right hand, he ascended from hell, and all the saints of God followed him (XVI-XIX).

The *Odes of Solomon*,[60] perhaps the earliest Christian hymn-book dating from the last quarter of the first century, provides a magnificent lyric statement on the harrowing of Hades as the decisive moment in the Christian redemptive process:

> I was not rejected although I was considered to be so,
> and I did not perish although they thought it of me.
>
> Sheol saw me and was shattered,
> and Death ejected me and many with me.
>
> I have been vinegar and bitterness to it,
> and I went down with it as far as the depth.
>
> Then the feet and the head it released,
> because it was not able to endure my face.
>
> And I made a Congregation of living among his dead;
> and I spoke with them by living lips;
> in order that my word may not fail.

---

[59] Mitra, 125-26.
[60] Rendel Harris, *The Odes and Psalms of Solomon* (Cambridge, 1909), 88

> And those who had died ran toward me;
> and they cried out and said, "Son of God, have pity on us.
>
> And deal with us according to your kindness,
> and bring us out from the chains of darkness.
>
> And open for us the door
> by which we may go forth to you,
> for we perceive that our death does not approach you.
>
> May we also be saved with you,
> because you are our Savior."
>
> Then I heard their voice,
> and placed their faith in my heart.
>
> And I placed my name upon their head,
> because they are free and they are mine (42:10-20).[61]

In another early Christianized Jewish apocryphal text, *The Martyrdom and Ascension of Isaiah* 3:15, it is not Jesus who descends into Hell but "the angel of the Church" into an unspecified location, which idea is not far from the Buddhist idea of the angel descending into the the netherworld.[62] What is important here is only the first-century Christian insertion in this Jewish work:

> And the guards who would guard the grave and the descent of the angel of the church which is in the heavens, whom he will summon in the last days; and that the angel of the Holy Spirit and Michael, the chief of the holy angels, will open his grave on the third day, and that the Beloved, sitting on their shoulders, will come forth and send out his twelve disciples, and they will teach all nations and every tongue the resurrection of the Beloved, and those who believe in his cross will be saved, and in his ascension to the seventh heaven from where he came.[63]

It seems that this classical doctrine of redemption as victory over the Devil and the liberation of mankind from the power of the Devil found in the early Christian teaching is a restatement of the Buddhist theory of the harrowing of Hell. However, there is a significant difference: in the Indian tradition, the souls in hell are

---

[61] Cited by Dominic Crossan, *The Cross That Spoke* (New York, 1988), 367-368.
[62] R. H. Charles, *The Ascension of Isaiah* (London: Black, 1900), xliv.
[63] Crossan, 369.

redeemed to be reborn on earth as in Virgil's *Aeneid*, since the Indians and Virgil refer to reincarnation as redemption from hell; in the Christian tradition, the redeemed are taken to heaven, it seems. However, in Matthew the redeemed appear not in heaven but on earth: "The tombs broke open and the bodies of many holy people who had died were raised to life. They came out of the tombs, and after Jesus' resurrection they went into the holy city and appeared to many people"(27:52-53).

17. Nature Miracle

17.1 Buddha

According to the *Lalitavistara* (vii), all movement in the world of nature and humanity ceases at the birth of Buddha. The half-opened flowers cease to bloom; birds pause in their flight; the wind stops blowing; the rivers no longer flow, when Buddha's holy feet touch the earth; sun, moon, and stars stand still; all human activity is paralyzed:

> When the Bodhisatva, immediately after his birth, advanced seven steps, innumerable millions then stood firm on that adamantine spot; incalculable millions of hundreds of thousands of Buddhas from ten quarters, of well-regulated feet, of mighty vigor, thoroughly exercised in the great religion.[64]

> The adamantine earth, possessed of vigor and might, stood still, when the great preceptor, the destroyer of decay and death, the noblest of physicians, the giver of the best medicine, standing on his two feet marked with a beautifully colored lotus and a wheel, advanced seven steps.[65]

17.2 Jesus

> And leaving her [Mary] and his sons in the cave, Joseph went forth to seek a Hebrew midwife in the village of Bethlehem. But as I was going (said Joseph) I looked up into the air, and I saw the clouds astonished, and the fowls of the air stopping in the midst of their flight. And I looked down towards the earth, and saw a table spread, and working people sitting around it, but their hands were upon the table, and they did not move to eat. They who had meat in their mouths did not put anything in; but all their faces were fixed upwards. And I beheld the sheep dispersed, and yet the sheep stood still. And the shepherd lifted up his hand to smite them, and his hand continued up. And I looked unto a river, and saw the kids with their mouths close to the water, and touching it, but they did not drink (Protoevangelion 13:1-10).

---

[64] Mitra, 126.
[65] Mitra, 131.

> In that hour everything ceased. There was total silence and fear. For even the winds stopped, they made no breeze; there was no motion of tree leaves; no sound of water was heard. The streams did not flow; there was no motion of the sea. All things produced in the water were quiet; there was no human voice sounding; there was a great silence. For the pole (or, people) itself ceased its rapid course from that hour. Time almost stopped its measure. All, overwhelmed with great fear, kept silent; we were expecting the advent of the most hight God, the end of the world[66] (A Latin Infancy Gospel, 72).

Indeed, Joseph brought the midwife, but after the birth of Jesus; in the *Abhinishkramanasutra*, Queen Maya was also attended by many women when she retired under the tree to give birth to Buddha.[67]

18. *The Taking of Seven Steps at birth*

18.1 *Buddha*

> Gods and men worshipped him with scented garlands, and said, "Great Being, there is here none like thee, much less superior anywhere." So having examined the four quarters, the intermediate quarter, the nadir and the zenith, ten quarters, and not seeing anyone like himself he said, "This is the northern quarter," and took seven steps....At the seventh step he stopped, and raising his lordly voice, he roared his lion-roar: "I am the chief in the world."[68]

18.2 *Mary*

> And the child increased in strength every day, so that when she was six months old his mother stood her on the ground to try if she could stand. And she walked [twice] seven steps and came to her bosom. And she took her up, saying: "As the Lord my God lives, you shall walk no more upon this ground until I take you into the temple of the Lord." (Protoevangelion 6:1).

It is interesting that the author of the *Protoevangelion* ascribes the miracle of the seven steps to infant Mary rather than to infant Jesus. The reason is that this work is devoted primarily to the infancy of Mary and only secondarily to the birth of Jesus; the author does not dwell on the childhood of Jesus in this work.

---

[66] Cartlidge and Dungan, 105.
[67] Beal, 43.
[68] *Nidanakatha* , Thomas , 33.

19. Marvelous Light/Star

19.1 Buddha

The presence of a marvelous and powerful light at the conception and birth of Buddha is recorded in the *Lalitavistara* and the *Majjhimanikaya*. This motif is found in the birth-stories of Krishna as well. As for Buddha,

> When, Ananda, the Bodhisatta was issuing from his mother's womb, then an illimitable glorious radiance, surpassing even the Deva-majesty of Deva, appeared in the world.[69]

> Then such brightness shone around, eclipsing the very sun and moon, and the Devas brought a white umbrella with an entire gold handle; it was large as a chariot wheel, with which to shelter him.[70]

> Then king Sudhodana assembling all the Sakyas investigated whether the boy would become a king, a universal ruler, or whether he would renounce the world to wander as an ascetic. And at the same time on the peak of the Himalayas dwelt a great sage named Asita, having the five attainments, together with his nephew Naradatta. At the moment when the Bodhisatta was born he beheld many marvelous wonders: the gods over the space of the sky making the word "Buddha" resound, waving their garments, and coursing hither and thither in delight. He thought what if I were to observe. He observing with his divine eye beheld all Jambudvipa, and in the great city called Kapila, in the house of king Sudhodana, the boy who had been born, shining with the brilliance of a hundred merits, honored by all the world, and adorned with the thirty-two marks of a great man. ... So the great sage Asita with his nephew Naradatta like a royal swan rose up and flew through the air to the great city of Kapilavatthu (*Lalitavistara*, vii).[71]

> As soon as the Bodhisatva was born, Mahesvaradeva turned to the Devas and spoke: "The Bodhisatva, the Great Being, has appeared in the world and will in a short time attain the highest and most perfect wisdom. Come let us go and greet him, do him homage, honor and praise him." Then Mahesvara, surrounded and followed by twelve hundred thousand Devas, after filling the whole great city of Kapilavastu with radiance, came to the palace where king Sudhodana's palace stood...and after saluting the Bodhisatva's feet with his head and throwing his upper garment over one shoulder, he walked round him some hundred thousand times, keeping his right side towards him, he took the Bodhisatva in his arms and spoke encouraging words to king Sudhodana. After Mahesvara with gods had thus performed the

---

[69] *Acchariya*, 123.
[70] Beal, 47.
[71] Thomas, 39.

ceremony of the great homage, he returned to his dwelling (*Lalitavistara*, vii).[72]

19.2 *Jesus*

And there were shepherds living out in the fields nearby, keeping watch over their flocks at night. An angel of the Lord appeared to them, and the glory of the Lord shone around them, and they were terrified (Luke 2:8-10).

And the midwife went along with him [Joseph], and stood in the cave. Then a bright cloud overshadowed the cave, and the midwife said, This day my soul is magnified, for mine eyes have seen surprising things, and salvation is brought forth to Israel. But on a sudden the cloud became a great light in the cave, so that their eyes could not bear it. But the light gradually decreased, until the infant appeared, and sucked the breast of his mother Mary (Protoevangelion 14:9-12).

After Jesus was born in Bethlehem in Judea, during the time of King Herod, Magi from the east came to Jerusalem and asked, "where is the one who has been born king of the Jews? We saw his star in the east and have come to worship him."...When he [King Herod] had called together all the people's chief priests and teachers of the law, he asked them where the Christ was to be born (Matthew 2:1-5).

Luke retains the Buddhist view that a light shone at the birth of Jesus, while Matthew converts the light into a star. Matthew obviously uses the Asita story and integrates it with the story of the Magi, while, as we shall see below, Luke retains almost entirely the Asita story.

20. *The Baby in Swaddling Clothes*

20.1 *Buddha*

Now at the time of Bodhisatva's birth, Sakra, with a beautifully fine Kasika garment, advanced and wrapped the body of the child in it, whilst the four Maharajahs, taking the child, wrapped thus in his swaddling clothes, brought him and showed him to his mother, "Now may men rejoice; the royal mother has brought forth a son; the Devas may be glad, much more may men."[73]

20.2 *Jesus*

While they were there, the time came for the baby to be born, and she gave birth to her firstborn, a son. She wrapped him in clothes and placed him in a manger (Luke 2:6-7).

---

[72] Ibid.
[73] Beal, 43-44.

It was after sunset, when the old woman and Joseph with her reached the cave, and they both went into it. And behold, it was all filled with lights, greater than the light of lamps and candles, and greater than the light of the sun itself. The infant was then wrapped up in swaddling clothes, and sucking the breasts of his mother Mary (Pseudo-Matthew 1:9-11).

The only point to be taken into consideration is that, though wrapping a child in clothes is such a common motif, this inconspicuous detail was not overlooked by Luke and Pseudo-Matthew, while Matthew ignored the detail.

21. *The Naming Ceremony*

21.1 *Buddha*

Then this idea struck King Suddhodana, "What name should I give to the Prince?" Then this occurred to him: "Since his birth everything has become profuse (*savarthasamriddhah*), let me name him sarvarthasiddha (one through whom every object has been attained)." Then with great ceremony and every propitious rite he declared, "Let the name of the Prince be Sarvarthasiddha," and named him accordingly (*Lalitavistara*, vii).[74]

21.2 *Jesus*

An angel of the Lord appeared to him in a dream and said: "Joseph,...you are to give him the name Jesus, because he will save his people from their sins" (Matthew 1:20-21).

On the eight day, when it was time to circumcise him, he was named Jesus, the name the angel had given him before he had been conceived (Luke 2:21).

22. *The Taming of Wild Animals*

22.1 *Buddha*

Buddha and Buddhist saints are often credited with the miraculous power of taming wild animals. Richard Garbe refers to *Cariyapitaka*, a selection of *Jataka* tales, with regard to a former existence of Buddha in the person of Sama the hermit. There Buddha relates:

While dwelling on the mountainside I drew to me lions and tigers by the power of friendship. I dwelt in the forest surrounded by lions and tigers, panthers, bears and buffaloes, by antelopes, deer, and wild boars. No creature was afraid of me, and I too feared no creature. The

---

[74] Mitra, 134.

CHAPTER THREE

power of friendship is my stay, and thus I dwell upon the mountainside.[75]

22.2 *Jesus*

They [Jesus and his family on the way to Egypt] came to a cave and wished to rest there. Mary dismounted and sat with Jesus in her lap....Suddenly a number of dragons came out of the cave, and all cried out in fear. Jesus got down from his mother's lap and stood before the dragons, which worshiped him....Jesus walked before them and bade them hurt no one....He said: "Fear not, neither conceive that I am a child, for I always was and am a perfect man, and it is necessary that all the beasts of the forest should grow tame before me. In like manner lions and leopards adored him and accompanied them, showed them the way, and bowed their heads to Jesus....The lions never injured their oxen and asses or the sheep they had brought from Judea (Pseudo-Matthew 16 and 17).

Though the canonical gospels refrain from dwelling explicitly on such marvels, Mark alluded in his gospel to the fact that wild animals behaved like tame animals in the company of Jesus: "And he was with wild animals" (Mark 1:13); that was during Jesus' sojourn in the desert, before the beginning of his public ministry.

23. *The Miracles of the Bending Tree and Gushing Water*

23.1 *Buddha*

Now, in the Lumbini Garden [where Buddha was born] there was one particular tree called a Palasa,... straight from top to bottom, and its branches spread out in perfect regularity.... Delighted at the sight, Maya rested awhile to admire it, and gradually approached under the shade of the tree; then that tree, by the mysterious power of Bodhisatva, bent down its branches, and, forthwith, the queen with her right hand took hold of one.[76]

Then there came forth from mid-air two streams of water, hot and cold, respectively, to refresh and cleanse the child's body as he stood there on the ground.[77]

23.2 *Jesus*

On the third day Mary saw a palm and wished to rest under it. When she was seated there she saw fruit on it, and said to Joseph that she would like to have some. Joseph said he was surprised that she should say that because the tree was so high; he himself was thinking more about water, of which they had very little left. Jesus sitting in Mary's

---

[75] Garbe, 76.
[76] Beal, 43.
[77] Beal, 47.

lap with a joyful countenance bade the palm give his mother of its fruit. The tree bent as low as her feet and she gathered what she would. He bade it rise again, and give them of the water concealed below its roots. A spring came forth and all rejoiced and drank of it (Pseudo-Matthew 20).

What is common in these related stories is that it is due to the power of the Masters that the trees bend and water gushes out—not due to any gifts associated with their mothers.

24. *The Fall of Idols*

24.1 *Buddha*

Buddha is called *Devatideva* (god above gods) in *Lalitavistara*. The chapter in *Lalitavistara* entitled "Taking to the Temple" expands this theme:

> Thus did King Sudhodana, amidst a mighty host of kings, with royal magnificence and kingly majesty, take the Prince to the temple, and enter it. Now, when the Bodhisatva set his right foot on the floor of that temple, all the inert images of the Devas, such as Siva, Skanda, Narayana, Kuvera, Chandra, Surya, Vaisravana, Sakra, Brahma, and the guardians of the quarters, rose from their respective places, and fell at the feet of the Bodhisatva. Thereupon, men and gods by hundreds of thousands burst into derisive laughter, and covered their faces with their clothes. The whole of Kapilavastu shook in six different ways. Celestial flowers fell in showers. Thousands of clarions resounded without a cause. And the gods whose images were in the temple made manifest their respective shapes and recited these gathas: "Never does the great mountain Meru...salute the footprint of a cow....How can then the great master of merit...salute the Devas?...Even as the mustard seed...so are the gods compared to him. Now, Bhikshus, on the entrance of the Bodhisatva into the temple, thirty-two hundred of thousands of Devaputras had their mind directed to...perfect Sambodhi (*Lalitavistara*, viii).[78]

24.2 *Jesus*

> And happy and rejoicing they came to the region of Hermopolis, and entered an Egyptian city called Sotinen. And since there was in it no one they knew whom they could have asked for hospitality, they entered a temple which was called the "Capitol of Egypt." In this temple stood 365 idols, to which on appointed days divine honor was paid in idolatrous rites.... But it came to pass that, when blessed Mary entered the temple with the child, all the idols fell to the ground, so that they all lay on their faces completely overturned and shattered. Thus they openly showed that they were nothing....When this was told to Aphrodosius,

---

[78] Mitra, 175.

the governor of that city,...he went up to blessed Mary, who was carrying the Lord in her bosom, and worshiped him, and said to his whole army and to all his friends: "If he were not the God of our gods, our gods would not have fallen on their faces before him, and they would lie stretched out in his presence. Thus they silently confessed him as their Lord (Pseudo-Matthew 22-24).

25. Healing Miracles

25.1 Buddha

Now the instant the Future Buddha was conceived in the womb of his mother,...the Thirty-two Prognostics appeared, as follows: an immeasurable light spread through ten thousand worlds; the blind recovered their sight, as if from desire to see this his glory; the deaf received their hearing; the dumb talked; the hunch-backed became straight of body; the lame recovered the power to walk; all those in bonds were freed from their bonds and chains; all fires went out in all the hells;...wild animals lost their timidity; diseases ceased among men; all mortals became mild-spoken.[79]

The diseased got rid of their ailments. The hungry and the thirsty had their hunger and thirst subdued. Drunkards had their drunkenness removed. The insane got their reason back. The blind got back their power of vision, and the deaf their hearing. Those who had deformities in their mouth or other parts of their bodies had those defects removed. The poor obtained wealth, and the bound their freedom from bonds (*Lalitavistara*, vii).[80]

25.2 Jesus

He went to Nazareth, where he had been brought up, and on the Sabbath day he went into the synagogue, as was his custom. And he stood up to read. The scroll of the prophet Isaiah was handed to him. Unrolling it, he found the place where it is written: "The Spirit of the Lord is on me, because he has anointed me to preach good news to the poor. He has sent me to proclaim freedom for the prisoners and recovery of sight for the blind, to release the oppressed, to proclaim the year of the Lord's favor." Then he rolled up the scroll, gave it back to the attendant and sat down. The eyes of everyone in the synagogue were fastened on him and he began by saying to them, "Today this scripture is fulfilled in your hearing" (Luke 4:16-21).

It seems that in the canonical gospels, Jesus reveals his miraculous powers not at the moment of his conception or birth, but only during his public ministry, which begins after his baptism. On

---

[79] *ntroduction to the Jatakas*, H. C. Warren, 43-44.
[80] Mitra 126.

the contrary, in the Buddhist traditions and the apocryphal gospels, the Masters begin to perform their miracles from the moment of their conception and/or birth.

26. Annunciation of Birth by a Woman

26.1 Buddha

When Buddha was born, many miracles took place in nature, as mentioned above. Mahanama and the Basita, the ministers of king Sudhodana, and the Brahmins were in consultation together, trying to figure out the meaning of these happenings. All at once, the midwife, who attended Queen Maya, came forth from Lumbini and cried out:

> "Oh! ye sons of Sakya! hurry away as fast as possible to Maharaja." Then the ministers replied, seeing her high spirits, "And what news shall we give him when we see him?... Is it good or bad?" To whom she replied, "Oh! Sakyas! it is wonderfully good news....The queen has borne a son...a child without peer on earth and the Devas are scattering flowers about him, and there is a heavenly light diffused about his person."[81]

26.2 Jesus

> Then the midwife cried out, and said, How glorious a day is this, wherein mine eyes have seen this extraordinary sight! And the midwife went out from the cave, and Salome met her. And the midwife said to her, Salome, Salome, I will tell you a most surprising thing, which I saw, A virgin hath brought forth (Protoevangelion 14:13-16).

> Jesus said, "Do not hold on to me, for I have not yet returned to my Father. Go instead to my brothers and tell them, 'I am returning to my Father and your Father, to my God and your God.'" Mary of Magdala went to the disciples with the news: "I have seen the Lord!" And she told them that he had said these things to her (John 20:17-18).

What is remarkable about these parallels is that the Protoevangelion retains the motif of the female messenger, while the Synoptic writers refuse to include it in their narratives. However, John, the most Buddhist of all the gospels, retains the motif, but deliberately makes her a bearer of the tidings of resurrection; that is perhaps because he does not have a nativity narrative.

---

[81] Beal, 46.

27. *Giving of Gifts*

27.1 *Buddha*

> Five hundred merchants with gold, silver, and precious stones arrived at the city; moreover, they had five hundred superb umbrellas, and five hundred golden dishes filled with different sorts of grain as tribute from five hundred different princes; on the delivery of which the bearers spoke thus: "Accept these things, O King! which we offer in respect for the Prince now born."[82]

27.2 *Jesus*

> After Jesus was born in Bethlehem in Judea, during the time of King Herod, Magi from the east came to Jerusalem and asked, "Where is the one who has been born king of the Jews?"...On coming to the house, they saw the child with his mother Mary, and they bowed down and worshiped him. Then they opened their treasures and presented him with gifts of gold and incense and of myrrh (Matthew 2:1-2, 9-11).

> And it came to pass, when the Lord Jesus was born at Bethlehem, a city of Judea, in the time of Herod the King; the wise men came from the east to Jerusalem, according to the prophecy of Zoroaster, and brought with them offerings: namely gold, frankincense, and myrrh, and worshiped him, and offered to him their gifts (Protoevangelion 3:1).

Of course, it was and still is a common practice in most societies to give gifts to babies on their birth. So it is difficult to claim that the gospel writers were influenced exclusively by the Buddhist tradition in this passage. It is, however, interesting that the evangelist uses the expression "from the East" in this connection.

28. *Presentation in the Temple*

28.1 *Buddha*

> At this time, not far from Kapilavastu, there was a Deva temple...at whose shrine the sakyas paid unwonted honors; then Sudhodana forthwith took the infant in his arms to this temple and addressed his ministers in these words, "Now my child may pay worship to the Deva." Then his mother ...took the child to pay the customary honors.[83]

> Now, Bhikshus, the Sakyas with their elders, both male and female, came together to King Sudhodana and thus addressed him: "May it please you majesty, the Prince should be taken tothe house of the Devas." The king said, "That is proper. Take the Prince to see it."...Then King Sudhodana entered his chamber, sent for the great matron Gautami, and

---

[82] Beal, 53.
[83] Beal, 44.

said to her, "Dress the Prince so that he may be taken to the temple" (*Lalitavistara*, viii).[84]

28.2 Jesus

When the time of their purification according to the Law of Moses had been completed, Joseph and Mary took him to Jerusalem to present him to the Lord (as it is written in the Law of the Lord, "Every firstborn male is to be consecrated to the Lord) and to offer a sacrifice in keeping with what is said in the Law of the Lord: "a pair of doves or two young pigeons" (Luke 2:22-24).

What is important here is not that Luke misinterprets the Jewish Law but that the motif of temple-presentation is preserved by Luke here; he also indicates that both parents are present at the ceremony, as in the Buddhist text.

29. Asita and Simeon

29.1 Buddha

The ascetic Asita had the memory of forty past cycles and forty to come, eighty in all, and seeing that the bodhisatta possessed the signs he called to remembrance whether he would become a Buddha or not, and knowing that he would certainly become a Buddha said, "this is a marvellous person," and smiled. Then calling to remembrance whether he should be able to see him when he had become a Buddha, he saw that he would not be able, but having died he could not attain enlightenment through a hundred or even a thousand Buddhas, and would be reborn in the formless world. And thinking "such a marvellous person, when he has become Buddha, I shall not be able to see; great verily will be my loss," he wept. The people seeing this asked, "our noble one just now smiled, and then began to weep. Can it be, revered sir, that there will be any misfortune to our noble son?" "There will be no misfortune to him. Without doubt he will become a Buddha." "Then why didst thou weep?" "Thinking that I shall not be able to see him when he has become Buddha; great verily will be my loss, and lamenting for myself I weep," he said.[85]

29.2 Jesus

Now there was a man in Jerusalem, whose name was Simeon, and this man was righteous and devout, looking for the consolation of Israel, and the Holy Spirit was upon him. And it had been revealed to him by the Holy Spirit that he should not see death before he had seen the Lord's anointed. And inspired by the Spirit he came into the Temple; and when the parents brought in the child Jesus, to do for him according to

---

[84] Mitra, 173-74.
[85] *Introduction to the Jatakas*; Thomas, 42.

the custom of the law, he took him in his arms and blessed God and said, "Lord, now lettest thou thy servant depart in peace, according to thy word; for mine eyes have seen thy salvation which thou hast prepared in the presence of all people, a light for revelation to the Gentiles, and for glory to thy people Israel." And his father and his mother marveled at what was said about him; and Simeon blessed them and said to Mary his mother, "Behold, this child is set for the fall and rise of many in Israel, and for a sign that is spoken against (and a sword will pierce through your own soul also), that thoughts of many hearts may be revealed (Luke 2:25-35).

The Asita-story closely parallels the Lucan story, and most scholars who have written on the possibility of Buddhist influence have accepted this passage as derived from the Buddhist account. In both accounts the sages allude to the greatness of the infant and prophesy their own death before the child will have grown up. It is even possible to see a verbal parallel in this case: both traditions refer to the spirit; in the Indian tradition, the sage arrives by air to the scene; in the biblical tradition, Simeon is brought to the Temple by the Spirit (*en to pneumati*).

30. *Illumination of Hearts*

The sage Asita says to King Sudhodana: "He will create the eye of knoledge for those whose eyes are enveloped in the dense darkness of utter ignorance. He will pluck out the dart of affliction from the sides of those who have been pierced by it...."(*Lalitavistara*, vii).[86] Luke changes this passage to: "The thoughts of many hearts may be revealed"(2:35).

31. *The Piercing of Heart and Assumption to Heaven*

31.1 *Buddha's Mother*

In the Buddhist tradition, the mother of Buddha dies seven days after his birth, besides experiencing pain in her heart after the birth of the child. *Lalitavistara* (vii) says:

> Then Bhikshus, on the seventh night after the birth of the Bodhisatva, Mayadevi departed this life. After her demise she was born among the thrity-three Devas...Because the span of her life was so ordained. The mothers of all former Bodhisatvas also died on the seventh night after their confinement. "And what was the cause of that?" "Because on the

---

[86] Mitra 142.

delivery of the well-grown Bodhisatva with all his organs complete, his mother's heart splits."[87]

The queen-mother, beholding her child born thus contrary to the laws of nature, her mind through fear, swayed between extremes. Not distinguishing the happy from the sad portents, again and again she gave way to grief.[88]

31.2 Jesus's Mother

Luke forebodes the death of Mary in the words: "And a sword shall pierce your own heart" (2:35). In the Christian tradition, after her death Mary was assumed to heaven in her body to be reunited with her son.

32. Anna and Shabari/Old Women

32.1 Ramayana

"Rama will visit they holy retreat; do thou receive him...with traditional hospitality. On beholding him, thou shalt attain the highest sphere from whence none returneth." "O Foremost of Men, thus did those blessed ascetics address me, and for thee I have gathered the wild fruits of diverse kinds that grow on the borders of Lake Pampa....Now thou hast seen the forest and hast heard all that thou didst desire to know; I will abandon my body so that I may approach those pure-souled ascetics whom I used to wait upon, to whom this hermitage belongs and whose servant I am."...Having received permission from Rama to depart, Shabari...cast herself into the fire, thereafter rising into the air like a bright flame....By virtue of her meditations she ascended to those sacred abodes where her spiritual preceptors, those high-souled ascetics, dwelt.[89]

And now the aged women of the long night in a confused way supplicating heavenly guidance, implored the gods to bless the child....And now near the spot within the garden, there was a Rishi, leading the life of an ascetic; his name was Asita.[90]

32.2 Jesus

There was also a prophetess, Anna, the daughter of Phanuel, of the tribe of Asher. She was very old; she had lived with her husband seven years after her marriage, and then was a widow until she was eighty-four. She never left the Temple but worshiped night and day, fasting and

---

[87] Mitra, 136.
[88] Buddhaghosha, *Life of Buddha* in the Chinese version of *Fo-sho-hing-Tsan-King*, trans. S. Beal, SBE XIX, 7-12.
[89] *Ramayana of Valmiki*, III, canto 74; trans. Hari Prasad Shastri (London, 1976),II, 157-58.
[90] Buddhaghosha, *Life of Buddha* in the Chinese version of *Fo-sho-hing-Tsan-King*, I. 39-70; trans. S. Beal, SBE XIX, 7-12

praying. Coming up to them at that very moment, she gave thanks to God and spoke about the child to all who were looking forward to the redemption of Jerusalem (Luke 2:36-38).

Shabari who lived near Pampa Lake wanted to see Rama before she went to heaven. She was granted the request after she showed Rama the hermitage built by Matanga. This well-known story from the popular epic seems to bear a close resemblance to the Anna-motif of the gospel episode. Buddhaghosha's version has the old women and Asita in the same chapter; so it is more than likely that the Mahayana versions of the Buddha, circulating along the silk-route, must have been known to the early Christians.

33. Lost and Found

33.1 Buddha

During the sowing festival, King Sudhodana and his courtiers took one hundred and eight plows and went to the fields, taking his young son with him.

> And in the field where the plowing was to be done was a solitary rose-apple tree of thick foliage and dense shade. Underneath this tree the king had a couch placed for the young prince, and spread over his head a canopy that was studded with gold stars.... Then he proceeded to the place where they were to plow.... Now the nurses who were sitting about the Future Buddha came out from behind the screen to behold the royal magnificence. And the future Buddha, looking hither and thither and seeing no one, arose in haste and sat him down cross-legged, and mastering his inspirations and his expirations, entered on the first trance. The nurses delayed a little, being detained by the abundance of good things to eat.... Suddenly the nurses remembered that they had left their young master alone; and raising the screen, they entered and saw the Future Buddha sitting cross-legged on the couch.[91]

> But now, having completed twelve years and being perfectly acquainted with all the customary modes of enjoyment,...it came to pass on one occasion that he was visiting the ...garden, and whilst there amused himself by wandering in different directions, shooting with his bow and arrow at whatever he pleased; and so he separated himself from the other Sakya youths.[92]

Though the first account does not give the age of the young prince, it emphasizes the religious dimension of the story; the second narrative gives the age of the young prince and describes the compassion the future Buddha feels towards a wounded bird.

---

[91] *Introduction to the Jatakas*, Warren, 54-55.
[92] Beal, 72.

33.2 *Jesus*

> Every year his parents went to Jerusalem for the Feast of the Passover. When he was twelve years old, they went up to the feast, according to the custom. After the feast was over, while his parents were returning home, the boy Jesus stayed behind in Jerusalem, but they were unaware of it. Thinking that he was in their company, they traveled on for a day. Then they began looking for him among their relatives and friends. When they did not find him, they went back to Jerusalem to look for him. After three days they found him in the temple courts, sitting among the teachers, listening to them and asking them questions (Luke 2:41-48).

Both the Christian and Buddhist stories identify the motif of losing and finding along with the religious dimension of the incident; both Masters are twelve at the time of this incident.

34. *Mother-Son Dialogue*

34.1 *Buddha*

> Then King Sudhodana entered his chamber, sent for the great matron Gautami, and said to her, "Dress the Prince so that he may be taken to the temple." "Please your majesty," said Gautami, and dressed the Prince. When the Prince was properly dressed, he innocently addressed his aunt, "Mother, where are you taking me?" "To the temple, my son, said she. Then the Prince, with a pleasant face and an arch smile, addressed these verses to his aunt: "On my birth all these three thousand regions trmbled; Sakra, Brahma, Suras...and Kumara saluted me by lowering their heads to the ground. Which are the gods then which are so much greater and nobler than I to whom you wish, mother, to send me? I am the god of gods, nobler than all gods. There is no god equal to me; how can there be one greater than I? For gratification of the people, mother, I shall go. By beholding me the crowd will be greatly exhilarated; even those who can exhibit wonders will respect me highly, and men and gods will know that I am the greatest god" (*Lalitavistara*, viii).[93]

34.2 *Jesus*

> Everyone who heard him was amazed at his understanding and his answers. When his parents saw him, they were astonished. His mother said to him, "Son, why have you treated us like this? Your father and I have been anxiously searching for you." "Why were you searching for me?" he asked. "Didn't you know I had to be in my Father's house?" (Luke 2:48-49).

> Then Jesus came from Galilee to the Jordan to be baptized by John. But John tried to deter him, saying, "I need to be baptized by you, and do you

---

[93] Mitra, 174.

come to me?" Jesus replied, "Let it be so now; it is proper for us to do this to fulfill all righteousness." Then Jesus consented (Matthew 3:13-15).

Both the Buddhist and Christian traditions share the same idea that the Master did not need the religious rituals since he was no ordinary person. The Christian narrative splits the idea into two episodes.

35. *The Infant Prodigy*

35.1 *Buddha*

At the age of eight, King Sudhodana appointed the legendary teacher Vishvamitra to instruct the young prince in the art of writing. The young prince addressed the teacher:

> My master, in what writing will you instruct me? Shall it be in the writing of Brahma Deva, Kharoshti, Akara, Mangala, Yava, Dravida,...or Sruta?...Of all these different styles of writing which does my master design to teach me?...Vishvamitra replied, "He has recited from beginning to end the names of different writing, which I have never heard of. Surely this is the Instructor of Devas and men." At this time, five hundred noblemen entered the school with the royal prince, and began to learn the sounds of different letters, on which occasion, the Prince... gave forth the sound of each letter.[94]

In the *Lalitavistara* version (ch. x), the young prince gives a list of sixty-four writing systems, including those of the Chinese and the Huns. When the boys repeat the alphabet, at each letter a moral truth is uttered.

> Then...when the Prince had duly grown up, he was taken to the writing school under a hundred thousand auspicious arrangements. He was accompanied and followed by ten thousand boys....All the Sakyas, led by king Suddhodana, proceeded in front of the Bodhisatva. With such a retinue did the Bodhisatva proceed to the school. Then he entered the school. Now Visvamitra, the schoolmaster, feeling the beauty and glory of the Bodhisatva to be insufferable, fell prostrate on the ground. Subhanga, a Devaputra..., held him by the right hand...and...said: "What avails him the mere knowledge of writing who is thoroughly versed in the fourfold path of the future, who is proficient in the knowledge of the cause and the effect of creation...? There is none in the three regions who can be greater than he in conduct; he is the greatest among all gods and men. You know not even the names of the writings which he learnt many millions of ages ago."...Now Bodhidsatva, taking up a tablet..., thus addressed the tutor Visvamitra: "Which is the writing, sir, which you wish to teach me: Is it the Brahmi writing; or the Kharoshti; or the

---

[94] Beal, 69-70.

Pushkarakshari; or the writing of the Anga?...Out of theses sixty-four kinds which is it, sir, that you wish to teach me? The schoolmaster Visvamitra, wonderstruck and deprived of all vanity and self-importance, recited these gathas with a cheerful face: "Wonderful this is of the Bodhisatva, the leader of men, that he should have learnt every sastra immediately on coming to the school! On coming to the school he has learned writings of which I do not know even the names..." In the presence of the Bodhisatava the teacher began to teach the boys the alphabet. When they pronounced the letter *a*, then resounded all the words—all sacraments are impermanent. On *á* being pronounced there resounded the welfare of one's own and of others. By the letter *i* the fullness of organs.[95]

35.2 *Jesus*

There was also at Jerusalem one named Zacheus, who was a schoolmaster. And he said to Joseph: Joseph, Joseph, why dost thou not send Jesus to me, that he may learn his letters. Joseph agreed....So they brought him to that master; who, as soon as he saw him, wrote out an alphabet for him. And he bade him say Aleph; and when he had said, the master bade him pronounce Beth....Then the Lord Jesus ...said to his master, Take notice how I say to thee; then he began clearly and distinctly to say Aleph, Beth, Gimel, Daleth, and so on to the end of the alphabet. At this the master was so surprised, that he said, Thou hast brought a boy to me to be taught, who is more learned than any master....

And when Joseph saw the understanding of child and his age, that he was growing to maturity, he resolved again that he should not remain ignorant of letters; and he took him and handed him over to another teacher. And the teacher said to Joseph: "First I will teach him Greek, and then Hebrew." For the teacher knew the child's knowledge and was afraid of him. Nevertheless he wrote the alphabet and practised it with him for a long time; but he gave him no answer. And Jesus said to him: "If you are indeed a teacher, and if you know the letters well, tell me the meaning of the Alpha, and I will tell you that of the Beta." And the teacher was annoyed and struck him on the head. And the child was hurt and cursed him, and he immediately fainted and fell to the ground on his face. And the child returned to Joseph's house....

And another teacher...took him with fear an anxiety, but the child went gladly. And he went boldly into the school and found a book lying on the reading desk and took it, but did not read the letters in it, but opened his mouth and spoke by the Holy Spirit and taught law to those that stood by. And a large crowd assembled and stood there listening to him, wondering at the grace of his teaching and the readiness of his words, that although an infant he made such utterances (Infancy Gospel of Thomas 20:1-15).

---

[95] Mitra, 192.

36. The Magis' Visit

36.1 Buddha

During his visit to the agricultural village, Prince Siddhartha went and sat under the shade of a Jambu tree, abosorbed in contemplation.

> At that time five foreign Rishis (wise men), who knew well the five conditions of things and were full of miraculous powers, were travelling in the air from the south towards the north. When they came over the noble grove they felt obstructed, and could not proceed. Feeling doubtful and horripilated, they recited:..."We are able to go without fail, to the abodes of the gods...how and by whose miraculous power is it that we are restrained?" Then the forest god that was there thus addressed...the sages: "Know that the son of the Sakya king, born of the race of the king of kings, resplendent as the morning sun,...the noblest of men, the adored of Devas...greater than ten hundred thousands of worlds, has taken possession of this grove, and is engaged in meditation, and his majesty counteracts the power of miraculous force." Then the rishis looked downwards, and beheld the Prince radiant in his beauty and glory....They approached the Bodhisatva and bepraised him in verses. One said: "The redeemer of those who are enthralled by affliction is born. He will acquire that religion wherewith he will disenthrall all creation." Another said: "There is born the great physician for those who are afflicted with disease and decay. He will acquire that religion wherewith he will wipe out birth and death." The Rishis, having praised the Bodhisatva with these verses, circumambulated his person by the right side, and passed away through the sky (*Lalitavistara*, xi).[96]

36.2 Jesus

> After Jesus was born in Bethlehem in Judea, during the time of King Herod, Magi from the east came to Jerusalem and asked, "Where is the one who has been born king of the Jews: We saw his star in the east and have come to worship him." When King Herod heard this he was disturbed, and all Jerusalem with him. When he had called together all the people's chief priests and teachers of the law, he asked them where the Christ was to be born. "In Bethlehem of in Judea," they replied."...After they had heard the king, they went on their way, and the star they had seen in the east went ahead of them until it stopped over the place where the child was. When they saw the star, they were overjoyed. On coming to the house, they saw the child with his mother Mary, and bowed down and worshipped him. Then they opened their treasures and presented him with gifts of gold and of incense and of myrrh. And having been warned in a dream not to go back to Herod, they returned to their country by another route (Matthew 2:1-12).

---

[96] Mitra, 183-184.

The similarities in the Buddhist and Christian narratives are significant. In both cases it is wise men who arrive and worship the boy who is addressed as king and god. In both stories the wise men need instructions to overcome their difficulty in proceeding farther. As the Indian wise men are prevented by the power of the Buddha and stops in the garden, the disappearance of the star in Matthew prevents the Magi from proceeding further. There are guides who will lead the wise men to the child in both traditions. What is most remarkable in the biblical passage is that there is a clear, probably unconscious, reference to the East and Eastern wisdom in the use the Persian word *magi*. One wonder whether the Gospel-writer is alluding here to his Oriental sources!

The differences are also significant. Jesus is still an infant in Matthew, whereas Buddha is already a young man in the Buddhist episode. The Indian wise men are travelling from the south to the north; the magi are traveling from the east to the west. There are only three magi in the Christian story; the three wise men probably represent the three major religions of the India: Buddhism, Hinduism, and Jainism—incidentally, in Khajuraho, India, there is a temple dedicated to these religions!--which must yield to the new god and his new religion. There is no King Herod in the Buddhist story, though there is King Kamsa in the story of the birth of Krishna. It is possible that Matthew incorporated elements from the Krishna story into the Buddhist story and judaized his version in order to proclaim the superiority of Jesus as the leader and king of the new religious movement.

37. *The Appellation of King*

Throughout his life Buddha was referred to as prince. In the visit of the five wise men mentioned above, the forest god referred to Buddha as "the son of the Sakya king, born of the race of king of kings." This passage is reminiscent of the query of the magi in Matthew: "Where is he who has been born king of the Jews?" (2:2).

I believe that the *Sela-Sutta* found in the Middling Collection and the Long Collection is a better illustration of where Buddha claims for himself the title of king as well as of the nature of the rdemptive function of Buddha, which seems to have been transferred to the Christian gospels:

> "I am a king, O Selo, an incomparable king of religion; by religion I set rolling a wheel, an irresistible wheel. What ought to be supremely known I know. What ought to be perfected I perfect; what ought to be renounced I renounce. Therefore, O Brahmin, am I Buddha. Discipline

thyself, O Brahmin. Hard to obtain is the appearing of fully enlightened ones repeatedly. He who indeed is hard in the world to obtain, in manifestation repeatedly, that fully enlightened one, O brahmin, am I— physician incomparable. Godlike, beyond measure, a crusher of the Devil's army. Having subjugated all enemies, I rejoice as one who hath nowhere a fear." "Thou art Buddha; thou art the master; thou art the sage who overcomest the devil; thou hast cast off all inclinations. After having crossed over thyself, hast thou ferried this human race across."[97]

The foregoing passage is reflected in the following gospel passages: "Pilate asked him, 'Art thou a king then?' Jesus answered, 'Thou sayest that I am a king. To this end have I been born , and to this end am I come into the world.'(John 18:37). "Now is the judgment of this world; now shall the prince of this world be cast out." (John 12:31). Throughout the gospels, Jesus appears as a physician. Further, the idea of Jesus overcoming the Devil has been discussed earlier in the section on the Harrowing of Hell.

38. *Mahaprajapati and Mary: Two Influential Women*

38.1 *Buddha*

Queen Mahamaya played a prominent role in the conception of Buddha. However, seven days after his birth, Mahamaya died in accordance with the custom that the mothers of bodhisatvas should die immediately after they had given birth. It was her sister, Mahaprajapati, Sudhodana's second wife, who brought up the young prince. She was one of the first coverts to the new way of life proclaimed by Buddha. Most importantly, she was the first nun ordained by Buddha. According to the *Anguttaranikaya*, iv, 274, it happened this way. After Buddha had made peace between the Sakyas and the Koliya, the widowed Mahaprajapati went to Buddha in Nigrodha park and asked that women might be allowed to become ordained nuns. Buddha refused three times and returned to Vesali. Then Mahaprajapati cut off her hair, put on yellow robes, and followed him there with other Sakya women. Ananda met them at the door and spoke in their behalf. When Buddha told Ananda that women are capable of the life of renunciation and asceticism, Ananda said: "If so, Lord, Mahaprajapati Gotami, the aunt of the Lord, was of great service: she was his nurse and fostermother, and gave him milk, and when his mother died, fed him from her own breast. It were good, Lord, for women to go forth..." "If, Ananda, Mahaprajapati will take upon herself the

---

[97] Cited by A. J. Edmunds, 83.

eight Strict Rules, let this be her ordination." Mahaprajapati accepted the rules and was admitted into the order as a nun.[98]

38.2 *Jesus*

In Luke's gospel Mary plays an active role in the conception of Jesus and after. When her pregnant kinswoman Elizabeth hails her as "blessed among women" and as "the mother of my Lord" (1:39-45), Mary responds with the Magnificant,a hymn of praise (1:46-55). In the presentation scene, the aged Simeon tells Mary: "A sword will pierce through your soul also" (Luke 2:35), perhaps characterizing her as hearing and doing God's word (1:38; 8:21). Luke also has a blessing on Jesus' mother from a woman in the crowd, which he applies to those who hear and keep God's word (11:27-28). Luke tells of an exchange between the boy Jesus and his mother in the Temple, in which he places God above his parents (2:21-40). Most importantly, Luke includes Mary among the women disciples praying in the upper room with the Twelve Apostles (Acts 1:41). Also, in the Fourth Gospel, Mary is associated with the disciples since she stands at the the foot of the cross with her sister, Mary of Clopas, and the beloved disciple (John 19:25-27).

In the light of all the parallels given above, one wonders whether the portrayal of Mary in Luke and John—as opposed to Mark who portrays her negatively (3:21-30; 6:4)—was perhaps subtly influenced by the Buddhist portrayal of Buddha's mother and fostermother.

39. *Preparing the Way*

39.1 *Buddha*

> Then Sudhodana Raja, having heard the words of the messengers of Supra Buddha, immediately issued orders to have all the road between Kapilavastu and Devadaho...made level, and freed from all weeds, pebbles, filth, and obstacles of all kinds; and to have the ground swept and sprinkled with scented water, and all kinds of flowers to be scattered along it....And she arrived at last at her father's house in the city of Devadaho.[99]

39.2 *Jesus*

> In those days John the Baptist came, preaching in the Desert of Judea and saying, "Repent, for the kingdom of heaven is near." This is he who was spoken of through the prophet Isaiah: "A voice of one calling in the

---

[98] *Vinaya-Pitaka* II: 253 ff.; E. J. Thomas, *The Life of Buddha*, 99-101.
[99] Beal, 42.

desert, 'Prepare the way for the Lord, make straight paths for him'" (Matthew 3:1-3).

Perhaps the difference between the two passages may appear to be too obvious: in the Buddhist tradition, the way is prepared for the mother of Buddha; in the Christian tradition the way is prepared for Jesus. However, it is good to bear in mind that the way is prepared for Maya who is carrying Buddha in her womb rather than just for herself. There is an interesting passage in the *Milindapanha* in which the earth becomes level ground as Buddha walks: "When the Lord was walking, this incognizant great earth elevated the low ground and flattened the high ground."[100]

40. Growing Up

40.1 Buddha

At this time Mahaprajapati, the royal prince's foster-mother, spake thus to the King: "As your majesty commands, my care over the child shall be most constant." Thus she sedulously attended him without intermission, as the sun tends on the mood during the first portion of each month till the moon arrives at its fulness. So the child gradually waxed and increased in strength; as the shoot of the Nyagrotha tree gradually increases in size, well-planted in the earth, till itself becomes a great tree, thus did the child day be day increase, and lacked nothing....In every place love of religion (the Law) increased and flourished as in the old times, when truth and justice were universally prevalent.[101]

40.2 Jesus

And when they had performed everything according to the law of the Lord, they returned into Galilee, to their own city, Nazareth. And the child grew and became strong, filled with wisdom; and the favor of God was upon him....And he went down with them and came to Nazareth, and was obedient to them; and his mother kept all these things in her heart. And Jesus increased in wisdom and in stature, and in favor with God and man (Luke 2:39-52).

This Lucan summation seems to reflect several episodes in the life of the young prince Siddhartha who displays his growth as a young man in the palace in the practice of meditation, martial arts, school, and statecraft.

---

[100] Cited by J. Duncan M. Derrett, "Greece and India: the Milindapanha, the Alexander-romance and the Gospels," *ZRGG* 19 (1967), 58.
[101] Beal, 64.

41. *Reference to signs*

41.1 *Buddha*

Buddha is recognized by others by the thirty-two signs that go with every Bodhisatva. The sage Asita tells Suddhodana: "Because, Maharaja, the Prince Sarvarthasiddha is endowed with the thirty-two signs of a great personage." "And what are the thirty-two signs?" "They are: (1)the Prince...has a coil of curly hair on his head....(2) His hair is of blackish deep blue color like the neck of the peacock...."(*Lalitavistara*, vii).[102]

41.2 *Jesus*

> "To you this day there is born in the city of David a Savior who is Messiah and Lord. And this will be your sign: you will find a baby wrapped in strips of cloth and lying in a manger" (Luke 2:11-12).

What is important in this passage is the notion of sign, which concentrates on the child and his recognizability by the people for whom the signs are intended. The child is found in special circumstances, which is the case with Buddha and Jesus. Buddha bears numerous signs in his body, while Jesus is recognizable only by the manger and his swaddling cloths. I like to add that it is the writer of the Fourth Gospel that uses the motif of sign as a means of recognition more effectively than the the Synoptic writers. For instance, in the post-resurrection account of Jesus' visit with the Apostles, the author uses the story of Thomas's unbelief to illustrate the importance of certain marks by which Jesus can be identified: "Thomas...declared: " Unless I see the nail marks in his hands and put my finger where the nails were, and put my hand into his side, I will not believe it." (20:25).

From the above-given long list of parallels, the objective reader would recognize that some of these parallels are more significant than others and that the cumulative evidence shows that the juxtaposition of these parallels is more than a fortuitous convergence of universal fokloric motifs simply because nowhere else do we see such a convergence of literary motifs. However, I realize that most conservative Christian scholars would argue that the Jewish heritage of the Old Testament can easily account for the composition of the infancy gospels, while the more liberal Western scholars would add Hellenistic writings to the Jewish sources consulted by the Christian writers of the gospels. What is common

---

[102] Mitra, 142-144.

to both schools of thought is that they as a rule refuse to examine the evidence of the Indian sources. So it is necessary to show that in contrast to the Indian traditions the Hebrew Bible and Hellenistic writings offer much less toward establishing the intertextuality of the infancy gospels so that future studies of New Testament writings may employ Indian sources for the elucidation of the textual history of the New Testament.

CHAPTER FOUR

INFANCY GOSPELS AND OTHER SOURCES

Though, by and large, the Christian Church rejects the Oral Torah, it retains the written Torah as the Old Testament, as the first covenant replaced by Jesus but continuous with the New Covenant established by Jesus through his death on the cross. Christians have always had an ambiguous attitude toward the Old Testament: though they have consistently refused to practice the Jewish Law, they have agreed to accept the text of the Hebrew Bible mainly for apologetical and exegetical reasons. Christians argue that the Messiah announced in the Old Testament is Jesus and use the Old Testament texts as proof-texts (*dicta probantia*) for this purpose: the Old Covenant and the Old Testament are not ends in themselves, but only means; they are of value only in their relation to the New Covenant and the New Testament; the meaning of the New Testament text becomes clear in the light of the text of the Old Testament in as much as both are revealed messages of one and the same God. In this the Christian theologians follow the lead of St. Augustine who suggested that the New Testament lies hidden in the Old Testament, and the Old Testament becomes clear in the New Testament. Thus Christian apologists tend to see a symbiotic relationship between the two scriptures so much so the Old Testament is the main—if not the only—source of the New Testament. Many Christian exegetes and theologians would say that it is not necessary to go outside the canonical Christian and Hebrew Scriptures in order to discover the sources and meaning of biblical texts. As Rev. Raymond E. Brown, the respected Catholic author of *The Birth of the Messiah* says, "The two evangelists [Matthew and Luke] could have written their infancy narratives without ever having heard or read such biographies [Greco-Roman biographies]—LXX forms of the stories of the Patriarchs, Moses, and David (enlarged by subsequent oral lore), plus some Jesus tradition and theological reflection could have given the orientation."[1] This view seems to be based on the theological perception that these two scriptures are the only inspired texts and that everything necessary for salvation is found in these scriptures. Brown, it is important to note here, does not exclude the role of

---

[1] R. E. Brown, "Gospel Infancy Narrative Research from 1976 to 1986," *Catholic Biblical Quarterly* 48 (1986), 477.

subsequent oral lore among the sources of the infancy narratives. However, he does not give any place at all to Indian sources in his magisterial study of the infancy gospels. Obviously, he wrote this study more as a theologian than as a comparatist. That is probably the reason he secured a *nihil obstat* and an *imprimatur* for his book. But literary critics look at the same texts without any theological preconceptions and look for sources and meanings wherever they can find them. I have already identified most of the Indian sources of the infancy gospels. My claim for these Indian sources can make a strong case only in comparison and contrast with the other real and alleged authoritative sources from the Old Testament and Hellenistic traditions. Let me briefly examine the claims of the Hebrew scriptures as the sole source of the narratives of the infancy of Jesus.

A. *Hebrew and Greek Sources*

Of course, the gospel writers did consult the Greek Old Testament extensively. In fact, there are numerous verbal parallels and literary motifs from the Hebrew Scriptures that the gospel writers have used. Some of these can be clearly seen in the infancy gospels. All these have been pointed out many times before. However, for purpose of comparison it is useful to cite the important ones in order to show that the Indian parallels are much more close to the gospel stories than many of the farfetched Hebrew or Hellenistic parallels. In other words, sometimes Old Testament parallels are closer to the New Testament, while at other times it is the Indian parallels that illuminate passages in the infancy gospels more clearly than Hebrew and Hellenistic sources, all of which are in the intertextual fabric of the text of the infancy gospels. To facilitate comparison, I shall follow a topical approach as in the previous chapter beginning with Matthew and ending in Luke.

1. *Pre-existence and Incarnation*

As mentioned in the previous chapter, the Christian idea of the incarnation of the Second Person of the Trinity has no better parallel in the Old Testament or Hellenistic sources than in the Indian religions, where Vishnu, the Second Person of the Hindu Trinity, became incarnate in Krishna and the divine Bodhisatva became man in Siddhartha Gautama. On the contrary, the Hebrew religion and the Hebrew Bible do not provide any clear support to the possibility of the incarnation of God simply on account of their doctrine of the total otherness or transcendence of the godhead. However, there are statements in the Hebrew Bible to the effect that God is father to his children. Certainly it was God who made Sarah, Leah, Rebecca, and Zipporah fruitful as the Spirit of God made Mary bear Jesus. And the New Testament notion of Jesus as God's beloved son is traced by Christian interpreters to Psalm 2:7: "Thou art my son; this day I have begotten thee." No one has seen this idea more clearly than Philo:

> And I will bring forward as a competent witness in proof of what I have said, the holy Moses. For he introduces Sarah as conceiving a son when God beheld her by himself; but he represents her as bringing forth her son, no longer to him who beheld her then, but to him who was eager to attain to wisdom, and his name is called Abraham. And he teaches the same lesson more plainly in the case of Leah, where he says that "God opened her womb." But to open the womb is the especial business of the husband. And she having conceived, brought forth, not to God, for he alone is sufficient and all-abundant for himself, but to him who underwent labor for the sake of that which is good, namely, for Jacob; so that in this instance virtue received the divine seed from the great Cause of all things, but brought forth her offspring to one of her lovers, who deserved to be preferred to all her other suitors. Again, when the all-wise Jacob addressed his supplications to God, Rebecca, who is perseverance, became pregnant by the agency of him who received the supplication; but Moses, who received Zipporah, that is to say, winged and sublime virtue, without any supplication or entreaty on his part, found that she conceived by no mortal man at all.[2]

One implication is that the gospel use of the term of God as Father may have its origin in the allegorical expressions of Hellenistic Judaism. The other implication is that Hellenistic Judaism helped the Christian writers make the tremendous leap from the allegorical sense to the literal sense by making Jesus a natural Son of God and the second person of the Trinity. Still that does not account for the notion of incarnation as found in the gospels, for which we find the best parallel in the Indian traditions, though the Indian traditions do not discuss the notion of divine sonship. The inference is that the gospels used Hellenistic as well as Indian traditions in their development of the notion of the incarnation of the Son of God.[3]

---

[2] *De Cherubim*, 45-47; Morton Enslin, "The Christian Stories of Nativity," *JBL*, 59 (1940), 327-328.

[3] Perhaps the contribution of Hellenistic religions in the fusion of the idea of a god-man or of a mortal who became eventually a god on account of his virtuous life

2. *Genealogy and Royal Origin*

Matthew introduces the whole narrative with the headline: "The book of the genealogy of Jesus Christ, the son of David, the son of Abraham" (1:1), which expression reminds us of Greek Genesis 5:1: "This is the book of the genesis of Adam." Here Matthew testifies that Jesus is a man and that at a certain stage his family is a royal family, the house of David, the bearer of messianic promises. Primarily, Matthew uses 1 Chron. 1:34; 2:1; 2:4, 5, 9, 10-15; 3:10-15, 17-19. Matt. 1:13-16 has names otherwise not known in the Hebrew scriptures, but names well known from Jewish sources of the Hellenistic period. The two motifs are common to the Hebrew and Indian traditions, the difference being that Buddha and Krishna were not only in title but also in reality princes or kings.

3. *Universal Salvation*

Though preoccupation with the salvation of the gentiles has never been a distinctive feature of mainline Judaism, there is some evidence of concern for the salvation of all nations as the establishment of God's reign among His people and the other nations of the world as in Isa. 49:25-26; 52: 6-10; 55:1-5; Jer. 31:31-34; Ezek. 36:22-32; 37:23-28. Particularly the apocalyptic writings dwell on this issue (Isa. 24-27). It is important also to note that Matthew's opening reference to Jesus as son of Abraham seems to imply the idea of universal salvation since Abraham, the progenitor of the whole people, is the bearer of the ancient promises: "By you all the families of the earth shall bless themselves" (Gen. 12:3). However, the idea expressed in Matthew 28:19: "Go therefore and make disciples of all nations" is closer to the Buddhist parallel cited earlier than to the Old Testament parallels.

4. *Virginal Conception*

There is no doubt that the gospel stories of the conception of Jesus by a virgin is influenced by the Greek Isaiah 7:14: "Behold, a virgin shall conceive and bear a son, and his name shall be called Emmanuel" (which means, "God with us"). After citing Isaiah, Matthew continues: "When Joseph woke from sleep,...he took his

---

(*theios aner*) to the idea of the immortal should also be mentioned in this context; see Charles H. Talbert, *What Is a Gospel? The Genre of the Canonical Gospels*, (Philadelphia, 1977, 25-52); W. L. Knox, *Some Hellenistic Elements in Primitive Christianity* (London, 1944), 22-23.

wife, but knew her not until she had born a son; and he called his name Jesus" (1:24-25). "The reason for the choice of *parthenos* in LXX is not known; later Greek versions read *neanis*, "a young person." Isa. 7:14 has nothing whatever to do with birth by a virgin. The LXX even uses *parthenos* for one who is not a virgin, cf. Gen. 34:3."[4] Further, "that a Jewish source preserves a tradition that Moses was born of a virgin is without foundation."[5] Therefore, in spite of the LXX evidence, the idea of virginal conception or *virginitas ante partum* was not germane to the Jewish tradition; the story was intended for the Greco-Roman and non-Jewish world, where stories of parthenogenesis or tales of divine impregnation of mortal women were fairly well known.[6] In fact, Greco-Roman literature abounds in the legends of the birth of gods by generation of a god with a mortal woman such as the birth of Hercules by the union of Zeus and Alcmene, of Pan by Hermes with a shepherdess, of Ion by Apollo and Creusa, of Romulus by Mars and Aemilia, of Asclepius by Apollo and Coronis, and of Augustus by a serpent-god and Atia.[7]

The gospel notion of *virginitas ante partum* is clearly stated in the *Lalitavistara*: ch.iii: "Sudhodana was the noblest among all the royal personages; he was of imperial family and absolutely pure in his body...She [Mayadevi] abided in penances like a hermit, always performing penances along with her consort. Having obtained sanction of the king, she had not entertained carnal wishes for thirty-two months."[8] It was during the period of abstinence that the miraculous conception of Buddha took place, according to one religious tradition of the Buddhists. So it is not correct to say that "ancient pre-Christian Buddhism knows nothing of the virginity of the mother of Buddha. She is a married woman who plainly conceives through traditional means."[9] Further, it is not true that the Christian version of the virginal conception is unique, as Boslooper in his excessive apologetic zeal states:

> What is common between Christian and "pagan" traditions is the idea of miraculous birth. In this sense they are parallel or analogous. There is a striking difference, however, between the Christian and non-Christian traditions. The Christian formula is unique. The idea that it contains—

---

[4] Samuel T. Lachs, *A Rabbinic Commentary on the New Testament* (Hoboken, 1987), 7
[5] Lachs, 7.
[6] For a good bibliography, see R. E. Brown, *op. cit.*, 119-121; Enslin, 317-338; Thomas Boslooper, *The Virgin Birth* (Philadelphia, 1962), 167-194.
[7] See E. S. Hartland, *The Legend of Perseus*, 2 vols (London, 1894).
[8] Mitra, 45-46.
[9] Boslooper, 138.

divine conception and human birth without anthropomorphism, sensuality, or suggestions of moral irregularity—is to be found nowhere in the literature of the world outside the canonical Biblical narratives. Rather than being an idea borrowed from other traditions, it is original with Christianity.[10]

Even anthropomorphism is not missing in the gospels: Just as the Buddhist scriptures represent the Bodhisatva as a white elephant, so do the gospel represent the Holy Ghost as a dove at the baptism of Jesus, as mentioned earlier, the only difference being the difference between the elephant and the dove. In fact, conception or some form of filiation is implied in "Thou art my beloved son; this day I have begotten thee," (Matt. 3: 16-17; Mark 1: 10-11), which version is found in many gospel manuscripts.[11]

Some versions of the Buddha story try to avoid anthropomorphism and serve as a model for conception through thought, assent, or word. For instance, *The Buddhacarita* of Asvaghosha says: "Then falling from the host of beings in the Tushita heaven, and illumining the three worlds, the most excellent of Bodhisatvas suddenly entered at a thought into her womb" (19).[12] Of course, Asvaghosha also continues to describe the phenomenon of this incarnation with the colorful metaphor of the white elephant; this type of writing reminds us of the combination of the anthropomorphic language of the Yahwistic tradition and the abstract style of Elohistic tradition in the book of Genesis.

The upshot of this comparison is simply that the Christian understanding of the virginal conception of Jesus is not significantly different from the Buddhist tradition.

5. *Virginitas in partu*

As for *virginitas in partu*, the canonical gospels are not explicit about it, though the apocryphal gospels and later Christian traditions are, as described earlier. As for this idea, there is no known Jewish or Hellenistic parallel that resembles the Buddhist description of the miraculous birth of Buddha, in which Mayadevi, the mother of Buddha, gave birth to her son from her right side. The real purpose of *virginitas in partu* was to show that not only the woman was inviolate during birth but also before birth; the virginal integrity during birth could prove miraculous conception, as we have seen earlier in Protoevangelion 14:14-28.

---

[10] Boslooper, 185-186.
[11] See *Gospel Parallels*, ed. Burton H. Throckmorton (New York, 1967),11.
[12] *Buddhist Mahayana Texts*, ed. E. B. Cowell (New York, 1969), 4.

The Christian tradition has no one else to thank for this idea but Buddhism.

6. *Virginitas post partum*

There is hardly anything unique about not having children after the birth of the firstborn in any religious traditions, except that a certain Christian tradition affirms this view after the fashion of the Buddhists. Indeed, the idea is not native to the Jewish religion nor to Hellenistic religions. That probably is the reason why many Christian scholars think that the verse "[Joseph] knew her not until she had borne a son" (Matt. 1:25) need not necessarily imply that Joseph did know Mary after she had borne her son. But they refer to texts like "His mother and his brethren stood outside" (Matt. 12:46) and "Are not his brethren James and Joseph and Simon and Judas" (Matt 13:55) and suggest Mary had other children.[13] On the other hand, mainline Catholic tradition affirms the perpetual virginity of Mary, which view, I believe, was more than likely a derivation from Buddhism.

7. *Dream Vision*

The Hebrew scriptures abound in dream vision parallels in birth stories which provided sufficient significant verbal as well as conceptual parallels for the Christian gospel writers for developing their versions of the conception and birth of Jesus. Undoubtedly, the classical birth stories of the great figures of the Old Testament, like those of Ishmael and Isaac (Genesis 16-17), of Samson (Judges 13), and of King Hezekiah (Isa. 7:14-16) function as style types and as subtexts of the gospel narratives. Some of the features of this style are the addressing of the person by name, the reassurance, allusion to the problem presented by the barrenness of the lady, the conception of a son, name-giving, and reference to the mission of the son. The verbal parallels from Isaiah 7 indicates clearly that Matthew had the oracle of the prophet in mind in describing the extraordinary circumstances surrounding Jesus' conception, birth, and mission.[14]

---

[13] See Herman Hendrickx, *The Infancy Narratives* (London, 1975), 35.
[14] Hendrickx, 34.

8. Angels at Conception

One may argue that the presence of God's messengers or angels at conception is a unique feature of the Hebrew Bible and the gospels. It is not so. The Buddhist *Mahavastu* has the following passage:

> Then, espying the queen on her bed, beautiful as a celestial maiden, throngs of devas [celestial beings] came down from their home in Tushita and alighted on the terrace....They said...What more do you want, O queen? O woman...who is ever undefiled, unsullied by what is foul...you are a worthy woman, supreme among women. And your son will be the Pre-eminent of men, who has abandoned lust and is rid of passion(7).[15]

This passage reminds us not only of the Annunciation scene in Luke but also of the words of Elizabeth to Mary: "Blessed art thou among women and blessed is the fruit of thy womb" (1:42). However, there is every reason to believe that the Old Testament stories also were in the mind of the evangelists when they composed the annunciation narratives.

9. The Visit of the Magi

Many scholars think that the magi episode in Matthew 2 is a *midrash* on Isaiah 41:2-3: "Who stirred up one from the east whom victory meets at every step? He gives up nations before him, so that he tramples kings under foot." Exegetes cite other biblical passages which could serve as fulfilment quotations for the magis' visit like the following:

> "May the kings of Tarshish and of the isles render him tribute, may the kings of Sheva and Seba bring gifts! May all kings fall down before him, all nations serve him!" (Ps. 72:10-11).

> "Kings shall see and arise; princes, and they shall prostrate themselves." (Isa. 49:7).

> "Arise, shine; for your light has come, and the glory of the Lord has risen upon you. For behold, darkness shall cover the earth, and thick darkness the peoples; but the Lord will arise upon you, and his glory will be seen upon you and nations shall come to your light, and kings to the brightness of your rising. Lift up your eyes round about, and see; they all gather together, they come to you; your sons shall come from far, and your daughters shall be carried in the arms. A multitude of camels shall cover you, the camels of Midian and Ephah; all those from Sheba shall come. They shall bring gold and frankincense, and shall proclaim the praise of the Lord." (Isa. 60:1-6).

---

[15] J. J. Jones, London, 1976), 6-7.

"A star shall come forth out of Jacob, and a scepter shall rise out of Israel." (Num. 24:17).

The influence of Num. 24:17 and Isa 60:1 is clear in the magi episode; perhaps even the parallel story of the visit of the Queen of Sheba to Solomon (1 Kings 10:1-13) may also be of some relevance here though King Herod is the antithesis of the wisdom of Solomon!

The story of the seer Balaam (Num. 22-24) is often cited as a parallel to the magi episode, particularly on account of the reference to the star of David. Hendrickx writes:

> Balaam was by profession an interpreter of dreams and therefore, a "magus" (Philo), coming "from the East"....While biblical tradition in general adopted a hostile view of Balaam, in Num 22-24 he is looked upon in a positive way. Balaam came from the East accompanied by two servants (Num. 22:22) who in the *Palestinian Targum* become fellow-magi, thus forming a party of three. The hostile king Balak intended to use the foreign magus Balaam (and his two companions) to destroy his enemy, but the magus honored Balak's enemy instead. This is very close to thevstory of Herod and the Magi. In fact both stories also end with the departure of the main characters.[16]

It is important to note here that the star in Num. 24:17 is a personification of the Davidic monarchy, while in Matt. 2:2 it is an astronomical phenomenon; and that Jewish writings interpret the star as a symbol of a person and not as a sign of his coming![17]

Some authors would see a connection between Matthew's story and Dio Cassius' account of the visit to Emperor Nero by Tiridates, king of Armenia in A.D. 66—some twenty years before the gospel was written--; he and his companions are elsewhere referred to as magi.[18]

Also, in later midrash, a story is told of a star which appeared at the birth of Abraham: "When our father Abraham was born, one star from the east came and swallowed up four stars of the four corners of the heavens. The wise men said to Nimrod: 'At this time a son is born to Terah and a nation will issue forth from him and will inherit this world and the world-to-come'."[19] Interestingly, Ptolemy refers to the Brahmins of India as *brachmanoi magoi* ;[20] so one cannot argue in all honesty that the magi-episode has nothing to do with India.

---

[16] Hendrickx, 42.
[17] See Hendrickx, 43.
[18] Hendrickx, 39.
[19] *Ma'ase Avraham*, 43 in Lachs, 9.
[20] Caldwell, 102.

138   CHAPTER FOUR

I am willing to accept the motif of the star, though not the expression *magus*, from these episodes. However, the story of the five wise men who visited Prince Siddhartha and worshipped him under the Jambu tree is much closer to the visit of the magi, except for the reference to the massacre of the innocents. In addition to that, here is an equally good Buddhist parallel from *Mahavastu*:

> When the child had entered the royal palace, the king bade his priest to fetch at once the wise men who were skilled in the rules and significance of sign. Learning this the saintly devas, called Mahesvaras, came on the scene....They stood quietly at the door of the king's palace and addressed the door-keeper: "Go in to Suddhodana and say to him, "Here are...men who know the rules and significance of signs, and they would enter, if it is your pleasure."...Suddhodana replied, "To be sure, let them with all speed enter within this noble palace."...Then the door-keeper...said,"His majesty is pleased, sirs, that you should at his behest enter the valiant king's palace."...One of them addressed the king, saying, "Let your majesty hear what the cause of our coming hither is. A son is born to you, O king, who is wholly faultless in body and who is judged fair by all the world and possesses to perfection the marks of excellence. For we, skilled in the science of signs, can recognize the marks of virtue and of vice. If it is not hard for you, we would see him who bears the marks of a Great Man." The king replied, "Come, see my son."...Then taking in his arms the Virtuous One,...he brought him....When the Mahesvaras observed from a distance the dignified approach of the Sasabala, they were thrilled with joy and bowed their heads crowned with glittering diadems to the ground (28).[21]

10. *The Massacre of the Innocents and Flight*

The rise of the new star often spelled destruction for the ruling monarch. During the reign of Nero, according to Suetonius,

> A blazing star [or comet—*stella crinita*], which is vulgarly supposed to portend destruction to kings and princes, appeared above the horizon several nights successively. He [Nero] felt great anxiety on account of this phenomenon, and being informed by one Balbilius, an astrologer, that princes were wont to expiate such omens by the sacrifice of illustrious persons, and so avert the danger forboded to their own persons, by bringing it on the heads of their chief men, he resolved on the destruction of the principal nobility in Rome.[22]

Nero not only did condemn the nobility but also banished their children from the city of Rome.

Of course, the motif of the vain attempts by ruling monarchs to prevent their fall from power by destroying the new-born child-

---

[21] J. J. Jones, II (London, 1976), 24-25.
[22] *Nero*, 36; Enslin, 330.

king appears in the birth stories of Zeus, Perseus, Oedipus, Romulus, Augustus, Moses, and the founder of the Fifth Dynasty of Egypt. Suetonius records:

> Julius Marathus [a freedman of Augustus of Oriental origin] is the author of the story that a few months before he [Octavian] was born, an omen at Rome came to public attention whereby it was announced that nature would give birth to a king of the Roman nation. In terror, the Senate decreed that no one born that year should be brought up. Those who had pregnant wives, because each had hopes for himself, saw to it that the edict of the Senate should not be registered in the treasury.[23]

Josephus adds this interesting note in his tale of the slaughter of the innocents in Egypt at the time of the birth of Moses—an element absent from the Exodus account:

> One of those sacred scribes, who are very sagacious in foretelling future events truly, told the king that about this time a child would be born to the Israelites who, if he were reared, would bring the Egyptian dominion low, and would raise the Israelites; that he would excel all men in virtue, and would attain a glory that would be remembered through all the ages. Which thing was so feared by the king, that, according to this man's opinion, he commanded that they should cast every male child which was born to the Israelites, into the river, and destroy it.[24]

It is also interesting to note that an apocalyptic work, *The Ascension of Moses*, talks about Herod and draws a parallel between Herod's destroying of his rivals and Pharaoh's killings to eliminate his rival Moses.[25] Raymond Brown writes:

> The most likely background is offered by the episode centered on Balaam in Num. 22-24. The setting is the plot of Balak, the Transjordanian king of Moab; he feared the Israelites who were being led by Moses out of Egypt sought to destroy them. Since I maintain that this pre-Matthean narrative based on Balak and Balaam was joined to a pre-Matthean narrative based on the birth of Moses, it is significant that both stories involve the attempt of wicked kings to destroy Moses. The Matthean Herod resembles both the Pharaoh and Balak.[26]

I venture to think that Matthew's reference to Herod's attempt to kill Jesus is an attempt at reading history backwards. From the apocryphal Gospel of Peter we know that it was King Herod who condemned Jesus; Matthew probably had this idea in mind when he was writing the infancy narrative!

---

[23] *Augustus*, 94; Enslin, 331.
[24] *Antiquities* II, ix, 2.
[25] Hendrickx, 49.
[26] Brown, 193.

The topos of flight for the preservation of the life of the child is also a familiar one, as in the stories of Zeus in the Dictean cave, of the woman arrayed with the Sun in the ancient Babylonian myth (Revelations 12), of the flight of the Olympian gods before Typhon, and of the flights of Isis, Leto, and Io to Egypt. Interestingly, Matthew refers to Hosea 11:1 in this story: "This was to fulfill what the Lord had spoken by the prophet, 'Out of Egypt have I called my son' (2:15). Hosea is referring here to God calling Israel, his son, from Egypt at the time of the Exodus; Matthew is using the Hebrew version rather than the Septuagint here! Naturally, the singular noun fits the context as well as his intention of representing Jesus as the second Moses and as the new Israel.

All told, these tales and citations do not provide all the details found in the story of Jesus as the combined stories of Krishna and Buddha do it with details such as birth in a manger at the time of tax-payment, dual births, King Kamsa's attempt to kill infant Krishna, and his exile from Mathura to Braj across the Yamuna, all of which have been pointed out in the previous chapter.

11. *Lucan Annunciation*

Biblical exegetes have made abundantly clear the apocalyptic character of the Lucan annunciation scenes involving Zechariah, Mary, and the shepherds. The book of Daniel (8-10) and its apocalyptic themes underlie the Lucan narrative. Hendrickx writes:

> The narrative has certain features of apocalyptic literature. A revelation is mediated by a celestial being to a human addressee to unveil a transcendent reality which nevertheless belongs to time and space. The annunciation follows an apocalyptic thought pattern. The viewpoint is eschatalogical; in the final analysis, the annunciation intends to relate an apocalyptic event. Beyond the narrative of the annunciation and the miraculous conception, the text intends to make of the angelic announcement the primordial revelation that the child about to be born is the fulfilment of the promises and the eschatological manifestation of God's power.[27]

Besides the apocalyptic themes, one can notice in Luke many verbal parallels not only from Daniel but also from 2 Samuel 7: 7-16 and other books of the Old Testament, which suggests that Luke has followed the style and outline of the annunciation narratives of

---

[27] Hendrickx, 70.

the Old testament, which has four elements: pregnancy, birth, name-giving, and future of the child. The following verbal parallels from 2 Samuel are noteworthy: "The Lord will make you a house...and I will make for you a great name...I will raise up your offspring after you, who shall come forth from your body, and I will establish his kingdom. He shall build a house for my name, and I will establish the throne of his kingdom forever. I will be his father, and he shall be my son...your throne shall be established forever"(2 Sam. 7:7-16).

However, the central theme of the incarnation of God is missing in all these Old Testament narratives. The main contribution of Indian religions to the annunciation stories is the concept of incarnation. I have noted earlier the other Buddhist parallels found in Luke's annunciation story.

12. *Visitation*

There are two points where the Buddhist and gospel traditions converge: one, in the visibility and recognition of the Master in the womb of the mother; two, the praise of the mother by the visitor. I have pointed out the first point, that of convergence, in the previous chapter. As for Elizabeth's salutation: "Blessed are you among women and blessed is the fruit of your womb" (Luke 1:42), there are the expressions: "most blessed" (Judges 5:24) and "O daughter, you are blessed by the Most High God above all women on earth" (Judith 13:23). Granting that these phrases were in the mind of the evangelist, let me point out that these utterances were not made in the context of a birth. However, I do not find a better parallel than the one in the Buddhist version, where heavenly men and women come to see and address the pregnant mother of Buddha. *The Mahavastu* reports:

> All these immortals ecstatically bowing their heads and raising their joined hands, lauded the virtuous Maya, the conqueror's mother, and alighted on the terrace. Then in great excitement a large throng of deva-maidens carrying fair garlands came, eager to see the Conqueror's mother, as she lay on the bed...They said..."She will bear a great man....You are a worthy woman, supreme among women. And your son will be the Pre-eminent of Men, who has abandoned lust and is rid of passion. What more can you want, O queen?" (7)[28]

---

[28] J. J. Jones, trans. *The Mahavastu*, II:7.

In this passage the context is the visit to a pregnant woman and women address the mother to be; above all, the pregnant woman is the mother of the Master as in the biblical story of visitation.

13. *The Magnificat*

The hymn (Luke 1:46-55) attributed to Elizabeth by some and to Mary by others is a literary mosaic of Old Testament texts. There is nothing comparable to this in the Indian birth stories. Though Hebraists would like to think that the entire hymn is based on the Old Testament, I have some reservation about verse 52: "He has put down the mighty from their thrones and exalted those of low degree." Neither 1 Sam. 2:7: "The Lord makes poor and makes rich; he brings low, he also exalts" nor Sir. 10:14: "The Lord has cast down the thrones of rulers and has seated the lowly in their place" which are suggested as its source, are not verbally as close as Hesiod, *Works and Days*, 6: "Lightly he [Zeus] bringeth low the mighty and lifteth up the humble."[29] An example like this shows that the evangelists must have consulted more than the Old Testament in their composition of the infancy stories.

14. *Jesus' Birth: Census, Manger, and Shepherds*

It is a fact that no Roman census for tax assessment was held in Judea before that of Quirinius in A.D. 6-7.[30] So there is neither Jewish nor Greco-Roman literary evidence to support a tax-related circumstance surrounding the birth of Jesus except the Indian parallel in which Krishna was born when his parents went to pay taxes.

According to Luke, "Mary wrapped him in swaddling cloths and laid him in a manger because there was no place for them at the inn" (2:7). For the commonplace motif of swaddling cloths I have noted a Buddhist parallel in the previous chapter. It is the Krishna-story that provides the motif of manger: Krishna was placed in the cowherd Nanda's house in Braj secretly by his father Vasudeva because there was no place for him anywhere else since the wicked king Kamsa's soldiers had been instructed to kill him as soon as he was born. There is one difference: in the gospel story the cowherds become shepherds, which adds a local color to the

---

[29] See also Euripides, *Troades*, 612-613.
[30] D. J. Hales, "The Roman Census and Jesus' Birth: Was Luke Correct? Part I," *Buried History* 9 (1973), 113-132; D. J. Hales, "The Roman Census and Jesus' Birth...Part II," *Buried History*, 10 (1974), 16-31.

narrative. Interestingly, in most traditional nativity scenes displayed throughout the world we find cows.

To explain the manger-motif by alleging crowding or Mary's need for privacy or a note of rejection is beside the point since there is little substantiation for such claims in statements or in the mood of the narration in Luke 2:1-20 or in what precedes.[31] The author's substitution of shepherds for cowherds was probably influenced by Micah 5:2-4, part of which he cites in the narrative; Micah 5:4 reads: "And he shall stand and feed his flock in the strength of the Lord, in the majesty of the name of the Lord his God." I do not discount the Old Testament references to manger and lack of shelter found in Isa. 1:13: "The ox knows its owner, and the cow its master's manger, but Israel does not know me; my people does not understand" and Jer. 14:8: "Why should you be like a stranger in the land, like a wayfarer who turns aside to tarry for the night?" But, again, these passages have nothing to do with a birth!

Luke's reference to the multitude of angels who announce or exult the birth of Jesus must have been influenced by the Buddhist narrative in which myriads of heavenly beings celebrate the birth of Buddha. On the other hand, the Old Testament references to the multitudes of heavenly hosts found in Daniel 7:10, "a thousand thousands served him, and ten thousand times ten thousand stood before him," and Jeremiah 19:13, "all the houses upon whose roofs incense has been burned to all the host of heaven" as well as Job 38:7, "the sons of God (angels) shouted for joy," have nothing to do with a birth! Further, the angelic message, "Peace on earth and good hope to mankind," has the best parallel in the Buddhist phrase used as the rationale for Buddha's birth: "This day Buddha is born for the welfare of mankind and to dispel the darkness of their ignorance."[32] In the *Suttanipata* the angels declare to Asita: "The Buddha-to-be, the best and matchless jewel, is born for the weal and welfare in the world of men, in the town of the Sakyas, in the region of Lumbini. Therefore are we joyful and exceedingly glad."[33]

15. *Presentation in the Temple*

Luke writes: "At the end of eight days, when he was circumcised, he was called Jesus, the name given by the angel before

---

[31] Hendrickx, 95.
[32] *Aaccharyabhutadhammsutta*, 123-124.
[33] See Garbe, 49.

he was conceived in the womb. And when the time came for their purification according to the law of Moses, they brought him up to Jerusalem to present him to the Lord; as it is written in the law of the Lord, 'Every male that opens the womb shall be called holy to the Lord' and to offer a sacrifice...'a pair of turtle-doves, or two young pigeons'." The circumcision, naming, and consecration of Jesus—as the first-born (Exodus 13:2,12) in the Temple (Luke 2:22-24)—are certainly very Jewish in their context. However, it is nowhere legislated that the child should be purified at the Temple, since there is a problem with Luke's use of "their purification" in the text. For Luke the presentation of Jesus was apparently very important, though he errs as to Jewish practice by connecting this presentation at the Temple with the law of the redemption of the firstborn[34]; perhaps Luke had in mind the dedication of Samuel by his mother Hannah at the temple of Shiloh (I Sam. 1:11, 22-28; see also Mal. 3). Perhaps Luke was also following the presentation story of Buddha in the temple, which could explain his confusion of the Jewish law of the redemption of the firstborn with the Indian practice of presentation!

16. *Simeon in the Temple*

The episode of Simeon's blessing is unknown in ancient Jewish literature unless one would demand to identify Simeon with the son of Hillel, the father of Rabbi Gamaliel, as suggested by A. Cutler.[35] Since there is no possible suggestion that an incident like this could be attached to Simeon's life in the rabbinic tradition, at best this is a far-fetched guess, and, therefore, Lachs is of the view that this position is "not reasonable" (33). I am willing to concede that there was probably an ancient custom for a rabbi to bless the child and that the passage suggests the idea of an old man who represents old times doing homage to a child who is to introduce a new era. There are perhaps some verbal echoes of Gen. 15:15: "[Abraham,] you shall go to your fathers in peace"; and of Gen. 46:30: "Now let me [Jacob] die since I have seen your [Joseph's] face" in the speech of Simeon who was "looking for the consolation of Israel" (Luke 2:25-30): "Lord, now let your servant depart in peace, according to your word, for mine eyes have seen your salvation." The concluding words of the *nunc dimittis* may have been inspired by Isa. 46:13: "I

---

[34] Lachs, 32.
[35] A. Cutler,"Does the Simeon of Luke 2 Refer to Simeon the Son of Hillel?" *JBR* 34 (1966): 29-35.

bring near my deliverance, it is not far off, and my salvation will not tarry; I will put salvation in Zion, for Israel my glory."

Perhaps Hellenistic tradition also has contributed some insight into this Lucan narrative. According to Gottfried Erdmann, the Simeon-motif was the point of contact between the biblical infancy narratives and the Hellenistic tradition of an Augustan golden age. "The Septuagint of Gen. 46:30 was the Old Testament basis of the Simeon motif which in III, 371 ff. of the *Sibylline Oracles* was united with a tradition whose root was in Isa. 52:7 ff. Both the author of the Lucan birth tradition and Virgil's *Eklogue* IV, 53-59, drew independently upon this tradition in the *Sibylline Oracles*.[36]

On the other hand, the whole Simeon episode is so much closer to the Asita story than to any Hebrew parallels. The Indian saint notices angels shouting for joy and learns from them that the Savior of the world has just been born on earth. Immediately he races to the birth-place of the child in a miraculous manner. He takes up the child in his arms and prophesies his future greatness, but immediately bursts into tears because he must die before the child has attained Buddhahood. Since Luke had already used the organic connection between the learning of the Savior's birth from the angels and the visit to the manger in the episode of the shepherds' visiting the child Jesus, he had every reason to omit Simeon's contact with the angels. Luke's expression that Simeon was "looking for the consolation of Israel" (2:25) is a bit puzzling. Fitzmyer thinks that "Luke does not further explain the 'consolation of Israel,' but it is to be understood as the post-exilic hope for God's eschatological restoration of the Theocracy to Israel."[37] But, as Lachs argues, "There is no support for this in the literature. This and similar phrases refer only to the restoration of the Second Temple."[38] However, the disputed Lucan expression makes sense when contrasted to the Indian story, where Asita tries to remember whether he would be able to see him when he has become a Buddha, he sees that he would not be able, but having died he could not attain enlightenment through a hundred or even a thousand Buddhas, and would be reborn in the Formless world. And thinking 'such a marvellous person, when he has become Buddha, I shall not be able to see: great verily will be my loss,' he weeps. Winternitz, who usually ignores loans in literature, thinks that the

---

[36] Boslooper, 184; see Gottfried Erdmann, *Die Vorgeschichten des Lukas- und Matthäus Evangeliums und Vergils vierte Ekloge* (Vandenhoeck & Ruprecht,1932).
[37] *The Gospel According to Luke.* Anchor Bible, 2 vols. (Garden City, 1981),I, 427.
[38] Lachs, 33.

146   CHAPTER FOUR

Asita-Simeon parallel in itself constitutes "one of the most striking Buddhist parallels to the Gospels" and regards it as "to some extent probable that the Buddhist legend was known to the author of the Christian narrative."[39] Roy Amore writes:

> I believe that the convincing evidence for the hypothesis of Buddhist influence here is that both the first and the last part of the Asita story occur in the Christian account. We might dismiss the similar stories of Asita and Simeon as coincidence, just as we might dismiss the similar stories of the angels rejoicing and speaking to Asita or the shepherds. But it is not merely coincidental that almost the whole of the Asita story appears in some form in the Lucan account. I suggest that the incident of Asita's conversation with the gods was the model after which the story of the shepherds in the fields was fashioned, and that the story of Asita in the palace is the model for the narrative about Simeon in the temple.[40]

17. *Anna from Asher*

Anna is the Greek form of Hannah, the mother of Samuel (1 Sam. 1:2) and is a prophetess. The passage probably alludes to Judith 8:4-8; 16:22-23 and Isa. 52:9. But there seems to be something out of place here. Fitzmyer writes: "This identifies Anna as a member of an outlying Northern tribe. What a prophetess from a tribe like Asher would be doing in the Jerusalem Temple is a bit puzzling."[41] In the Indian parallel of Shabari, the problem of distance is easily solved because Rama goes far south to visit the holy woman who has been waiting patiently for him before her death, which occurs immediately after her vision of the divine Rama. It seems likely that Luke has transferred the death of Shabari to the famous *nunc dimittis* phrase of Simeon.

18. *The Precocious Jesus*

Form-critical analysis has shown that the story of Jesus as an infant prodigy (Luke 2:41-52) was an isolated story lifted from somewhere else and placed into the context of Luke 2 with some editorial work in which verses 40 and 52 provide the framework.[42] In fact, the Lucan narrative of the twelve-year old boy in the Temple may have parallels in the traditional stories of youthful prodigies. Dibelius writes:

---

[39] Garbe, 49.
[40] Roy Amore, *Two Masters, One Message* (Nashville, 1978), 155.
[41] Fitzmyer, 43.
[42] Hendrickx, 113.

> The trait of the precocity of a hero, a wise man, or a saint, who even in youth shows the promise of his later calling, and thereby shames, or at least astonishes his elders, is naturally widespread....Si Usire in Egypt, at twelve years old, can read the magic books....Josephus at fourteen is visited by high priests and eminent persons desiring to hear his exegesis of the law, and Rabbi Eleazar ben Hyrkanos was found in the school by his father who meant to disinherit him. The legend of Jesus, moreover, points in no way to anything beyond itself. As the future teacher of the people, Jesus even in youth can take part in the discussions of the rabbis, and, as the future Messiah, He knows Himself to be at home in the Temple as the house of His Father. The legend obviously arose where Jesus was both teacher and Messiah.[43]

But the question why Luke does not tie the episode of the missing Jesus with some other Old Testament passage as he frequently tries to do with the other episodes remains. The answer is that there is no corresponding parallel in the Bible. What is particularly puzzling is the mention of twelfth year as in the story of Buddha who was found missing at twelve. According to Avot 5:21, a male attains his religious maturity at thirteen when he has to observe the mizvot of the Torah. Lachs writes:

> A child who did not need the ministration of his mother could be obligated to observe the Law at an earlier age. Furthermore, since there is such a dependency here and in the birth story of John the Baptist on the birth story of Samuel, it is significant that Josephus states that the beginning of Samuel's prophetic period started during his twelfth year.[44]

As indicated in the previous chapter, Luke only hints at the precocity of Jesus unlike the apocryphal Infancy Gospel of Thomas which uses the Buddhist material extensively.

19. *Other Motifs in the Canonical Gospels*

In the previous chapter I have identified many other interesting common motifs in the canonical gospels and Indian traditions. Some of these parallels are so commonplace that they may appear to be coincidental. However, the cumulative effect of these parallels should be and are taken into consideration in this study.

20. *The Apocryphal Traditions*

As pointed out in the previous chapter, the parallels between the Christian apocryphal gospels and Indian traditions are the most striking. These items are as important as the canonical

---

[43] Martin Dibelius, *From Tradition to Gospel* (New York, 1965), 107-108.
[44] Lachs, 34.

parallels from a literary point of view for the simple reason that they are all contemporary Christian documents evincing common religious and literary traditions and not just developments of the existing canonical gospels.[45] Here I would like to dwell briefly on two prominent apocryphal motifs, Jesus' power of levitation and his descent into Hell, which are not toally uncanonical simply because they are referred to less graphically in the canonical tradition.

20.1 *Levitation*

The canonical gospels refer to Jesus and Peter walking on the sea as in Mark 6:45-51, John 6:16-21, and Matthew 14:22-33. For example, John wrties: "And when evening came, his disciples went down unto the sea....And the sea was rising by reason of a great wind that blew....When...they had rowed about five and twenty or thirty furlongs, they beheld Jesus walking on the sea, and drawing night unto the boat; and they were afraid" (John 6:16-20). The apocryphal Acts of John has the following: "I will tell you yet another glory, brethren; sometimes when I meant to touch him I encountered a material, solid body; but at other times again when I felt him, his substance was immaterial and incorporeal, and as if it did not exist at all....And I often wished, as I walked with him, to see his footprint in the earth, whether it appeared—for I saw him raising himself from the earth—and I never saw it"(93).[46] We find the idea of Jesus' docetic body also in John 20:26: "A week later his disciples were in the house again, and Thomas was with them. Though the doors were locked, Jesus came and stood among them" and in the episode of Jesus' escape from the hands of his enemies who tried to throw him down the cliff at Nazareth (Luke 4:28-30).

All these Christian ideas, including those of the resurrection and ascension of Jesus, have been foreshadowed or anticipated in the Buddhist and Hindu views of the levitation of supernatural beings. For instance, Buddha, the liberated being (*arhat*), describes his supernatural powers (*siddhi,iddhi*, or *labdhi*) as follows in the second *sutta* of *Dighanikaya*:

I, brethren, can realize (*pratyambhu*) whatever countless powers I will; being many, I become one, and having seen many become also one; seen or unseen, I can pass through a wall or a mountain as it were air; I can

---

[45] Helmut Koester and James M. Robinson, *Trajectories Through Early Christianity* (Philadelphia, 1971), 158-204.
[46] *New Testament Apocrypha*, ed. Edgar Hennecke and W. Schneemelcher, II (Philadelphia, 1964), 227; see Henri de Lubac, *Aspects of Buddhism* (London, 1953), 86-130.

sink into the earth or emerge from it as though it were water; I can walk on the water as it were solid earth; I can move through the air like a bird; I can touch with my hands the sun and moon; I have power with respect to my body even so far as unto the Brahma world.[47]

This idea of the gods' bodies levitating is a commonplace in traditional Indian literature, and it can be seen in the story of Nala and Damayanti and in the view that the way a supernatural being is identified is that it can stand poised in the air.[48]

20.2 *Descent into Hell*

That Christ's descent into hell was a favorite theme for the Christians can be seen particularly from the creedal statement: "He descended into Hell." There are four major canonical texts which are mentioned often as referring to this event, but, according to Dominic Crossan, "it is most unlikely the subject is contained in any of them."[49] These texts are Colossians 2:15: "He disarmed the principalities and powers and made a public example of them, triumphing over them." Ephesians 4:8-9, citing Pslam 68:18 says: "Therefore it is said, 'When he ascended on high he led a host of captives, and he gave gifts to men.' (In saying, 'He ascended,' what does it mean but that he also descended into the lower parts of the earth? He who descended is he who also ascended far above all the heavens, that he might fill all things)." 1 Peter 3: 18-20 says: "For Christ also died for our sins once for all;...he went and preached to the spirits in prison, who formerly did not obey." 1 Peter 4:6 says: "This is why the gospel was preached even to the dead that though judged in the flesh like men, they might live in the spirit like God."

The apocryphal Gospel of Peter 10:39-42 has the following:

> And whilst they [the guards] were relating what they had seen, they saw again three men come out from the sepulchre, and two of them sustaining the other and a cross following them, and the heads of the two reaching to heaven, but that of him who was led of them by the hand overpassing the heavens. And they heard a voice out of the heavens crying, 'Thou hast preached to them that sleep,' and from the cross there was heard the answer, "yea."[50]

Of course, the emphasis in the creedal and Petrine descent into hell or harrowing of hell is on how Jesus despoiled the demonic

---

[47] Cited by A. K. Coomaraswamy, *Hinduism and Buddhism*, 69; see also W. Norman Brown, *Indian and Christian Miracles of Walking on Water* (Chicago, 1928), 15.
[48] Jataka 546.
[49] *The Cross That Spoke* (New York, 1988), 363.
[50] Cited by Crossan, 362.

powers of hell and liberated the holy ones. In the absence of any other known sources and in the presence of the Buddhist tradition mentioned in the previous chapter, the logical conclusion is that this idea of redemption was suggested to the Christian writers by the Buddhist tradition. About the originality of the Christ's descent into hell, Jean Danièlou writes:

> The descent into hell was a subject of central importance for Jewish Christianity....The most frequent view in the ancient world placed the habitations of the dead...in the regions under the earth, the *inferi* strictly so-called. It is to these regions that the term "Hell" in the phrase "Descent into Hell" refers, and the purpose of the Descent, in Jewish Christian thinking was to enable Christ after his death to preach deliverance to the righteous who were imprisoned there....This doctrine appears to be purely Jewish Christian; it in fact constitutes a dogmatic development which was to be accepted by the common tradition, and finally included in the Creed."[51]

As I have pointed out in the previous chapter, the idea of Christ's descent into hell is not a Jewish concept but a Christian one which is derived from Buddhist sources. But since it is found in the Apostles Creed, the idea is genuinely orthodox and Christian. However, in order to safeguard the sanctity and purity of the canonical gospels, most Christian scholars refuse to acknowledge any relationship between the canonical scriptures and Indian religious literatures. They cannot brook the suggestion that the canonical gospels might have come in contact with pagan literature. On the other hand, in the face of overwhelming evidence they are willing to admit that the apocryphal gospels were influenced by India.[52] It was the pioneering efforts of Richard Garbe who was convinced that there was a direct relationship between Buddhistic legends and the apocryphal gospels that had accomplished this apparently "impossible" conversion in Western attitude toward the East. His main reservation to accepting major borrowings on the part of the canonical gospels from Buddhism was based on the historical apprehension that the Mahayana written traditions were later than the canonical gospels. As we have seen before, in fact, the Mahayana stories and doctrines are much anterior to the composition of the canonical gospels as we know them today. Garbe writes:

---

[51] J. Danièlou, *A History of Early Christian Doctrine before the Council of Nicaea*, Vol I. *The Theology of Jewish Christianity* (Philadelphia, 1964), 233).

[52] Boslooper, 147.

The parallels with Buddhist tales in the Apocrypha are of an altogether fabulous character and differ essentially from those in the canonical Gospels. Here we have to do with miracle tales of a genuinely Indian cast....These tales come mainly from later Buddhism, the so-called Mahayana, and their transference to the apocryphal Gospels can be laid to direct communication, whereas the few Buddhist narratives that have found admission into the canonical Gospels belong to original Buddhism, the Hinayana, and have been transmitted over indirect routes.[53]

Unfortunately, Garbe did not have much to say about the relationship between the birth-stories of the Christian and Indian traditions, which I have tried to remedy in this work rather extensively. But he has pointed out a number of obvious parallels between Christian and Indian traditions in the Christian apocryphal legends, and I have tried to complement Garbe in in this area also. For example, I have included in this study some other striking analogies not mentioned by Garbe like the following: In both traditions the child chooses his parents; the White Elephant or the White Bird symbolizes conception; the gem is a common term for the unborn child; at conception and birth the same wonders take place in the natural world; the birth is virginal and miraculous; the child announces at birth who he is and takes seven steps; there is heavenly annunciation at birth; the idols in the temple fall as soon as the divine child enters; the child can read the letters of the alphabet and knows more than his teacher.

B. *Biographical Theory*

What is most fascinating about these analogies is that in no other religious traditions including Hellenistic and Jewish religions do we see so many striking common motifs. It is precisely for this reason that I reject the view that these common traditions are merely variations of archetypes or of the same mythical or hagiographical structures. The well-known and the most influential proponent of the hagiographical theory is Martin Dibelius. According to him, the points of agreement between the Buddha legends and the stories about Jesus, arise not from the phenomenon of one serving as the source of the other, but from the "law of biographical analogy." Dibelius writes:

---

[53] Garbe, 72.

> It need cause no surprise if the essential element of the Simeon-legend had a parallel in at least *one* other legendary sphere, namely in that of the Buddha. For the law of biographical analogy which causes many lives of saints to be composed in a similar manner...is obviously active when a holy man, while still a child, is recognized by an aged seer. Thus Asita, according to several sources, spoke a prophecy about the child which later became the Buddha, according to which this child would bring wisdom and light and destroy the darkness of ignorance. The idea is too widespread to justify a theory of direct dependence. Since Asita is brought by magic power into the palace and Simeon is driven by the Spirit into the Temple, since Asita takes the child to his bosom and Simeon takes it into his arms, and since Asita bewails his approaching end and Simeon prepares himself now willingly for death, it appears to me that these related traits make literary interdependence possible but do not prove it. Much more probable is the supposition that the development of the Legend followed the same law in the former as in the latter case. The same holds good also of other analogies of less importance, such as the prophecies about Augustus.[54]

It is undeniable that there is a great deal of truth in this approach as well as in the psychological theory of mythical archetypes propounded by Jung and Otto Rank who have correctly observed that the general unanimity of these myths may be accounted for in the very general nature and behavior of the human psyche rather than in primitive community and migration.[55]

I agree, for instance, that the idea of the miraculous birth and of miracles found in all religions can be accounted for by the biographical and psychological theories. Or, several other parallels—even up to two dozen—can be accounted for by the law of biographical analogy. I am even willing to grant that it is possible to find the same two dozen parallels within a biography or hagiography in all traditions. But here we are talking about four dozen parallels in four short chapters and these four dozen parallels are not found in all traditions except two. This is precisely what I have tried to demonstrate in this comparative study of Indian religions and the Christian gospels. In this book I have dwelt only on the infancy gospels; in my future studies I shall show hundreds of close parallels between the life and teachings of Jesus and the life and teachings of Buddha. In the light of all this overwhelming evidence, the problem of borrowing or literary interdependence will not go away. The cumulative evidence of hundreds of parallels cannot easily be brushed aside or explained away without doing violence to evidence and without being

---

[54] Dibelius, 127-128.
[55] Otto Rank, *The Myth of the Birth of the Hero* (New York, 1959), 7-10.

dishonest. As Edward Said puts it in a wider perspective, "the contemporary intellectual rightly feels that to ignore a part of the world now demonstrably encroaching on him is to avoid reality."[56]

W. Norman Brown has made a careful comparative study of the Indian[57] and Christian (Matt. 14:12-23; John 6:16-21) miracles of walking on the water and has addressed the theory of the independent origin of the same idea or fiction in different cultures. He finds that both traditions illustrate the miraculous idea of walking on the water and the efficacy of faith; both have two main characters: the disciple who has faith and the Master on whom the faith rests; both show faith functioning and disfunctioning; the main difference is that in the Christian tradition the disciple does not renew the faith in the same episode, whereas in the Buddhist tradition the disciple renews faith and restores the miracle. There is no question on the issue of which tradition is older: the Buddhist story is represented on the Sanchi stupa built c. 250 B.C., while the Christian stories date only from the first century even in its oral form. Brown writes:

> For although a single idea of fiction might arise spontaneously in different quarters of the world, it is wholly unlikely that parallel stories containing a number of similar ideas woven together into a coherent whole should so originate. If we regard the incidents and psychic motifs of stories as units, we may say that similar units may exist independently in widely separated communities, but similar groupings of incidents are not likely to exist independently. Empiric observation bears this out. There is very little likelihood that stories came from Eurasia to the American Indians before the time of Columbus; hence it is only in keeping with this fact that there is so little correspondence between the folk-tales of the Old World and the New except what can clearly be traced back to the result of known contact. The two bodies of fiction are essentially dissimilar.

> Thus it is barely possible that in India and Palestine there should have arisen in each without reference to the other the notion that human beings may miraculously walk on the water. More, each might independently have got the purpose of illustrating some religious notion by means of a miracle based upon that belief. But that they should separately have combined this notion and this purpose in a story, have used them in connection with the same doctrine, faith, and have developed stories closely similar in incident is so improbable as to be almost impossible. Finally that both should carry their story to the same most unusual conclusion, namely the cessation of the miracle on the

---

[56] Edward Said, *Orientalism* (New York, 1978), 109.
[57] *Lalitavistara*, ch. 26; *Digha Nikaya* 3.94; *Mahavagga* 1.20.16; *Mahavagga* 8.15; *Jataka* 49; etc.; see Norman Brown, *The Indian and Christian Miracles of Walking on the Water* (Chicago, 1928), 10-29 for a translation of the Indian texts

diminution of faith, is completely incredible. For in that a coincidence between the experiences of Peter when his faith grew weak and of the Buddhist lay disciple in the same circumstances lies the most cogent reason for considering the two legends connected....To find this sort of most recondite handling of miraculous material at all in two separate bodies of religious literature should arouse suspicion, but to find it...attached to similar stories seems to me compelling testimony that the two stories are genetically connected.[58]

Max Müller is an interesting figure in this regard. Toward the end of his life, this brilliant Indologist who was at home in both the Western and Eastern traditions, was on the point of accepting the theory of Buddhist influences on the New Testament. In the miracles of Peter walking on water and of Jesus feeding a multitude with five loaves, "he finds an agreement with the Buddhist parallels 'that can be accounted for by some historical contact and transference only'; in these cases 'we could hardly deny that communication and exchange must have been...we can hardly fall back on mere chance.'"[59]

Garbe suggests that probably Gnosticism was the common ground where the Indian and early Christian traditions met. About the Gnostic origin of the apocryphal gospels he writes:

> Most of these are of Gnostic origin, which also accounts for the assimilation of the demonstrably Buddhistic tales, for the Gnostic sects arose under strong Buddhistic influences. These influences are clearly evident in the Gnostic conceptions of numerous spirit-worlds and heavens, which were derived from the cosmogony of later Buddhism. For instance, the system of Basilides (first half of the second century) is completely saturated with Buddhism, as demonstrated by J. Kennedy. It regarded suffering as the basis of all existence, accepted the transmigration of souls with the law of retribution, and conceived personality as a complex of five constituent parts, corresponding to the five Buddhist Khandhas or Elements of Being—to mention only the most conspicuous borrowings from Buddhism. E. Lehmann calls Gnosticism the "Western conduit of Oriental speculation, which brought all sorts of miscellany into early Christian church and among them some things of which Christianity has never been able to rid itself of."[60]

In the last two chapters I have shown the presence of Indian texts in the infancy gospels and contrasted them with the other subtexts to recognize once again that the gospel writers had used non-Jewish sources in their writings in various proportions. Now it is necessary to show the role the Indian texts play in the Christian

---

[58] W. Norman Brown, 59-60.
[59] Garbe, 25-26.
[60] Garbe, 71.

writings and the rationale the gospel writers followed when they incorporated them into their works. Then in the last two chapters I shall trace the story of the contacts between India and the West, especially in the context of Gnosticism, to account for the presence of Indian religious ideas in the writings of early Christians, at least in the sense that India was vivid in the consciousness of the West.

CHAPTER FIVE

INDIAN SUBTEXT: TEXT AND CONTEXT

Authors do not live in a total vacuum. They take up and use words, phrases, sentences, and discourse already written and spoken by others. For example, the gospel writers have quoted passages and phrases from the Old Testament. I have also tried to demonstrate that the same evangelists have made use of other sources, particularly Indian traditions. Naturally such alien elements in a text can have a significant bearing on its interpretation. Needless to say that the presence of Old Testament quotations and Old Testament references in the New Testament leads one to suggest that the books of the New Testament are Jewish and Eastern documents. But the Greek language, in which these books were written, would insinuate that they are Western works, intended primarily for a community that used an Aryan language like Greek rather than Hebrew, in which the Jewish rabbis continued to compose the Oral Torah: the Mishna and the Talmud. In contrast, the gospel writers preferred to use the Greek Septuagint rather than the Hebrew Scriptures. To put it differently, the gospels are in a sense Western documents dealing with the East. Naturally, the question arises: What did the gospel writers do to their Indian or Eastern sources?

A. *Orientalism*

One way to answer the question is simply to say that the gospel writers did not use Indian sources. In support one can claim that these writers do not acknowledge these Oriental texts. However, in the face of the overwhelming evidence presented in the previous chapters, it is hard to subscribe to that kind of categorical misstatements. I agree that the gospel writers do not identify their Buddhist or Hindu sources. However, what I see is a concealed presence of Indian ideas and motifs in the gospels. In this case the gospel writers' use of Indian ideas is like Michel Foucault's appropriation of Martin Heidegger and Oriental texts. Many commentators see Heidegger as one of the more prominent influences on Foucault, and, as Manfred Frank has demonstrated it, it goes a long way toward explaining Foucault.[1] Yet Foucault never mentions Heidegger, thus concealing his source! Schaub writes about Foucault's use of Oriental sources, which Foucault himself does not acknowledge:

> Foucault rarely refers explicitly to the Orient...It is because the Oriental discourse in Foucault's work is almost always hidden...Foucault would conceal such appropriated knowledge all the more rigorously if he considered it 'subjugated" and "subversive" at the same time. For him, there is no dichotomy here. In his view repressed and forbidden knowledge can have the most explosive potential for subverting power. Much of his work is concerned with excluded and forbidden codes or discourses. They become hidden, according to Foucault, when interdictions are brought to bear against them within certain intellectual cultures. Thus they become the silent underground of the official discourses. Foucault himself has termed such concealed codes "esoteric in...structure("La Folie" 16). In the West, Oriental thought systems are often regarded as esoteric theologies rather than as philosophies."[2]

I suggest that the situation of the gospel writers' use of the Indian sources is somewhat similar: they deliberately conceal these Oriental sources, which were esoteric and forbidden in the early Church because of their close association with the esoteric thought of Gnosticism which was the primary purveyor of Oriental wisdom and in whose midst early Christian writings arose—I shall treat the problem of Gnosticism in a later chapter. What is important to note here is that, like Foucault, the gospel writers have reduced the Oriental texts and all their other sources to the level of a subtext. They subordinate, subjugate, and conceal such appropriated knowledge, which I call "subtext." This type of behavior is a manifestation of what Edward Said and others call "Orientalism," the commonest of the Western perceptions of the Orient. Said writes:

> Ideas, cultures, and histories cannot be seriously understood or studied without their force, or more precisely their configurations of power, also being studied....The relationship between Occident and Orient is a relationship of power, of domination, of varying degrees of a complex hegemony, and is quite accurately indicated in the title of K. M. Panikkar's classic *Asia and Western Dominance*. The Orient was Orientalized not only because it was discovered to be "Oriental" in all those ways considered commonplace...but also because it *could be*—that

---

[1] Manfred Frank,*Was ist Neostrukturalismus?* (Frankfurt, 1984 in Uta Liebmann Schaub, "Foucault's Oriental Subtext," *PMLA*, 104 (1989), 307.
[2] Schaub, 307.

is, submitted to being—made Oriental. There is very little consent to be found, for example, in the fact that Flaubert's encounter with an Egyptian courtesan produced a widely influential model of the Oriental woman; she never spoke of herself, she never represented her emotions, presence, or history. He spoke for and represented her. He was foreign, comparatively wealthy, male, and these were historical facts of domination that allowed him not only to possess Kuchuk Hanem physically but to speak for her...My argument is that Flaubert's situation of strength in relation to Kuchuk Hanem was not an isolated instance. It fairly stands for the pattern of relative strength between East and West, and the discourse about the Orient that it enabled (5-6)....Too often literature and culture are presumed to be politically, even historically innocent; it has regularly seemed otherwise to me, and certainly my study of Orientalism has convinced me (and I hope will convince literary colleagues) that society and literary culture can only be understood and studied together. In addition, and by an almost inescapable logic, I have found myself writing the history of a strange, secret sharer of Western anti-Semitism. That anti-Semitism and Orientalism resemble each other very closely is a historical, cultural, and political truth.[3]

How curiously right is Said when he says that anti-Semitism and Orientalism go together. Indeed, we find both in the Christian gospels. Since so much ink has already been spilt on anti-semitism in the gospels, I shall not touch the issue of religious anti-Semitism at all except to state that there is a general scholarly consensus that in the gospels the Jews—high priests, pharisees, and Sadducees are condemned for their role in the crucifixion of Jesus.[4] As for literary anti-Semitism, I view it as part of Orientalism. When the gospel writers use the books of the Old Testament, as a rule they do not identify them at all except in the case of prooftexts; instead, they reduce it to the level of subtexts by concealing and subjugating them to their purpose as most artists do out of an unremitting ambition to master the text. Take for example the *Magnificat*. It is a veritable mosaic of Old Testament quotations for the most part; the author of the piece does not care to identify his biblical as well as his classical sources; in fact, by metamorphosing it he has made it to look like his own creation. A similar situation obtains in the Christian apocryphal description of Jesus as an infant prodigy at school. In the Indian version, the different writing systems are mentioned; in the Christian version,

---

[3] Said, 27-28.
[4] E. P Sanders, *Jesus and Judaism* (Philadelphia, 1985), 341-354. has a good bibliography

different letters of the Hebrew alphabet are recorded instead. However, Child Jesus discusses the mystical meaning of the letters as in the Indian tradition. In the Gospel of Thomas and in the narrative of *Lalitavistara*, the teacher falls unconscious at the appearance of the miraculous child in the school. The young Jesus, indeed, discomfits, subjugates, and dominates the old man. Similarly, the gospel version subjugates and dominates the Hebrew and Indian sources.

The degree of subjugation and domination of sources is not the same in the apocryphal gospels as in the canonical gospels. The apocryphal gospels tend to follow the Indian sources fairly closely by changing fewer details, as our comparison has already demonstrated. Since the similarities between the apocryphal gospels and the Indian sources are more obvious than in the case of the canonical gospels, critics are willing to see a literary interdependence in their case. The canonical gospels, on the other hand, seem deliberately to obscure their Indian sources by ignoring most of the details of the Indian texts and by concealing their sources. Naturally, the hand of the editor is at work here. But why does the editor try to obscure his sources? Maybe the author/editor wants to appear original, maybe not. Maybe he wants to exclude the outsider or the *hoi polloi* from getting inside as in Kafka's parable "Before the Law" found in *The Trial*. Mark, I think, provides the clue to this kind of obscurity deliberately intended by the gospel writer in his Parable of the Sower: A man went out to sow; some of his seed fell by the wayside and was eaten by the birds; some fell on stony ground, where it grew without rooting and was scorched by the sun; some fell among thorns, which choked it; and some fell on good ground, yielding at harvest thirty, sixty, and a hundredfold. "He that hath ears, let him hear." Later, the disciples, baffled by this enigmatic parable, asks Jesus about the meaning of the parable. Jesus replies that they who are instructed in the mysteries of the Kingdom need not be addressed in parables, but those outside are addressed only in parables, "*so that* (*hina*) seeing they may see and not perceive, and hearing they may hear but not understand, *lest* (*mepote*) at any time they should turn and their sins be forgiven them" (Mark 4:11-12). By the way, let me point out that the Parable of the Sower itself is originally a Buddhist parable—more about it in another study. In spite of the editorial changes made by Matthew in this Markan passage, where he changes *hina* to *hoti* (because), substitutes Mark's subjunctive with the indicative, and supplies Isa. 6:9-10 to gloss over Mark's *mepote*, Matthew himself practices the essential ambiguity in his own gospel in the use of his other sources. My point simply is that all narrative is dark and often intentionally so: It reveals and at the same time it conceals, and the authors/editors have their reasons for obscuring their narratives; sometimes they spell out their reasons as Mark had done—outsiders must stay stay outside and be damned—, but often they do not. [5]

I am not finding fault with the gospel writers for practicing obscurity by concealing their sources; rather I am trying to understand the philosophy of their discourse and the religious system they subscribed to. Recent New Testament scholarship has convincingly shown that the gospels form a separate literary genre, in which the authors have integrated various subtexts to create their own texts in the process of creating their own theological system within the church. Since we have the gospels as transmitted by the church, we have every reason to believe, as Gerhardsson argues convincingly, that the church through the evangelists shaped, altered, doctored, and edited the contents of the gospels.[6] In this sense a religious text is the product of a textual community or the product of a system. The authors are not independent writers with no affiliation to a church; they are spokesmen for the churches which they represent and defend as missionaries do. Undoubtedly, they are inventive and original artists; they are not mere editors skilled in the use of scissors and paste pot. They are more: they are creative narrators who tell their story with a sense of unity and continuity. They use their borrowed texts as subtexts to stand as integral strands in the new text, providing unity, development, and coherence of meaning. As a result, often it is difficult to name subtexts as Indian, Hellenistic, or rabbinic, so much so that for hundreds of years—until the advent of form criticism—Christian readers of the infancy gospels have looked upon them as one continuous narrative by one single author and interpreted the text as part of their unique religious system.

One can infer the presence of a system within a community of religious texts because it is impossible to have a text without a system. This system is made up of three essential components: ethnos, ethos, and ethics. Jacob Neusner writes:

---

[5] See Frank Kermode, *The Genesis of Secrecy* (Cambridge, 1979),23-47.
[6] Birger, Gerhardsson, *The Origins of Gospel Traditions* (Philadelphia, 1979.

When writings such as those of the Judaic canon have been selected by the framers of a religious system, and, read all together, those writings are deemed to make a cogent and important statement of that system, hence, the category, "canonical writings." I call that encompassing, canonical picture a "system," *if and when* it is composed of three necessary components: an account of a world view, a prescription of a corresponding way of life, and a definition of the social entity that finds definition in the one and description in the other. When those three fundamental components fit together, they sustain one another in explaining the whole of a social order, hence constituting the theoretical account of a system. Systems defined in this way work out a cogent picture, for those who make them up, of *how* things are correctly to be sorted out and fitted together, of *why* things are done in one way, rather than in some other, and of *who* they are that do and understand matters in this particular way. When, as is commonly the case, people invoke God as the foundation for their world view, maintaining that their way of life corresponds to what God wants of them, projecting their social entity in a particular relationship to God, then we have a religious system.[7]

B. *Jesus Movements*

The religious system that created the infancy gospels including the apocryphal ones but later rejected the apocrypha and which in turn was fashioned by the gospels is called today Christianity. With the person of Rabbi Yeshua (Jesus) it started out as a renewal movement(s) within Judaism—Hellenistic and Palestinian—and was nurtured by the immediate as well as later followers of Jesus over a rather long period of time between 30 and 150 A.D. Originally a Palestinian phenomenon, the Jesus movement came to be known as Christianity after about 85 A.D., with the expulsion—voluntary and/or involuntary—of the Jesus people from the synagogue.

The Jesus movement was not itself a monolithic movement, nor were the Christian texts created by one person in one place. Most Christian scholars today would like to believe that the gospel attributed to Matthew was written in Syria by an unknown Greek-speaking Jewish Christian at the end of the first century in a mixed community of Jewish and gentile descent.[8] Mark was probably written a few years earlier, again in Syria.[9] The Gospel of Luke was

---

[7] Jacob Neusner, *The Systemic Analysis of Judaism* (Atlanta, 1988), 29-30.
[8] Raymond Brown, 45.
[9] Burton Mack, *The Myth of Innocence*, (Philadelphia, 1987), 318.

written in a gentile community at the end of the first century, and Luke's work is markedly different from Matthew among other things in the absence of Hebrew words, of local Palestinian color, and of direct Old Testament quotations.[10] Since all the earliest gospel fragments come from Egypt, it is quite possible that the gospels were written in Egypt. Most of the apocryphal infancy gospels in their present form are also Christian products or written by different members of the Jesus Movement with Gnostic associations probably before the canonical gospels in Egypt and other places. Though in their incipient stage these gospels were associated with the amorphous Jesus movements, in their second-century stage of redaction, they came to be called Christian works.

1. *Ethnos*

The Jesus movement started out within the ambiance of Judaism long before the creation of the written gospels. Later the written gospels gave religious legitimacy to the Jesus movement and contributed significantly—along with other sociological, political, and economic forces—toward the creation of the new religious entity, Christianity, which became separate from Judaism.

The Jesus movement started out within Judaism, and it can be defined by relating it to another contemporary powerful and influential movement within Judaism, the group of Pharisees, who are presented as the enemies of Jesus in the gospels. It should be noted that the group of Pharisees "assumes importance in our eyes out of proportion to its place in the gospels because the kind of Judaism that emerges from the first century draws heavily upon the methods and values imputed to the Pharisees in the later rabbinic literature."[11]

Both groups were expressions of the religion of Israel. The gospels view the members of the Jesus movement as the family of Jesus, "the body of Christ," who shared all their possession with one another as members of a close-knit family would. The Pharisees were different. They were not a family. Though they appear as a political party in Josephus' writings, they "were characterized by their adherence to certain cultic rules.[12]

---

[10] Brown, 235.
[11] Neusner, *Systemic Analysis*, 91.
[12] Neusner, "*Systemic Analysis*, 91.

2. Ethos

In their world views both movements were similar and different. The view of the Hebrew scriptures that Israel was one large family descended from a single set of ancestors was common to both. The Jesus people accepted this view and defined the "true" Israel as the family of Jesus, as made up of those—Jews only at first, but gentiles were included later—who accepted Jesus as the Messiah— important for the Jewish members of the movement—and Jesus the Christ as the Son of God who rose from the dead. Being God and Messiah, Jesus saved Israel and the rest of mankind by saving them from the slavery of Satan and sin. Faith on the part of the believers brought them all together into Jesus' family, which is also the family of David, Jacob, Isaac, and Abraham who shared the faith. The Pharisees, on the other hand, looked upon Israel as a holy people, sharing a holy way of life—cultic and moral— prescribed in Mosaic Torah. While the Jesus people emphasized salvation, the Pharisees stressed sanctification and cultic purity. "The Pharisees were a sect and had developed a peculiar perception of how to live and interpret life. They acted in their homes as if they were priests in the temple....They lived...as if they had to obey at home the laws that applied to the Temple."[13]

3. Ethics

In their ethics, both groups followed the Torah selectively. In fact, very little more can be said with certainty about the development of early "Christian" moral teaching. Even the so-called Christian norm of non-retaliation was derived from the Hebrew scriptures according to Paul. He argues that, since vengeance is the Lord's according to Deuteronomy (32:35), Christians must never avenge themselves. In principle, the ethics of the Jesus movement is not in any way unique; much of their "revolutionary" ethical teaching is found in the Buddhist scriptures—I shall show this in my forthcoming book. In practice, however, passages such as Ephesians 5:22 - 6:9 suggest that "Christians" drew up "rules for households" (*Hausstafeln*) that are rooted in Jewish and non-Jewish ethical teaching. "But to risk a conclusion, we are in the presence of an abortive development,"[14] as

---

[13] Neusner, *Systemic Analysis*, 98.
[14] James L. Kugel and Rowan A. Greer, *Early Biblical Interpretation* (Philadelphia, 1986), 129.

in the case of the abolition of private property and the practice of the socialist ideal in Acts 4: 32.

With the coming of more and more gentiles into the fold of the Jesus movement and in their efforts to accommodate them, the Jesus people began to give up increasingly the practice of sacrifices, circumcision, and other Mosaic customs like the observance of the Sabbath and food laws. The crucial practical matter where the Jesus movement made their critical break with traditional Judaism was the institution of the Eucharist, which substituted for the most important rite of the Israelite cult, the daily whole-offering, even before the destruction of the Temple. It is quite possible that the rite of the Eucharist itself was instituted only after the destruction of the Temple as a substitute for the whole-offering and retroactively applied to the time of Jesus.

C. *Context: Confrontation and Self-Definition*

The tendency of all great religions, like that of great nations and large families, is to tolerate differences as far as possible, especially if the leadership is magnanimous, compassionate, and understanding. If the statement of Rabbi Gamaliel in Acts 5: 34-39 is any indication, the Judaism of the Pharisees tolerated the Jesus movement within the larger group. However, when the survival of the nation/religion itself is at stake, especially in the face of attacks from without—"It is better for one man to die than for the nation to perish" (John 18:14) as in Caiaphas' prophecy—, there is always a tendency to suppress internal dissent by oppressive methods such as persecution, inquisition, excommunication, and even execution. In tense times, dissenters within a religious community have the tendency to claim that they are the true "Israel" or "Christians" or "Islam" and to set up parallel administrative structures within the religious organization. Then the establishment would be forced to persecute and excommunicate the dissidents and parade the miscreants as a deterrent example in front of the faithful. But over a period of time, the persecuted minority would acquire more admirers, adherents, and converts on account of their conviction, dedication, and perseverance in the face of persecution. As their numbers grow, the dissenters would establish themselves as a separate religion within a religion or state within a state.

Separation of the new group is a mutual movement; most often it is not the result of unilateral action, but the result of a long period of alienation of affection, culminating eventually in a declaration of independence and an act of excommunication. Such, I believe, is the case of the establishment of the Jesus movement as Christianity, as a separate religion.

As the Jesus movement grew stronger in number and more nonconformist or heretical in their ethos and practices, they began to appear as a schism and as a heresy within the body politic of the first-century Judaism which was dominated by the Pharisees. During this time the messiah-movements threatened the very existence of Judaism as these movements pitted a divided Jewish community against the mighty and ruthless Roman imperial power. After the failure of the Jewish revolt against the Romans in the sixties and the destruction of the Temple in 70, there was very little room for much pluralism in the Jewish religion, as the Pharisee group attained exclusive domination. Some factions in the Jesus movements became more rebellious by challenging some of the basic tenets, the authority, and the power of the Pharisees; for instance, gentiles among them rejected circumcision and dietary laws and substituted the Eucharist for the whole-offering. Above all, the Jewish Christians claimed that Jesus was not only the Messiah but also the only begotten Son of God. As the Jesus people gradually alienated themselves from the mainstream of Pharisaic Judaism, the main body not only frowned upon them but even possibly included them among the *minim* (heretics). "Around the year 85, the twelfth of the *Eighteen Benedictions (Shemoneh Esreh*: one of the principal prayers in the synagogues) was formulated so as to include a curse on *minim* or heretics, including, or even primarily, Jews who believed in Jesus as the Messiah—['May the Nazarenes and the heretics be suddenly destroyed and removed from the Book of Life']" A Christian invited to pronounce the benedictions would be unable to proclaim the twelfth. Thus identified, he would be excluded from the synagogue.[15] On the contrary, Urbach, Kimmelman, and Maier argue that the *minim* did not include the Jewish Christians.[16]

---

[15] Brown, 46; W. D. Davies, *The Setting of the Sermon on the Mount* (Cambridge, 1964), 275 ff.; J. L. Martin, *History and Theology in the Fourth Gospel* (New York, 1968), 31 ff.
[16] Charlesworth, *Pseudepigrapha* , 82.

In any case, there was really no compelling practical reason for the gentile Christians to be closely associated with Judaism. As they became more powerful and more independent and as the center of Christianity shifted from Jerusalem westward to Rome, a rift between Judaism and the Jesus people became natural and unavoidable, geographically and ideologically. So at the time the gospels were being composed, the Jesus movement was already on the margins of first-century Judaism; they were in it, yet not out of it. On the one hand, they still loved Judaism, the Mother Church, the ancestral home of Jesus, his mother, and his closest associates. On the other hand, they hated her because she was acting as a stepmother towards the gentile Jesus people. They naturally asked themselves: Should we stay or shall we leave? They stayed awhile; they felt they could not stay much longer, for they refused to conform to the Jewish faith and continued to proclaim that Jesus was the Messiah and the Son of God. The Pharisees could tolerate the view that Jesus was the Messiah, but they could not compromise on the view that Jesus was God or God's son. Neusner writes:

> Jews grudgingly recognized that Christianity was not merely another paganism, but in their awareness festered Tarfon's allegation that Christians knew God but denied him, knew the Torah but did violence against its meaning. Today we recognize in these implacably negative projections signs of frustration, anger at someone who should know better than to act as he does, a very deep anger indeed.[17]

No wonder then that the Pharisees probably excommunicated the Jewish Christians. In William Green's view, the Jews had expelled only one group, the Jewish Christians, from their community, whereas they had tolerated all other radical messianic movements. Most likely Green is right: the Jesus movement was not just any messianic movement; it denied the basic tenet of Judaism that Yahweh alone is God; for the folks in the Jesus movement, Jesus was also God, which was an unforgivable blasphemy and intolerable heresy in Judaism. That is the reason why Jesus appears in the rabbinic writings in an very unfavorable light.

Surprisingly the rabbis pay little attention to Jesus in general. The chief tannaitic scholar who talks about Jesus is Rabbi Eliezer, whose mentor, Rabbi Yohannan Ben Zakkai, was a contemporary of Jesus. In the Talmud—the commentary on the Mishna of the first

---

[17] *Systemic Analysis*, 90.

two centuries A.D. contained in the Jerusalem (fourth century) and the Babylon (fifth century) versions—Jesus is not mentioned by name; Jesus is referred to as a "certain person," as "Balaam," as "Ben Stada," or as "Ben Pandira." The Talmud contains many polemical statements such as that Jesus was the illegitimate son of an adulteress by a Roman soldier named Pandira or Panthera and that none came forward in his defence during his trial.[18] Joseph Klausner summarizes the tannaitic or the earlier interpretation of Jesus found in the Talmud:

> There are reliable statements to the effect that his name was Jeshua of Nazareth; that he "practiced sorcery" (i.e. performed miracles, as was usual in those days) and beguiled and led Israel astray; that he mocked at the words of the Wise [the officially sanctioned interpreters of the Law]; that he expounded scripture in the same manner as the Pharisees; that he had five disciples; that he said he was not come to take aught away from the law or to add to it; that he was hanged (crucified) as a false teacher and beguiler on the eve of the Passover which happened on a sabbath; and that his disciples healed the sick in his name.[19]

Later interpretations of the Talmud and the Midrash are much more polemical in nature and more discrediting to the Jesus heresy. R. T. Hereford summarizes this later Jewish testimony:

> Jesus, called a Notzri [the Nazarene], Ben Stada, or Ben Pandira, was born out of wedlock. His mother was called Miriam, and was dresser of women's hair. Her husband was Pappos ben Jehudah. Her paramour was Pandira. She is also said to have descended from princes and rulers, and to have played the harlot with a carpenter....Jesus had been Egypt and brought magic thence. He was a magician, and led astray and deceived Israel. He sinned and caused the multitude to sin. He mocked at the words of the wise and was excommunicated. He was tainted with heresy....He called himself God, also the son of man and said that he would go up to heaven. He made himself to live by the name of God....He was tried in Lud as a deceiver and as a teacher of apostasy....He was tried in Lud on the eve of Pesah, which was also the eve of the Sabbath. He was stoned and hung, or crucified....He was punished in Gehinnom by means of boiling filth....He was a revolutionary. He was near to the kingdom....He is excluded from the world to come.[20]

Naturally, all these allegations and accusations indicate the Jewish hostility towards the Jesus movement. Probably it was the

---

[18] See Joseph Klausner, *Jesus of Nazareth* (New York, 1926), 17-54.
[19] Klausner, 46; cited by Howard Kee, *Jesus in History* (New York: Harper, 1970), 40.
[20] Herford, *Christianity in Talmud and Midrash*, Clifton: Reference Book, 1966), 348-349; cited by Howard Kee, 40-41.

gentile membership of the Jesus movements that precipitated the crisis of excommunication. Chadwick writes:

> The existence of the Gentile mission was an embarrassment in the mission of the Jewish Christians to their own countrymen (Rom.11:28 illustrates this point); and their position was not helped by the attitude of some of their Gentile brethren who had no desire to stress their debt to Judaism and were inclined to the unconciliatory view that the destruction of Jerusalem by the hated Romans in A.D. 70 was nothing but the unmerited judgement of providence for the murder of Jesus, which was itself only the last of a long line of stiff-necked refusals of God's word in the prophets. The Jewish nation's rejection of the Messiah was discovered to be the subject of Old Testament prophecy just as much as the world-wide mission of the Church as the people of the Messiah. Accordingly, there came into being a tradition of interpretation of the Old Testament which concentrated upon prophetic denunciations of mere externalism in religion and upon the observance of feasts and ceremonies...The Mosaic Law was not God's permanent will, but a temporary and provisional measure.[21]

Obviously, this expulsion increased the bitterness "Christians" felt toward the Pharisees who excommunicated them. Of course, the Pharisees had good reasons for doing what they had done. But the Jewish Christians were angry. This anger found its expression in the gospels; Matthew, for instance, portrays the Pharisees as the murderers of Jesus! Nevertheless, some Jewish Christians continued to practice their Jewish religion by observing sabbaths, circumcision, and other Jewish feasts. In the fourth century there were some Jewish churches in Syria. It is their *Gospel according to the Hebrews*, which magnifies the position of James, Jesus' brother, that Jerome translated into Latin.[22] One such Jewish Christian community, the Cnanaya Catholics who claim their origin from Thomas of Cana, a relative of Jesus, is still very much alive and active in Kerala, South India.

The gospel writers' anger toward the Jews is one element of the complex context of the theological and apologetical thinking and reasoning of these men. On the one hand, they resented the Jews who expelled them and tried to tackle the problem of the right of the Jesus movement to exist independently of the synagogue. On the other hand, they still cherished their Jewishness for the personal reason that it was part of their ethnic heritage and for the practical reason that it was useful in the preaching of Jesus'

---

[21] Henry Chadwick, *The Early Church* (London, 1988), 21-22.
[22] Chadwick, 22.

message of salvation to the Jews. This double dimension can be seen in the apologetic overtones and didactic intent of the Christology of the infancy narratives.

By presenting Jesus as the son of David and as the divine Messiah, Matthew proposes to the Jews that they need not expect another Messiah and that Jesus, and not Moses, is the fulfillment of all future expectations of the nation. Perhaps Matthew is also trying to prove to the synagogue which opposed the Jesus movement that God had foretold the career of Jesus. In chapter 1: 22-23, Matthew cites the Old Testament directly by introducing the citation with the words: "All this took place to fulfill what the Lord had spoken by the prophet who said. ..." In Matthew there are fourteen of these citations, five of which (1: 22-23 citing Is. 7: 14, 2: 5-6 citing Micah 5: 1 and 2 Sam. 5: 2, 2: 15 citing Hosea 11: 1, 2: 17-18 citing Jer. 31: 15, and 2: 23 citing Isa. 4: 3 and Judges 16: 17) are found in the infancy narrative. Some of the citations refer to minor details in Jesus' career as if to imply that the whole of Jesus' life, down to the minutiae, were foreordained by God.

In fact, during the formative period of Christianity—from the time of the Apostles to the time of Ireneus—Christian writers were obliged to come to terms with the Hebrew scriptures—not the Oral Torah—because the written scriptures represented the authority of God for their practices and beliefs. Naturally, the Jewish Christians rejected the Oral Torah since it was a living tradition founded on the authority of the living rabbis, whose authority they rejected except that of Rabbi Jeshua (Jesus). On their part, Christian writers took over the role and authority of the Jewish sages and interpreted the scriptures in a "Christian" sense. They used the Hebrew scriptures to demonstrate that Jesus was the fulfillment of Israel's hope.

The Christians took three different approaches in this endeavor: (1) the Hebrew scriptures prophesy Jesus Christ and the events in his life, as explained above; (2) the scriptures foreshadow Christ; (3) the scriptures are an allegory of the Christian truths.

It is primarily to find a warrant for the Christian message of salvation and to present the person of Jesus as savior not only of the Jews but of the entire mankind that these Christians needed the Hebrew scriptures. For instance, 1 Corinthians 5: 1-11 argues that the core of the message of salvation—the death and resurrection of Jesus—is not only supported by empirical evidence but are "in accordance with the Scriptures." It is, however, by no means clear what constitutes the scriptural proof for the resurrection in 1

Corinthians 15: 4. The "third day" could find support in Hosea 6: 2 ("On the third day he will raise us up" or Jonah 1: 17 ("Jonah was in the belly of the fish for three days and three nights"). But Psalm 110:1 seems to be the central verse at issue here: "Sit at my right hand till I make your enemies your footstool." Acts 2: 34-35 preserves this passage as a proof text for Jesus' resurrection and his exaltation as Christ and Lord. In the same context Mark uses Daniel 7: 13, along with Psalm 110: 1, in Jesus' answer to the high priest's question whether he is the Christ: "I am; you will see the Son of Man seated at the right hand of Power, and coming with the clouds of heaven" (14: 62).

Another example of the Christian apologetic is the application of the metaphor of the rejected stone to refer to Jesus' death and resurrection in Mark 12: 10-11 (immediately after the parable of the wicked husbandman) and in Acts 4: 11. In Jesus' lament over Jerusalem (Mt 23: 39; Luke 13: 35), Psalm 118: 26 ("Blessed is he who comes in the name of the Lord") is used in the eschatological sense.

The same tendency can be found in the infancy narratives. There are constant allusions there to Hebrew scriptures. In fact, the gospel writers are saturated in the Hebrew scriptures. For instance, Luke's infancy stories remind his readers of the story of Samuel's birth, while Matthew's reminds them of Moses' birth. The figures of Adam, Abraham, Isaac, Jacob, Moses, and David hover over the gospel portrayal of Jesus.

It would be fair to argue that the gospel writers used only Hebrew scriptures if it could be proven that the gospel audience were just the Jewish folk. In reality, the gospels were written by Jewish Christians for Jews and gentiles whose world view was thoroughly permeated by a cosmopolitan culture. So the gospels had to make sense not only for Jews but also for non-Jews.

In order to make the person and message of Jesus acceptable to non-Jews, the gospel writers had to speak a language intelligible and acceptable to this non-Jewish audience. One such attempt consisted in constructing a synthesis of the new Christian religion with Platonism. Paul who wanted to be all things to all men characterizes this approach in his reported speech given at Athens (Acts 17: 16-31). In the Letters of Paul, as Henry Chadwick points out, "we can see a masterly attempt to retranslate the Palestinian gospel into the religious idiom of the surrounding world."[23] In John's

---

[23] Chadwick, *Early Christian Thought and the Classical Tradition*, (Oxford, 1984), 4

prologue, the neoplatonic Logos becomes God incarnate and the light who enlightens every man coming into the world, and is the principle of rationality and order in the cosmos (John 1: 1-18). The diffused popular philosophy of the first and second centuries was an eclectic affair "not bound within either the straitjacket of school orthodoxy or the requirements of rigid internal consistency."[24]

The best example of this cosmopolitan cultural figure of the time is Philo, who takes for granted the philosophical *koine* of the blend of Platonic metaphysics, Stoic ethics, and Aristotelian logic.

As the studies of Martin Hengel and other scholars show, Philo was not an exception but rather the rule of the times. Hengel writes:

> From about the middle of the third century BC *all Judaism* must really be designated 'Hellenistic Judaism' in the strict sense, and a better differentiation could be made between the Greek-speaking Judaism of the Western Diaspora and Aramaic/Hebrew-speaking Judaism of Palestine and Babylonia. But even this distinction is one-sided. From the time of the Ptolemies, Jerusalem was a city in which Greek was spoken to an increasing degree. The Maccabean revolt changed little here, and in the New Testament period between Herod and the destruction of AD 70 it must have had quite a considerable minority who spoke Greek as their mother tongue....These circumstances make the differentiation between 'Palestinian' and 'Hellenistic' Judaism, which is one of the fundamental heuristic principles of New Testament scholarship, much more difficult; indeed, on the whole it proves to be no longer adequate. We have to count on the possibility that even in Jewish Palestine, individual groups grew up bilingual and thus stood right on the boundary of two cultures. This problem arises not only with Jerusalem, but also with Galilee.[25]

The gospels indicate that the close associates of Jesus were Galileans. Galilee had been annexed by the Hasmoneans only in 104-103 B.C. and then ruled by Rome from 63 B.C.. Yet Galilee was quite a cultural mix due to its geographical location at the southern tip of Phoenicia. Major caravan routes to Damascus, Tyre, Caesarea, Samaria, Antioch, and the Transjordan passed through Galilee, which was marked by Hellenistic cities founded by the Seleucid.[26]

One of the characteristics of this Hellenism, which denotes the mixture of Greek and Oriental cultures, was the universalism of the wise man: the wise man was the citizen of the world through a

---

[24] Chadwick, 6.
[25] *Judaism and Hellenism*, trans. John Bowden I (Philadelphia, 1974), 104-105.
[26] Burton Mack, *A Myth of Innocence* (Philadelphia, 1987), 65-67.

common education and a shared mythology. Meleager of Gadara composed this epigram: "Tyre gave me birth, but Gadara was my home, that new Athens in the land of the Assyrians.... If I was a Syrian, what matter? The world is the home of mortals, and a chaos bore all men, my friend."[27]

The flourishing intellectual life of the province of Syria produced the Cynics Menippus, Meleager, and Oenomaus from Gadara; the Sceptic Heracleitus from Tyre; the Epicureans Zeno from Sidon and Philodemus from Gadara; the Peripatetics Diodoret from Tyre, Boethius from Sidon, and Nicolaus from Damascus; the Stoics Posidonius from Apamea, Antiochus from Ashkelon, Antipater from Tyre, the teacher of Cato the Younger, and so on.[28]

Hellenistic universalism is also evident in the religion of Galilee. Theissen writes:

> Greek mythology was transplanted to Syria and Palestine, or native traditions were given a Greek interpretation. Thus the story was told in Joppa of how Perseus freed Andromeda on a rock there....Scythopolis prided itself on being the place where Dionysus was brought up....In Samaria, in the first century AD, Simon Magus could give out that his consort was a reincarnation of Helen....In the same region, Heracles and Astarte were later held to be the parents of Melchizedek in the Old Testament....Apollo was worshipped in Gaza and Astarte in Ashkelon as the heavenly Aphrodite....During the Hellenistic reform Yahweh was even worshipped as Zeus in Jerusalem and Samaria....Hellenistic culture sensed the same god behind the various divine figures.[29]

The Hellenistic reform movement tried to set up a gymnasium in Jerusalem (2 Maccabees 4: 9); the Maccabean reaction put an end to it; the Maccabeans also suppressed the beginnings of religious tolerance, including the emperor cult of the Roman era.

During the Hellenistic era, some people failed to make the distinction between philosophical eclecticism and religious syncretism. The cosmopolitan, Hellenized Philo could accept eclecticism, but he would not tolerate syncretism in belief and cult. In fact, when he begins to speak of God, the Hellene gives way to the Hebrew, and against syncretism he has uttered several warnings.[30]

It is easy to understand that the gospel writers shared the Jewish as well as the Hellenistic heritage of their culture. The

---

[27] *Anthologia Graeca*, 7. 417. 1 ff.
[28] Gerd Theissen, *Sociology of Early Palestinian Christianity* (Philadelphia, 1985), 88.
[29] Theissen, 89.
[30] Chadwick, 7.

Jewishness of the gospels consists in the pious, though selective and unorthodox, transmission of the revered text and certain traditions. For instance, there are fifty-seven scriptural quotations in Mark 11-16, of which thirty-three are from the prophetic books. Of the 160 scriptural allusions in Mark, half are from the prophets.[31] Obviously, this literary dependence on the prophetic corpus implies that the author of the gospel spent a great deal of time in the interest of establishing a certain relationship between the prophets and the gospel-story of Jesus.

Indeed, the Hellenism of the gospel writers manifests itself in their eclecticism of religious traditions and their openness to other non-ethnic intellectual influences, as we have seen before. In all this they did not simply create a patchwork of religious traditions about Jesus. Theirs was "a highly conscious scholarly effort in fabricating a new text by taking up strands from textual patterns that belonged to the multifaceted cultural fabric of...[their] traditions."[32] There was a great deal of energy, research, and search for hermeneutics involved during the composition of the gospels. Burton Mack writes about the gospel of Mark:

> It was composed at a desk in a scholar's study lined with texts and open to discourse with other intellectuals. In Mark's study were chains of miracle stories, collections of pronouncement stories in various states of elaboration, some form of Q, memos on parables and proof texts, the scriptures, including the prophets, written materials from the Christ cult, and other literature representative of Hellenistic Judaism....One might imagine Mark's study as a workshop where a lively traffic in ideas and literary experimentation was the rule for an extended period of time....The story was a new myth of origins.[33]

One of the major cultural forces that contributed to the religious syncretism of the period during which the new literary myth of the Christians was taking shape was Gnosticism, which I shall discuss in the following chapter.

---

[31] Howard Kee, *Community of the New Age*, (Philadelphia, 1977), 45.
[32] Mack, 323.
[33] Mack, 322-323.

CHAPTER SIX

GNOSTICISM, THE NEW TESTAMENT, AND INDIA

The gospel writers and the Jesus movement which they represented were less than orthodox; they were eclectic in their preaching and writing. Undoubtedly they themselves would be the first to admit that they had consulted other sources when they wrote their works, as Luke did in the prologue of his gospel. In their own eyes they did only what all writers do: They had composed organically whole and systematically structured books, explaining the reality of the risen Jesus and expounding his teachings, which were the cornerstone of the faith of the Jesus movements they represented. Unlike the syncretist, who is a mere collector of religious ideas, the gospel writer, being an imaginative writer, organized his motifs, themes, and ideas according to governing principles.

But in the eyes of others they were religious syncretists or charlatans. That was why they were declared heretics by the Pharisees. Though the Christians professed their belief in monotheism, they rejected the Jewish version of monotheism; the Christians affirmed that Jesus was God, the Son of God who became man through his birth from Virgin Mary. The incarnation of God on earth, the expectation of a divine Paraclete after the fashion of the Buddhists, and the conception of virgin birth were alien to Jewish religious thought; it was then concluded that these ideas, not being native to the Jewish religion, must have been invented or borrowed from non-Jewish religions and integrated into the belief-system of the new movement. However, seen from the inside through the eyes of the believers, these were revealed ideas, though for the authors of the books and for the leaders of the movement, it was eclecticism, but no syncretism. Therefore, seen from the outside, early Christianity "could be" interpreted as a form of syncretism especially on account of its close resemblance to the various Gnostic sects. In fact, many of the leaders of the second-century Gnostic movements were themselves prominent Christians like Valentinus, who was a candidate for the prestigious position of the Bishop of Rome.

A. *Gnosticism*

The cultural milieu in which Christianity emerged as a distinct religion was not only Judaism but also Hellenism, which in its broad sense denotes the mixture of Greek (Western) and Oriental cultures from the time of Alexander. Though the term "Christian" was employed only in the second century, there were followers of Jesus or Jesus movements in the first century, as we have seen above. The terms "Christian" and "Christianity" are used sometimes in this book for the sake of convenience to refer to the followers of Jesus in the first century. My theory of the influence of Indian religious thought on early Christianity can be described as a Hellenistic phenomenon, as a meeting of the East and the West in the Mediterranean area. It is like the presence of the Greek language in the Hebrew Scriptures (LXX) and the New Testament and like the impact of Greek culture on Judaism and Christianity in general. This chapter zeroes in on the nature of the Indian impact on Christianity by identifying the intellectual movement known in current biblical scholarship as Gnosticism, which specialized in fusing Eastern and Western ideologies and which served as a conduit between India and the intellectual life of the Mediterranean world. As Jean Sedlar points out, "Interestingly, the Gnostic sects are also those which show the greatest affinity with Indian thought. The resemblances are often striking: in the broader Gnostic attitude of world-alienation as well as in specific items of doctrine and in the life-style of Gnostic practitioners."[1]

There are good reasons for considering Christianity itself as a gnostic movement at least as an example of perennial gnosis or perennial philosophy (perennial love of wisdom). Geddes MacGregor writes:

> The ancient gnosis that I would call the perennial gnosticism does have a motif, a theme, a principle that governs the judgments the gnostic makes and that gnostics have always made about religious ideas, practices and beliefs. Gnosticism indeed constitutes a specific understanding of what religion is about, and the ancient gnosis that this understanding is called is perennially...expressed in gnostic movements and tendencies from the dawn of recorded history of religions down to the present day. It is closely allied to the mystical element in religion.[2]

In this broadest sense, every religious person is a gnostic inasmuch as he holds the spiritual elements in man and the

---

[1] Sedlar, 124.
[2] Geddes MacGregor, *Gnosis*, 31-32.

universe in high esteem and considers the spiritual dimension more important than the material world.

In the narrowest sense, the term *Gnostic* usually refers in the language of the Church Fathers to a few heretical teachers and sects that flourished from the second to the seventh century, such as Valentinus, Basilides, and several others who tried to absorb into Christianity certain mythological and speculative currents of thought in vogue. Though Harnack described Gnosticism as "the acute Hellenization of Christianity," Christian theologians describe it as "the verbal Christening of paganism." As George Mac Rae puts it,

> However many Christian ideas are used or misused by the Gnostics, Gnosticism remains essentially a form of paganism. Its Christian elements are on the surface only. The language and images of Christianity are used, but the essence of the Christian message is ignored completely. One must think of a vast religious spirit of atmosphere...a spirit essentially pagan which absorbed select elements from Christianity as indeed it absorbed something from most of the other religions it encountered.[3]

Probably truth stands somewhere in the middle: Gnosticism is both pagan and Christian.

Until the mid-eighteenth century all our knowledge of Gnosticism was derived from the descriptions, fragments, and short works of Gnostics contained in the refutations of the Gnostics by patristic writers like Ireneus of Lyons (late second century), Hegesippus (second century), Tertullian (d. after 220), Clement of Alexandria (d. before 215), Hippolytus of Rome (d. 235), Origen (d.253-54), Eusebius (fourth century), Epiphanius (fourth century), and Ephrem (d. 373). This negative, fragmentary picture of Gnosticism and Gnostics were supplemented since the discovery of original Gnostic texts from the middle of the eighteenth century, culminating in the major find of important Gnostic texts from Nag Hammadi, Egypt, in 1946. The Askew Codex contains the best known *Pistis Sophia*; the Bruce Codex contains the *Books of Jesus*; the Berlin Codex contains *The Gospel of Mary*, *The Sophia of Jesus Christ*, and *The Apocryphon of John*. The Nag-Hammadi find consists of 13 codices containing some 51 Gnostic works such as Valentinus' *Gospel of Truth* and *The Gospel of Thomas*.

The major Gnostic leaders who were attacked by the Church Fathers were Basilides, Carpocrates, Valentinus, Marcion, and

---

[3] George Mac Rae, "Gnosticism," *The New Catholic Encyclopedia*, 524.

Bardesanes, all of whom lived in the second century. Of these, Basilides and his son founded a sect in Alexandria, Egypt. Carpocrates, a contemporary of Basilides, was known for his worship of icons and the practice of magic. The most famous Gnostic Valentinus, who was the author of numerous books, was an Egyptian who taught in Rome. Marcion, who wanted to establish a church, taught that the world was evil and that it was the work of a demiurge, whom he identified with the God of the Old Testament; the Marcionites were characterized by strong asceticism and by their vehement opposition to the Old Testament.[4]

The Gnostics are characterized by one trait: they are hard to define because of the diversity of the sects and differences of views among them as well as "because of the extreme complexity of the religious phenomenon itself."[5] In this sense, defining Gnosticism is like defining Christianity. Speaking of the Valentinians, Ireneus writes: "Let us now look at the inconstant opinion of these, how when they are two or three they do not say the same things about the same subject, but give answers contrary both in words and in meanings."[6] It is more than likely that Ireneus was not interested in understanding them nor did he understand them; he was more interested in refuting them. Be that as it may, modern scholars have tried to understand the Gnostic movements and define them. According to Hans Jonas, "A Gnosticism without a fallen god, without benighted creator and sinister creation, without alien soul, cosmic captivity and acosmic salvation, without the self-redeeming of the deity—in short, a Gnosis without divine tragedy will not meet specification."[7] Jean Daniélou postulates the mind-matter dualism as the essential feature of Gnosticism.[8]

According to MacRae, the distinguishing features of Gnosticism are dualism, emanationism, and salvation through esoteric knowledge.[9] He discusses Gnosticism under five headings: God, the world, man, salvation, and morality: The God of the Gnostics is the totally other, the absolutely transcendent deity, who has nothing to do with the creation and the running of the world. God and the

---

[4] See George Mac Rae, "Gnosticism," *The New Catholic Encyclopedia*, R. M. Grant, *Gnosticism: A Sourcebook of Heretical Writings from the Early Christian Period* (New York, 1961); J. Doresse, *The Secret Books of the Egyptian Gnostics* (New York, 1960); Hans Jonas, *The Gnostic Religion* (Boston, 1963), passim.

[5] Mac Rae, 523.

[6] Ireneus, *Adversus Haereses* 1.11.1.

[7] Hans Jonas, *The Gnostic Religion* (Boston, 1963); cited by Mac Gregor, 21.

[8] Jean Daniélou, *The Theology of Jewish Christianity* (London, 1964), 73.

[9] Mac Rae, 525.

universe are opposed to each other as light and darkness and as good and evil. Between God and men are a large number of spiritual and phenomenal beings, some of whom are called Archons or "rulers." The creator of the visible world is the Demiurge. The material world is the result of the fall of Sophia, one of the spiritual beings, who is attracted to evil matter and produces the Archons. There is a divine spark in man, which descends from the pleroma of God and which tries to ascend to God from the world of matter. The process of ascent or liberation starts through the instrumentality of Gnosis or knowledge, not necessarily through grace or faith. The role of the redeemer is to come among mankind and reveal to them the saving knowledge; this redeemer is a semi-divine being, who only appears as human. The knowledge he communicates is an esoteric knowledge, which is intended only for those who are capable of being saved by it. As for their lifestyle, it is hard to accept the charges of immorality and of antinomian libertinism that their enemies have accused them of.[10]

T. P. van Baaren, recognizing that a short definition of Gnosticism is impossible, lists sixteen characteristics as descriptive of the movement. The following traits supplement Mac Rae's views: Gnosis is not primarily intellectual, but an insight which is necessary for salvation; it is more than philosophical knowledge; it is the esoteric, revealed knowledge glorified during the Hellenistic period (mysteries, Hermetica, New Testament, magical papyri); it is a saving act which redeems the knower: "The beginning of perfection is the knowledge of Man, but the knowledge of God is complete perfection."[11]; "If anyone has knowledge, he is from above."[12] The Bible is interpreted allegorically; there is a tendency to downgrade the Old Testament. The world is regarded with pessimism; it is the work of a demiurge who brought it about in ignorance of God's will. Human beings are of three kinds: (i) those who possess full gnosis and are capable of full salvation; (ii) those who have faith (*pistis*) and have a limited capacity for salvation; (iii) those who are fully absorbed in the cares of this world and are consequently incapable of salvation. Gnostics make a clear distinction between *pistis* and *gnosis*. The mind-matter dualism generally leads to a severely ascetical mode of life or to libertinism. Gnosticism is a religion of revolt. Gnosticism appeals to the desire to belong to an elite group. When the Christological

---
[10] Ireneus, *Adversus Haereses*, 1.6.2-3.
[11] Hippolytus, *Refutatio* V.6.6.
[12] Nag Hammadi Codex I.3.22.1.

question arises, the tendency to distinguish sharply between Christ as "heavenly savior" and the "man Jesus" is prominent, leading to docetism. Christ as a Redeemer is himself redeemed (*salvator salvandus*). Salvation consists in the complete emancipation of the spiritual from the corporeal.[13]

Without denying the elitist, syncretist, esoteric, and ascetic attitudes of the Gnostics, I am inclined to accept the view of Frederik Wisse that the Gnostics were primarily teachers of rival schools of thought rather than heresiarchs and that they were pushed out of the Church not primarily for their unbelief but for political reasons since the tradition of picturing Gnostics as sectarians with distinctive doctrines goes back only to Justin Martyr.[14] Gnostics and Gnosticisms were probably rival "despised" teachers like the Sophists of ancient Greece, or like the Thomistic, Scotist, Suarezian, and Augustinian schools of philosophy in the history of scholastic thought. It can be reasonably assumed that monastic communities served as havens for much heterodox thought since they were and still are not directly under the bishops, who were and are usually the guardians and enforcers of orthodoxy. The discovery of the Nag-Hammadi texts in the vicinity of a Pachomian monastery seems to support this perception. Elaine Pagels thinks that the monks who lived in the monastery may have included the Nag-Hammadi texts within their devotional library.[15] She writes: "In 367, when Athanasius, the powerful Archbishop of Alexandria, sent an order to purge all 'apocryphal books' with 'heretical' tendencies, one (or several) of the monks may have hidden the precious manuscripts in the jar and buried it on the cliff of Jabal al-Tarif, where Muhammad 'Ali found it 1,600 year later."[16] Obviously, the Gnostic teachers coexisted, lived side by side with the rest of the Christians, and found at least limited acceptance and toleration in the larger Christian community until certain powerful bishops or self-styled guardians of the "official" Church teaching, which was in its incipient stages at that time, decided to take action against them. Wisse writes:

---

[13] U. Bianchi, *Le Origini dello Gnosticismo* (Leiden: Brill, 1967), 178-80.

[14] Frederik Wisse, "Prolegomena to the Study of the New Testament and Gnosis," in *The New Testament and Gnosis*, eds. A.H.B.Logan and A.J.M.Wedderburn (Edinburgh, 1983), 138-145.

[15] E. Pagels, *The Gnostic Gospels* (New York, 1981), 145; F. Wisse, "Gnosticism and Early Monasticism in Egypt, in "*Gnosis: Festschrift für Hans Jonas* (Göttingen, 1978), 431-440.

[16] Pagels, 145.

> For Justin the word *hairesis* may still have carried the meaning "school" in the sense of a teacher who attracted a number of disciples or followers. Justin himself headed such a school in Rome and there can be little doubt that this applied also to Valentinus, Basilides, Ptolemy, and Marcion. When such teachers were "excommunicated" the result would not automatically be the birth of a sect characterized by a distinctive teaching at variance with emerging orthodoxy. This would only be the case if the conflict was basically doctrinal and if the teacher in question imposed an authority structure on his followers similar to the one in orthodoxy. We have good reason to believe that this was seldom the case....The real reason for the expulsion of some of the heads of "schools" was more likely a conflict with the church authorities over the right to teach than over heresy. This may lie behind Tertullian's report that Valentinus left the church when he failed in his bid to become the bishop of Rome [*Val.*4]; it is unlikely that his teaching was orthodox before his break with the church and became heretical only afterwards. Rather it would appear that in the middle of the second century the bishop of Rome began to limit the freedom of the various "schools" which had operated unchecked in the city up to that point, and which may have caused unrest among the believers as well as tension with the hierarchy. As a consequence Valentinus and Marcion were forced to leave, and their teaching which had been tolerated before was now declared heretical. Heresy at this point was not yet teaching which conflicted with official doctrine, but rather the distinctive teaching of persons who were no longer in communion with the church.[17]

According to the Church Fathers, the founder of the Gnostic Movement was Simon Magus, the Samaritan, who appears in Acts 8:9-24 as a magician who tried to bribe Peter.[18] He was reported to have written a book called *The Great Tidings*, to have claimed that he was a divine incarnation, and to have made his disciples practise a libertine way of life. Hippolytus in his treatise against heresy quotes from Simon's book, which reveals plainly Gnostic ideas: God as totally the other, individual souls as reflections of this God, world-creation through a series of intermediaries, and the notion of Ennoia as incarnate wisdom or as wisdom held captive in Helen.[19] One of his disciples was the Samaritan Menander who claimed to be a savior sent from above.

What is remarkable about the tradition of Simon Magus is the suggestion that there existed some form of Gnosticism already in the first century. Recent studies of the Pauline and Johannine works by scholars and the recent discovery of additional Gnostic documents at Nag-Hammadi increasingly confirm the view that

---

[17] Wisse, 139-140.
[18] Jonas, *Gnostic Religion*, 103, thinks that there are two Simons.
[19] Jonas, *Gnostic Religion*, passim.

during the New Testament times already there existed varieties of Gnosticism in the Mediterranean world. Robert McL. Wilson in his well-known book *The Gnostic Problem* (1958, 1964) argues that no movement springs as full-grown like Athene from Zeus' head but that a movement develops by stages and that ideas which were later stigmatized as Gnostic may not have struck at an earlier period as heretical. He would apply the term *gnosis* to the New Testament period not as a system but as a pervasive atmosphere which enveloped all contemporary religions and philosophies to a certain extent. Wilson writes:

> In short, Gnosticism in the broader sense is a general tendency of the period which saw the birth of Christianity, and makes its presence felt in various ways in all the thoughts of the time. In a narrower sense, the name is applied to certain types of speculation which appeared in the first two centuries of the Christian era, and whose chief characteristic was the assimilation of Christianity more or less completely to the ideas of the contemporary world. These Christian Gnostics thus apply to the Christian Gospel the ideas of the wider Gnosticism around them.[20]

Elsewhere, Wilson shows inclination to concur with the views of the older scholars in this field who thought that Christian Gnosticism arose as an "attempt to express Christianity in Hellenistic terms, without the safeguards which Paul and his fellow-laborers imposed upon their work. Speculations of a Gnostic type, as has been said, were already current before Christianity appeared on the scene, and there were in later days pagan systems closely akin the to the Christian Gnosis."[21] James M. Robinson in his introduction to the edition of the Nag-Hammadi library, after noting "the long-standing debate among historians of religion as to whether Gnosticism is to be understood as only an inner-Christian development or as a movement broader than, and hence independent of, and perhaps even prior to Christianity," states clearly: "This debate seems to be resolving itself, on the basis of the Nag-Hammadi library, in favor of understanding Gnosticism as a much broader phenomenon than early Christian heresy-hunters would lead one to think."[22]

As for the ideological origins of the Gnostic movement, there is not enough evidence to argue that the varied theological and philosophical ideas have had their original home in Judaism

---

[20] Wilson, 263.
[21] Wilson, 68.
[22] James M. Robinson, ed., *The Nag-Hammadi Library in English* (San Francisco, 1977), 6.

especially since the Christian forms of Gnosticism show strong anti-Jewish bias. It cannot, however, be denied that Gnostic ideas can be found in the Qumran scrolls of heterodox Jews.[23] On the other hand, Gnostic ideas are more pagan than Jewish.

On the issue of the various sources of Gnosticism, MacRae makes the following generalizations:

> Gnosticism grew out of the confrontation of a broad syncretistic movement which flourished especially in Egypt, in Syria and Asia Minor, and eventually in Rome, with Christianity. The syncretism consisted in a tendency to adopt into one pattern of thought elements from all the religions and philosophies current in the Hellenistic world. To this amalgam ancient Iranian religion contributed the cosmic dualism that forms a basic element of nearly all varieties of Gnosticism. From Egypt came elements of the cult of Isis and Osiris; from Babylonia the influence of astrology and the planetary gods; from Syria, Greece, and Rome cultic features of the mystery religions and magic; from Judaism a host of Old Testament figures and many variations on the creation story; and from Greece, again, the philosophical currents of Stoicism and Neo-Pythagoreanism....Finally, Christianity lent to the Syncretistic movement the role of the Savior Christ.[24]

MacRae is not quite right about Christianity's contribution of the Gnostic soteriology. Also, he ignores the important contribution that the Indian thought has made to the rise and development of Gnostic thought in the Hellenistic world. Take, for instance, Gnostic soteriology. The notion of the Gnostic savior is older than Christianity, and is therefore independent of Christianity as well as of Judaism which does not possess such a soteriology. The Gnostic idea of the descending redeemer, on the other hand, is found in Buddhism and Hinduism. Therefore, Christian soteriology must be derived from Hinduism and Buddhism via Gnosticism. Recently Kurt Rudolph argued without making any reference to Hinduism and Buddhism:

> The idea of a descending Redeemer is a strange, Hellenistic one for the original Christian kerygma as well; it is, I think, connected with the beginnings of Gnostic thinking; it is found already in Paul's writings and then above all in the Fourth Gospel. Probably it would still be hard to decide here who gave and who received. At any rate Christology (and soteriology) as attested in the New Testament was born when Gnostic and Hellenistic ideas were already in the air.[25]

---

[23] Sedlar, 140-144.
[24] Mac Rae, 528.
[25] Kurt Rudolph, "'Gnosis' and 'Gnosticism'," in *The New Testament and Gnosis*, eds. A. H. B. Logan and A. J. M. Wedderburn (Edinburgh, 1983), 30.

What is important to note here is that the Christian writing of the first and second centuries "reflects the growth and emergence of Christian thought and conduct in a dialogue with its environment involving agreement and disagreement. Part of this environment was undoubtedly a Gnostic viewpoint, not only in matters of ideology and theology, but also on practical matters."[26] There is probably much truth in the statement that underlying Gnosticism is the assumption that all religions are equally true because all are myths symbolizing the very same eternal verities. The Gnostics seem to have fused together elements from Buddhism, Hinduism, Zoroastrianism, Judaism, Hellenism, and Christianity. In this context van Baaren's assessment of the origin of Gnosticism is credible:

> Gnosticism is a historic development of the last centuries before and the first centuries after the beginning our era, taking place in the countries surrounding the Mediterranean, roughly coinciding with the Roman Empire, and forming part of the syncretistic religious situation in this time and this place. It is, of course, of great importance to discover the historic sources of gnosticism, but not always, perhaps not very often, is this knowledge essential for our understanding of gnosticism as it is found in our sources because the history of religion teaches us that in many cases foreign elements are accepted only to be treated as part of the borrower's own religion with complete disregard or misunderstanding of their original significance and function. This then is a matter in which each instance is to be judged on its own merits and where no sweeping generalizations are feasible. Historically considered, gnosticism has many roots. I am not yet convinced by any theory deriving gnosticism mainly or even exclusively from one source. Iranian, Near Eastern, Greek, Judaic, and Christian influences have all cooperated in the formation of gnosticism.[27]

There are two theses implied and to be further clarified in the brief discussion of Gnosticism in this study: one, the Christian scriptures, canonical and non-canonical, were written in a Gnostic milieu so much so Gnostic ideas and allusions are found in several Christian scriptures; two, Gnosticism and Buddhism/Hinduism have numerous ideas in common so much so Gnosticism must have borrowed a good many of them from the earlier Indian thought since no other religious system offers such an array of Gnostic ideas.

---

[26] Rudolph, 31.
[27] Th. van Baaren, in U. Bianchi, 176.

B. Gnosticism and the Christian Scriptures

The logion of Matthew 11:25-27: "At that time Jesus answered and said: I confess to thee, O Father, Lord of heaven and earth, because thou hast hid these things from the wise and prudent, and hast revealed them to little ones. Yea, Father, for so hath it seemed good in thy sight. All things are delivered to me by my Father. And no one knoweth the Son, but the Father; neither doth any one know the Father, but the Son, and he to whom it shall please the son to reveal him" is difficult to explain in its Matthean setting;[28] its language clearly suggests Gnostic overtones in spite of its affinities to Qumran texts, which also use Gnostic words.[29]

The "Pauline" Pastoral Epistles refer to Gnostics who are the "opponents." The writer is warning against Gnostics as a general threat. The orthodox Epistle 2 Timothy repudiates two Gnostic Christians at the beginning of the second century:

> Avoid empty and worldly chatter; those who indulge in it will stray further and further into godless discourse, and the infection of their teaching will spread like a gangrene. Such are Hymenaeus and Philetus; they have shot wide of the truth in saying that our resurrection has already taken place, and are upsetting people's faith (2:16-18).

The view that the Christian's resurrection has already taken place as a spiritual reality is advocated in the Gnostic *Treatise on Resurrection*, the *Exegesis on the Soul*, and the *Gospel of Philip* in the Nag-Hammadi library.[30]

A number of these Gnostic preachers tried to impress women (2 Timothy 3:6) and expected payment from their clients (Titus 1:11); they engaged in speculative myths (1 Timothy 1:4; 4:7; 2 Timothy 4:4; Titus 3:9) and claimed a higher esoteric knowledge (1 Timothy 6:20); they were ascetics who disdained creation (1 Timothy 4:3 ff).[31] The First Epistle to Timothy clearly states that the Gnostic heretics were confusing Christian believers with "godless chatter and contradictions of what is falsely called gnosis" (1 Timothy 6:20); this type of Gnostaicism was an encratite movement which showed its contempt for the body and for all matter by prohibiting

---

[28] Mac Rae, 522.
[29] W. D. Davies, "'Knowledge' in the Dead Sea Scrolls and Matthew 11:25-30," *Harvard Theological Review* 46 (1953): 113-139); Menahem Mansoor, "The Nature of Gnosticism in Qumran," in U. Bianchi, 389-400.
[30] Robinson, 4-5.
[31] F. Wisse, 142.

marriage and the eating of many kinds of foods (4:3).[32] Wisse points out that Hymenaeus and Philetus, the two leaders,

> are most likely the real opponents of the author. He laces them in the context of the despised Gnostics just as the heresiologists did with their contemporary opponents. The author also used the clever device, perfected by the heresiologists, of linking the contemporary Gnostics with the "heretics" of the past. For the Paulinist author these are the circumcision party (Titus 1:10), the teachers of the law (1 Timothy 1:7) whom the great Apostle had already refuted.[33]

In Second Corinthians Paul battles also against the striving after false wisdom (2 and 3), against a rigorous abstinence (7), against a misdirected sense of freedom (8-10), and against the denial of bodily resurrection (15), all of which can be traced back to a basic Gnostic attitude.

One important reference found in the Deutero-Pauline Epistle to the Colossians is the concept of the worship of the Angels, Principalities, and Powers. Hans-Martin Schenke thinks that this notion of the worship of angels is Gnostic-inspired. He writes:

> According to the general world view of Gnosticism, the Gnostics themselves, though in principle already redeemed, are nonetheless subject to the domination of the Archons. Between the realm of light and the world of humans lies the domain of the Archons, who are opposed to the light above and to the light that is in humans as soul or spirit. The Redeemer has secretly passed through the realm of the Archons, has brought humans the redeeming knowledge, and at his triumphal return above has prepared for the Gnostic the way through the realm of the Archons into the realm of light....Probably the "angels" or "principalities and powers" to which the "worship" of our heretics is directed correspond to these Archons of Gnosticism.[34]

Similarly in the case of Ephesians, Schenke sees traces of Gnosticism:

> Again further Gnostic or mythological conceptions are applied to Christ: Ephesians 2:14-18—the breaking down of the dividing wall between the world above and the world below by the Redeemer...; 4:8-10—the return of the redeemer into the world of light and the triumph over the Archons...; 5:25b—32 the church as the Savior's female partner to be redeemed. The Gnostic background of this last passage must of course be seen much more concretely than it appears, e.g. in Schlier.[35]

---

[32] Rudolf Schnackenburg, "Early Gnosticism," in *Jesus in His Time*, ed. H. J. Schultz (Philadelphia, 1971), 139.
[33] Wisse, 143.
[34] Schenke, in *New Testament and Gnosis*, 11-12.
[35] H.-M. Schenke and K. M. Fischer, *Einleitung in die Schriften des Neuen Testaments*, I (Berlin, 1978-7) in *New Testament and Gnosis*, 13.

186 CHAPTER SIX

Helmut Koester has discussed the impact of Gnosticism on Q—the celebrated source of Matthew and Luke—1 and 2 Corinthians, Ephesians, Hebrews, the Pastoral Epistles, and 2 Peter as well as Nag Hammadi Codex . He writes:

> In the tradition of the sayings of Jesus, Gnosticism appears in the emphasis upon, and the predominance of, wisdom sayings, and in the spiritualizing of the eschatological sayings of Jesus. The *Gospel of Thomas* offers this interpretation of the sayings under the apostolic authority of Thomas, a tradition that seems to have continued under the name of this particular apostle in communities in Syria....Within the circle of Johannine churches, gnostic interpretation is again tied to the sayings of Jesus, which were used for the development of dialogue materials in which Jesus speaks about the presence of eschatological salvation, mediated through himself as the revealer from the heavenly world of the Father, the home of all those who are able to hear his voice. The basic concept of the hymn, used by the author of the Gospel of John for his prologue, demonstrates the intimate connection between the myth of Wisdom and the gnostic understanding of Christian revelation. A fully developed gnostic christology, however, does not appear until later among the opponents of 1 John and in the *Acts of John*, where it took shape in explicit controversy with the Gospel's attempts to amalgamate the concept of the gnostic revealer with the kerygma of the death and resurrection of the earthly Jesus.[36]

Most scholars today readily admit that the Gospel of John includes more Gnostic elements than any other books of the New Testament. The Gnostic environment of this gospel is a viable alternative to the often-suggested Qumran context according to Schenke:

> In the question as to the background of the Fourth Gospel, in any case the Gnostic and the Essene...worlds must remain alternatives. And against Qumran, which has clear advantages with regard to the age of the attestation, there is the argument that precisely the main point, the special Christology of the Fourth Gospel, is generally recognized to be in no way derivable from Qumran, whereas New Testament scholarship needs precisely a place where the whole of the strange statements of the Fourth Gospel are intelligible....The author takes up the dualistic conception that every person has a place of origin, be it from God or from the devil, and that one reveals this origin in one's conduct. In the formulation "to come from," "to be born from God," the ethical dualism is rooted in Gnostics, not in Qumran. In Qumran mankind is determined by the power for which one decides: God or Belial. But in Gnosticism on the other hand one is determined by one's place or origin: light or darkness. Or, put otherwise: in Qumran the dualism is an apocalyptic historical occurrence, in Gnosticism a metaphysical definition of one'

---

[36] H. Koester, *Introduction to the New Testament* , 2 vols (Philadelphia: Fortress, 1982), II: 208.

essence. In spite of all attempts to affirm Qumran as the sphere of influence, one must hold to the view that the Johannine circle is in this matter clearly influenced by Gnosticism. It has taken over this dualism and made it its own, but not in a cosmological interest, but rather in a soteriological and practical, ethical interest.[37]

In Schenke's view, the Gnosticism of John is not Gnosticism pure and simple, but rather a toned-down Gnosticism. It is "the stump of a fully developed Gnosticism whose roots and limbs have been cut off in order to suspend it in a Christian framework. This is clearest...in that Jesus...promises again and again to reveal what he has seen and heard from the Father, without ever fulfilling this promise."[38]

In Kurt Rudolph's view, Gnosticism is deeply rooted in the Fourth Gospel and the Johannine Epistles: The redeemer is presented in the garb of a gnostic redeemer; dualism—of light and darkness, truth and lie, "above" and "beneath," God and devil— pervades the entire narrative. Mankind is divided into two classes: those who know God and thus coming from him and those who do not know him and are of this world or of the devil. Knowledge is identified with faith; freedom from the world is freedom from sin (John 8:31-36), and resurrection has already taken place in the act of faith (John 5:24; 11:25). "The view, advocated by E. Käsemann, that in the author (or authors) of the Johannine writings a heretic has found a place as a Christian witness within the New Testament is, under these circumstances, fully justified. The author...'is a Christian gnostic who possessed the altogether unimaginable boldness to write a gospel of the Christ experienced by him, who addresses the world of Gnosis'."[39]

What is more important to point out in this regard about the Fourth Gospel is that its anti-Jewishness is perhaps due to its Gnostic strain.[40] Though one may strongly argue that John is an anti-Gnostic work in its present form, it is noteworthy that the Gnostics seized it, probably in its earlier versions, and interpreted it to fit their views. Origen wrote his own commentary on John against the first Gnostic commentary of Heracleon (Schnackenburg, 140). Also Paul—Tertullian branded him as *haereticorum apostolus*—was championed by the Gnostics, which seems to suggest that Paul as

---

[37] Schenke, in *New Testament and Gnosis*, 16.
[38] Schenke, 15.
[39] Rudolph, *Gnosis: The Nature and History of Gnosticism* (New York, 1987), 306.
[40] See Pheme Perkins, *The Gnostic Dialogue*. (New York, 1980), 16-17.

well as John was considered a kindred spirit by the Christian Gnostics.

What we see in the Gospel of John and in the Epistles of Paul is not just Gnosticism pure and simple but rather an uneasy alliance between Hellenistic Gnostic thought and Jewish Christianity. Bultmann sees struggles between various tendencies in the "syncretistic" early Christianity, which he describes as follows:

> The person of Jesus is sometimes defined in terms of Jewish and apocalyptic categories, sometimes as the "Lord" of cultus, as a mystery deity, sometimes again as the Gnostic redeemer, the pre-existent being from the heavenly world, whose earthly body is only an outward garb. This explains why the "rulers of this world" failed to recognize him, as only "his own" can. The Christian community is sometimes described in Old Testament categories as the people of God, the true seed of Abraham, sometimes in Gnostic categories as the "body of Christ," in which individuals are incorporated by means of the sacraments of baptism, and the Lord's Supper. Of course, some of these concepts are confined to particular writings or groups of writings in the New Testament (which varies a great deal in its language and thought). But they are also to be found side by side or in combination in the same author, especially in Paul and the Epistle to the Hebrews.[41]

What I have tried to do in this section is to show traces of Gnosticism in the canonical books of the New Testament. It is unnecessary to demonstrate again the obvious and generally accepted fact that many of the texts discovered at Nag-Hammadi are Gnostic texts written and used by Christians. This is because, as Martin Krause argues, "Gnosticism and Christianity accommodated themselves to one another in Egypt, in keeping with the syncretistic mode of thinking of the Egyptians in all ages and not for the first time in late antiquity. This resulted in a Christian Gnosticism which left its mark in Christian Gnostic writings."[42] However, in spite of co-existence, often opposition surfaced; there is enough evidence for this in the works of Tertullian and Ireneus. Naturally, the opposition was mutual. Just as the Pauline corpus, Tertullian, and Ireneus attacked the Gnostics, some of the Nag-Hammadi authors criticized the so-called orthodox Christians. The *Second Treatise of the Great Seth* complains against orthodox Christianity, contrasting it with the "true church" of the Gnostics: "We were hated and persecuted not only by those who are ignorant

---

[41] Rudolf Bultmann, *Primitive Christianity in Its Contemporary Setting* (Philadelphia, 1983), 178-179.

[42] Martin Krause, "The Christianization of Gnostic Texts," in *New Testament and Gnosis*, 187-188.

[pagans] but also by those who think they are advancing the name of Christ since they were unknowingly empty, not knowing who they are, like dumb animals."[43] "The *Apocalypse of Peter* has Christ criticize the orthodox as follows:

> They will cleave to the name of a dead man, thinking that they will become pure. But they will become greatly defiled and they will fall into a name of error and into the hand of an evil, cunning man and a manifold dogma, and they will be ruled heretically. For some of them will blaspheme the truth and proclaim evil teaching. And they will say evil things against each other....But many others, who oppose the truth and are the messengers of error, will set up their error and their law against these pure thoughts of mine, as looking out from one (perspective), thinking that good and evil are from one (source). They do business in my word....*And there shall be others of those who are outside our number who name themselves bishop and also deacons, as if they have received their authority from God.* They bend themselves under the judgment of the leaders. These people are dry canals (italics mine).[44]

When the Roman empire embraced the orthodox brand of Christianity, the Gnostics became an endangered species. About the time the Nag-Hammadi library was being collected, Epiphanius, the Bishop of Cyprus, reported how authorities suppressed the Gnostics:

> I have had a brush with this sect myself, beloved, and got my information about its customs in person, straight from the mouths of its members. Women who believed this nonsense offered it to me, and told me the kind of thing I have been describing. In their brazen impudence, what is more, they tried to seduce me, like that vicious, wicked Egyptian woman who was married to the chief cook—I was young, and this made me attractive to them....For the women who told me about this salacious myth were outwardly very charming, but all the devil's ugliness was in their vile minds. However, the merciful God saved me from their depravity. Then, while I was at it, I read their books, understood what they really intended and was not entrapped as they had been; their literature left me unmoved. And I promptly reported these people to the local bishops, and found which of them were masquerading as members of the church. And so they were driven out of the city, about eighty of them, and it was cleansed of their rank, thorny growth.[45]

All this shows that Gnosticism was a force reckoned with in the New Testament times and an intellectual tradition to be reckoned with in our own understanding of the formation of the books of the New Testament.

---

[43] See Pagels, 123.
[44] Robinson, 5.
[45] Robinson, 5.

C. *Gnosticism and Indian Thought*

I have justifiably argued above, though not in great detail, that the New Testament writers were quite aware of Gnostic ideas and Gnostic sects. As for the non-Christian sources of Gnosticism, there is general agreement that they are quite varied. For instance, the *Paraphrase of Shem* and the *Apocalypse of Adam*, Sethian documents, may simply be outgrowths of a Jewish Gnostic group. Other texts in the Nag-Hammadi library, like *Zostrianos*, *Marsanes*, and *Allogenes* show philosophic and Neoplatonic orientations. There are then Hermetic texts like the *Discourse on the Eighth and Ninth*.[46] However, so far scholars have not made any serious research and study on the relationship between Gnostic thought and India except for a handful of minor references to the possible interaction between Gnostic and Indian religious thought.[47] The obvious reason for this scholarly neglect is the difficulty of the undertaking. Unlike the corpus of the Gnostic texts, the Indian sources are voluminous. A comparative study of Indian and Gnostic texts is not only provocative but also infinitely enriching to biblical scholarship and intellectual history. In the following pages I can only give intimations of the complexities of the issue and the rewards awaiting future scholars. As Dryden would put it, here is God's plenty.

Common to both is the conviction that a correct insight into the self and the nature of the world liberates the human soul from them and effects a reunion with the Transcendent which is ultimately the Self itself. First I will list some features that are common to the Indian and Gnostic traditions—many of which are the ones pointed out by Conze (652-665)—, then develop the notions of radical dualism, gnosis, salvation, and the role of the redeemer in both traditions, and finally give some illustrative examples from Indian works and Christian scriptures:

1. The divine being is indefinable and infinite.
2. There is an opposing principle of evil, which is matter.

---

[46] Robinson, 7-9.

[47] Isaac Jacob Schmidt, "Über die Verwandtschaft der gnostisch-theosophischen Lehren mit den Relgionssystemen des Orients, vozüglich dem Buddhaismus" (Leipzig, 1828),IV:1-25 ; J. Doresse, *The Secret Books of the Egyptian Gnostics* (New York, 1960), 284-285; G. Woodcock, *The Greeks in India*, London, 1966), 157-158); Jean Sedlar, 124-139; G. Tucci, *Tibetan Painted Scrolls*, I(1949); Edward Conze, "Buddhism and Gnosis," in Ugo Bianchi, 631-667.

3. There is also a principle of good which is opposed to the principle of evil.

4. The infinite communicates with matter in a series of emanations.

5. The cosmos is the result of of the descent of the spirit into matter.

6. Deliverance of spirit from matter is effected through asceticism and contemplation leading to gnosis or wisdom.

7. Gnosis is not merely intellectual knowledge, but seeing God or God-realization.

8. This gnosis is the realization by the soul of its heavenly origin and is a gift of the Redeemer who has descended from the realm of light to teach the way of deliverance or remembrance.

9. This gnosis is also piety, and piety to the Redeemer leads to gnosis.

10. The perfect man is free from the world and is master of himself, for he has realized the truth, has passed from death to life, and has risen from the natural and put on the spiritual state.

11. The Gnostic Satan is a tempter of holy men.

12.There is a sharp division between the aristocracy of the perfect/elect and the ordinary folk of hearers. In Buddhism there are the monks and aryas or the spiritually awakened as opposed to the ignorant and children, especially the hearers (*sravakas*).

13. In the Mahayana tradition wisdom is personified and worshiped as prajnaparamita who plays a role similar to the role Sophia plays in the Gnostic tradition.

14. Both systems are fond of connecting serpents to wisdom.

15. Both rely on the power of secret formulas (*mantras*).

16. Both place great emphasis on light.

17. Salvation is likened to awakening, and consequently there is a tendency to regard this world as a dream or as unsubstantial. Incidentally, I wonder whether the two following biblical episodes have veiled Gnostic associations: the scene in Gethsemene where Jesus prays awake and tells the Apostles, "Could you not watch one hour with me?...Watch and pray so that you may not enter into temptation; the spirit is indeed willing but the flesh is weak" (Matt. 26:38-41) and the scenario of the resurrection of Lazarus where Jesus tells his disciples that he is going to wake up Lazarus (John 11:11-13).

18. In both systems, sexual intercourse played a decisive role in the gradual deterioration of mankind.[48]

19. The two following passages that use the metaphor of gold in the context of the divine spark in humans are tantalizingly similar. "As gold sunk in filth will not lose its beauty but preserve its own nature, and the filth will be unable to impair the gold."[49] "Supposing that gold belonging to a man on his travels had fallen into a place full of stinking dirt. As it is indestructible by nature, it would stay there for many hundreds of years."[50]

20. The Indian doctrine of the multiple divine incarnations is found in the Bactrian Gnostic doctrine according to which the son of God was not incarnated for the first time in Bethlehem, but was incarnated before and will be incarnated again in the future, as mentioned in Hippolytus' *Philosophoumena*.[51]

21. The Gnostic elect's predilection for monastic life was probably patterned after the monastic life of the Buddhist monks.

22. The theory of Buddha's triple body seems to underlie the Alexandrian Christians' speculations about Jesus' transcendental body, St. Paul's mystical body, and especially Mani's triple Jesus. The three forms of Jesus are (i) transcendental, corresponding to Buddha's *dharmakaya*, (ii) historical, who only apparently underwent the Passion, corresponding to the *nirmanakaya*, (iii) Jesus *patibilis*, similar to Buddha's *sambhogakaya*.[52]

23. "How could anyone miss the resemblance between the theme of the seduction of the celestial Archons by the Virgin of the Light—a favorite theme with both Gnostics and Manichaeans—and the episode of Vishnu changing himself into a dazzling courtesan, in order to get back from the *asuras* (the Titans) the ambrosia they had stolen [read: obtained rightfully] after the churning of the Sea of Milk?"[53] And Doresse is right.

24. "How, above all, could one neglect another extraordinary feature—that, in the mythology of the *Mahabharata*, there is a White Mountain, Svetaparvata, situated in the regions beyond the darkness of this world? For there, again, is the Mountain of Lights, dear to Zoroastrian, Gnostic and Mandaean traditions. And the Seven Guardians whom the Mandaeans located precisely there,

---

[48] Conze, 664.
[49] See Jonas, 271
[50] Conze, *Buddhist Texts*, 182-183.
[51] Conze, 664.
[52] Conze, 664-65; see also H. de Lubac, *La rencontre du Bouddhisme et de l'occident*, 9-32.
[53] Jean Doresse, *The Secret Books of the Egyptian Gnostics* (New York, 1960),284.

where the Gnostics also knew them to be, now appear to us—though doubtless the same—in the form of serpents with seven heads."[54]

Fundamental to all forms of Gnosticism is the assumption that God cannot but be good and the world is full of suffering and hence evil. Since effect is somehow contained in the cause, God who is pure light and goodness cannot be the maker of the world and everything in it lest he be tainted with evil. In the Eastern variant of Gnosticism, this basic dualism is radical: The beneficent deity (Pirit or Father Goodness) is co-eternal with and co-equal to the maleficent deity (Darkness, Matter, or Satan). At some point fragments of light which are human souls were seduced by Darkness and became embedded in matter. By contrast, on the Western front, there is a single principle of the cosmos, which allowed itself to emanate into a demiurge which in turn produced one angel, then another angel, and so on. Among these lower emanations is the demiurge which created the world. Since all these intermediaries are not the same as each other, they are finite and hence somewhat prone to evil not only in the metaphysical sphere but also in the moral universe. Since God has refrained from creating the evil world, he is not evil at all. With the soul's long association with matter, it forgets its true nature, becomes "numb," "drunk," and "asleep." This extreme dualism seems to be diametrically opposed to the Greek conception of orderliness in the cosmos as well as to the Hebrew view of the universe as good and as created by God.

According to the Gnostics, ignorance is the root of all evil, and suffering. As the *Gospel of Truth* puts it, "Ignorance...brought about anguish and terror. And the anguish grew solid like a fog, so that no one was able to see. For this reason error is powerful." (17.10-16).[55] In fact, many people live in a state of complete oblivion and confusion until they receive knowledge. The *Gospel of Truth* describes this state of affairs in the "Nightmare Parable":

> They were sunk in sleep and found themselves in disturbing dreams. Either (there is) a place to which they are fleeing, or, without strength, they come (from) having chased after others, or they are involved in striking blows, or they are receiving blows themselves, or they have fallen from high places, or they take off into the air though they do not even have wings....When those who are going through all these things wake up, they see nothing, they who were in the midst of these disturbances, for they are nothing. Such is the way of those who have

---

[54] Doresse, 284-285.
[55] *The Nag Hammadi Library* (*NHL*), ed. James M. Robinson (San Francisco, 1977), 38.

cast ignorance aside as sleep, leaving [its works] behind like a dream in the night...This is the way everyone has acted, as though asleep at the time when he was ignorant. And this is the way he has come to knowledge, as if he had awakened (29.8-30).[56]

This ignorance is primarily lack of self-knowledge, and self-ignorance is a form of self-destruction:

If one does not [understand] how the fire came to be, he will burn in it, because he does not know his root. If one does not first understand the water, he does not know anything....If one does not understand how the wind that blows came to be, he will run with it. If one does not understand how the body that he wears came to be, he will perish with it....Whoever does not understand how he came will not understand how he will go.[57]

Every human being bears within himself the potential for self-knowledge and self-fulfillment. Jesus says in the *Gospel of Thomas*: If you bring forth what is within you will save you. If you do not bring forth what is within you, what you do not bring forth will destroy you" (45.30-33).[58] He continues:

The Kingdom is inside of you, and it is outside of you. When you come to know yourselves, then you will be known, and you will realize that you are the sons of the living Father. But if you will not know yourselves, then you dwell in poverty, and it is you who are that poverty (32.19-33.5).[59]

This knowledge of the self is at once knowledge of God because the true self of a person is divine because it is a part of God. According to Hippolytus, Simon Magus claimed that each human being is a divine dwelling place, "and that in him dwells an infinite power...the root of the universe."[60] This knowledge of divine makes the knower enlightened as to his own divinity. Allogenes explains his own process of spiritual development: "[I was] very disturbed, and [I] turned to myself....[Having] seen the light that [surrounded] me and the good that was within me, I became divine" (52.8-12)[61] In the *Book of Thomas the Contender*, the Saviors tells Thomas:

Now since it has been said that you are my twin and true companion, examine yourself that you may understand who you are, in what way

---

[56] *NHL* 38; E. Pagels (143-169) develops these ideas at length to whom I am indebted to many of the Gnostic references that follow.
[57] *Dialogue of the Savior* 134.1-22 in *NHL*, 234.
[58] *NHL*, 126.
[59] *NHL*, 118.
[60] Hippolytus, 6.9.
[61] *NHL*, 446.

you exist, and how you will come to be. Since you are called my brother, it is not fitting that you be ignorant of yourself and to know that you have understood, because you had already understood that I am the knowledge of the truth. So while you accompany me, although you are uncomprehending, you have (in fact) already come to know, and you will be called "the one who knows himself." For he who has not known himself has known nothing, but he who has known himself has at the same time already achieved knowledge about the Depth of the All (II.7).[62]

It follows from these considerations that knowledge in the Gnostic context has a religious and supernatural meaning, and *Gnosis* means primarily knowledge of God experienced in a state of illumination. Since redemption for the Gnostic believer consists in freedom from the bonds of matter, which is ignorance, it is removed by means of the knowledge of self which is identified with God. But this knowledge is often mediated through the Revealer or the Redeemer, who is often the risen Jesus who has descended from the realm of Light. But it is the disciple himself who must bring about his enlightenment. In the *Discourse on the Eighth and the Nineth* the student reminds his spiritual master of a promise: "[O my father], yesterday you promised me [that you would bring] my mind into [the] eighth and afterwards you would bring me into the ninth. You said that this is the order of the tradition." The teacher assents, but reminds him that the disciple himself must bring forth the understanding. As they join in prayer, first the master enters a trance; then the disciple follows suit:

When he had finished praising he shouted, "Father Trismegistus! What shall I say: We have received this light. And I myself see the same vision in you, I see the eighth and the souls that are in it and the angels singing a hymn to the ninth and its powers.... I pray to the end of the universe and the beginning of the beginning, to the object of man's quest, the immortal discovery....I see myself! I have received power from thee. For thy love has reached us.[63]

This Gnostic world-view reflects many ideas basic to Hinduism and Buddhism. I shall give a brief outline of the essential religious teachings of classical India of the pre-Christian times on the relationship between God and the human being in the context of human salvation through gnosis.

The essential primary doctrine of the Upanishadic literature is an idealistic monism, which consists in the assertion that all is one and that the phenomenal world is unreal. Only Brahman, the

---

[62] *NHL*, 189.
[63] *Discourse on the Eighth and the Ninth* 58.31-61.2 in *NHL* 295-296.

unknown self, is real. The human self, which imagines itself to be distinct from all other selves, is in error; in reality it itself is the Supreme Self, the Brahman. The purpose of human life is to overcome ignorance with regard to this doctrine and realize the Brahman-Atman identity: "His form is not capable of being seen; with the eye no one sees Him. They who know Him thus with the heart, with the mind, as abiding in the heart, become immortal."[64] "He is a universal deity who Himself is the universe which He includes within His own being. He is the light within us, *hrdyantar jyotih*."(*Rg Veda*, X. 121.2).[65] "Higher than this is the Brahman, the supreme, the great hidden in all creatures according to their bodies, the one who envelopes the universe, knowing Him, the Lord, (men) become immortal (*Svetasvatara*, III.7). "When Brahman is known...birth and death cease" (*Svetasvatara* II.15). "He who sees the true nature of Brahman...is freed from all fetters" (*Svetasvatara* VI.12-15). Here I would like to quote two passages, one from the *Brhadaranyaka Upanishad* and the other from a post-Buddha writing that should remind us of the "Nightmare Parable" of Gnosticism cited earlier:

> Verily, there are just two states of this person (the state of being) in this world and the state of being in the other world. There is an intermediate third state, that of being in sleep-dream. By standing in this intermediate state one sees both those states, of being in this world and of being in the other world. Now whatever the way is to the state of being in the other world, having obtained that way one sees both the evils of this world and the joys of the other world. When he goes to sleep he takes along the material of this all-embracing world, himself tears it apart, himself builds it up; he sleeps (dreams) by his own brightness, by his own light. In that state the person becomes self-illumined (IV.3.9).[66]

In the third station of Deep Sleep there is no empirical consciousness, but an identification with the Brahman. The same Upanishad, on which Gerard Manley Hopkins's "Windhover" is probably based, continues:

> As a falcon or eagle having flown around in the sky becomes weary, folds its wings and is borne down to its nest, even so this person hastens to that state where he desires no desires and sees no dream....This is his form which is free from craving, free from evils, free from fear. As a man when in the embrace of his beloved wife knows nothing without or within, so the person when in the embrace of the intelligent self (Brahman) knows nothing without or within. That,

---

[64] *Svetasvatara*, IV.20; Radhakrishnan, 23.
[65] Radhakrishnan, 23.
[66] Radhakrishnan, 257.

verily, is his form in which his desire is fulfilled, in which the self is his desire, in which he is without desire, free from any sorrow. There in that state a father is not a father, a mother is not a mother, the worlds are not the worlds, the gods are not the gods, the Vedas are not the Vedas....He is not affected by good; he is not affected by evil, for then he has passed beyond all the sorrows of the heart....This is his highest goal; this is his highest treasure; this is his highest world; this is his greatest bliss. (III.3.19-33).

This last passage seems to underlie the following coda from the Gospel of Thomas, which should be understood in a mystical sense:

Jesus saw infants being suckled. He said to His disciples, "These infants being suckled are like those who enter the Kingdom." They said to Him, "Shall we then, as children, enter the Kingdom?" Jesus said to them, "When you make the two one, and when you make inside like the outside and the outside like the inside, and the above like the below, and when you make the male and the female one and the same, so that the male not be male nor the female female; and when you fashion eyes in place of an eye, and a hand in place of a hand, and a foot in place of a foot, and a likeness in place of a likeness; then will you enter the Kingdom" (22).[67]

The following text from the *Gaudapada*, which describes a fourth state of being, reverses the symbols of waking and sleeping; the true awakening is a sleeping to the world:

Dreams and sleep belong to the two first,
A dreamless sleep is the possession of the third,
Neither dreams nor sleep does he who knows it
Ascribe to the fourth.

The dreamer's knowledge is false,
The sleeper knows nothing at all.
Both go astray; where all this vanishes
There the fourth state is reached.

It is in the beginningless illusion of the world
That the soul sleeps: when it awakes,
Then there awakes in it the eternal,
Timeless and free from dreams and sleep alike.[68]

It became gradually clear that such a lofty metaphysical doctrine was intelligible only to the elite who alone had the

---

[67] *NHL*, 121.
[68] Cited by A. K. Coomaraswamy, *Buddha and the Gospel of Buddhism* (New York, 1964), 192.

leisure to devote their lives to the pursuit of contemplative life. Naturally, the the lay people were left out this world of contemplation and the life of perfection. Hence later Upanishads, like the *Svetasvatara*, developed a secondary doctrine, a theistic doctrine, which does not convey the secret of the highest knowledge but offers a path of salvation to all and sundry, as a concession to the masses who see multiplicity in the universe: the individual human soul, created by or emanating from the Supreme, is distinct and free, and when it becomes enlightened it will return to the Supreme Soul (*paramatman*) whence it was derived. The Supreme is that "from which these beings are born, that by which they live and that into which, when departing, they enter" (*Taittiriya Upanishad*).[69] This theistic secondary doctrine, thus, avoids ultimate duality.[70]

A good example of the secondary doctrine, which bears close resemblance to some of the metaphors of the Gnostic mythology, is found in the *Maitri* Upanishad:

> Verily, that subtle, ungraspable, invisible one, called the person, dwells here in the body with a part of himself with previous awareness even as the man who is fast asleep awakes of his own awareness. Now, assuredly that part of him, which is entirely intelligent in every person is the spirit which has the marks of conception, determination, and self-love, *Prajapati* called Visva....Verily, in the beginning Prajapati stood alone. He had no happiness, being alone. Then, meditating on himself, he created numerous offspring. He saw them to be like a stone, without understanding, without life, standing like a post. He had no happiness. He then thought to himself, "let me enter within in order to awaken (enlighten) them." He made himself like the wind and sought to enter into him. Being one, he could not do it. He divided himself fivefold and is called *prana, apana, samana, udana, vyana* (five kinds of breath). (II.5-6).[71]

The secondary doctrine contained in the Upanishads led to the dualistic Samkhya philosophy, which is one of the six orthodox systems of Hindu philosophy; it was founded by the sage Kapila (c. 500 B.C.) and has had a profound influence on Buddhism and subsequent Indian Philosophy. It is useful to note here that the monistic system of the Upanishads and the dualistic system of Samkhya are preserved in the Eastern and Western versions of Gnosticism.

The Samkhya system rejects the notion of *Isvara*, the personal creator, and starts with the postulate that there are two uncreated

---

[69] Cited by Radhakrishnan, *The Bhagavadgita*, 22.
[70] Paul Deussen, *The Philosophy of the Upanishads* (New York, 1966.
[71] Radhakrishnan, 801-803.

substances: matter which is real, in opposition to the Upanishads, and an infinite multitude of individual souls. The material universe is traced back to a first cause, which is *prakrti*, primitive matter, from which the universe is evolved. Each material substance is composed of three properties (*gunas*) in different proportions: *sattva* (light and joy), *rajas* (pleasure and pain) and *tamas* (darkness and inertia). *Purusha* is the second principle that accounts for the souls which are included in the *Purusha*. Samkhya bases this doctrine on the concept of *satkaryavada*, which means that the effect exists in the cause since something cannot come out of nothing. The first product of *Prakrti* is *Mahatattva* or the Great Principle (similar to the Demiurge), which is the first manifestation of the universe. Each soul becomes intertwined with *Prakrti* and begins its individual career. This happens by the sheer presence of the soul or by virtue of its nearness, which "seduces" matter to itself; this idea is almost identical to the idea of the seduction of the Archons by the Virgin of Light, referred to earlier by Doresse. The soul, being pure spirit and eternally unchangeable, remains in the most complete passivity, in harmony with its nature. Since the soul is totally impassive, it is matter that is changing all the time. As soon as the soul is united with the body or matter, consciousness erupts. And all conscious existence is suffering since there is no pain unless there is awareness or sensation. Even pleasure conceals pain in its womb and leads to suffering. However, it is not the nature of the soul to suffer or feel pain; it is the connection between the soul and matter that is the source of suffering. It is all due to "want of discrimination," or to our failure to recognize the essential distinction between the soul and matter. Since the "want of discrimination" is the root of all evil, the means of deliverance is the "discriminating knowledge" of the absolute difference between soul and matter:

> When once we have recognized that it is in matter that everything which happens takes place, that the soul, the *ego*, has no part in any movement or change, any suffering or sorrow, and stands aloof from it all, and that the soul is just as little affected by rebirth and death as by the other processes in the inner organ, release is at once attained. For the soul of the wise matter ceases to be active, as the dancer ceases to dance when the spectators are satisfied.[72]

The *Bhagavadgita* combines the various philosophical and religious schools of thought and develops a synthetic philosophy

---

[72] "Samkhya," *Encyclopedia of Religion and Ethics*, 191.

of salvation, which deals with the three ways of salvation: the way of knowledge (*jnana*), the way of the unselfish discharge of duty (*karma*), and the way of devotion (*bhakti*). The *Gita* develops this triple approach to meet the needs and aspirations of different human beings in this world. Suffice it to say that for the development of notion of salvation in the Synoptic New Testament, the last two ways are very important, whereas for the Gnosticism of the elites only the way of knowledge is relevant; on the other hand, for the Fourth Gospel the way of knowledge is is as important as the way of devotion.

On the ideal or metaphysical level, The Upanishads, the philosophers, and the *Gita* look upon deliverance as attained by means of knowledge. Radhakrishnan writes:

> At the human level action is caused by desire or attachment, *kama*. The root cause of desire is *avidya* or ignorance of the nature of things. The roots of desire lie in the ignorant belief in the individual's self-sufficiency, in the attribution of reality and permanence to it....To escape from bondage we must get rid of ignorance, which is the parent of ignorant desires and of ignorant actions. Vidya or wisdom is the means of liberation from the chain of *avidya-kama-karma*.[73]

In Indian thought as well as in Gnosticism, wisdom is the direct experience which occurs as soon as the obstacles to enlightenment are removed. That is what happens to Arjuna when he learns wisdom from his Master Krishna and is thereby illumined in the *Gita*; here a personal god manifests himself as a human being, propounds his teachings, and demands from his disciple faith and love towards him. Not only in the Bhagavata religion of the worshippers of Krishna but also in other expressions of Hinduism as well as Buddhism, the spiritual teacher, or *guru*, plays an important role—as in Gnosticism. Respect shown to the teacher is very old in India: perfect obedience was expected from the disciples, and the master's voice was to be considered as the voice of God.

The strife between darkness and light, between the principles of good and evil, or between Christ and Satan which is at the heart of Gnostic mythology, Johannine theology, and early Christian soteriology seems to be a development of the Indian traditions about the battle between the gods (*devas*, the bright ones) and the Asuras, where the gods are finally victorious, in spite of many previous setbacks, as in the Buddhist myth of the opposition

---

[73] Radhakrishnan, 52.

between Buddha and Mara. I intend to discuss the subject of the Indian sources of Gnosticism in greater depth in a future study.

The purpose of this brief discussion has been to show that Gnostic ideas are more closely allied to Indian thought than to any other religious philosophies identified so far. It is useful to point out some close textual parallels found in the Gnostic and apocryphal texts to confirm this point.

One of the tenets of Gnosticism is that Jesus possesses esoteric knowledge—the occult-knowledge tradition about Jesus. This idea, which is hinted at by Mark (14:28; 16:7) and Matthew (28:8-20) in the post-resurrection appearances of Jesus who shares his secret information with his close associates in private sessions, is fully developed in the apocryphal works. In the Infancy Gospel of Thomas 20:1-15, Jesus sets his teacher straight about the hidden meaning of the letters of the alphabet:

> There was also at Jerusalem one named Zacheus, who was a schoolmaster. And he said to Joseph: Joseph, Joseph, why dost thou not send Jesus to me, that he may learn his letters. Joseph agreed....So they brought him to that master; who, as soon as he saw him, wrote out an alphabet for him. And he bade him say Aleph; and when he had said it, the master bade him pronounce Beth....Then the Lord Jesus...said to his master, Take notice how I say to thee; then he began clearly and distinctly to say Aleph, Beth, Gimel, Daleth, and so on to the end of the alphabet. At this the master was so surprised that he said, Thou hast brought a boy to me to be taught, who is more learned than any master....

> And when Joseph saw the understanding of the child and his age, that he was growing to maturity, he resolved again that he should not remain ignorant of letters; and he took him and handed him over to another teacher. And the teacher said to Joseph: "First I will teach him Greek, and then Hebrew." For the teacher knew the child's knowledge and was afraid of him. Nevertheless he wrote the alphabet and practised it with him for a long time; but he gave him no answer. And Jesus said to him: "If you are indeed a teacher, and if you know the letters well, tell me the meaning of the Alpha, and I will tell you that of the Beta." And the teacher was annoyed and struck him on the head. And the child was hurt and cursed him, and he immediately fainted and fell to the ground on his face. And the child returned to Joseph's house....

> And another teacher...took him with fear and anxiety, but the child went gladly. And he went boldly into the school and found a book lying on the reading desk and took it, but did not read the letters in it, but opened his mouth and spoke by the Holy Spirit and taught law to those that stood by. And a large crowd assembled and stood there listening to him, wondering at the grace of his teaching and the readiness of his words, that although an infant he made such utterances.

In the life of Buddha we find that when the prince was eight years old, King Sudhodana appointed the legendary teacher Vishwamitra to instruct the young prince in the art of writing. The young prince addressed the teacher:

> My master, in what writing will you instruct me? Shall it be in the writing of Brahma Deva, Kharoshti, Akara, Mangala, Yava, Dravida,...or Sruta?...Of all these different styles of writing which does my master design to teach me?...Vishwamitra replied, "He has recited from beginning to end the names of different writing systems, which I have never heard of. Surely this is the Instructor of Devas and men." At this time, five hundred noblemen entered the school with the royal prince, and began to learn the sounds of different letters, on which occasion, the Prince...gave forth the sound of each letter.[74]

In the *Lalitavistara* version (ch. x), the young prince gives a list of sixty-four writing systems, including those of the Chinese and the Huns. When the boys repeat the alphabet, at each letter a moral truth is uttered.

> Then...When the Prince had duly grown up, he was taken to the writing school under a hundred thousand auspicious arrangements. He was accompanied and followed by ten thousand boys....All the Sakyas, led by king Sudhodana, proceeded in front of the Bodhisatva. With such a retinue did the Bodhisatva proceed to the school. Then he entered the school. Now Visvamitra, the schoolmaster, feeling the beauty and glory of the Bodhisatva to be insufferable, fell prostrate on the ground. Subhanga, a Devaputra..., held him by the right hand...and...said: "What avails him the mere knowledge of writing who is thoroughly versed in the fourfold path of the future, who is proficient in the knowledge of the cause and the effect of creation...? There is none in the three regions who can be greater than he in conduct; he is the greatest among all gods and men. You know not even the names of the writings which he learnt many millions of ages ago."...Now Bodhisatva, taking up a tablet..., thus addressed the tutor Visvamitra: "Which is the writing, sir, which you wish to teach me: Is it the Brahmi writing; or the Kharoshti; or the Pushkarasari; or the writing of the Anga?...Out of these sixty-four kinds which is it, sir, that you wish to teach me? The schoolmaster Visvamitra, wonderstruck and deprived of all vanity and self-importance, recited these gathas with a cheerful face: "Wonderful this is of the Bodhisatva, the leader of men, that he should have learnt every sastra immediately on coming to the school! On coming to the school he has learned writings of which I do not know even the names..." In the presence of the Bodhisatva the teacher began to teach the boys the alphabet. When they pronounced the letter *a*, then resounded all the words—all sacraments are impermanent. On *á* being pronounced there

---

[74] Beal, 69-70.

resounded the welfare of one's own and of others. By the letter *i* the fullness of organs.[75]

If the parallel given above is striking in Gnostic-Indian similarities, the one that follows is spectacular on the same grounds.

One of the oldest of the Gnostic gospels is the Apocryphon of John, which shows affinities with the Samkhya philosophy and in which the circumstances of the revelation made to John is described vividly.

> It happened one day when John went up and came to the temple that a pharisee named Arimanius approached him and said to him, "Where is your master whom you followed" And he said to him, "He has gone to the place from which he came." The Pharisee said to him, "This Nazarene deceived you with deception and filled your ears with lies and closed your hearts and turned you from the traditions of your fathers. When I, John, heard these things, I turned away from the temple to a desert place and I became greatly grieved. Straightway...behold the heavens opened and the whole creation which is under heaven shone and the world was shaken. And I was afraid, and behold I saw in the light a youth who stood by me. While I looked at him, he became like an old man. And he changed his form again, becoming like a servant. There was not a plurality before me, but there was a likeness with multiple form in the light, and the forms appeared through each other, and the likeness had three forms. He said to me, "John, John, why do you doubt, and why are you afraid? You are not unfamiliar with this likeness, are you? That is to say, be not timid! I am the one who is with you forever. I am the Father, I am the Mother, I am the Son. I am the unpolluted and incorruptible one. Now I have come to teach you what is and what was and what will come to pass, that you may know the things which are not revealed and the things which are revealed and to teach you the perfect man. Now, then, lift up your face that you may receive the things which I shall tell you today....And when I asked to know it he said to me, "The Monad is a monarchy with nothing above it. It is he who exists as God and Father of everything, the invisible one who is above everything, who is imperishability, existing as pure light which no eye can behold (II.l).[76]

In what follows, Jesus, as revealer, teaches John about the Aeons, the immeasurable Light, the ineffable Thought, the indefinable Spirit, and the process of creation.

The Indian text that interests us here is *The Bhagavadgita*. This great Upanishad starts with a circumstance similar to the one found in the Gnostic work. Arjuna is downcast and sad because in the ensuing Battle of Kurukshetra he would be forced to kill his own

---
[75] Mitra, 183-184.
[76] *NHL*, 99-100.

kinsmen; he casts away his bow and arrows, his spirit overwhelmed by sorrow. To him thus overcome with pity, Krishna speaks the words of *brahmavidya* (the science of the Absolute). The Blessed Lord [Krishna], developing Samkhya theory and yoga practice, says:

> Thou grievest for those whom thou shouldst not grieve for, and yet thou speakest words about wisdom. Wise men do not grieve for the dead or for the living. Never was there a time when I was not, nor thou, nor these lords of men, nor will there ever be a time hereafter when we all shall cease to be. As the soul passes in this body through childhood, youth and age, even so is its taking on of another body. The sage is not perplexed by this....He who thinks that this slays and he who thinks that this is slain; both of them fail to perceive truth; this one neither slays nor is slain....Arjuna said: "Thou art the Supreme Brahman...the eternal, the first of the gods, the unborn, the all-pervading....Thou shouldst tell me of Thy divine manifestations, without exception, whereby, pervading these worlds, Thou dost abide in them....How may I know Thee?...Krishna said: "I am the beginning, the middle and the very end of beings....Of letter, I am the letter A and of compounds I am the dual. I also am imperishable Time....There is no end to my divine manifestations. Whatsoever being there is, endowed with glory and grace and vigor, know that to have sprung from a fragment of My splendor."...Arjuna said: "I desire to see Thy divine form."...The Blessed Lord said: "Behold, O Partha, My forms, a hundred-fold, a thousand-fold, various in kind, divine, of various colors and shapes....But thou canst not behold Me with this human eye of yours; I will bestow on thee the supernatural eye. Behold My divine power."...Having thus spoken...the great lord of all yoga revealed to Partha His Supreme and Divine Form....If the light of a thousand suns were to blaze forth all at once in the sky, that might resemble the splendor of that exalted being. There the Pandava beheld the whole universe with its manifold divisions gathered together in one, in the body of the God of gods....Arjuna said: "In Thy body, O God, I see all the gods and the varied hosts of beings as well, Brahma, the Lord seated on the lotus throne and all the sages and heavenly nagas....I behold Thee as one without beginning, middle or end, of infinite power, of numberless arms, with the moon and the sun as Thine eyes, with Thy face as a flaming fire, whose radiance burns up this universe."(passim).

This vision of the transformation of Krishna is found in a variation in the Buddhist *Lotus Sutra* also. In all these works, as in the transfiguration episode in the canonical gospels, the living master is presented as the sole revealer of the hidden truth.

Another important Christian gospel, the Gospel of Thomas, which originated in encratite circles, shows clear evidence of the influence not only of Gnostic theology but also of Indian thought. The one hundred and fourteen collected logia of Jesus are designated as "the secret sayings which the living Jesus spoke" and "whoever finds the interpretation of these sayings will not experience death." According to the Gospel of Thomas, the basic religious experience is not only the recognition of one's divine identity, but more specifically the recognition of one's origin (the light) and destiny (the repose). In order to return to one's origin, the disciple has to become separate from the world by "stripping off" the fleshly garment and passing by the present corruptible existence; then the disciple can experience the new world, the kingdom of light, peace, and life. Jesus says to to his disciples in the Gospel of Thomas: "When you disrobe without being ashamed and take up your garments and place them under your feet like little children and tread on them, then will you see the Son of the Living One" (37).[77] This passage should remind us of the same garment metaphor Paul uses in his epistle to the Colossians where he asks his disciples to put off the old man in order to put on the new man (3:8-10). Jesus says to Thomas: "I am your master. Because you have drunk, you have become intoxicated from the bubbling spring which I have measured out." This passage bears close resemblance to what the Jesus of the Fourth Gospel says: "If any man thirst, let him come unto me and drink. As the Scripture has said it, out of the belly of the man who believes in me shall flow rivers of living water" (7:38). In fact, there is no scripture passage that says what the Fourth Gospel attributes to Jesus except the Buddhist Scripture (*Patisambhida-maggo*, I:53). Jesus of Thomas says; "Blessed are the solitary and elect, for you will find the Kingdom. For you are from it, and to it you will return....We came from the light.... Split a piece of wood, and I am there. Lift up the stone, and you will find me there." This last logion of Jesus is reminiscent of the story of the incarnation of Vishnu as Narasimha (man-lion), who came out of the split wood and killed the atheist Hiranyakasipu, the asura father of Prahlada.[78]

One difference I notice between the canonical gospels and the Gnostic apocryphal gospels is that the former seem to try hard to hide their Indian/Gnostic sources, whereas the latter sometimes almost verbatim repeat their Indian sources; the reason for this difference could very well be that the canonical gospels were more heavily edited by orthodox censors than the apocryphal works which were much more open to Eastern influences in the formulation

---

[77] *NHL*, 122.
[78] *Bhagavatapurana* , VII.

of their religious thought. Much of this editorial activity was a feature of the second century. An interesting example of this type of action we find in Tatian, who left the Church in 138 to form his own group. He prepared his own canon, which included a single gospel, which, according to F. C. Burkitt, was a drastically edited version of the Gospel of Luke.[79] In his version Marcion removed all Jewish "perversions" in order to create the true gospel. Tatian also wrote his harmonic version of the gospel, the *Diatessaron*, from the Syriac gospels in the middle of the second century. No copy of this gospel—except in its Armenian version—nor the commentary on it written by Ephrem—except in a few fragments—is extant. All the copies of this gospel were destroyed by church authorities as evidenced in the attestation of Theodoret, Bishop of Cyrrhus on the Euphrates in A.D. 423, when he himself ordered the removal of 200 copies of the *Diatessaron* from the churches of his diocese.[80] What is clear from these is simply that the Catholic Church in the second century formed its own official canon by first declaring the fourfold gospel as canonical after having made necessary changes in them.[81]

One wonders why the Church Fathers were so vehemently opposed to the Gnostics, their fellow Christians, and why they would edit out as much Gnosticism as possible from the canonical gospels. Apart from the real reasons which are probably political, they give a good theological reason: Gnosis is from the devil! For instance, Eusebius of Caesarea (264-339) makes the classic formulation of this view:

> Like brilliant lamps the churches were now shining throughout the world, and faith in our Savior and Lord Jesus Christ was flourishing among all mankind, when the devil who hates what is good, as the enemy of truth, ever most hostile to man's salvation, turned all his devices against the church. Formerly he had used persecutions from without as his weapon against her, but now that he was excluded from this he employed wicked men and sorcerers, like the baleful weapons and ministers of destruction against the soul, and conducted his campaign by other measures, plotting by every means that sorcerers and deceivers might assume the same name as our religion and at one time lead to the depth of destruction those of the faithful whom they caught,

---

[79] *Cambridge Ancient History*, XII (London, 1939): 452-454, cited by Howard Kee, *Jesus In History* (New York, 1970),250.
[80] See Kee, 252.
[81] Kee, 250.

and at others, by the deeds which they undertook, might turn away from the part to the saving world those who were ignorant of faith."[82]

At the head of these agents of the devil stand the Gnostic Simon Magus, his son Menander who engendered the double-headed and double-tongued serpent, according to Eusebius, Saturninus of Antioch and Basilides of Alexandria. These founded "ungodly heretical schools," the former in Antioch and the latter in Egypt. As Kurt Rudolph points out, "with the help of this line of descent, the rise and expansion of the gnostic heresy was explained for subsequent ages."[83]

An important corollary that follows from this short comparison of Gnostic and Indian texts is that the literary genre of the dialogue of the Gnostics is patterned after the Indian dialogues of the Upanishads, and especially of the *Bhagavadgita* and the Buddhist *sutra*, where we have a teacher or revealer instructing the ignorant disciples in the mysteries of Supreme Wisdom (*jnana-gnosis*) and where the *sutra* is created as a string of logia. On the Indian side there are also some pedagogical and philosophical question-answer dialogues as in some Gnostic texts.[84]

One Greek writer and contemporary of the Gnostic teachers (c. 225 B.C.), Hippolytus who came to Rome from Alexandria, obviously knew Indian religious thought and recognized the indebtedness of the Gnostics to Indian thought. He wrote about the Indian Brahmins:

> There is...with the Indians a sect composed of those philosophizing among the Brahmins. They spend a contented existence, abstain both from living creatures and all cooked food, being satisfied with fruits; and not gathering these from the trees, but carrying off those that have fallen to the earth. They subsist upon them, drinking the water of the river Tazabena. But they pass their life naked, affirming that the body has been constituted a covering to the soul by the Deity. These affirm that God is light, not such as one sees, nor such as the sun and fire; but to them the Deity is discourse, not that which finds expression in articulate sounds, but that of the knowledge through which the secret mysteries of nature are perceived by the wise. And this light which they say is discourse, their god, they assert that the Brahmins only know on account of their alone rejecting all vanity of opinion which is the soul's ultimate covering. These despise death, and always in their own

---

[82] Eusebius, *Ecclesiastical History* IV.7; cited by Kurt Rudolph,*Gnosis: The Nature and History of Gnosticism* (New York, 1987), 276.

[83] Rudolph, 276.

[84] See Pheme Perkins, *The Gnostic Dialogue* (New York, 1980) for an analysis of the structure of the Gnostic dialogues. I intend to develop the ideas alluded to in this paragraph in a later study.

peculiar language call God by the name which we have mentioned previously, and they send up hymns to him. But neither are there women among them, nor do they beget children. But they who aim at a life similar to these, after they have crossed over to the country on the opposite side of the river, continue to reside there, returning no more; and these also are called Brahmins. But they do not pass their life similarly, for there are also in the place women, of whom those that dwell there are born, and in turn beget children. And this discourse which they name God assert to be corporeal, and enveloped in a body outside himself, just as if one were wearing a sheep's skin, but that on divesting himself of body that he would appear clear to the eye. But the Brahmins say that there is a conflict in the body that surrounds them, and they consider that the body is for them full of conflicts; in opposition to which, as if marshalled for battle against enemies, they contend, as we have already explained. And they say that all men are captive to their own congenital struggles, viz., sensuality and unchastity, gluttony, anger, joy, sorrow, concupiscence, and such like. And who has reared a trophy over these, alone goes to God; wherefore the Brahmins deify Dandamis, to whom Alexander the Macedonian paid a visit, as one who had proved victorious in the bodily conflict. But they bear down on Calanus as having profanely withdrawn from their philosophy. But the Brahmins, putting off the body, like fishes jumping out of water into the pure air, behold the sun.[85]

The ascetic ideal of the Indian monks was well known in the Christian world in the second century. Certainly it did not originate in Judaism since the theory and practice of the mortification of the body, sexual abstinence, and the glorification of poverty are alien to the letter and spirit of the Judaism of the Old Testament.[86] It is not certain that the Essenes and the Therapeutae of the first century B.C.-A.D. who practised celibacy, poverty, and asceticism were really Jews at all, as I shall show in the next chapter. In the second century there were sectarian Christians known as "encratites" ("self-controlled") who forbade marriage and counselled abstinence from meat. It is these Gnostic encratites who are chastised by Paul in 1 Timothy 4:1-4:

> The Spirit clearly says that in later times some will abandon the faith and follow deceiving spirits and things taught by demons. Such teachings come through hypocritical liars, whose consciences have been seared as with a hot iron. They forbid people to marry and order them to abstain from certain foods, which God created to be received with thanksgiving by those who believe and know the truth.

---

[85] Hippolytus, *Refutation of All Heresies*, I.21 in Alexander Roberts and James Donaldson,*The Ante-Nicene Christian Library*, (New York, 1926) V:21-22.

[86] Bernhard Lohse, *Askese und Mönchtum in der Antike und in der alten Kirche* (Munich, 1969), 80-84; Sedlar, 235.

Ireneus, too, would assail these Gnostic encratites for teaching the same false doctrines, for they "set aside the original creation of God, and indirectly blame Him who made the male and female for the propagation of the human race."[87] I Hippolytus, as well, knows about these encratites. He writes:

> Others, however, styling themselves encratites, acknowledge some things concerning God and Christ in like manner with the Church. In respect, however, of their mode of life, they pass their days inflated with pride. They suppose that by meats they magnify themselves, while abstaining from animal food, and being water-drinkers, and forbidding to marry, and devoting themselves during the remainder of life to habits of asceticism. But persons of this description are estimated Cynics rather than Christians, inasmuch as they do not attend unto the words spoken against them through the Apostle Paul in [1 Tim. 4:1-5].[88]

According to Ireneus, the leader of the encratites was the Syrian Tatian, a convert to Christianity, who taught that Christians should renounce all their property, abstain from meat and wine, and renounce marriage which is another word for fornication. The encratites found support for their life-style in the gospels. Not only the Gospel of Thomas but also the Synoptic Gospels say that there will not be any marriage after the Resurrection since the redeemed souls will be like angels in heaven.(Matt. 22:30; Mark 12:25; Luke 20:34-35). In Luke's version, the elect abjure marriage even in this life: "They who shall be accounted worthy to obtain the other world and the resurrection from the dead, neither marry nor are given in marriage" (20:35). Drawing the logical conclusion that, since the resurrection had already taken place, only the unmarried could be saved, Origen in the third century carried this form of asceticism too far to the point of self-castration, which resulted in his excommunication.[89]

What is remarkable about all the encratites is that Hippolytus connects the ones of his times to the ones whom Paul apparently condemned and that they shared the same views. Hippolytus also has an answer to their origins. He says: "Their [encratites'] opinions have been formed not from the Holy Scriptures but from themselves and the Gymnosophists among the Indians."[90] Indeed, Hippolytus who could speak with such clarity and authority on the Indians also spoke with clarity and authority on the Gnostic-

---

[87] reneus, *Adversus Haereses*, I.28 in *Ante-Nicene Christian Library* V.100.
[88] *Refutation* VIII.13; *ANCL* V:124.
[89] Sedlar, 241-242.
[90] Ibid., VIII; *ANCL* V.117

encratitic teachings. Evidently he knew what he was talking about. Particularly striking is his use of the garment symbolism, according to which the Brahmins regarded the body as a clothing for the soul. This metaphor is found in the *Bhagavadgita* II:22: "Just as a person casts off worn-out garments and puts on others that are new, even so does the embodied soul cast off worn-out bodies and take on others that are new."[91] On this point Sedlar who says that "his explanation for Brahmin practices betray the influence of Gnosticism, e.g. his statement that the Indian ascetics regard the body as clothing for the soul suggests Gnostic garment-symbolism" (242-243), is wrong: It is Gnosticism that was influenced by the Indian thought simply because the *Gita* is much older that the Gnostic writings.

The upshot of this comparative study is the plain perception that the Gnostic teachings seem to appear very Indian. Indeed, they do. No wonder, Elaine Pagels asks the right questions and suggests an answer:

> Does not such teaching—the identity of the divine and human, the concern with illusion and enlightenment, the founder who is presented not as Lord, but as a spiritual guide—sound more Eastern than Western? Some scholars have suggested that if the names were changed, the "living Buddha" appropriately could say what the Gospel of Thomas attributes to the living Jesus. Could Hindu or Buddhist tradition have influenced gnosticism? ...The British scholar of Buddhism, Edward Conze, suggests that it had. He points out that "Buddhists were in contact with the Thomas Christians (that is, Christians who knew and used such writings as the Gospel of Thomas in South India."...Trade routes between the Graeco-Roman world and the Far East were opening up at the time when gnosticism flourished (A.D. 80-200); for generations, Buddhist missionaries had been proselytizing in Alexandria.[92]

The answer suggested by Elaine Pagels is not anything really new. A fair number of writers in the Greek language, over a period of several centuries since the time of Alexander, expressed the view that Oriental wisdom—of Egypt, Chaldea, Persia, Palestine, and India—had influenced classical Greek Philosophy and later Hellenistic thought since Oriental/Indian civilization had antedated that of Greece.[93] It is quite likely that Indian ideas could have travelled to the Mediterranean Roman empire where Christian scriptures were composed during an eclectic period. As

---

[91] Radhakrishnan, 108.
[92] Pagels, xx-xxi.
[93] Edward Zeller, *A History of Greek Philosophy*, trans. S. F. Alleyne (London, 1881), I: 26-49; Sedlar, 20.

Charles Eliot argues, "a number of Buddhist legends make their appearance in the...gospels and are so obviously Indian in character that it can hardly be maintained that they were invented in Palestine or Egypt and spread thence Eastwards."[94]

There exists some external circumstantial evidence that supports the Indian-Gnostic connection. Between 1897 and 1903 Greek fragments of the Gospel of Thomas were discovered at Oxyrhyncus (nos. 1, 654, 655) in Upper Egypt. One of the Oxyrhyncus papyri contains a play based on a fictitious event that takes place in India.[95] Also, the suggestion of an Indian presence in Egypt seems to have an ally in Philo. His description of the Therapeutae seems to support the hypothesis that Indian Buddhists of the Theravada group(*Thera* means "elders" or "arahats" (the perfect); *vada* means "doctrine.") which "embraced the speculative life," emphasized salvation through gnosis, and had their own books were active near Alexandria during the time of Philo.[96]

The issue, then, that is raised by my references to the presence of Indians in Alexandria and of Indian religious ideas in Gnostic writings and in Christian gospels needs clarification. Is the presence of Indians and of Indian books in Egypt where most of the earliest Gnostic and Christian writings were discovered an impossible dream or the fiction of the imagination of Philo and Hippolytus, or is it a tenable theory that can be supported with historical evidence? The answer is that the Indian presence in the Mediterranean world was a widely acknowledged fact of life in Western literature, especially during the formative period of Christianity and the New Testament.

---

[94] Charles Eliot, *Hinduism and Buddhism* (London, 1921), III, 441.
[95] See *Journal of Royal Asiatic Society* (1904), 399 ff. The play is a good illustration of what Edward Said calls "Orientalism."
[96] Philo, *A Treatise on Contemplative Life* in *The Essential Philo*, ed., Nahum N. Glatzer (New York, 1971), 311; F. C. Conybeare, *About the Contemplative Life* (London, 1895).

CHAPTER SEVEN

INDIA AND THE WEST IN ANTIQUITY

Geographically speaking, the terms "Asia," "East," and "India" were imprecise in the European imagination of antiquity. Before the age of the great discoveries, these terms were used so interchangeably that Egypt was sometimes pictured in maps as situated in Asia, which stood as a synonym for India.[1] Sometimes Parthia included India as well. This means that when Matthew speaks about the magi from the East, it is possible that he means India; so also when the Acts of the Apostles describes the nationalities of the God-fearing Jews who were in Jerusalem for the Pentecost, he probably includes Indians among the people from Asia and Parthia (Acts 2:9-10). In spite of their lack of scientific knowledge of India, educated people in antiquity knew a great deal about the land and its people.

A. *India and the Old Testament*

India is mentioned in Esther 1:1 and 8:9 as the eastern boundary of the Persian Empire under Ahasuerus (c. fifth century B.C.) and in 1 Maccabees 6:37 in a reference to the Indian mahouts of Antiochus's war elephants (second century B.C.). Otherwise there are no explicit references to India in the Old Testament. However, archeological evidences of the Kulli culture of Baluchistan indicate that from c. 2800 B.C. there were contacts between Mesopotamia and the great cities of the Indus civilization.[2] At the sites of ancient Sumerian cities of Kish, Lagash, and Ur, archeologists have discovered typical objects of the Indus civilization that indicate there existed a flourishing trade in spices between India and Mesopotamia. The presence of Indian ivory objects of foreign workmanship discovered in Mesopotamia suggests that they were imported from India. Since commerce by its nature is mutual, it is probable that the cultural interaction was mutual between these geographical regions.

---

[1] Donald F. Lach, *Asia in the Making of Europe*, I (Chicago, 1965), 4.
[2] Stuart Piggot, *Prehistoric India to 1000 B.C.* (Harmondsworth, 1950), 207-208; cited by Sedlar, 3.

There are some indirect references to India in the Old Testament. According to 1 Kings 9:26-28, King Solomon's navy (c. 1000 B.C.), sailed to Ophir to fetch gold. Since Ophir is *Sopheir/Sophara* in the LXX, since *Sophir* means India in Coptic, and since gold was plentiful in the mountains north of Punjab in Northwest India, it is generally accepted that Ophir was a port in India. Sedlar writes:

> In favor of Ophir as India are the facts that the geographer Ptolemaios (Ptolemy) notes an " Abiria" (Ophir?) at the mouth of the Indus, that Buddhist writings refer to the coast around Bombay as " Sovira" (possibly Ptolemaios' " Supara"), and that the Jewish historian Josephos (first cen. A.D.) identifies the Biblical " Sopheir" with the Indian " Land of Gold."[3]

Certain other Indian products, such as ivory, the peacock, and the monkey going to King Solomon's court suggests that they must have originated in India. I Kings 10:22 explicitly states that every third year King Solomon's navy, together with King Hiram's, brought him " gold, silver, ivory, apes, and peacocks." The Old Testament words for peacock *tuki*, for ivory *shen habbim*, and for the ape *kof* all seem to be derived from their Indian counterparts *tokei*, *ab*, and *kapi* respectively. [4] Indian textiles and fragrances also seem to have made their way to the world of the Old Testament: Proverbs 7:17, Ps. 45:8, and Song of Solomon 4:14 refer to the Indian fragrant wood called aloes (Heb. *ahalim* by a term derived from Sanskrit *agaru* and from cognates in Tamil and Malayalam; the Greek *sandalon* is a derivative of the Sanskrit/Malayalam *chandana*;[5] ancient Babylonian texts refer to linen as *sindhu* (*sindon* in Greek, meaning "Indian"); Isaiah 3:23 refers to *sadin* for fine linen.[6] Rice was brought to European ports from South India; the word *rice* is a shortened form of the Spanish *arroz*, derived from the Arabic *aruz*; the Greek *oruza* and the Latin *oryza* are perhaps derived from Arabic or from the Tamil *arisi*.[7] As Sedlar argues, "the juxtaposition of three or four products known to be found in India, together with the sailing of Solomon's ships to "Ophir," lends weight to the supposition that sea-commerce with

---

[3] Sedlar, 5.
[4] Robert Caldwell, *A Comparative Grammar of the Dravidian or South-Indian Family of Languages* (London, 1913), 88-89; Max Müller, *The Science of Language* (New York, 1891), I: 188-191.
[5] Caldwell, 89.
[6] J. Kennedy, "The Early Commerce of Babylon with India," *JRAS* (1898), p. 252; J. Sayce, *Hibbert Lectures* (1887).
[7] H. G. Rawlinson, *Indian Historical Studies* (London: Longmans, 1913),165-166.

India already was in existence."[8] It may be added that the Greek word *drachma*, which is found in many vernacular languages, is derived from the Prakrit *dramma* and the modern *dam*, which survives in the modern English expression, " I don't give a *damn*."

Not only part of King Solomon's wealth but also some of his wisdom seems to have been derived from India. For instances, there are some passages in chapter 30 of the book of Proverbs attributed to Solomon, besides the famous judgement of the legendary king.

Who has gone up to heaven and come down? Who has gathered the wind in his fists? Who has bound up the waters in a garment? Who has established all the ends of the earth? What is his name, and what his son's, if thou knowest?(Proverbs 30:4).	Who knows or who here can declare whence has sprung—whence this creation—from what this creation arose, whether any made it or not? He who is in the highest heaven is its ruler. He verily knows, or even he knows not. (*Rg Veda*, 10:129).
The horseleech has three daughters; they say always, "Give, give." There are three things never sated,yea, four that never say "enough." Sheol is never sated with the dead, nor the womb's gate with men, earth never sated with water, and fire says never "enough"(30:15).	Fire is never sated with fuel nor the streams with the ocean, nor the god of death with all creatures. Nor the bright-eyed one with men.(*Panchatantra* 1: 153).
There are three things too wonderful for me, yea, four which I know not: the way of an eagle in the air...the way of a ship through the sea (30:18-19).	The path of ships across the sea, the soaring eagle's flight Varuna knows. (*Rg Veda*).

---

[8] Sedlar, 5.

Under three things earth trembles, and four it cannot bear: Under a servant when master, and a fool filled with meat, under an odious woman wedded, and a handmaid heir to her mistress (30:21-23).	A bad woman wedded, a friend that is false, a servant become pert, and a house full of serpents, make life unsupportable (*Hitopadesa* 2:7).[9]

A few Indian stories also have found their way into the books of the Old Testament, two of which are interesting. Of these two the first one is associated with Solomon and the other with Daniel.

The first story deals with the famous Judgment of Solomon (1 Kings 3:16-28). To settle the issue of to whom the live baby belongs, the king gives the order:

> "Cut the living child in two and give half to one and half to the other." The woman whose son was alive was filled with compassion for her son and said to the king, "Please, my lord, give her the living baby! Don't kill him!" But the other said, "Neither I nor you shall have him. Cut him in two!" Then the king gave his ruling: "Give the living baby to the first woman. Do not kill him; she is his mother."(25-27).

The Indian parallel found in Jataka 546 (*Mahosadha*) is illuminating. A goblin woman carried the child of a woman who was bathing in a tank near Sage Mahosadha's (Bodhisatva) house. The mother of the baby pursued the goblin and brought the matter to the attention of the sage.

> When he heard the story, although he knew at once by her red unwinking eyes that one of them was a goblin, he asked them whether they would abide by his decision. On their promising to do so, he drew a line and laid the child in the middle of the line and bade the goblin seize the child by the hands and the mother by the feet. Then he said to them, "Lay hold of it and pull; the child is hers who can pull it over."They both pulled, and the child, being pained while it was pulled, uttered a loud cry. Then the mother with a heart which seemed ready to burst, let the child go and stood weeping. The sage asked the multitude, "Is it the heart of the mother which is tender towards the child or the heart of her who is not the mother?" They answered, "The mother's heart."Is she the mother who kept hold of the child or she who let it go?"They answered, "She who let it go."[10]

---

[9] Joseph Jacobs, *The Fables of Aesop* (London, 1889), 132-33.
[10] *Jataka Tales*, eds. H. T. Francis and E. J. Thomas (Bombay, 1970), 300.

The second story in the Bible that is related to a Jataka tale *Mahosadha Jataka* (546) is that of Susanna in the Book of Daniel (13:1-64). Susanna, the beautiful wife of Joachim, is the object of the adulterous passion of two elders or magistrates of the court, who are constantly looking for an opportunity to be alone with her. As she takes a bath in the garden, they give her the choice of submitting to them or facing prosecution for adultery. Since she rejects their demands, she is accused, tried, convicted, and condemned to die. In response to her prayers, God sends young Daniel to defend her. He interrogates the two elders separately, proving their guilt; the court condemns them to death in Susanna's place. In the course of defending Susanna, Daniel asks the first elder: " 'Under what tree did you see them conversing together?' He said, 'Under a mastic tree.' After having him put aside, Daniel asked the second one, 'Under what tree did you see them conversing together?' He said, 'Under a holm tree.'" (54-58).

Jataka 546 has an interesting parallel—it has also a variant in the *Panchatantra*—to the story of Susanna, though it differs from the Hebrew narrative in many details. The dwarfish Golakala has worked for seven years in a certain house and obtained Dighatala as his wife. One day, on their way to visit her parents, they come to a swollen river, which they are afraid to cross. A stranger Dighapitthy, who falls in love with Dighatala, accosts them and promises to take them across the flooded river. First Dighapitthy carries the woman across the river; by the time they reached the middle of the river, the woman has already agreed to love the stranger and marry him. As soon as they reach the opposite shore, they begin to carry on as husband and wife. The husband who sees that he is cuckolded is humiliated. A little later, the irate husband somehow manages to cross the river, which he finds to be shallow. He catches up with them and asks his wife to give up her paramour. She refuses and claims that Dighapitthy is her real husband. Mahosadha, the Bodhisatva, hears about the quarrel and offers to mediate; the quarreling parties agree. He cross-examines each of the three separately in the hearing of the crowd:

> He sent for Dighapitthi and asked him his name. Then he asked the wife's name, but he not knowing what it was, mentioned some other name. Then he asked him the names of his parents and he told them, but when he asked him the names of his wife's parents he, not knowing, mentioned some other names. The Great Being put his story together and had him removed. Then he sent for the other and asked him the names of all in the same way. He, knowing the truth, gave them correctly. Then he had him removed and sent for Dighatala and asked her what her name

was and she gave it. Then he asked her her parents' names and she gave them correctly, but when he asked her the names of her husband's parents' names, she talked at random and gave wrong names. Then the sage sent for the other two and asked the multitude, "Does the woman's story agree with Dighapitthy or Golakala?" They replied, "With Golakala." Then he pronounced his sentence, "This man is her husband, and the other is the thief."[11]

The Book of Kings was probably edited during the Babylonian Captivity in the sixth century, and Daniel in the second century B.C. Incidentally, Jataka 339 speaks of a voyage from India to Baveru (Babylon). Since the Jataka stories are pre-Buddhist in origin and since India was in contract with Babylonia from the second millennium, it is more than likely that India must be the source of these tales—the problem of folktales will be discussed more at length later in this chapter.

B. *India and the Greek World: Before Alexander*

The Greek world of 1500-1000 B.C. portrayed in the Homeric epics is similar to the heroic world of the Indian Vedas. The warriors ride in chariots, and some of their gods bear similar names like Ouranos-Varuna, Kore-Gauri, and Zeus-Dyaus. Many of these cultural similarities are obviously due to their sharing the common Indo-European culture which they carried with them to different parts of Europe and Asia during the First *Völkerwanderungszeit*. It is not likely that these different Indo-European nations, like Greece and India, continued to maintain their ancient cultural ties traversing over vast geographical expanses after they had left their homeland behind in Central Asia. It is, however, possible that a small amount of trade linked Greeks and Indians. Several times Homer mentions objects, like tin and ivory, that obviously came from India since the Greek names of these articles are similar to Indian ones.[12] Though Homer confused India and Ethiopia, Herodotus (fifth century) knew the distinction between Ethiopians and Indians, both of whom served in the Persian army that the Greeks had fought at Marathon (480 B.C.).[13] In the fourth century,

---

[11] *Jataka Tales*, 301-302.
[12] J. W. McCrindle, *Ancient India as Described by Megasthenes and Arrian* (London, 1877), 3-4.
[13] Herodotus, VII.65-66); Loeb edition, III. 379-381.

Ctesias used the term interchangeably.¹⁴ In a sense this identification of Indians with Ethiopia can be justified since a large number of Indians in South India, namely, the Dravidians, trace their origins to Upper Egypt.¹⁵

Herodotus in his *History* relied on both oral and written records of the East.¹⁶ He consulted works such as *Arimaspea*, a poem by Aristaeus, and for his physical description of India, he relied largely on Hecateus of Miletus, the geographer from the fifth century. He placed Indians on the easternmost point of the known world and made the Indus River flow southeastward with no conception of the peninsular shape of the country. He portrayed the Indians as made up of many nations speaking different languages, with the fair Aryans living in the north and the blacks in the south. He referred to Indian cotton and to incredible stories such as that of the gold-digging ants; from his reference to the Indians paying tribute to Persia with gold, it is to be inferred that parts of India were under Persian dominance at least for a while even before the time of Alexander.

Around 400 B.C. Ctesias, the first author of a separate work on India, wrote his *Indica* in which he tried to correct Herodotus. Being a medical doctor by profession, he had spent eight years at the Achaemenid court of Artaxerxes Memnon, where he had the opportunity to acquire a good deal of information on India for his *Indica*. After his return to Greece he wrote a large historical work on Persia, *Persica*, and a smaller work on India. Both these works have not survived except in fragmentary citations and in some large excerpts made by Bishop Photios in the ninth century.¹⁷ He knew that India contained elephants, monkeys, parrots, and other huge birds. But Ctesias also helped perpetuate many fantastic myths about India by describing oriental animals and monsters in detail. He portrayed Indians as satyrs, some of them living to be 200 years old, and grossly exaggerated the size of the country. He described the sun in India as very hot and very large, compared to other places. The fables and traditions of Ctesias were recorded and bequeathed to the Middle Ages by Pliny.¹⁸

---

[14] McCrindle, 4 n.

[15] Zacharias P. Thundy, "The Egyptian Osiris Myth and the Tamil *Cilappadikaram*," *Tamil Civilization*, 1 (1983), 83-90.

[16] Rawlinson, 38-42; J. E. Powell, *The History of Herodotus* (London, 1930) *The Cambridge History of India*, I, 396.

[17] Sedlar, 12.

[18] F. Jacoby, "Ctesias," *RE* 11 (1875), 203-35; Lach, 7.

Some religious and philosophical ideas from India seemed to have filtered into Greece during this time, probably through the agency of merchants or more probably through the West's contact with India's wandering holy men. According to the later testimony of Eusebius (260-340 A.D.) who got it from Aristoxenos (320-300 B.C.), Socrates conversed with an Indian holy man in Athens. The Indian asked Socrates what kind of a philosopher he was. When Socrates replied that he investigated human affairs, the Indian laughed and said: " No one is able to observe human affairs if he is ignorant of divine affairs."[19]

There are striking similarities in some of the philosophical ideas shared in common by the Greeks and the Indians of this period.

As for the essence of the ultimate being or the foundation of the universe, the Indian Upanishadic texts (700 B.C. to 100 B.C.) speculated that it must be Brahman: the whole world is Brahman; everything originates from it and returns to it, and it is the subtle essence that inheres in everything.[20] Like the Indians, the Ionian philosophers were very much interested in the *arché* or *Urstoff* of the universe. Thales declared this primary substance to be water; Anaximenes claimed it to be air. On the contrary, Anaximander suggested that it is the Boundless or the Infinite, which is imperishable, inexhaustible, indestructible, and endless. In this conception of the prime substance, Anaximander came closest to the Upanishadic philosophers. Herakleites of Ephesus (536-470 B.C.) identified the *Urstoff* with fire, which is in constant flux; thus all things are forms of fire. This fire-image is close to the heart of the teaching of Buddha, who in his famous "Fire Sermon" declares that all things are on fire. The Eleatic Parmenides (470 B.C.) developed the idea of Being at the root of everything whose only quality is existence. The Parmenidian emphasis on Being as opposed to Non-Being could be related to the dualistic Samkhya philosophy only in the sense that he rejects the Samkhya dualism and subscribes to the Upanishadic monism.[21]

The idea of metempsychosis that the spirits or souls of the deceased move around and inhabit animals or plants is a fairly widespread belief among Indians of the Hindu, Jain, and Buddhist

---

[19] Eusebius, *Evangelicae Praeparationis*, XV.xi.3; A. J. Festugière, Grecs et sages orientaux," *RHR* 130 (1945): 34-36; cited by Sedlar, 14.
[20] See supra ch. 6.
[21] Sedlar, 16-21.

religious persuasions since the time of the Upanishads. This idea was known in Greece as early as the fifth century B.C., in Orphism and Pythagoreanism. Plato in the fourth century refers to it as an "ancient tradition."[22] The idea is attested in the *Brhadaranyaka Upanishad* of the seventh century B.C. The basic Upanishadic idea is that all souls are subject to the law of karma, which implies that all souls are involved in the process of transmigration until their final release which can be accomplished only through gnosis or mystical knowledge. It also implies that the present condition of every being is the direct result of the being's karma or of the quality of its behavior in its past existence and that the soul becomes successively purified through a series of rebirths—and idea which is found in a modified form in the Catholic notion of purgatory. What is remarkable about the Greek idea of metempsychosis is that the Greeks themselves considered the idea a foreign one. According to Herodotus, the Greeks learned it from Egypt.[23]

A special feature of the worldview of the Jews, Christians, and Zoroastrians is that time is linear and that this universe is unique and unrepeatable. On the contrary, in classical Greece as well as in India the recorded belief has been that time is cyclical and that the universe is periodically created and destroyed. In the Hindu view, the great age (*mahayuga*) is divided into four lesser ages of progressive decline: *Krta, Treta, Dvapara,* and *Kali.* The present age, *Kaliyuga,* will come to an end with the appearance of Kalki, the incarnation of Vishnu, who is to bring about another *Krta Yuga*.[24] The Buddhists call the great age *mahakalpa,* which is divided into four lesser cycles called *asamkheyas* (immensities); the great age is destroyed by fire and water, successively, but only to be renewed. This age was considered by the earlier Buddhists as the last after the birth and death of Gautama Buddha who will never again be reincarnated; however, the beginning of a new age is associated with the coming of the future Buddha, Maitreya who appears as the Paraclete in the Gospel of John and as the Christ with the second coming in the Book of Revelations.[25] Hesiod has made the Greek view popular in his *Works and Days* with his

---

[22] *Phaedo* 70 cd.
[23] Herodotus II.123.
[24] *Vishnu Purana* IV.24; R. F. Gombrich, "Ancient Indian Cosmology," in C. Blacker and M. Loewe, eds. *Ancient Cosmologies* (London, 1975), 121.
[25] H. C. Warren, *Buddhism in Translations,* 315, n.1; Sedlar, 42-46.

notion of the four ages of gradual physical and moral decadence: Golden Age, Silver Age, Bronze Age, and Iron Age. The Greeks also had the idea of cyclic scheme in world ages since the time of Anaximander in the sixth century B.C.[26] Plato also taught the view that world-destruction occurs alternately by fire and by water, and at regular intervals.[27] They saw the creation and destruction of the worlds patterned after the cyclical change of seasons in the earthly year.[28]

The idea of the deterioration of the quality of life implied a pessimistic view toward the present life and a desire to escape by looking forward to deliverance from the cycle of becoming. The ascetic ideal was always held in esteem in India from the Vedic times. One Rg-Vedic hymn (136) describes the naked ascetics wearing "garments soiled of yellow hue" and "all sky to look upon." The digambara Jain monks still today go about naked. These monks also practiced severe austerities in order to obtain enlightenment and freedom. So asceticism was viewed as a means of attaining gnosis or sacred knowledge which would lead to deliverance. Two popular forms of asceticism are abstinence from marriage and all sexual activities and vegetarianism. Not only in India but also in Greece, these two forms of asceticism were practiced.

Many Greek cults required that the participants in divine worship be chaste; only chaste priests and priestesses were allowed to serve the virgin goddesses Athena and Artemis. Eleusinian mystery cult also required chastity from initiates; the Pythagorean Brotherhood, which practiced vegetarianism, allowed sexual relations only for procreation.[29] It is to be pointed out that the Greek ideal of chastity was of temporary duration and that continence as well as vegetarianism played only a minor role in Greek society compared to the Indian ideal.[30] One often wonders whether the ubiquitous half-naked Indian gymnosophist whom the reader encounters in classical Greek literature as an ascetic ideal has anything to do with the beginnings of the Greek ideal of chastity and vegetarianism. An interesting version of the Alexander-Dandamis meeting has been attributed to historian Arrian of the second century B.C. In this episode the Brahmins

---

[26] Sedlar, 43.
[27] *Timaeus*, 22c.
[28] Sedlar, 44.
[29] Sedlar, 37.
[30] Sedlar, 37.

describe their life-style as follows: They live in forests and dress in leaves, sleep on bare ground, observe chastity and silence, abstain from meat and cooked food, eat just the fruits of the earth, drink only water, continually sing hymns, and despise the pleasures of the senses.[31]

It is a fact that many Greeks give the Orientals at least some credit for the contributions they have made to Greek thought and ideals. Zeller writes: "The Greeks themselves were inclined from early times...to grant the peoples of the Orient, the only ones whose intellectual culture preceded their own that they had a share in the origination of their philosophy. In the early days it is only individual doctrines which in this manner are derived from the Orient."[32]

This Greek recognition of Oriental contribution should be seen as a sign of the classical Greek's readiness to learn from alien sources; the Greek word *historia* implies curiosity, openness for the alien, the other, and journeys outside Greece since Greek philosophers and historians were supposed to have travelled to foreign countries in search of wisdom.[33] The earliest recorded use of the word "philosophize" occurs in the context of travel for the sake of theory.[34] Pythagoras, the alleged inventor of the word "philosophy," is reported to have travelled widely and to have been the recipient and transmitter of Oriental wisdom.[35] Herodotus, Plato, and Aristotle also emphasize the Greek debt to the Orient while they equally stress the independence of Greek thought. Though Plato never mentions India in his writings, he himself is reported in later literature to have travelled to India.[36]

The Orient in the thought of the early Greek philosophers was primarily Egypt, the storehouse of ancient learning; however, a little later the geographers Scylax and Ctesias, who were in the service of Persian kings, brought Indian topography and mythology closer to Greece. For instance, Ctesias' "dog-headed" creatures correspond to the Sanskrit *Sunamukha* or *svamukha*, those with "blanket ears" are the Sanskrit *karnapravarana*, and the "one-

---

[31] Günther Christian Hansen, "Alexander und die Brahmanen," *Klio* 43-45 (1964), 364; Sedlar, 72
[32] E. Zeller, *Die Philosophie der Griechen in ihrer geschichtlichen Entwicklung*, I (Darmstadt, 1963), 20; cited by Wilhelm Halbfass, *India and Europe* (Albany, 1988), 5.
[33] Halbfass, 5.
[34] Herodotus I.30.
[35] Diogenes Laërtius I.12; Halbfass, 6.
[36] Herodotus I.60 and Halbfass, 6.

footed" creature is the Sanskrit *ekapada*.³⁷ In Halbfass's assessment, "some ideas which later generations associated frequently and commonly with Indian religion and the Indian way of life, such as vegetarianism...and the contempt for death, already emerged in the pre-Alexandrian image of India."³⁸ What is, therefore, clear from the few references cited above is that the religion and philosophy of India had not yet played a major role in the development of Greek thought until the end of the fourth century B.C.

C. *India and the Greek World: After Alexander*

Alexander (356 - 323 B.C.)who had learned something about Asia from his tutor Aristotle broke through the Persian defences that separated the Greek world from India and waged a military campaign in northwest India. Alexander's conquest served as a watershed in the Greek understanding of Asia and brought the Indian subcontinent into direct communication with Greece.³⁹ A court historian kept daily records of Alexander's campaign up to the year 327 B.C. The philosopher Callisthenes of Olynthus accompanied Alexander and wrote about his exploits till his departure from Bactria to India. Four factual histories of Alexander's campaigns were written after Alexander's death by eyewitnesses: by Nearchos the admiral, by Onesikritos the chief pilot, by Aristobolus the architect, and by Ptolemy the general and later founder of the famous Egyptian dynasty named for him. Besides being glorifications of Alexander, these accounts were also faithful reports about India. Though they are not available in their original versions, Arrian's *Indica* (c. 150 A.D.) preserved much of the information contained in them. At least twenty of Alexander's contemporaries wrote histories about him.⁴⁰ The tendency of these historians was to portray Alexander along the existing literary parallels of the heroes of the Trojan War, which

---

[37] K. Karttunen, "The Reliability of the Indica of Ktesias," *Studia Orientalia* 50 (1981):105-107; Halbfass, 453.

[38] Halbfass, 11; W. Reese, *Die griechischen Nachrichten über Indien bis zum Feldzuge Alexanders des Grossen* (Leipzig, 1914), 66 ff.; Wecker, "India," *RE* 9 (1916), 1264-1325.

[39] W. W. Tarn, *Alexander the Great* (Cambridge, 1948), I, Pt. 2.

[40] C. A. Robinson, Jr. "The Extraordinary Ideas of Alexander the Great," *American Historical Review* 62 (1957): 326-327; L. Pearson, *The Lost Histories of Alexander the Great* (London, 1960); J. R. Hamilton, "Cleitarchus and Aristobolus," *Historia* 10 (1961): 448-458.

convention was a commonplace in the literature of the period. Facts were soon mixed up with fancy in the Alexander romances which became popular after the death of Alexander; Cleitarchus of Colophon and Pseudo-Callisthenes of Alexandria (c. A.D. 200) composed such works that later fired the popular and literary imagination of the Middle Ages.[41]

Alexander conquered not merely to destroy and plunder, though, of course, he sought military glory in all his campaigns. Being the recipient of the best education of his time from Aristotle, he was an admirer of culture and literature. For him conquest was also a means for scientific discovery; that was the reason he included writers and scientists in his military campaigns.[42] Alexander really wanted to conciliate those whom he had conquered and attempted an amalgamation process in government, religion, military, and art. Accordingly, he sometimes wore Persian dress and adopted Persian imperial ceremonial at the Macedonian court; he appointed many non-Greeks to important positions in government administration; he ordered the teaching of the Greek language to native youths; above all, he promoted intermarriages between Persians and Greeks, himself setting the example by marrying the Persian princess Roxane. In many conquered territories he established Greek garrisons, which naturally served as the outposts of Hellenic civilization.[43] The natural outcome of this syncretist movement on the part of Alexander was that the mixed generation of later Greek rulers deliberately tried to fuse Greek and Oriental cultures: they erected buildings and planned towns in the Greek style and treated native deities as identical with Greek deities with similar features. This Hellenism sponsored by Alexander was characterized by syncretism, tolerance, cosmopolitanism, and openness to foreign ideas.[44]

Obviously Alexander had intended to make northwest India a permanent part of his empire; it was for this purpose that he had established a dozen satrapies with Macedonian governors and with garrisons to support them. However, events after his death did not live up to his expectations. Two years after Alexander's death, the Asian satrapies became independent and started to fight among themselves. Finally, by 304 B.C. Seleucus Nicator emerged

---

[41] E. H. Haight, *Essays on the Greek Romances* (New York, 1945).
[42] Tarn, 145-146.
[43] Tarn,133, 233.
[44] Sedlar, 56-60.

victorious from these internecine battles and felt strong enough to challenge the Indian king Chandragupta (c. 321-297 B.C.) who had already annexed the Greek territory in India to the Maurya empire which he had founded. Since a military victory proved impossible, Seleucus concluded a treaty with Chandragupta and recognized the Indian king's sovereignty over Punjab and ceded the territories of Gandhara, Gedrosia, and parts of Arachosia to the Mauryan in exchange for 500 war elephants and the matrimonial alliance of Chandragupta with a Syrian princess;[45] this treaty proved beneficial to Seleucus later because he was able to defeat his rival Antigonos at the battle of Ipsos in 301 B.C. with the help of Chandragupta's war elephants.[46] This alliance became the beginning of a long-standing friendly relationship between the Maurya and the Seleucid dynasties. From the friendly and amusing correspondence that followed, the following facts emerge: Chandragupta sent Seleucus some powerful Indian drugs; Bindusara requested of Antiochus a consignment of "figs, Greek wine, and a sophist"; to which the monarch replied that while delighted to send figs and wine, he could not deal in sophists since it was not in good form for the Greeks to do so.[47] The Seleucids sent several ambassadors to the Mauryan court of Pataliputra in the Magadha country where Buddhism as well as Hinduism flourished; two of these, Daimachos and Megasthenes, wrote books about India. Though Daimachos' work has disappeared completely, Megasthenes' work has survived in many fragments and has served as an important source of the West's knowledge about India.

The Greek Satrapy of Bactria in the mean time became an independent state under the Greek Diodotus and incorporated the famous Buddhist cultural center of Takshasila (Taxila) into the Greek kingdom. About 170 B.C. Bactria was divided into East and West Bactria with rival rulers in power. The famous Menander, celebrated in the Buddhist *Milindapanha* as a patron Buddhism and as a Buddhist, ruled in Takshasila in the late second century B.C.

---

[45] Plutarch, "Alexander," 62.2 in *Plutarch's Lives* (Loeb), VII. 401.
[46] Tarn, 96.
[47] Rawlinson, 208.

1. *More Knowledge About India*

Three major results of the Macedonian invasion and the Greek occupation of northwest India were the acquisition and dissemination of knowledge about India, the establishment of an influential hybrid Hellenistic civilization in Bactria, the Greeks' encounter with the Indian wise men, and the spread of Buddhism in central Asia.

The major source of the West's knowledge about India was Megasthenes. He could write with the authority of an eyewitness on the geography, climate, customs, and culture of the Indians. Later historians tended to accept everything Megasthenes said and continued to talk about the extreme temperatures of India, of its mighty rivers, of the absence of the Great Bear from the night sky, of the monsoons, and of the pearls collected in south India. Sugar cane, precious stones, cotton, spices, and drugs found in India made the Greeks consider India as a wealthy country. Wonderment about India grew apace with Megasthenes' description of the huge banyan trees, deadly snakes, man-like monkeys, and enormous elephants. Megasthenes also wrote about the bright-colored cotton clothes that people wore, the diet of rice and meat, and the absence of wine. He distinguished the fair-skinned Aryans of the north from the dark-hued southerners. Megasthenes talked about the "philosophers" as the smallest but the highest class among the seven groups of people he encountered in India. He observed the practice of polygamy, the fascinating ritual of *sati*, and many other customs and laws of the people, which constitute one of the valuable sources for the study of ancient law in India.[48]

Eratosthenes, the famous librarian at Alexandria from about 234-196 B.C., collated all the available information about the topography of India and included it in his *Geographica*, a work which is lost now, but summarized by Strabo along with criticisms of it by Hipparchus.[49] Eratosthenes was the first writer to present India as a peninsula; he described Ganges as flowing eastward to the ocean, shortened the dimensions of both Ganges and Indus, and indicated the existence of the island Taprobane (Sri Lanka/Ceylon).[50]

---

[48] Lach, 10.
[49] James O. Thomson, *History of Ancient Geography* (New York, 1965), 158-167.
[50] Thomson, 135.

2. Bactria

Our major sources of information about the Indo-Greek kingdoms of Bactria are numismatics and archeology, apart from the Buddhist work *Milindapanha* and the art of Gandhara. In general, what Sedlar says about Bactria's culture is worth citing:

> Greek rule in Bactria and India produced a partial amalgam of Greek and native forms of life and thought. In the 3rd and 2nd centuries B.C. this region—modern Afghanistan and northern Pakistan—was very far from being an economic and cultural backwater. Bactria under Greek rule was a flourishing country of many towns and cities; its capital, Baktra (modern Balkh) was a great entrepôt for trade between Babylon and India. In the 3rd century B.C. Chandragupta's grandson Asoka sent Buddhist missionaries to Bactria, where he erected rock inscriptions composed in Greek by someone who was obviously familiar with the vocabulary of Hellenistic philosophy. A thousand years later (7th cen. A.D.) the Chinese pilgrim Hsüan Tsang counted one hundred Buddhist monasteries and three thousand monks in the city of Baktra alone.[51]

The Bactrian coins issued by the earliest rulers were all in pure Greek style, but in India they issued a bilingual coinage, with legends in both Greek and Kharoshti scripts, which shows the hybrid nature of the Bactrian people and culture.

In 1964-65, archeologists uncovered the remains of a Greek city at Ai Khanum at the confluence of the ancient Oxus river and one of its tributaries. It was perhaps founded by Alexander himself or one of the Seleucids; it could even be the Alexandreia-on-the-Oxus mentioned in Ptolemy's *Geography*; that city was destroyed by fire about 100 B.C. Excavations revealed a Greek palace, a gymnasium, the tomb of a prominent citizen, and a Greek inscription of the maxims from the Temple of Delphi.[52] The presence of the Greek style of architecture is evident in the layout of Sagala, the capital city of Menander in Punjab and at Sirkap in Takshasila as well. The assimilative nature of the Bactrian culture can be seen in the way these Greek kings carried themselves; for instance, Menander's coins represent him as a *chakravartin*, as the supremely wise Indian ruler like Asoka or Buddha himself. The Indian work *Milindapanha*, written c. 150-100 B.C., claims that Menander became a convert to Buddhism and a disciple to Nagasena. An Indo-Chinese tradition says that he took the yellow robe in his old age

---
[51] Sedlar, 62; Thomas Watters, *On Yuan Chwang's Travels in India* (London, 1904-05), I: 108.
[52] Paul Bernard, "Ai Khanum on the Oxus: a Hellenistic City in Central Asia," *PBA* 53 (1967): 71-95; Mortimer Wheeler, *Flames over Persepolis* (New York, 1968), 75-87.

and died an *arhat* (the confirmed saint of the Christian theology typified by Jesus' Apostles). According to Plutarch, at Menander's funeral, seven nations disputed for a share of his ashes as at that of Buddha, which they later buried under stupas in their own countries—the Gospel of John seems to refer to this story in the episode of the soldiers' casting of lots for the seemless garment of Jesus.[53]

What is remarkable here about the Bactrian culture as testified by the Indian author is that the Indian testimony agrees with the evidence of the coins: the Greeks of Bactria were not merely domineering colonialists but open-minded people who integrated themselves with the culture and religion of India.

The Saka (Scythian) kings who supplanted the Greeks in Bactria after 135 B.C. continued the synthesis of Greek and Indian culture with their own in the region which now extended as far as Mathura. They retained the Greek administration and employed Greek artisans and artists; they used the Seleucid calendar and Macedonian names of months.

The Parthians, the rulers of an independent kingdom in eastern Persia, replaced the Sakas in Bactria by the beginning of the first century. The Parthians, too, continued the Hellenistic tradition in art, architecture, and administration while retaining Greek as the *lingua franca*.

By the middle of the first century B.C. the Kushans, who lived in the vicinity of Bactria, conquered the Parthians, but continued the same policy of cultural amalgamation. The archeological remains of the Kushan city of Surkh Kotal in Afghanistan reveal a synthesis of indigenous and Greek architectural motifs. For instance, though the city's general architecture is un-Greek, much of the building ornamentation is Greek; Kushan coins show images of various Indian, Greek, and Persian gods.[54] Evidence of Greek material articles found at Sirkap indicates a flourishing trade between the Parthians and the Greek world.[55] Interestingly, the most influential of the Kushan kings, Kanishka (late-first century B.C.) was a patron of Buddhism, which means that the Buddhist religion and culture were very much alive and active in northwest India and that there was mutual interaction between the Hellenistic and Buddhist cultures.

---

[53] Rawlinson, 216.
[54] Sedlar, 65.
[55] John Marshall, *A Guide to Taxila* (Cambridge, 1960), 28-31.

This interaction of Indo-Greek cultures is nowhere more evident than in the Mahayana Buddhist art of Gandhara. Up until the first century B.C. the Buddhists refrained from depicting Buddha in human form; instead, they used symbols like Buddha's wheel of law, his footprints, his umbrella, or the bodhi tree to represent him. It seems that the impetus to portray Buddha as a human being came from the influence of Greek art during the Parthian period. The Gandhara art portrayed Buddha in the fashion of a Greek god, in Greek drapery, mingled with Indian features such as *ushnisha* This phenomenon indicates that already by the first century B.C., if not earlier, Buddha was worshipped as a god in the Mahayana Buddhism of Northwest India. Sedlar writes:

> Thus the Buddha, formerly not portrayed at all, came to resemble the Greek god Apollo or a Roman emperor in heroic pose draped in a toga. The statues were drawn on classic proportions, following Hellenistic models for the physiognomy, the gestures, and the drapery, while the reliefs employ that narrative style commonly found in western Asia for recounting the life-stories of historical or religious heroes. But in every case the themes were Indian, depicting scenes from the Buddha's life and exemplifying his powers as a saviour.[56]

Some of the statues created at Gandhara were clearly the work of Greek artists. Rawlinson writes: "Zeus does duty as Kubera, Pallas Athene as an Indian attendant. Purely Greek themes like Hercules and the Lion, Ganymede and the Eagle, Tritons, Centaurs, and so forth, are reproduced with no attempt at concealment."[57]

Gradually, in the course of the Kushan era, the statues were sculpted more and more by native craftsmen who were farther removed from the original Greek influence since the statues became more Indian and less Greek. This tendency would indicate that the Indian culture was becoming more inclined in the second and third centuries to reject foreign influences on their art and culture. Meanwhile the Hellenized statues of Buddha spread all along the trade routes throughout most of northwest India and east Asia.

3. *The Indian Gymnosophists*

I referred above to the meeting of the Bactrian king Menander with the Buddhist sage Nagasena, which is the subject matter of the *Milindapanha*. Before Menander, Alexander himself had met

---

[56] Sedlar, 66-67.
[57] Rawlinson, 222.

some of these Indian wise men who are known in Greek writings as the gymnosophists of India. What is important to note about these philosophical encounters is the Greeks' openness to accept the possibility of a philosophical partnership of debate with and instruction in the wisdom of India.

Who are these gymnosophists? They are mostly men who left the world to walk on the path that leads to the attainment of perfection or *arahatta* or *nirvana* (*nibbana*). Long before the time of Gautama Buddha, there were in India religious men and women who were known as "wanderers" (*Parivrajakas* or *Paribbajakas*), who are to be distinguished from forest-dwelling hermits (*vanaprasthas*)celebrated in the Upanishads and the epics. Some of these were known also as *sramanas* or pilgrims whose only motto was "keep on going." Some of these ascetics were called *sannyasins* (renouncers) when they were seen practicing the ideal of total renunciation. A person could enter upon this stage of life when he felt he was ripe for it instead of waiting till old age and retirement. This way of life implied a dying to to the world; hence funeral rites were performed when the renouncers left home and took to the open air.[58] In the *Upanishads* some of these ascetics appear as sages or *rishis* like Yajnavalkya and Uddalaka, who having practiced asceticism attained transcendental wisdom and whose role in society was to teach this truth to their disciples. Buddha resembles these Upanishadic sages.[59]

The wanderers travelled about singly or in bands; sometimes they would stop at certain public lodgings for the discussion of theological issues. "Thus we hear of the wandering mendicant Potthapada, who on a certain occasion was dwelling at the hall put up in Queen Mallika's Park for the discussion of systems of opinion, the hall set round with a row of Tinduka trees, and known by the name of 'The Hall'. And there was with him a great following of mendicants; to wit, three hundred mendicants."[60] These wandering monks followed the teachings of one leader and travelled together. Some of them were followers of Mahavira like the Niganthas (Jain monks), the Gotamakas (probably the

---

[58] A. K. Coomaraswamy, *Hinduism and Buddhism* (Philadelphia: American Philosophical Society, n.d.), 29-30.

[59] Patrick G. Henry and Donald K. Swearer, *For the Sake of the World: The Spirit of Buddhist and Christian Monastaicism* (Minneapolis, 1989), 72-75.

[60] T. W. Rhys Davids, *Dialogues of the Buddha*, i.224 in A. K. Coomarswamy, *Buddha and the Gospel of Buddhism* (New York, 1964), 152.

schismatic followers of Devadatta, Buddha's cousin), Buddhist monks, and Brahmanical groups. Of these the followers of Buddha later developed into an Order and religion, the *sangha* and religion of Buddhism. They were all ascetics, characterized by celibacy and voluntary poverty. Some of the Jain monks, dating from the seventh century B.C., still now abandon all worldly possessions including clothing and subject the body to intense suffering and mortification; at their initiation their hair is pulled out by roots; they meditate in full sunlight of a hot summer day and maintain an uncomfortable posture for several hours a day. The Ajivakas were more notorious for their austerities than the Jain monks. A. L. Basham describes the lone Ajivaka as follows:

> Naked and solitary, he fled like a deer at the sight of men. He ate refuse, small fish, and dung. In order that his austerities should not be disturbed he took up his abode in the depths of the jungle. In winter he would leave his thicket and spend the night exposed to the bitter wind, returning to the shade as soon as the sun rose. By night he was wet with melted snow, and by day with the water dripping from the branches of trees. In summer he reversed the process, and was scorched by the sun all day, while at night the thicket shielded him from the cooling breeze.[61]

Onesikritos, the pilot of Alexander's fleet, is the first reported author who describes the Greeks' encounter with the Indian gymnosophists. According to Onesikritos, Alexander heard about the ascetic exploits of the Indian wise men and dispatched the author to make contact with them. Having met them in the outskirts of the city of Takshasila, he invited them to an audience with Alexander. We do not know whether these men accepted the invitation or not. However, in a manuscript written about 100 B.C. we find the story of such a meeting.[62] In the first century A.D. Plutarch included it in his *Lives*. In this story Alexander has taken ten sages as prisoners and asks them each a question with the stipulation that if anyone fails to answer the question satisfactorily he will be put to death. Some of the questions and answers are these: "Which are most numerous, the dead or the living?" "The living, because the dead do not exist." "Which is the most cunning of the beasts?" "The one which men have not yet found

---

[61] A. L. Basham, *History and Doctrine of the Ajivakas* (London, 1951), 111; cited by Henry and Swearer, 78.

[62] Papyrus Berl. 13044, cited by J. Duncan M. Derrett, "Greece and India: the Milindapanha, the Alexander-romance and the Gospels," *Zeitschrift für Religions- und Geistesgeschichte* 19 (1967), 49,51.

out." "Which is stronger, life or death?" "Life is stronger than death because it supports so many miseries."[63] A second-century A.D. document discovered in Cairo describes Alexander's meeting with the Brahmin Dandamis who criticizes the Greek life-style of wearing clothes, meat-eating, drinking, avarice, war, and subjugation of other peoples. He tells Alexander to renounce his kingdom and live the life of an ascetic recluse. Though Alexander approves of the ascetic life-style, he refuses to follow the advice of Dandamis for practical reasons, citing the responsibilities of his kingly office.[64]

The gymnosophists were known not only for their stoic attitudes towards pain and pleasure but also for their contempt for death. The gymnosphist Kalanos exemplified this attitude better than anyone else. Kalanos reportedly went with the Greeks on their return from India. In Susa he immolated himself, like Hercules before him, by his own free will in front of the whole populace.[65] Clearchos also found the gymnosophists' defiance of death as their distinctive characteristic.[66] The topos of the defiance of death is repeated by Cicero, who says that Indian sages spend their lives naked, can easily withstand heat and cold, and burn themselves without a sigh of sadness.[67] Cicero refers also to *sati*, the custom of self-immolation practiced by Indian women who follow their husbands into the funeral pyre, a custom also referred to by Aristobolus, the historian of Alexander, and later by Plutarch, Diodorus, Philo, and Seneca.[68]

The Greeks seemed to have known different kinds of Indian sages. According to Strabo, Alexander's admiral Nearchos divided them into two classes: political advisors and investigators of nature (XV.1.66). Megasthenes divides the Indian sages or sophists into two groups: the Brahmanas and Sarmans; the former represent a consistent philosophy and a more civilized way of life, while the latter are renouncers who practice a radical and uncompromising life-style. Megasthenes also says that the Brahmins knew all

---

[63] Plutarch, "Alexander," 69: Loeb VII. 405-409; cited by Sedlar, 71.
[64] Hansen, 364; Sedlar, 72.
[65] Hansen, 358-360.
[66] Halbfass, 12.
[67] *Tusculanae disputationes* V.7:"Quae barbaria India vastior aut agrestior? In ea tamen gente primum ei, qui sapientes habentur, nudi aetatem agunt et Caucasi nives hiemalemque vim perferunt sine dolore, cumque ad flammam se adplicaverunt, sine gemitu aduruntur"; Flavius Josephus, *De bello Iudaico* VII.352 ff; Halbfass, 13.
[68] Halbfass, 13.

those doctrines concerning nature which were subsequently taught by the Greeks.[69] Later, Flavius Josephus would present the Jews as descendants of Indian philosophers.[70] The *samanaioi* of Clement of Alexandria are obviously Buddhists.[71] Also, Porphyry's reference to the Brahmanas and Samanas indicates that the people of the Hellenistic world were not totally unfamiliar with the distinction between Hindus and Buddhists.[72] It is possible to raise the question whether the Greek philosopher Pyrrhon of Ellis (365-275 B.C.), the reputed founder of Scepticism in Greece, who, according to Diogenes Laërtius (2nd cent. A.D.), accompanied Alexander's army to India, had contacts with the Indian ascetics. Perhaps Diogenes is correct that Pyrrhon's encounters with the Indians led to his love of solitude and to the formulation of the Sceptic thesis that knowledge is impossible and that the wise person should suspend judgment on all questions, for Diogenes bases his claim on information provided by Pyrrhon's followers.[73] Whether Pyrrhon was influenced by India or not, the proposition that the Greek philosophers of the time were aware of the religions and philosophies of India is tenable.

4. *Buddhism in Central Asia*

According to legend, it was a disciple of Ananda who brought Buddhism to Gandhara in Bactria fifty years after the death of Buddha. According to Hsüan-tsang, it was two merchants, Trapusha and Bhallika, who were the first to offer food to Buddha after his enlightenment and who became his followers, that preached Buddhism in the area; this legend seems to have some etymological evidence: the town of Bahlika (Bhalk) is perhaps derived from the name Bhallika. It is quite possible that Buddhists were in the area during the invasion of Alexander since Onesikritos encountered fifteen Indian ascetics in the outskirts of Takshasila, Bactria, as mentioned earlier. From the time of the Mauryas (300-150 B.C.), there is enough archeological evidence to support the view that there were Buddhist monks in the northwest from the third century B.C. Hinüber writes:

---

[69] Halbfass, 15.
[70] *Contra Apionem* I.178 ff.
[71] *Stromateis* I.17.3 ff.
[72] *De abstinentia* IV. 17 ff.; Porphyry quotes the Gnostic Bardaisanes.
[73] "Pyrrhon" IX.61 in Diogenes, *Lives* II.475; cited by Sedlar, 75.

> Asoka's inscriptions in Kharoshti characters at Shabazgarhi and Mansehra, and those in Greek and Aramaic, bear witness to his missionary zeal. He seems to have been the first to build stupas here; that of Dharmarajika in Taxila, dating back to the period of of the Maurya empire, became a centre of Buddhist scholarship. The pilgrim Hsüan-tsang records several stupas in the Punjab area, and archaeology confirms that they go back to Mauryan times. Legends relating to the building of these stupas mostly refer to episodes in the former lives of the Buddha, so that th north-west became associated with his previous existence, as east India was associated with his last.[74]

After the successive invasions of the Sakas and the Parthians, the Kushanas in the first century B.C., promoted Buddhism, while the earlier Greek, Saka, and Parthian administrations at best tolerated it. According to Edward Conze, "Buddhism had by the second century B.C. been well established in Central Asia. Khotan, Kucha, Turfan, etc., were at the time flourishing centres of culture owing to the caravan routes which went through them. The establishment of Buddhism on the great silk routes was an event of decisive importance for its future propagation in East Asia."[75] At the latest, from the first century A. D. Buddhism pushed its frontiers across the whole of north India and parts of Chinese Turkestan and Afghanistan. The Kushana emperor Kanishka built large stupas near Prusupura (Peshawar), much admired by the Chinese pilgrims, and even convened a Buddhist Council. A few monasteries dating to that period have been unearthed. Klimkeit writes:

> From the northwest India Buddhism spread through what is now Afghanistan to the areas beyond the Oxus to the Tarim Basin. Not only the adherents of Mahayana, but also of Theravada schools settled in the oasis towns of Central Asia. Thus the Vaibhashikas, a branch of the Sarvastivadins, were strongly represented in Kucha, maybe also in Turfan....It is clear that in and since his [Kanishka's] time the faith from India established various important centers between the Indus and Oxus. Of the Iranian people in Central Asia, it was especially the Parthians and Sogdians who were open to the foreign religion and who spread it further to the east. Indicative of the situation is the fact that a Parthian prince of Arsacide blood, stemming from Bukhara, whose name is transmitted to us as An-Shi-Kao, travelled to China in 148 A.D. both on a religious and diplomatic mission. An especially important role in the spread of the Buddhist faith to the east was played by the Sogdians.

---

[74] Oskar von Hinüber, "Expansion to the North: Afghanistan and Central India," in *The World of Buddhism*, eds. Heinz Bechert and Richard Gombrich (New York, 1984), 100.

[75] Edward Conze, *A Short History of Buddhism* (London, 1964), 63.

An east Iranian people with centers around Samarkhand and Bukhara, they possessed a string of commercial settlements all along the northern and southern silk routes leading into the heartland of China....Remnants of Buddhist and Christian literature are both preserved in Sogdian. Besides the Parthians and Sogdians, the Sakian Iranians, living especially in and around Khotan, were followers of the Buddhist faith. In Khotan, Theravada and Mahayana were both represented, the latter predominating. Along with the Khotanese, Sanskrit was used as an ecclesiastical language.[76]

Up to the end of the nineteenth century hardly anything was known about the Buddhist presence in central Asia. However all this changed by a string of discoveries beginning with that of the Gandhari *Dhammapada* (1889). It was followed by Sir Aurel Stein's pre-World-War-I expeditions which uncovered quite a library of Buddhist texts before World War I. Besides many minor discoveries since then, one spectacular find came from Naupur near Gilgit. Here some shepherds unearthed some sixty manuscripts on birch-bark, paper, and palm leaf, containing fifty different texts along with a complete copy of the *Mulasarvastivada-Vinaya* in Sanskrit. These manuscripts date from the sixth century.[77]

Though there does not survive any earlier manuscript from this area, there is the first-century A.D. Gandhara image of Buddha flanked by two Bodhisatvas, probably Maitreya and Vajrapani; its inscription seems to mention the transfer of merit (Hinüber, 104). Manichean documents from the Parthian region supply evidence for this lack of knowledge about Buddhism and Hinduism in the area for the earlier period.

Right from the beginning, Mani (216-276) had strong affinities with Buddhism and Christianity. He considered himself an apostle of Christ like Paul and Thomas and recognized the place and role of Jesus and Buddha in the divine plan of redemption, though his religion superseded them all;[78] Mani spent at least one year in northwest India, where Buddhism was influential; a Turfan document discovered in Central Asia attests to Mani's travel to

---

[76] Hans-J. Klimkeit, "Christian-Buddhist Encounter in Medieval Central Asia," in *The Cross and the Lotus*, ed. G. W. Houston (Delhi, 1985)10-11; O. Hansen, "Die buddhistische Literatur der Sogdier," *Handbuch der Orientalistik* I, 4 (Leiden: Brill, 1968): 83-99.
[77] Hinüber, 100-104.
[78] Sedlar, 208-234.

India.[79] According to the Turfan document, he converted a Buddhist ruler to his faith. The king hailed him as Buddha (Parthian *bwd*) and as the path to salvation.[80] Mani's familiarity with Indian ideas finds support in Al-Biruni's statement that Mani learned about the doctrine of reincarnation in India.[81] What is important to note here is that there are several Buddhist terms found in the Parthian and Sogdian Buddhist documents, such as Parthian *mwxs* for Sanskrit *Moksha*, Parthian *pwn* for Sanskrit *punya*, and Turkic *mitrii burxan* for Buddha Maitreya.[82]

The spread of Buddhism in Central Asia seems to have followed the trade routes on land. From Western Asia to India an all-land route was feasible until the first century A.D. when these routes were effectively blocked by the rulers in Persia.[83] Sedlar describes the extent of this trade route:

> The most important routes converged upon the great metropolis of Seleukia on the Tigris. Although far inland, Seleukeia was a deep-water port connected by canal with the Euphrates; it was the nerve-center for important trade routes leading in every direction across Asia. Arriving from Smyrna, Antiocheia, or places between, at Seleukeia the traveller could either continue overland or sail down-river, then via the Persian Gulf and the Arabian Sea to India. By land the principal route led through Baktra (Balkh), then via the passes of the Hindu Kush to Kapisa (near Kabul), Thakshasila, Sagala, Mathura, and finally Pataliputra (Patna) on the Ganges.[84]

Probably the spread of Buddhist and Hindu ideas to the West was facilitated more by sea than by land for the simple reason that travel was easier on water than on land because of the relative freedom from highway robbery. In fact, since there is more historical evidence for sea travel between India and the West, it is reasonable to assume that Indian missionaries and wise men travelled with trade caravans, as it happened later during the sixteenth and seventeenth centuries when missionaries accompanied European merchants to the Americas and Asia. The Buddhist monks were wandering missionary-minded mendicants by

---

[79] W. Sundermann, "Zur frühen missionarischen Wirksamkeit Manis," *AOASH* 24 (1), p. 88; Mani himself claimed to have travelled the whole land of India (*Kephalia*, trans. H. J. Polotsky and A. Böhlig, *MHSMB* (Stuttgart, 1940), I. 184; Sedlar, 211.

[80] Mary Boyce, *A Reader in Manichean Middle Persian and Parthian* (Leiden, 1975), 36; Klimkeit, 19.

[81] Al-Biruni, *India* I. 54 ff.: Klimkeit, 19.

[82] Klimkeit, 19-21.

[83] Mortimer Wheeler, *Rome Beyond the Imperial Frontiers* (London, 1954), 154.

[84] Sedlar, 87.

profession; Buddha himself reportedly gave them permission to travel with caravans even during the rainy months when the monks were supposed to stay in monasteries, according to the *Vinaya*; the reason probably was that certain trade trips took more than three months. There is sufficient evidence to attest that a significant volume of trade was carried on between India and the Greek world.

D. *Indians in the Greco-Roman World*

Even before Alexander's time, Indians were known to have been in Greece, like the Indian who disputed with Socrates and the Indian contingent in Xerxes' army of invasion (480-479 B.C.); so also Indian curios like colorful peacocks and parrots had been introduced into Greece in earlier times.[85] With the Macedonian's invasion, trade in Indian ivory and spices began.[86] After Alexander's death, trade continued, but it fell into the hands of intermediary powers along the travel route from India reaching Alexandria in Egypt.

Early in the third century B.C., a Greek army officer Patrocles travelled to India and brought useful information about that land.[87] Perhaps it was from him that the Geographer Eratosthenes (late 3rd century B.C.) gathered his information about the physical contours of the country, the existence of Sri Lanka, the mouth of Ganges, and the Monsoons.[88] There is evidence that Ptolemy II (c. 285-246 B.C.), who extended his naval power in the Red Sea, exchanged ambassadors with the Mauryan emperors of India. He displayed Indian women, dogs, oxen, parrots, and peacocks during his triumphal procession which took place in Alexandria 271-270 B.C. ; later, Ptolemy IV (221-203 B.C.) had a luxurious river-boat embellished with Indian stones built for himself.[89]

During the second century much of the trade between India and Alexandria was conducted through intermediaries, like Arabia Felix (Yemen), the town of Moscha, and the island of Socotra. According to Agatharchides of Alexandria (c. 110 B.C.), merchants

---

[85] Lach, 11.
[86] W. W. Tarn, *The Greeks in Bactria and India* (Cambridge, 1951), 361-362.
[87] Strabo, *Geography* II.3.3-5; Sedlar, 84.
[88] Strabo, *Geography* XV.1.11-14.
[89] Athenaeus, *Deipnosophistae* 196-201; Loeb II, 387-411; George F. Hourani, *Arab Seafaring in the Indian Ocean in Ancient and Early Medieval Times* (Beirut, 1963), 22-24).

from Patala, a port at the mouth of the Indus, used to visit Socotra.[90]

Strabo (c. 63 B.C.-A.D. 21), the author of six historical books on Asia in Greek and a conserver of earlier geographers, reports that about this time the Ptolemies of Egypt sent Eudoxos of Kyzikos on a trade mission to India. In this expedition the Greeks were assisted by a shipwrecked Indian captain rescued from the Egyptian waters; they went to India and purchased precious stones and fragrances.[91] Strabo also gives information of a flourishing trade between Egypt and India in the first century B.C. during the Roman rule. He himself accompanied one such trade trip down the Nile to Ethiopia, where goods were transferred overland to Myos Hormos on the Red Sea. About this time Alexandrian merchants used to send about 120 ships to India.[92] Obviously, the *pax romana*, ushered in by Emperor Augustus (27 B.C.-A.D. 14), helped cut down the incidence of Arab piracy on the high seas and improve direct trade relations between India and the Roman empire.[93] It is to be mentioned in passing that Pomponius Mela, the first Latin geographer whose work has survived, has nothing significant to add to the West's knowledge of India.[94]

Another factor that assisted the Alexandrian sailors in their trade with India was their own discovery of the possible utilization of the southwest monsoon winds in making the voyage across open sea in record time.[95] According to Pliny, the voyage from the Arabian port of Cane to Muziris in South India took only forty days.[96] The port of Muziris that Pliny is talking about is not Cranganore on the west coast, but Muziris in the Pandian kingdom on the east coast at the mouth of River Kaveri, the reason being that it is extremely dangerous to dock ships on the west coast during the monsoon season. A flotilla of hundred plus ships naturally discouraged the pirates.

A first-century (A.D.) work, the *Periplus of the Erithraean Sea* ("Circuit of the Indian Ocean"), an anonymous Greek work

---

[90] Hourani, 22.
[91] Strabo,*Geography* II.3.3-5.
[92] Strabo, XV.1.4; Loeb VII.5; P. Thomas, "Roman Trade Centers on the Malabar Coast," *Indian Geographical Journal* 6 (1931-32): 230-240.
[93] M. P. Charlesworth, "Some Notes on the *Periplus Maris Erythraei*," *Classical Quarterly* (1928), 97.
[94] Lach, 14.
[95] Tarn, *Bactria and India*, 369.
[96] Pliny, *Natural History* VI.26; Loeb II.419.

originally written in Egypt by a Roman subject around 50, gives clear, concise, and accurate information about Roman trade with India. The author talks about harbor facilities, political conditions, customs duties, and merchant wares in the different places along the trade route to India.[97] The writer, who uses first-person pronoun in parts of the book, may have travelled with the merchants on a trip to India. At the port of Barygaza, the author says, the Greeks traded wine, copper, tin, lead, coral, topaz, gold, silver, sweet clover, and other items which were exchanged for a profit with the money of the country. The king of land purchased from the Greeks silver vessels, singing boys, beautiful maidens for his harem, fine wines, and thin clothing. In his description of Muziris, he says that the port city abounds in ships sent there with cargoes from Arabia and with the boats of the Greeks.[98] A fourth-century map known as the Peutinger Table shows a temple dedicated to divine Augustus at the mouth of River Kaveri, which suggests that there were Romans living there in the first century B.C.[99]

Linguistics and literature supply some supporting evidence to Greek trade with India. As mentioned before, many Greek words for Indian products, such as those for cinnamon, ginger, cloves, rice, brown sugar, camphor, nard, apes, sapphire, emerald, opal, lapis lazuli, and sandalwood, have corresponding cognate words in Tamil, Malayalam, and/or Sanskrit.[100] The Tamil epic of *Cilappadikaram* refers to Greek ships which brought gold to Muziris and left laden with pepper, to Greek mansions at the mouth of Kaveri river, to the Greek carpenters who built a palace for the Tamil king, and to Greek bodyguards in the service of the Tamil king.[101]

Archeological evidence also indicates that the Greeks and Romans engaged insignificant trade with south India. One typical site that has yielded much evidence for Western trade activity in

---

[97] *Periplus of the Erithraean Sea*, trans. Wilfred H. Schoff (New York, 1912); K.A. Nilakanta Sastri, *Foreign Notices of South India* (Madras, 1972); Sedlar, 91.
[98] Sastri, 57.
[99] Martin P. Charlesworth, "Roman Trade with India: A Resurvey," *Studies in Roman Economic and Social History in Honor of Allan Chester Johnson* (Princeton, 1951), 142; cited by Sedlar, 93.
[100] Karl Lokotsch, *Etymologisches Wörterbuch der europäschen Wörter orientalischen Ursprungs* (Heidelberg, 1927); R. Caldwell, *Dravidian Languages*, 89-91; Sedlar, 93.
[101] V. Kanakasabbhai Pillai, *The Tamils Eighteen Hundred Years Ago* (Madras, 1966), 16-38; Sedlar, 93-94.

the first century was the port of "Poudouke" (modern Pondicherry) mentioned by *Periplus* and the Ptolemy.[102] Sedlar writes:

> Poudouke by the middle of the first century A.D. was a brick-built emporium with extensive storage and manufacturing facilities. To this port came Indian ships carrying precious stones from Ceylon, silks and spices from the Ganges region. Greek merchants arriving overland from the Malabar coast met them there. Fairly superficial digging at the site of Poudouke has unearthed enormous quantities of Western material, indicative of the large volume of commerce conducted at this place. Articles of Mediterranean origin—most notably the Italian red-glazed "Arretine" pottery, which went out of production about 45 A.D.—are here suddenly super-imposed upon a purely native and local culture. The excavations at Poudouke provide striking confirmation of the older literary evidence that the reign of Augustus at Rome witnessed a significant upsurge in the Indo-Mediterranean trade.[103]

Hoards of Roman coins have been excavated in different parts of south India, especially those from the period of Augustus to Nero. Just recently, archeologists excavating around the South Indian state of Andhra Pradesh have unearthed more than 15,000 Roman gold and silver coins bearing the impressions of the Roman emperors Augustus, Tiberius, Nero, and Plotina, the wife of Trajan. The most rewarding single dig was at Akkenapalli in Nalgonda district, where more than 1,000 Roman gold and silver coins were unearthed.[104] It seems that Indian kings and merchants considered the Roman coins primarily as gold and silver bullions and as capital reserves rather than as a means of exchange since these coin hoards also had jewelry and other valuables and since much of the trade was in the nature of barter.

The increased trade between Rome and India in the first century resulted in a huge trade deficit for Rome with the outflow of gold and silver from the empire. This situation caused some serious concern for the Roman economists. According to Pliny, who wrote during Vespasian's reign (69-79 A.D.), "the maritime commerce between India and the Roman empire caused the export of over 50 million sesterces ($5,000,000) annually to India, or 100 million sesterces ($10,000,000) for India, China, and the Arabian Peninsula taken together."[105] Emperor Tiberius complained to the Roman senate in a letter about this financial drain due to the purchase of

---

[102] *Periplus* 60; Ptolemy, *Geography* I.14.
[103] Sedlar, 94.
[104] *India Abroad*, May 12, 1989, p. 22.
[105] Sedlar, 94.

female slaves and luxury items like Kashmir wool, ivory, pearls, tortoise shell, silk, and precious stones.[106] Pliny lamented: "This is the sum which our luxuries and our women cost us."[107] Alaric's demand that the Roman emperor pay him "three thousand pounds of pepper" as ransom of Rome seems to suggest that there was vigorous trade going on between Rome and India even in the fifth century, that is, even after the disastrous division of the empire in 364.[108]

One disappointing feature of the Rome-India trade is that we do not find much evidence of Indian material goods on the Roman soil. The reason for this is probably that India exported to Rome mostly perishable consumer goods like Chinese silk, spices, and similar things. Even so, an ivory statuette of the Indian goddess Lakshmi was unearthed in Pompeii in 1939; it was probably brought to Italy before A.D. 79.[109] As Lach points out, in Italy the chief port for Indian wares was Puteoli (Pozzuoli) near Naples, where Domitian had a warehouse constructed in A.D. 92 to store Indian spice and silks; later he improved a highway that connected Puteoli with Rome.[110]

While silk from China, processed in Syria and Egypt, was the staple item of the land trade, pepper and the other spices were the major items of trade from India. Pepper was used for cooking and for manufacturing drugs. Pliny writes:

> It is quite surprising that the use of pepper has come so much into fashion, seeing that in other substances which we use, it is sometimes their sweetness and sometimes their appearance that has attracted our notice; whereas, pepper has nothing in it that can plead for recommendation to either fruit or berry; its only desirable quality being a certain pungency; and yet it is for this that we import it all the away from India! Who was the first to make trial of it as an article of food?[111]

The answer to Pliny is that since pepper was and still is a spice used in South India and elsewhere, probably the Western traders who went to India learned to use it as a digestive and as a preservative from the Indians who had been using pepper for these purposes for a long time. Like pepper, ginger was also used as a

---

[106] Tacitus, *The Annals of Imperial Rome* III.53.
[107] *Natural History* XII.84.
[108] Rawlinson, 151.
[109] A Maiuri, "Statuetta eburnea de arte indiana a Pompei," *Le arti* 1 (1938-39): 111-115; Lach, 15.
[110] Lach, 15.
[111] Pliny, XII.14; cited by Lach, 16.

digestive; the Romans used it to spice dried fish. Cinnamon was used as a perfume, unguent, and condiment—the Romans thought it came from Africa! Frankincense and myrrh, the gifts of the Magi, were also thought to be products of India, even though they are actually gum resins from Africa and Arabia. What is interesting to suggest here is that the author of the Gospel of Matthew probably thought that the Magi were from India since their gifts, including gold for which India was famous from the time of Solomon, were putatively Indian.

This trade between India and the West also facilitated travel in both directions. Of course, the fact that goods were exchanged between these parts of the world indicates that those objects did not get there on their own but that people from the respective areas carried those with them. Besides this obvious conclusion, there is also some literary evidence for the presence of Indian travellers in the West and of Western travellers in India.

1. *Indians in the West*

As for Indians in Greece, the first documented evidence before the time of Alexander is that of the wise man who disputed with Socrates. After the time of Alexander, the first information comes from the edicts of Emperor Asoka (c.274-236 B.C.). His inscriptions show that he dispatched envoys to the Greek kings of Syria, Egypt, Macedonia, and Cyrene, who were cited by their names, for the purpose of preaching the Buddhist *Dharma*. In the Shabazgarhi edict, the king repents the war with Kalinga that caused immeasurable suffering to the military and civilian population and says:

> Thus these ills are of all men in equal shares but felt most by His Sacred Majesty. There is again no country where do not exist these classes, viz., Brahmana and Sramana ascetics, except among the Yonas [Ionians or Greeks]. There is no place in any country where there is not a faith of people in one or other of the sects. Therefore, even a hundredth or the thousandth part of all those people who were wounded, slain, or carried off captives, in Kalinga, would now be considered grievous by His Sacred Majesty. Nay, even if any one does mischief, what can be forgiven is considered as fit to be forgiven by His Sacred Majesty. Even those forest peoples who have come under the dominions of His Sacred majesty—even these he seeks to win over to his way of life and thought. And it is said unto them how even in his repentance is the might of His Sacred Majesty, so that they may be ashamed of their crimes and may not be killed. Indeed, His Sacred Majesty desires towards all living beings freedom from harm, restraint of passions, impartiality and cheerfulness. And what is *Dharma-vijaya*, moral conquest, is considered by His

Sacred Majesty the principal conquest. And this has been repeatedly won by His Sacred Majesty both here in his dominions and among all the frontier peoples even to the extent of six hundred yojanas where are the Yona king, Antiochos by name, and, beyond that Antiochos, the four kings named Ptolemy, Antigonos, Magas, and Alexander; below, the Cholas, Pandyas, as far as Tamraparni. Likewise, here in the king's dominion, among the Yonas and Khambojas, among the Nabhakas and Nabhitis, among Patinikas, among the Andhras and Palidas, everywhere are people following the religious injunction of His Sacred Majesty. Even those to whom the envoys of His Sacred Majesty do not go, having heard of His Majesty's practice, ordinances, and injunctions of Dharma, themselves follow, and will follow, the Dharma. The conquest that by this is won everywhere, that conquest, again, everywhere is productive of a feeling of Love. Love is won in moral conquest. That love may be, indeed, slight, but His Sacred Majesty considers it productive of great fruit, indeed, in the world beyond.[112]

As this edict indicates, in the early part of the third century the Hindu Brahmins and the Buddhist Sramanas were not known to reside in the Greek states except among the Greeks in the dominion of Asoka, that the king sent his emissaries also for moral or religious propaganda. The reference to Brahmins and Sramanas seems to suggest that both religious personnel—Hindu, Jain, and Buddhist—were included among the king's embassies and that the host countries had the opportunity to learn from all three religious representatives. There is no extant literary indication about the success or continuation of this mission in the Western world. It is quite probable that these missionaries—probably the wanderers called *paribhajakas*, mentioned frequently in the Pali scriptures, must have made many proselytes and left some lasting impression on some people in the Hellenistic nations. As mentioned earlier, the fact that Clement of Alexandria and others had inherited this distinction between Brahmanas and Sramanas—a very common distinction found in the Buddhist scriptures as *samana-brahmana* (religious teachers)—could suggest that some of these Indian sages were still to be found in the Hellenistic world after the time of Ashoka. Some archeological evidence seems to support the view that a colony of Indians existed at Memphis as early as 200 B.C.[113]

The descendants or successors of the Indians are found in the Egypt of the first century A.D. The evidence for this statement comes from the testimony attributed to Apollonius of Tyana by

---

[112] Radha Kumud Mukerjee, *Asoka* (Delhi, 1962), 164-169.
[113] Flinders Petrie in *Man* 8 (1908):129; cited by J. Edgar Bruns, *The Art and Thought of John* (New York, 1969), 117.

Philostratos. Apollonius, according to Philostratos, went to Egypt to visit the gymnosophists who lived in upper Egypt. The most remarkable thing about these gymnosophists is that these men were ashamed of their Indian heritage and therefore openly considered themselves Egyptians. Apollonius rebukes them for this behavior:

> If I deal in riddles, the Science of Pythagoras allows it; riddles are in the tradition of him who discovered the lessons contained in the Language of Silence; and you yourselves assisted Pythagoras to formulate this Science during the time when, yourselves originally Indians, you approved the Indian way. But, for shame of the reason whereby the anger of the earth made you come hither, you chose to disguise the truth that you were Ethiopians of Indian origin, and took every means to this end. This is why you have stripped yourselves of all your native fashion of dress, as though thereby you stripped yourselves of being Ethiopians; and have resolved to worship in the Egyptian manner instead of your own; and have dscended to speak in such unbecoming terms of the Indians, as though it were not a scandal for you to derive from an origin which you denounce as scandalous. Aye, not even yet have you amended this perversity; you have made a foul and scurrilous exhibition of it this very day, in saying that the Indian practices are worthless, mere sorcerers' terrors and sorcerers' lures for eye and ear, and in showing yourselves stupidly indifferent to the fame of any Science before you know the quality of it. Not that I mean to say a single word in defence of myself—my highest wish is to be as the Indians esteem me—but I do not permit the Indians to be attacked.[114]

2. *The Therapeutae*

Philo Judaeus' (20 B.C. - 50 A.D.) description of the Therapeutae of Alexandria seems to support the hypothesis that the Therapeutae were Indian Buddhists of the Theravada group which "embraced the speculative life" or emphasized salvation through gnosis.[115] According to Philo, "with regard to etymology, they are called therapeutae...either because they profess an art of medicine more excellent than that in general use in cities...or else because they have been instructed by nature and the sacred laws to serve the living God."[116] Obviously, Philo does not know why they are called by the name therapeutae. He is not clear whether they are

---

[114] Philostratos, VI.11; trans. J. S. Phillimore (Oxford, 1912), II, 111-112.
[115] Philo, *A Treatise on Contemplative Life* in *The Essential Philo*, ed., Nahum N. Glatzer (New York, 1971), 311; F. C. Conybeare, *About the Contemplative Life* (London, 1895.
[116] Philo, 311.

Jewish ascetics; they are like God-fearing Jews who lead a virtuous life. He only says that they "devoted their whole life and themselves to the knowledge and contemplation of the affairs of nature in accordance with the most sacred admonitions and precepts of the prophet Moses."[117] What he is trying to do is to contrast them against the degenerate Greeks! Because the Therapeutae were like good Christians, Eusebius would later identify them with the earliest Christian Church of Alexandria and with the beginning of Christian monasticism.[118] What is most striking about the therapeutae is that, besides using their books for study, they followed the discipline of Buddhist monasticism—the combination of cenobitic life with study and contemplation, celibacy, celebration of festivals, fasting, and vegetarianism—for both male and female. The Therapeut sabbath is none other than the uposatha-sabbath the Buddhists monks observe; the "Pentecost" they celebrate is the Visakha celebration of the birth, renunciation, and the *parinibbana* of Buddha held on the full moon of the month of Visakha, which corresponds more or less to the Jewish month of Pentecost; Philo's "old virgins" are none other than the Bhikhunis of the Buddhist Order. Most importantly, the word *therapeuta* itself is a Buddhist word. *Therapeuta* is the Hellenization of the Sanskrit/Pali word *theravada;* they were probably the successors of the missionaries whom Emperor Asoka sent to Egypt, to the kingdom of Ptolemy, in the third century as Theravada medical missionaries. Greek, which does not have corresponding sounds for the labio-dental voice fricative v and the apico-dental fricative ∂, changed the Indian v and ∂ to Greek p and t respectively; for instance, Clement of Alexandria changed *Buddha* into *Boutta*; p, of course, is only the voiceless form of the bi-labial voiced stop b. The v of the Malayalam word *karuva* appears as p of *karpion* (cinnamon) in Ctesias.[119] Further, the Greek word *therapeia*, from which the modern English words *therapy* in the meaning of "medication" is derived, is closely related to *therapeuta* (healer), because the theravada monks whom Asoka sent abroad were by profession healers. The evidence for this comes from one of Asoka's rock edicts, the Girnar Edict, which reads:

---

[117] Philo, 325.
[118] Eusebius, *Historia Ecclesiastica*, II.17; II.18.7
[119] I intend to develop this hypothesis more extensively in a later article especially with reference to the Buddhist origins of Christian monasticism in Egypt.

> Everywhere within the dominion of His Sacred and Gracious Majesty the King, and likewise among the frontagers such as the Cholas, Pandyas, Sativaputra, the Keralaputra, what is known as Tamraparni, the Greek King, Antiochos, and those kings, too, who are the neighbors of that Antiochos—everywhere have been instituted by His Sacred and Gracious Majesty two kinds of medical treatment—medical treatment of man and medical treatment of beast. Medicinal herbs also, those wholesome for man and wholesome for beast, have been caused to be imported and to be planted in all places wherever they did not exist. Roots also, and fruits, have been caused to be imported and to be planted everywhere wherever they did not exist. On the roads, wells also have been caused to be dug and trees caused to be planted for the enjoyment of man and beast.[120]

The Asokan missionary monks living in sangharamas could very well be the therapeutic monks living in the monasteries of Alexandria. Philo, who traces the etymology of therapeuts to healing and divine worship, tells us how widespread they were:

> There are many parts of the world in which these folks are found, for both Greece and the barbarian lands must needs have their share in what is good and perfect. They are, however, in the greatest abundance in Egypt, in every one of the so-called departments [districts], and especially round about Alexandria. The principal persons draw up their colony from all quarters as to a fatherland of Therapeuts, unto a well-regarded spot which lies on Lake Marea, on a somewhat low hill, very well situated both with regard to security and the mildness of the air.[121]

We do not know exactly how many such monks were there in Egypt in the first century B.C. But we do know from the accounts of Rufinus and Jerome that the vast desert of the Nile Valley was the haven for thousands of monks, that Oxyrhyncus harbored ten thousand monks and two thousand nuns, and that Necchia, forty miles from Alexandria, had five thousand monks.[122] It could very well be true that these therapeuts were a few of the Buddhist monks who reportedly went to Sri Lanka on the occasion of the consecration of the famous Buddhist tope at Ruanwelli (160-137 B.C.) According to the Buddhist Chronicle *Mahavamsa*, Buddhist monks came from all parts of the world including "30,000 from the vicinity of Alasadda, the capital of Yona country."[123] If Alasadda mentioned here is Alexandria—which seems the case—, then

---

[120] Mookerjee, *Asoka*, 131-132.
[121] Philo 315-316; see also Arthur Lillie, *India in Primitive Christianity*, 165.
[122] Lillie, 165.
[123] Lillie, 174.

Philo's therapeuts must very well be Buddhist theravada monks residing in Egypt; on the other hand, this Alasadda could also be the Alexandreia-on-the-Indus.[124]

In this connection, I would like to add that the Essenes, the kindred monks of Palestine, also had some Buddhist affinities since their name corresponds to the Prakrt *ishi* for the Sanskrit *rishi* or to *isino* and *Isayo*, the two plural forms of a common Pali term for the Buddhist, and since their life-style was patterned after that of the Buddhist monks, as Samuel Beal had suggested.[125] However, I am more inclined to argue that the word *essene* is derived rather from the Sanskrit word *sannyasi*, which represents the life-style of the Essenes in this context. It is worthwhile to point out here that Philo himself did not know the etymology of *Essene*. He says that the Essenes "derive their name in my opinion by an inaccurate trace from the term in the Greek language for holiness (*Essen* or *Essaios—Hosios*, holy), inasmuch as they have shown themselves pre-eminent by devotion to the service of God."[126]

At the end of the first century A.D., the orator Dio Chrysostom, addressing the Alexandrians, made reference to the "Indians who view the spectacles with you and are in your midst on all occasions."[127] His statement that these Indians were held in low repute by their fellow countrymen could indicate that they, who "came by trade" were probably merchants of the lower vaisya caste, inferior to the Brahmins and the Kshatriyas. Dio Chrysostom also refers to Indian epics—probably the *Mahabharata* and *Ramayana* —which he obviously mistakes for the Greek epics. He writes: "It is said that the poetry of Homer is sung by the Indians, who had translated it into their own language and modes of expression, so that even these Indians are not unacquainted with the woes of Priam and the weeping and wailing of Andromache and Hecuba, and the heroic feats of Achilles and Hector, so potent was the influence of what one man had sung."[128] In the Indian epic of *Mahabharata*, the characters of Arjuna and Karna correspond to Achilles and Hector respectively; the lament of Kunti for her son Karna and the lament of Gandhari for all her

---

[124] Rawlinson, 34-35.
[125] S. Beal, *Abstract of Four Lectures on Buddhist Literature in China* (London, 1882), 163; Edmunds, 135.
[126] Cited by Lillie, 173.
[127] *Oratio* 37; Loeb, III, 211; Bruns, 118.
[128] Dio Chrysostom, Orations LIII.554; cited by H. G. Rawlinson, *Intercourse Between India and the West* (New York, 1971), 169-170.

dead children should remind one of the sad plight of Andromache and Hecuba; so also the rape of Helen is similar to abduction of Sita by Ravana in the *Ramayana*. But the question whether certain Greek literary motifs were borrowed from India remains highly debatable.[129]

On the Indian side, Sanskrit and Pali works make frequent references to sea-voyages; a bas-relief at Bharhut, of the second century B.C., shows two boats on the rough sea, each containing three men, pulled by oars; the *Milindapanha* and the *Mahaniddesa* record the naval stations visited by the seafarers; the Buddhist Jataka tales describe merchants' travels to strange lands.[130]

The first-century Latin writers mention the presence of Indian embassies to Rome. Diplomatic missions have appeared occasionally at the courts of the following emperors: Augustus, Claudius, Trajan, Antoninus Pius, Septimius Severus, Elagabalus, Aurelian, Constantine, Julian, and Justinian.[131] These embassies probably had political and commercial motives, like regulating the trade between Rome and India and coordinating opposition to Parthia, the enemy of Rome. The Romans seemed to have interpreted such missions rather as an acknowledgement of the imperial majesty of Rome by foreign nations. So Augustus claimed on his Ancyra inscription that "to me were sent embassies of kings from India, who had never been seen in the camp of any Roman general."[132] Horace thought this historical embassy so important that he mentioned it in his ode on the secular games in 17 B.C.[133]

One of the really remarkable Indian embassies to Augustus was that of the south-Indian king Pandion, who sent a letter written in Greek to Augustus. This embassy met Augustus at Samos in 21 B.C. Strabo reports:

---

[129] Tarn, 380-381; A. B. Keith, *A History of Sanskrit Literature* (Oxford, 1928), 352-357; cited by Lach, 12.

[130] Haripada Chakraborti, *Trade and Commerce of Ancient India* (Calcutta, 1966); R. K. Mukerjee, *Indian Shipping: A History of the Sea-borne Trade and Maritime Activity of the Indians from the Earliest Times* (Bombay, 1957), 19-54; Jean Filliozat, "Échanges," *Revue Historique* (1949), 7; H. G. Rawlinson, "India in European Literature and Thought," in G. T. Garratt, ed., *The Legacy of India* (Oxford, 1937), 17-18; Sedlar, 81.

[131] J. W. McCrindle, *Ancient India as Described in Classical Literature* (Westminster, 1901), 167, 213-214.

[132] Evelyn Schuckburgh, *Augustus: The Life and Times of the Founder of the Roman Empire* (London, 1903), appendix, no. 31; Sedlar, 81-82.

[133] Edmunds, 119.

> Nikolaos Damaskenos says that at Antioch by Daphne he met with the Indian ambassadors who had been sent to Augustus Caesar. It appeared from the letter that their number had been more than merely the three he reports that he saw. The rest had died chiefly in consequence of the length of the journey. The letter was written in Greek on parchment and imported that Poros was the writer, and that though he was the sovereign of 600 kings, he nevertheless set a high value on being Caesar's friend and was willing to grant him a passage wherever he wished through his dominions, and to assist him in any good enterprise. Such, he says, were the contents of the letter. Eight naked servants presented the gifts that were brought.[134]

Pandion's ambassadors were accompanied by a holy man, who subsequently burned himself in a funeral pyre like his compatriot Kalanos of old who performed self-immolation in Athens. The epithet engraved on his grave identified him as Zarmanochegas (*sramanacharya*), or the master ascetic; this Indian from Bargosa (Broach) could very well have been a Buddhist interpreter or a Brahmin ascetic. It is of some interest here note the suggestion of Bishop Lightfoot that St. Paul had this incident in mind when he wrote: "If I give my body to be burned, and have not love, it profiteth me nothing" (1 Cor. 13:3).[135]

Interestingly, a Sri Lankan embassy during the reign of Claudius (c.41-54 A.D.) came about when one of Claudius' tax-collectors was blown off his Red Sea course and ended up in Sri Lanka.[136] According to Pliny,

> In the reign of the Emperor Claudius ambassadors came to his court therefrom, and under the following circumstances. A freedman of Annius Plocamus, who had farmed from the treasury the Red Sea revenues, while sailing around Arabia was carried away by gales of wind from the north beyond Carmania. In the course of fifteen days he had been wafted Hippuri, a port of Taprobane, where he was humanely received and hospitably entertained by the king; and having in six months' time learned the language, he was able to answer the questions he was asked. The king particularly admired the Romans and their emperor as men possessed of an unheard-of love of justice, when he found that among the money taken from the captive the denarii were all of equal weight although the different images stamped on them showed that they had been coined in the reigns of several emperors. This influenced him most of all to seek an alliance with the Romans, and he accordingly

---

[134] Strabo, *Geography* XV.1.73; McCrindle, 77-78; cited by Sastri, 46.
[135] A. J. Edmunds, *Buddhist and Christian Gospels* (Philadelphia:Innes, 1908), 120.
[136] Sastri, 47-50.

dispatched to Rome four ambassadors, of whom the chief was a Rachia (Rajah).[137]

Obviously, the Indian missions made a great impression on the Greek world; otherwise they would not have been mentioned by Greek and Roman historians. Their exotic gifts, their religions, their merchandise of spices and silk, and the feats of their ascetics made the Greeks and Romans aware more than ever of the presence of the East in their midst. It is true that the Greek traders were probably more interested in quick and high profits than in the philosophies and religions of India. Nevertheless, knowledge about India continued to increase in the West and continued to whet the curiosity of people for more knowledge about that exotic country.

E. *Western Travellers in India*

1. *Non-Christian Witnesses*

The third-century sophist Philostratos gives a long description of Apollonius of Tyana's first-century travels in India. According to Philostratos, Apollonius travelled widely and visited India, where he spent four months and was instructed in the wisdom of the Brahmins. Apollonius' travel purpose was the attainment of wisdom. He said to the Brahmins: "I consider that your lore is profounder and much more divine than our own," and he asked that he be taught: "Will you teach me then...all this wisdom?"[138] The Indian king Phraotes wrote to Iarchus, his Indian master, a letter in Greek regarding the intentions of Apollonius: "Apollonius, wisest of men, yet accounts you still wiser than himself, and is come to learn your lore. Send him away therefore when he knows all that you know yourselves, assured that nothing of your teachings will perish, for in discourse and memory he excels all men."[139] Apollonius himself acknowledged his gratitude to his Indian hosts in the letter he wrote to Iarchus as he left India:

> I came to you on foot, and yet you presented me with the sea; but by sharing with me the wisdom which is yours, you have made it mine even to travel through the heavens. All this I shall mention to the Hellenes; and I shall communicate in my words with them as if you were present,

---

[137] Pliny, *Natural History* VI. 14.84-88; McCrindle,102; cited by Sastri, 50.
[138] Philostratos, *Life of Apollonius*, III.16; Loeb I.263.
[139] *Life of Apollonius*, II.41; Loeb I.227.

unless I have in vain drunk the draught of Tantalus. Farewell, ye goodly philosophers.[140]

Apollonius lived like the ascetics of India, professing his belief metempsychosis and practicing vegetarianism, and claiming that the Pythagorean way of life had come from India via Egypt.[141] In a conversation with the future emperor Vespasian, he said that he followed the religion of the Indians.[142]

What is to be inferred from this is not that everything Philostratos says about Apollonius is true, but that Philostratos had genuine information about India and that Apollonius of the first century also knew and admired India. According to the testimony of Lucian of Samasota, in the middle of the second century A.D., Demetrius, the Greek philosopher, also went to India and settled down among the Brahmins.[143]

Philo (d. A.D. 50), mentioned above, also knew about the Indian gymnosophists and admired their natural philosophy; he thought they deserved as much praise as Abraham.[144] Apuleius (A.D. 160-170) also was favorably impressed the customs and aspirations of the gymnosophists.[145] Plutarch had reservations in his approval of the gymnosophists' way of life, partly due to his Orientalism.[146]

It is quite likely that the Neo-Platonists of Alexandria also could have come under the influence of Indian thought. Plotinus (203-270), the outstanding exponent of this philosophy, was such an admirer of Indian wisdom that, in an effort to learn from the magi of Persia and the Brahmins of India, he attached himself to the Roman emperor Gordianus III who was then marching with army to Asia. Plotinus did not reach India, but barely escaped with life when Gordianus was murdered in Mesopotamia.[147] Plotinus must have had some knowledge about Indian philosophy; otherwise he would not have embarked for India. Probably Plotinus, who spent most of his life in Alexandria, learned it from books available at the famous Alexandrian library or from Indians who lived in

---

[140] *Life of Apollonius* III.51; Loeb I.337.
[141] *Life* VIII.&; Loeb I.303-305.
[142] *Life* V.30; Loeb I.533.
[143] Lucian, *Toxaris* , 34.
[144] *Philo*, ed. F. H. Colson, Loeb Library IX.62-66; cited by Thomas Hahn, "The Indian Tradition in Western Medieval Intellectual History," *Viator* 9 (1978), 213-234.
[145] *Florida*, cited by Hahn, 216.
[146] Plutarch, *Life of Alexander* 8.65; Hahn, 216; see Sir Edward Bysshe, *Palladius de Gentibus Indiae* (London, 1665) for a collection of ancient texts.
[147] Sedlar, 200.

Alexandria or from his master Ammonius Sakkas, whose disciple he was for eleven years.[148]

Ammonius, according to Eusebius, was a Christian who turned pagan. Perhaps the clue to his paganism can be gleaned from his sobriquet—"Sakkas"—which corresponds to no other Greek word, like the word *therapeuta* discussed earlier. As Erich Seeberg has argued, the word cannot mean "sack wearer," or any other known Greek word; he thinks that "Sakkas" is a variation of the Indian word "Sakya," the tribal name of Buddha the Sakya Muni whose followers are known by the phrase "sons of the Sakya."[149] It is quite possible that Ammonius was a Greek Buddhist! Ammonius was also the teacher of the Origen, whose writings also show affinities to Indian thought.[150]

There is, however, one dissenting voice, which rejects the Oriental origins of Greek wisdom, among the Greeks. It is that of the third-century (A.D.) Greek doxographer Diogenes Laërtius, who refutes the thesis that philosophy had its origin among barbarians like the Persians, Chaldeans, Egyptians, and Indians. Wilhelm Halbfass assesses the worth of Diogenes' contributions:

> Diogenes' reputation is that of a compiler; he presents and arranges his materials without any deeper understanding, and he does not provide philosophical perspectives of his own. His discussion of the origin and autonomy of Greek philosophy follows mostly older opinions. He neglects the "latest views" of his contemporaries in this matter. Neoplatonist, Neopythagorean, Jewish and Christian philosophers, who responded to this question with new intensity while presenting the relationship between Greek and Oriental culture in new and different perspectives and contexts, receive only slight attention in Diogenes' discussion. Diogenes is Hellenizing and "classicist" in approach. Further, in spite of his "compilatory" style, his personal position in the controversy with which he introduces his work is unambiguous: the origin of philosophy, in his view, is Greek, nothing but Greek. He goes on to state that the term "philosophy" itself defies all attempts at translation into Oriental, "barbaric" languages.[151]

---

[148] Eunapius, "Life of Plotinos," in Kenneth S. Guthrie, ed., *Plotinos, Complete Works* (London, 1918), 7-8; Sedlar, 199.

[149] Erich Seeberg, "Ammonios Sakkas," *Zeitschrift für Kirchengeschichte* 50 (1941), 140-142; Sedlar, 201.

[150] Henri de Lubac, *Aspects of Buddhism*, trans. George Lamb (London, 1953); *La Rencontre du Bouddhisme et de l'Occident* (Paris, 1952); "Textes alexandrins et bouddhiques," *RSR* 27 (1937): 336-351.

[151] Halbfass, 3; Diogenes Laërtius, *Lives of Eminent Philosophers* I.7; IX.61.

2. Christian Witnesses

There should be some truth in the Christian legends about the visits of Thomas and Bartholomew, the Apostles of Jesus. These men could have travelled to India in the company of merchants either by land or by boat.

The Indian account of the St. Thomas Christians of the Malabar coast says that Thomas landed at Kodungalloor (Cranganore) in 52 A.D., converted twelve Brahmin families to Christianity, founded seven churches on the west coast, and then died the death of martyr at Mylapore, near Madras, on the east coast. These Indian traditions are found in the third-century *Acts of Judas Thomas*, probably composed at Edessa. The story of Thomas is as follows:

After the death of Jesus, the disciples divided up the world for evangelization by casting lots; India fell to Thomas' lot. Thomas was not happy about this assignment. Meanwhile Jesus sold Thomas as a slave to the merchant Habban who was going to India. The merchant and the Apostle travelled together to the capital of King Gundaphar, who asked Thomas to build a royal palace and advanced him large sums of money. Thomas spent all the money on the poor. When called to account for the money, Thomas said that he had already built the royal palace, not on earth, but in heaven. The incredulous king threw Thomas in prison. About this time, the king's brother died and appeared in a dream to the king and showed him the palace that Thomas built for him in heaven. The repentant king released Thomas from prison and accepted Christianity. Later, Thomas was martyred by a king called Mazdai (a Persian name), who objected to his queen's conversion to Christianity. On the contrary, according to the traditions of the St.-Thomas Christians of Kerala, Thomas was assassinated by enraged Brahmins, who were envious of Thomas's proselytizing successes. Thomas's body was buried at Mylapore, but later it was moved to Edessa.[152]

Apart from the local traditions of the St. Thomas Christians, the earliest testimony of the presence of Christians in larger India comes from Bardaisanes' *Book of the Laws* (196 A.D.), which mentions Christians in the Kushan country.[153] Eusebius (260-340 A.D.) claims that the Alexandrian Pantainos preached

---
[152] M. R. James, "The Acts of Thomas," in *The Apocryphal New Testament* (Oxford, 1924); Leslie W. Brown, *The Indian Christians of St. Thomas* (Cambridge, 1956); Eugene Tisserant, *Eastern Christianity in India* (Bombay, 1957).

[153] Sedlar, 182.

Christianity in India some time about 190 A.D.; according to Eusebius, Pantainos discovered that Bartholomew (Mar Thoma?) had preceded him there and had left a Hebrew (Aramaic?) copy of the Gospel of Matthew.[154]

There are also some other early Christian testimonies that attest to the knowledge early Christians too had of India. Clement of Alexandria (d. 215), for example, writes of the Indian philosophers:

> Philosophy, a thing of the highest utility, flourished in antiquity among the barbarians, shedding its light over the nations. And afterwards it came to Greece. First in its ranks were the prophets of the Egyptians; and the Chaldeans among the Assyrians; and the Druids among the Gauls; and the Samanos among the Bactrians; and the philosophers of the Celts; and the Magi of the Persians, who foretold the Savior's birth and came to the land of Judea, guided by a star. The Hindu gymnosophists are also in the number, and the other barbarians philosophers. And of these there are two classes: some of them called Samanos, and others Brahmins. And those of the Samanos who are called forest-dwellers neither inhabit cities nor have roofs over them, but are clad in the bark of trees, feed on nuts, and drink water in their hands. They know neither marriage nor begetting of children, like those now called Encratites. There are also among the Hindus those who obey the precepts of Buddha (Boutta), whom, on account of his extraordinary sanctity they have exalted into a god.[155]

Elsewhere Clement expresses a lower opinion of the Indians' natural philosophy and cites them as an example of vain asceticism.[156] However, Clement would reverse himself later, depending on his need, and refer to the spiritual courage of the Indians manifested in their encounter with Alexander the Great.[157] The third-century *Recognitiones*, associated with Clement of Rome (d. A.D. 97), also regard the Brahmins favorably: "Similarly, among the Bactrians and in the regions of India are large multitudes of Brahmins, who, following the traditions and laws and customs of their elders, do not commit adultery or murder; neither do they worship idols nor eat meat nor get drunk nor harbor malice, but always fear God."[158]

---

[154] Eusebius, *Ecclesiastical History* V.9-10; Loeb I. 461-463; Sedlar, 180-181.
[155] *Stromateis* I.15; PG 8.777; cited by A. J. Edmunds, 144.
[156] *Stromateis*, 3.7; PG 8:1164.
[157] *Stromateis*, 4.7; PG 8.1263.
[158] The *Recognitiones* survive only in a Latin translation of the original; PG 1.1410; see Thomas Hahn, *art. cit.*

By the third century, when the Christian Church had begun to be dominated by the Western apologists, Orientalism began to creep into their thinking. Tertullian (A.D. 220), who wrote some books in Greek, knew about the Indian Brahmins, but scorned their naturalness or primitivism.[159] Hippolytus included the Brahmins among the heretics outside the fold of the elect. His detailed treatment of the doctrine of the Brahmins shows that he must have had some first-hand knowledge of Indian religions. Jean Filliozat argues that Hippolytus was familiar with the *Maitri Upanishad*, and uses Hippolytus as a basis for the possibility of extensive contact between East and West in the first Christian centuries.[160] Prudentius (A.D. 410) sees the wisdom of the gymnosophists as a symbol of vanity.[161] It is understandable that Augustine (A.D. 432) who publicly renounced his Oriental Manichean heritage should be harsh in his criticism about the Orient; he thought that no good could come out of Indian wisdom.[162] On the same issue of the Brahmins, Augustine's mentor, Ambrose, however, held a different view. In a letter to Simplicianus, Ambrose compared himself favorably to the Indian: "Non enim de contemptu mortis libros philosophorum depromo, aut gymnosophistos Indorum, quorum prae caeteris Calani laudatur responsum Alexandro, cum juberet sequi."[163]

In contrast to the Western Christian Fathers, the Eastern Christians had profound respect towards the wisdom of India and were desirous of learning from India. Two examples are worth mentioning here. They are Bardaisanes (154-222) and Basilides (early second century), who considered themselves good Christians, though their enemies, like Clement and Hippolytus, branded them as heretics and Gnostics. Basilides held the doctrine of karma and reincarnation; he was reported to have taught that even the martyrs suffered for their sins since all souls come into the world tainted with the sins of their past existence. His notion of the soul as a compound of appendages is similar to Buddhist doctrine of the

---

[159] *Apologeticus* 42.1; PL 1.490-491:"Neque enim Brachmanae aut Indorum gymnosophistae sumus, silvicolae et exules vitae."
[160] Jean Filliozat, "La doctrine des Brahmanes d'après Saint Hippolyte," *Revue de l'histoire des religions* 130 (1945): 59-91.
[161] Prudentius, *Hamartigenia* 402-403; PL 59.1040.
[162] *De civitate Dei* 15.20; PL 41.463: "Et Indorum Gymnosophistae, qui nudi perhibentur philosophari in solitudinibus Indiae, cives ejus mundi sunt, et a generando se cohibent. Non est enim hoc bonum nisi cum fit secundum fidem summi boni, qui Deus est."
[163] Ambrose, *Epistola* 37; PL 16.1138.

skandhas. His view of the the indescribability of God is analogous to the upanishadic teaching of the *nirguna* Brahman, who is devoid of all attributes and qualities.[164]

As Porphyry's testimony indicates, Bardaisanes was the author of a book on India from which a few citations have survived. His description of the Brahmins and the Sramanas preserved by Porphyry is quite accurate. He carefully distinguishes between Brahmin priests and Buddhist monks; the former receive wisdom by succession, by being born into a caste, while the latter receives it by choice and election. To paraphrase Porphyry:

> Of the philosophers, some dwell on mountains, others near the Ganges River. They eat fruits, cow's milk or rice, but under no circumstances touch animal food, which would denote extreme impurity and impiety. They spend their days and much of their nights in hymns and prayers to the gods. Each has his own cottage and lives for the most part alone. Often they do not speak for many days; moreover, they engage in frequent fasts....The ascetics, however, have expressly chosen their status. Anyone wishing to join them must announce his intention to the ruler of his native place, then abandon the city and all his property. He will not return to his wife and children, or pay any further attention to them. The wife will be supported by her relatives, and the children by the king. The ascetics live outside the city and spend their days in pious conversation. They reside in houses and temples (monasteries) built for them; by the king, and of which they are stewards. Like the Brahmins they eat rice, bread, fruits, and herbs; all are unmarried and without possessions. They willingly await death, sometimes seeking it out when they are neither ill nor oppressed. Both Brahmins and ascetics are greatly revered by other Indians. The king himself visits the holy men; in times of danger he asks for their prayers.[165]

F. *India's Debt to the Greeks*

All that I have said about the indebtedness of the West to India may sound like a case of "Occidentalism," an expression of the Orient's superiority over the Occident as though the East had never learned or borrowed anything from the West during antiquity. Not so. Of course, the East did learn much from the West since the Renaissance but even during the Hellenistic times. Besides having learned from the Greek artists of Gandhara, India has also learned much from Greek astronomy. Early Indian scientists are

---

[164] Sedlar, 168-170; Sir Charles, Eliot, *Hinduism and Buddhism* (New York, 1957), 423.
[165] Sedlar, 174; see Porphyry, *On Abstinence from Animal Food*, trans. John Dryden and A. H. Clough (Philadelphia, 1908), 171-172.

quite explicit about it. "The Yavanas are indeed barbarians," says the *Gargi Samhita*, "but astronomy originated with them, and for this they must be venerated as gods."[166] Two of the five Indian astronomical treatises (*siddhantas*), the *Romaka siddhanta* and the *Paulika siddhanta* are manifestly Greek; the former is named after *Romaka* , "a famous city," which is none other than Rome, which is alluded to several times in in the *Brihatsamhita* and *Pancha Siddhantika* of Varahamitra; the latter is named after Paul of Alexandria (4th century A.D.).[167] The *jamitra*, or the seventh place on the horoscope, by which the astrologer predicts happiness for the married person, is the Greek *diametron*. Similarly, many of the names of the planets and of the signs of the zodiac, like *Kriya* for the Greek *Krios*, *Tavuri* for *Tauros*, *Jituma* for *Didmos*, *Pathona* for *Parthenos*, *Ara* for *Ares*, *Heli* for *Helios*, *Asphiyit* for *Aphrodite* and *Himna* for *Hermes*, are also of Greek origin.[168] In this connection, it should be mentioned that the Greeks also knew of Indian astronomy already in the second century B.C. The most astonishing piece of evidence is an inscription of the late second century B.C. found during the excavations of the theater at Miletus; this calendar of the heliacal risings and settings of certain fixed stars mentions the name *ho Indon Kallaneus* in a list of earlier authorities.[169] It is fair to say that "astronomy and astrology in India are not indigenous sciences, but are local adaptations and developments of Mesopotamian, Greco-Babylonian, and Greek texts."[170]

It is possible to argue that Indian classical drama also may owe some thing to Greece since the Greek language and art were known in northwestern India. Indian drama has the word, *yavanika* ("Greek curtain"), which seems to suggest some indebtedness to Greek dramaturgy. The Indian author of the play *Toy Cart* (*Mricchakatika*), a play similar to the New Attic Comedy, may have seen Greek plays performed; like the Greek critics before him, Bharata in his *Natya Sastra* lays down the rule that no more five characters appear on the stage at the same time; the Indian *Vidushaka* and the *vita* of Indian drama can be compared to the

---

[166] Cited by Rawlinson, 225.
[167] H. G. Rawlinson, *Intercourse Between India and the Western World* (New York, 1971), 173.
[168] Rawlinson, 225; David Pingree, "Indian and Pseudo-Indian Passages in Greek and Latin Astronomical and Astrological Treatises," *Viator* 7 (1976): 142-195.
[169] Pingree, 144.
[170] Pingree, 142.

parasite and pimp of Greek comedy; also, like the Greek plays, Indian drama eschews the portrayal of violent scenes on stage. Further, at Ramgarh, a small Greek amphitheater was unearthed.[171]

G. *Evidence of Fables*

Fables, which are humorous beast stories with "morals," provide striking evidence for interaction between India and the Mediterranean world of antiquity. Of course, it is true that many similar folktales have originated independently of one another in different parts of the world. It is also true that many folktales have travelled in both directions—from India to Europe and from Europe to India—without any one paying attention to pedigree for the simple reason that wisdom or folklore is the common possession of all mankind. In this book, however, I am interested in the question of pedigree in folktales since I am grinding the historical axe to prove a point. One particular story, with a distinctive pedigree, that has travelled from India to the West is the legend of Barlaam and Iosaphat, which entered the Western Christian world as the story of an Indian prince converted to Christianity. In actuality, it is but a reworked story of the life of Buddha in the Christian garb, and not a parallel legend of independent origin.[172]

From the time of Herodotus, other Indian stories have been reported in Greek literature. In Herodotus, a man named Hippokleides lost his bride on the very day of betrothal by dancing in an indecent manner in front of her father (VI.129); this episode reminds us of the biblical episode of the indecent dance of David before the Ark of the Covenant performed in sight of Michal, his wife and daughter of King Saul (2 Samuel 6). Obviously both stories are transferences from the Indian fable (Jataka 32) where the daughter of the swan, the king of birds, chose the peacock as her husband; when the peacock begins to dance, he exposes his back side; outraged by this shameless behavior, the swan refuses him his daughter as bride. According to Winternitz,

> The fable seems to have travelled across Persia to Greece at an early date....That the story was brought to India by the Greeks when they

---

[171] Rawlinson, 226-227.
[172] David M. Lang, *The Wisdom of Balahvar, A Christian Legend of the Buddha* (London, 1957).

were ruling Bactria, as C. H. Tawney conjectures, I regard as improbable for the reason that it is easier to explain a fable being referred to human situations than to create a fable out of a personal anecdote. Then too the peacock is proverbial in India for being typically shameless, since he bares his back parts when he dances."[173]

Another Herodotan anecdote (III.119) concerns a woman faced with the choice of saving the life of her husband, child, or brother; she selects her brother as in a common Indian story found in the Jatakas and the *Ramayana*.[174] The argument is the same on the Indian side as well as on the Greek side which also includes a variation of this story in Sophocles' *Antigone*, 909-912; it is that the brother is irreplaceable since the woman can acquire another husband and another child. Pisschel accepted an Indian origin of the story as early as 1893.[175]

A third story concerning a thief who managed to steal from the treasury was rewarded by the king himself is found in the Jatakas and other Indian collections.[176]

The folklore issue is simply this: Were the Greek fables contained in Aesop's collection influenced by their Indian counterparts in the Buddhist Jataka stories and the Indian *Panchatantra*? There are two questions that concern us here: One, is it chronologically feasible for the Indian fables to have influenced the Greek fables? Two, how many of the Greek fables can really be said to have been influenced by the Indian fables?

As for chronology, no literary version of Aesop's fables is known to have existed before the fourth century B.C., when Demetrius of Phaleron, the founder of the famous Alexandrian Library, was reported to have collected them into a handbook, which is no longer extant.[177] It was actually Phaedrus, writing in the first century A.D. and Babrius writing in 235 A.D. who compiled the so-called Aesop's fables and made them available to the European world. Joseph Jacobs writes about the provenance of *Aesop's Fables*:

> The fables known as *Aesop's Fables*, which have spread throughout Europe, can be traced back to a collection in Latin and German published soon after the invention of printing by Heinrich Stainhowell,

---

[173] Cited by Garbe, 27.
[174] Garbe, 27; Sedlar, 101.
[175] Cited by Garbe, 27.
[176] Herodotus II.121; W. R. Halliday, "Notes upon Indo-European Folk-Tales and the Problem of Their Diffusion," *Folk Lore* 34 (1923): 138; Sedlar, 101.
[177] Ben Edwin Perry, ed., *Babrius and Phaedrus* (Cambridge: Loeb Library), XIII, lx; Sedlar, 102.

printed about 1480, and, within the next ten years, translated into Italian, French, Dutch, English (by Caxton), and Spanish. This consists of a life of Aesop (connected with the legend of Ahiqar), four books derived from a mediaeval collection of fables known as *Romulus*, a selection of the fables of Avian, some from a previous selection made by Ranutio, others called "extravagant," and two collections of rather coarse anecdotes from Poggio and Petrus Alphonsi. The *Romulus* has turned out to be entirely mediaeval prose renderings of Phaedrus, a Greek freedman of Augustus, who flourished in the early years of the 1st century A.D. It contains survivals of Phaedrine fables which are no longer extant in verse form, such as "The Town and the Country Mouse," "The Ass and the Lap-Dog," and "The Lion and the Mouse." It may accordingly be said that our *Aesop* is Phaedrus with trimmings.

Besides these prose renderings of Phaedrus, which form the bulk of the modern European *Aesop*, there exist a number of Greek prose renderings which were, for a long time, supposed to be the original *Aesop*, but have been proved by Bentley and others to have been derived from a metrical collection in choriambics by one Valerius Babrius, tutor to the son of the Emperor Severus, who flourished about A.D. 235, and part of whose fables were discovered on Mt. Athos by Minoides Menas in 1840. Babrius, in his preface, refers to two sources—Aesop for Hellenic fable, and Kybises for "Libyan" fable; and Jacobs has suggested that the latter collection ran to about one hundred in number, and was derived directly or indirectly from a Sinhalese embassy which came to Rome about A.D. 52.[178]

On the Indian side, there are the Buddhist Jataka stories, purportedly stories told by Buddha, which were themselves derived from the earlier Hindu collections. In written form they cannot be older than the fourth century A.D., perhaps. But there is evidence for postulating a much earlier existence for them. On several Buddhist stupas in India we find carved representations of scenes from some of the Jataka tales and fables. The earliest and most important of these monuments is the stupa of Bharhut (250 B.C.), where scenes and titles of at least twenty-eight tales have been identified, several of the so-called Aesopic fables among them.[179]

It is no longer feasible to hold the view that all the Indian fables were brought to India by the Greeks, as Benfey used to argue.[180] Benfey was quite convinced of the Greek origin of the

---

[178] Joseph Jacobs, "Fable," *Encyclopaedia of Religion and Ethics*, V: 676; Joseph Jacobs, *Fables of Aesop* (London, 189.
[179] H. T. Francis and E. J. Thomas, *Jataka Tales*, iii.
[180] Theodor Benfey, *Pantschatantra, fünf Bücher indischer Fabeln, Märchen und Erzählungen* (Leipzig, 1859).

fables that he assigned the date 200 B.C. to the compilation of the Jataka tales since that could be the earliest date for the Greek fables to have arrived in India. Then came the discovery of the Bharhut stupa and other archeological finds, which demolished the theory of Benfey. The monuments proved the existence of a great body of Indian fables independent of any Greek source.[181]

It is a matter of debate as to the exact number of European folktales that are derived from India. Rhys Davids thinks that almost all of Aesop's fables were probably derived in one way or another from Indian sources.[182] Jacob's calculation shows that 56 of the 260 Aesopic fables have Indian counterparts.[183] In 1957, Laurits Bødker pointed out that there are only 20 Indian tales that are closely related to the European tales.[184] According to Jacobs, there are at least a dozen fables in the Greek collection which exhibit distinctive Indian features and, therefore, seem to be derived from Indian sources: "The Wolf and the Crane," "The Ass in the Lion's Skin," "The Wolf and the Lamb," "The Peasant and the Snake," "The Crow and the Fox," "The Dog with the Meat," "The Weasel as Bride," "The Grateful Eagle," "The Goose that Lays the Golden Eggs," "The Bald Man and the Fly, " "The Oak and the Reed," "The Belly and Members," "The Two pots," and "The Cat Turned into a Maiden." The main criterion for assigning these tales' place of origin to India is that the tales' protagonists suggest an Indian environment with birds, beasts, and ideas native to India.[185] Jacobs quotes Jataka 30, 32, 34, 45, 136, 143, 146, 189, 215, 294, 308, 374, 383, and 426 as important parallels to Aesop's fables.[186]

The critical problem is to determine whether the Greek fable is derived from the Indian fable or the other way. As Jacobs points out, the solution to this problem is given by the thirty fables found in the Talmud and the *Midrash Rabbah*, a rabbinical commentary on the Torah. Except in three or four cases, all these have parallels in Greek fables, in Indian fables, or in both. When the Jewish version is found in both, it invariably follows the Indian version rather than the Greek. For instance, one of the Talmudic fables is that of the Lion and the Crane as in the Indian collection rather

---

[181] Francis and Thomas, iii.
[182] T. W. Rhys Davids, *Buddhist Birth Stories* (New York, 1977), xxxii
[183] Joseph Jacobs, "Fable, *Encyclopedia of Religion and Ethics* V.677
[184] Laurits Bødker, "Indian Animal Tales: A Preliminary Survey," *Folklore Fellows Communications* 68, No. 170 (1957), 4.
[185] Sedlar, 105.
[186] Francis and Thomas, iv.

than that of the Wolf and the Crane as in the Aesopic collection.[187] In the case of "The Two Pots," the Talmudic proverb (*Esther Rabbah* 2) "If a stone falls upon the pot, woe to the pot; if the pot falls upon the stone, woe to the pot," resembles the Indian *Panchatantra* verse, "Like a stone that breaks a pot, the mighty remain unhurt," rather than the Greek fable we are familiar with.[188] As for the Indian fables in the *Midrash Rabbah*, Francis and Thomas write:

> On Gen.26:26 is told the fable of the Egyptian partridge, which extracts a bone from the throat of a lion, as in Jat. 308, not a wolf, as in Aesop...On Esther 3:6, a bird, which builds its nest on the sea-shore that was threatened by the waves, tries to bale out the water with its beak, and is rebuked by another bird. Cf. Jat. 146, which is without a parallel in Aesop. On Esth. 3:1 is told the story of a man who had a she-ass, its foal, and a sow. To the latter he gives unstinted food, but to the others in proportion. The foal inquires of its mother why the idle sow should be so fed. The ass replies, the hour will soon come when you will see the sow's fate, and understand that it was well fed not out of favour, but for a disgraceful end. When the feast comes, the fatted sow is killed, and the moral explained to the foal. So in Jat. 30,...an ox and its younger brother take the place of the ass and foal. But in Aesop, a heifer pities a working ox. At the feast it is taken to be slaughtered, and the ox smiles and points the moral.[189]

Since the Talmudic fables show close Indian affinities, it should be assumed that the rabbis knew Indian fables. In fact, the Talmud (*Synh*. 38b)itself mentions that Rabbi Meir of the middle of the second century, knew 300 hundred fox fables.[190] It is practically impossible for the rabbis to have translated the Greek fables first into Hebrew and then taken them to India. The process must have been in the reverse order since the Indian fables are earlier than the first collection of Aesopic fables made by Demetrius of Phaleron. Jacobs writes:

> Quite apart, however, from the Talmudic evidence, the probabilities are in favor of India on general grounds. India is the home of incarnation, and it was, therefore, natural for the Indians to imagine animals acting as men, whose predecessors they were, whereas in Greece such a belief was at best a "survival," and no longer living in the thoughts of the people. The existence of the "moral" in the the fable properly so called may be traced back to the *gathas*, which formed the nucleus of the *Jatakas*,

---

[187] Cited by A. J. Edmunds, 124.
[188] See Jacobs, 676.
[189] Francis and Thomas, v.
[190] Joseph Jacobs, *The Fables of Aesop* (London, 1889) I, 120

the two "Stories of the Present and Past" being given as explanations of these metrical morals. The possibility of the same fable having arisen independently in the two countries may be at once dismissed. Two minds in different countries may hit upon the same story to illustrate a simple wile of woman or a natural act of revenge, but it is in the highest degree improbable that two moral teachers, trying to inculcate the dangers of the lowly vying with the proud, should express it by the imagery of two pots floating down astream. In one case, indeed, we have practically absolute evidence of the direct derivation of classical fables from India. There is a fable of "The Farmer and the Serpent," in which the farmer receives benefits from the serpent, but he or his son strikes it, which brings the friendship to an end. This occurs both in Latin (*Romulus* ii, 10), derived from Phaedrus, and in Greek...derived from Babrius. Both forms, however, are imperfect, whereas the Indian, given in the *Panchatantra* (iii,5) assigns the motive for every incident, and practically combines the Greek in the Latin forms, which are thus shown by Benfey...to have been derived from it.[191]

The Libyan fables (*Logoi Lubikoi*), which is part of the Babrius collection and which was used by the rabbis, is attributed to a mysterious Kybises. Who is this Kybises? There is no such writer known in antiquity. He is believed to be a Libyan by the name of Kybisias, Kybisios, or Kybisses. Babrius couples him with Aesop: "The first, they say, who spoke fables to the sons of the Hellenes was Aesop the wise, and the first who spoke fables to the Libyans was Kibysses."[192] I would suggest that *Kybises* is a corruption of the Indian word *Hitopadesha*, just like Pilpay, alias Bidpai, the other author of the Indian fable collection; we know *bidpai* is a corruption of the Sanskrit *Vidvan*, which means the "philosopher," (Vishnusarman), the reputed author of the *Hitopadesha*. In sum, one of the sources of the collection known as "Aesop's Fables" is the Indian *Hitopadesha* and the Indian fables were already known in the Mediterranean region during the first century A.D.

The moral of the story of the fables is simply that a fable, though it will not be repeated in another country with the same details, cannot be invented twice. If two fables are almost identical or rather very similar on important points, then one must have been derived from the other. In the case of at least a dozen beast fables of the Greek and Jewish world, it can be concluded that they were originally Indian fables.

---

[191] Jacobs, 677.
[192] Cited by Jacobs, *Aesop's Fables*, 121.

H. *Conclusion*

In this chapter I have examined various facets of the mutual interaction between India and the Western world from third millennium B.C. to the third century A.D. The emphasis has been on the period after the invasion of India by Alexander in the fourth century. The evidence shows that the influence has been mutual, with Mesopotamia giving more to India in the second millennium B.C. and the Hellenistic world receiving more from India than it gave. The reason for this is simply that there was an advanced civilization in Mesopotamia in the second millennium, and since then with Alexander's invasion power shifted to India, Palestine, and Alexandria until the whole picture changed with Augustus' Roman empire in the first century B.C. Contacts between India and the West increased during the Hellenistic times in a significant way so much so many Greek writers came to accept as an article of faith that their philosophy originated in Egypt and India. Already by the time of Hesiod, the Eleatic philosophers, and Plato, Indian religious ideas like metempsychosis seem to have been known in Greece. This hypothesis seems tenable in view of the chronological anteriority of the Indian Upanishads, Buddhism, and Jainism which taught the doctrines of karma and reincarnation. Alexander's invasion in the fourth century B.C. increased dramatically the Greeks' factual knowledge of India with eyewitness reports and with later Greek embassies in India like that of Megasthenes. Of course, Alexander would not have undertaken the invasion of India had he not enough reliable information about its potential for him and the Macedonian empire. The great upsurge of Indo-Greek trade increased cultural and religious contacts as well. The written accounts about the Indian ascetics by the Greeks and the sensational suicides of Kalanos and Zarmanochegas (Sramanacharya) made the Greeks look at Indian religions more seriously than ever. Jean Sedlar thinks that during the Hellenistic period the Greek attitude toward Indian ascetics and Indian wisdom underwent a subtle change: from the older version of viewing the Indian ascetics as being merely clever and worldly to the new view of seeing the Indians as possessing a serious ethical-ascetic doctrine.[193] Meanwhile the volume of trade increased dramatically between

---

[193] Sedlar, 279.

India and the West via Alexandria, which also resulted in the transmission of fables in both directions. The first century B.C. and first century A.D. were probably the peak point for Indo-West contacts. During this century many Indians seemed to have settled down in Alexandria just as Greeks did in India. Philo wrote about the Indian Buddhist monks of the therapeutae, while Dio Chrysostom talked about ordinary Indian residents in the city. One remarkable find dating to the first century is a papyrus fragment of a Greek play taking place in India. One of the Oxyrhyncus papyri (413) contains the story of a Greek lady named Charition shipwrecked on the Coast of South India.[194] The king of that country addresses his retinue by the words "Indon promoi" (chiefs of the Indians). Being familiar with Dravidian languages, I can identify some of the words that have given trouble; *kottos* is Tamil/Malayalam *kuti* meaning "drink"; and *zopit* is Tamil *sappitu*, which means "eat" and *brathis* is Tamil *varatha* meaning "foreigners" in the pejorative sense. It is remarkable that this play dates from the first century A.D., that it is found at Oxyrhyncus where one could find Indians, and that Greeks and Indians coexisted in that environment. A remarkable coincidence in this connection is that between 1897 and 1903 Greek fragments of the Gospel of Thomas were also discovered at Oxyrhyncus (nos. 1, 654, 655) in Upper Egypt. The appearance of the Gnostic-encratitic Gospel of Thomas in the Indian environment seems to suggest that Gnosticism was also a byproduct of Indian thought. Hippolytus, whose testimony was discussed in the previous chapter, claimed expressly that the doctrines of the Gnostic Christian Encratites were compounded not out of the Holy Scriptures, but from their own views and from those of the Gymnosophists among the Indians.[195]

In sum, at least the educated people of the period knew India well and could even identify Indian doctrines as Indian. Therefore, there existed really no insurmountable barrier preventing Christianity and Indian religions from influencing each other during the formative years of Christianity.

---

[194] G. P. Grenfell and A.S. Hunt, *The Oxyrhyncus Papyri*, Part III (London, 1903): 41-55; D. L. Page, *Select Papyri*, Loeb Library, III (Cambridge, 1950), 336-349; Eugen Hultzsch, "Remarks on a Papyrus from Oxyrhyncus,"*Journal of Royal Asiatic Society* (1904), 399-405; L. D. Barnett, "The Alleged Kanarese Speeches in P.OXY. 413," *Journal of Egyptian Archaeology* 12 (1926): 13-15.

[195] Hippolytus, *Refutation of Heresies*, vii, Intro; ANCL, V.117.

However, there exists in the West a mental barrier or the prejudicial "Orientalism" that would protest against the view that it is quite possible and even probable that Indian thought could have influenced the Christian gospels. In the first place, there is the theological position which holds the view that the Bible, being an inspired book, is entirely the work of God and even dictated by God. Most modern scholars would accept the view that the Bible is inspired, but they would add that it has also a human author who used all kinds of human resources to put the book together. However, these same scholars would reject summarily the possibility of the influence of India on biblical and Greek thought. This they do not out of intellectual honesty but rather out of prejudice. For instance, W. G. Rutherford, the editor of *Babrius*, in his introduction rejects the possibility of Indian influence in a few contemptuous phrases. How is it possible, he asks, that a nation so original as the Greeks should be indebted for their fables to the childish Orientals, with their page after page of weak moralising, capped by a so-called fable? And so, with a lofty wave of the hand, he bids the Indians go to their appropriate diet (*kunes pros meton* is his phrase)."[196] A similar mental block, which is probably a case of the attack of the Hegelian virus, is to be found in the words of the New Testament scholar C. B. Caird who wrote in 1962: "I should have thought that the Indian notion of N. T. dependence on Buddhism was due simply to a deficient historical sense. I certainly know of no N. T. scholar outside India who would give such an idea credence for a minute."[197] I have shown above that Indian traditions are much older than the Christian gospels. Further, there is no intrinsic improbability that the gospel writers could not have imitated, consciously or unconsciously, materials which had some real relevance to the themes of the birth, mission, teaching, and miracles of Christ they were handling. They acted in their literary composition the way we do today. We read literature of all sorts, consult all available sources, dismember our sources, clip the wings and tails of these oral and written texts, patch them up together, summarize and paraphrase our sources, sometimes conceal them, and all the time try to create new stories and new poems out of them, thereby appearing as their original authors, as self-begotten.

---

[196] Cited by Joseph Jacobs, *Aesop's Fables*, 105.
[197] Cited by J. Duncan M. Derrett, "Greece and India: the Milindapanha, the Alexander-romance and the Gospels," *ZRGG* 19 (1967), 34.

In the case of the gospel writers, since I have shown their dependence on Indian sources with a wealth of material not found in comparable measure even in their much-acclaimed biblical and Greek sources, the issue must not be summarily dismissed. For the birth-stories of Jesus found in the canonical and apocryphal gospels, the primary giver was India and the receiver Christianity for the simple reason Christianity was an upstart movement with little to give while Hinduism and Buddhism were already well-established religions with their own rich theologies and mythologies and were in a better position to give than in any desperate need to receive. Besides, Indians and Indian religions were already basically ethnocentric especially after Hinduism had developed into a pan-Indian phenomenon by the time of the rise of Buddhism. Being ethnocentric, the Indians experienced all things foreign as marginal to their center of identity and excluded themselves from foreign elements by withdrawing within the bounds of their tradition which was significantly sufficient and relatively superior in their eyes to foreign elements up until the days of the British Raj. Subsequently, during the nineteenth and twentieth centuries Hinduism in India and Buddhism in Sri Lanka came under the strong influence of Western Christianity so much so during this period both Hinduism Buddhism received back from Christianity all that they had given Christianity in its formative period and perhaps more.

EPILEGOMENON

PRE-TEXT AND PRETEXT

In his seminal study "Odysseus' Scar," Eric Auerbach compares the styles of Homer and the Bible and concludes:

> The two styles, in their opposition, represent basic types: on the one hand fully externalized description, uniform illumination, uninterrupted connection, free expression, all events in the foreground, displaying unmistakable meanings, few elements of historical development and of psychological perspective; on the other hand, certain parts brought into high relief, others left obscure, abruptness, suggestive influence of the unexpressed, "background" quality, multiplicity of meanings and the need for interpretation, universal-historical claims, development of the concept of the historically becoming, and preoccupation with the problematic. Homer's realism is, of course, not to be equated with classical-antique realism in general; for the separation of styles, which did not develop until later, permitted no such leisurely and externalized description of everyday happenings; in tragedy especially there was no room for it; furthermore, Greek culture very soon encountered the phenomena of historical becoming and of the "multilayeredness" of the human problem and dealt with them in its fashion; in Roman realism, finally new and native concepts are added....Since we are using the two styles, the Homeric and the Old Testament, as starting points, we have taken them as finished products, as they appear in the texts; we have disregarded everything that pertains to their origins, and thus have left untouched the question whether their peculiarities were there from the beginning or are to be referred wholly or in part to foreign influences.[1]

Auerbach compares only the Old Testament with Homer. Hence what he says about the Old Testament is only partially true of the New Testament. So many stylistic, linguistic, and cultural changes took place during the intertestamental times. In the case of the gospels, their origin cannot be conceived of as an organic development of the Old Testament except perhaps in apologetical and theological terms. The environmental impact of Hellenism, which was characterized by Gnosticism, was of fundamental importance to the origins of the New Testament, which was written in Greek and was obviously intended rather for Greek-speaking peoples than for "barbarians." The difference of the literary style of the New Testament can be easily seen by comparing it with the style of the Jewish Oral Torah of the Mishna, which was written

---

[1] Erich Auerbach, "Odysseus' Scar," *Mimesis* (New York, 1946), 19-20.

by Jewish rabbis in Hebrew about the same time the gospels were redacted. Both the Mishna and the gospels take the Written Torah for granted where they are relevant. But the appeal to prooftexts is sparing in both works. Interestingly, the Mishna records minority opinions as against the opinion of the anonymous majority views; the gospels, on the contrary, are a record of Jewish minority views disguised as the official exegesis of the Old Testament itself. The significant difference between the two is that the Christian gospels stressed the matter of salvation and the Jewish Mishna the importance of sanctification. Jacob Neusner writes:

> When Christianity came into being, in the first century, one important strand of the Christian movement laid stress on issues of salvation, in the gospels maintaining that Jesus was, and is, Christ come to save the world and impose a radical change on history. At that same time...the Pharisees emphasized issues of sanctification, maintaining that the task of Israel is to attain that holiness of which the Temple was a singular embodiment. When in the gospels, we find the record of the Church placing Jesus into opposition with the Pharisees, we witness the confrontation of different people talking about different things to different people.[2]

So, when we compare the Judaisms of the time after the Destruction of the Temple in 70 A.D., two movements stand out: Pharisaic Judaism and Christian Judaism. Both movements developed in the same geographical area and cultural milieu. Of the two only the former called themselves Jews and continued to maintain their Jewish identity by retaining the Written Torah of the Mosaic covenant in its entirety, while the latter took on the new name of Christians and claimed a new law and a new covenant. The former accepted traditional Judaism while the latter modified it to the point of almost rejecting it and of being excommunicated by the establishment. The rejection was mutual and almost total. While Pharisaic Judaism continued to worship Yahweh as the only one and true God, the Christians began to worship Jesus as the Incarnate Son of God. In place of the traditional Jewish monotheism the Christians introduced the notion of the Trinity and an incipient cult of Mary, who would be later canonized as the Mother of God. Further, the Christians substituted the Eucharist for the whole-offering. In short, the Christians developed a new theology, a new mythology, and a new worship system centering around the person of Jesus and away from Yahweh. Obviously, these new Christian developments were not a natural outgrowth of or organic evolution

---

[2] Jacob Neusner, *From Testament to Torah* (Englewood Cliffs, 1988), 62-63.

from mainstream Judaism since Christianity was rejected as a heresy by the Pharisees.

Christianity was, therefore, an innovation, a revolution, a new religion with its own ethos, ethics, and ethnos. In fact, the Christian theology of incarnation and its soteriology were not derived from the Jewish Bible. Most of its ethics, which is drastically contrasted in the Sermon on the Mount, is found in Buddhism and Hinduism—I intend to discuss this point in my forthcoming book. Most importantly, the ethnic composition of early Christianity shows a very large number of foreigners among them if the Acts of the Apostles is a reliable indicator.

What then characterized the new Christian movement in the eyes of the Jews was its foreignness. This foreignness of Christianity was due to its foreign elements and foreign influences, which were what gave Christianity its uniqueness and separated it from Judaism. If the Christian gospels are different in content, genre, and style from the Old Testament, except perhaps for its disputed midrashic orientation, it is all due to a great extent to foreign influences notwithstanding the original contributions of the authors of the gospels.

In my work I have tried to address only the question of the origins of the Christian gospel narratives of the infancy of Jesus and suggested that these texts owe a great deal to sources other than the Hebrew Scriptures. This foreign influence was there in the gospels from the beginning and remained there in spite of various redactions, revisions, and censorship.

I identified this case of foreign influence on the gospel texts as a case of intertextuality, which is evident from the composite nature of the gospel text and in its intertextual structure. In the gospels, too, as in Old Testament narratives, we find inadequate externalization of authorial thoughts, obscurity, abruptness, fault lines, and suggestive influence of the unexpressed sources in abundance. The reason for all this is that the books of the New Testament, especially the Synoptic gospels, are not the work of one author at a given point in time, but rather that they show evidence of multiple authorship, of the use of various oral and written subtexts, of redactional activity, and final editorial work. All these different stages in the formation of the books of the New Testament can be conveniently encapsulated in the words *pre-text* and *pretext*. The matter of the gospel narratives is called pre-text and the principle of integrating this matter is identified as pretext, the guiding artistic principle of form, without the pejorative moral connotation of the term.

Such a deconstructive criticism of the gospel text suggests that these books are not just theological works but primarily literary works with a textual history, relating different texts to one another in an intertextual format. Joel Rosenberg writes about the Old Testament: "the Bible's value as a religious document is intimately and inseparably related to its value as literature. This proposition requires that we develop a different understanding of what literature is, one that might and should give us some trouble.[3] Indeed, the Bible as a literary text does give us readers and critics trouble since we see in it "a complete interfusion of literary art with theological, moral, or historiosophical vision, the fullest perception of the latter dependent on the fullest grasp of the former."[4] However, in order to show the complete interfusion of literature and theology, we have to take the text apart or rather we have to distinguish one from the other like the divine from the human in Jesus Christ and Gautama Buddha. Of course, we distinguish only in order to reunite; we destruct only in order to reconstruct.

In this book I have tried to distinguish a few elements of the literary craft of the evangelists by tracing the contours, sources, and substance primarily of the Indian subtexts that make up the texture of the infancy gospels. I distinguish between the literary and the theological in order to highlight both since both are ever-present realities in the gospels. Doing violence to one diminishes the beauty and destroys the integrity of the other. Similarly, overemphasizing one to the point of asserting that the Bible is only theology or the Word of God does a disservice to the text. My own study may appear as a self-contradiction in this regard since it seems to overemphasize the literary. Let me make it clear: My intention has not been to minimize the theological at all even though I have deliberately tried not to stress the theological. I did so simply because Christian scholars have already done it over and over again. Besides, I do not have much to add to the existing theological literature on the Infancy gospels.

In the past Christian scholars have tended to subordinate the literary aspect of the gospels to its "unique" theology to the point

---

[3] Joel Rosenberg, "Meanings, Morals, and Mysteries: Literary Approaches to the Torah," *Response* 9: 2 (Summer, 1975), 67-94; cited by Robert Alter, *The Art of the Bibliczl Narrative* (New York, 1981), 19.

[4] Robert Alter, *The Art of the Biblical Narrative* (New York, 1981), 19.

that they have dwelt exclusively on the "uniqueness" and "originality" of the gospels as though the gospels were conceived like Athena in the divine imagination with minimal human agency. Many modern biblical scholars have tried to stem this theological tide by trying vociferously to pile up the literary, extra-biblical sources of the Christian scriptures. I added my voice to this growing critical chorus to proclaim that the New Testament is not Western literature, pure and simple, but rather still very much Eastern. This is not just because the gospels were composed in the East by Orientals but because they were extensively influenced by their Oriental sources of which India and its religions were an integral part. My analysis of the Infancy gospels shows that this influence was deep and pervasive. I am inclined even to suggest that the Christian writers must have been familiar, not just vaguely but thoroughly, with the Indian religions. I could do this kind of analytic work only within the liberal framework of modern literary criticism which endorses the methods of deconstructionism, intertextuality, and new historicism in comparative literary studies.

The *Listenwissenschaft* method I used in order to pile up parallels—some convincing and central, while others conjectural and tangential—shows the intricacies of intertextuality and the composite nature of the biblical narrative, which is an accepted premise in all biblical criticism, both old and new, the difference being that the old or the theological school admits only Old Testament subtexts, while the new historical-critical school is willing to look at extra-biblical subtexts—oral and written. Modern criticism readily admits the centrality of extra-canonical Jewish works as well as Hellenistic works in the intertextual structure of the books of the New Testament.

The closer we look at the text of the gospels, the more intrigued we are by the its intricately composite or intertextual narrative style. Without denying the fact that the books of the New Testament are literary wholes in their own right, we have to come to terms with another fact that they are made of elaborately layered materials. As for the Pentateuch, the scholarly consensus now is that those books were put together from different oral traditions and from different written texts over a period of some five centuries. The various ingenious scholarly reconstructions aside, the structural analyses of of most books of the Bible tell us that the text we have is not of one hand done in a single moment in time. Robert Alter articulates this view about the nature of the composite artistry of the Old Testament eloquently:

> A century of analytic scholarship has made powerful arguments to the effect that where we might naively imagine that we are reading a text, what we actually have is a constant stitching together of earlier texts drawn from divergent literary and sometimes oral traditions, with minor or major interventions by later editors in the form of glosses, connecting passages, conflations of sources, and so forth. The most eminent instance of this composite character of the biblical text has been found by scholars in the first four books of the Pentateuch which, on the evidence of style, consistency of narrative data, theological outlook, and historical assumptions, have been extensively analyzed as a splicing of three separate primary strands—the Yahwistic Document (*J*), the Elohistic Document (*E*), and the Priestly Document (*P*). *J* might date back to the tenth century B.C.E.; *E* could be about a century later, *P* would appear to be the work of a tradition of priestly writers, not one author, that begins fairly early in the First Temple period and continues into the sixth and fifth centuries B.C.E.[5]

The books of the New Testament, especially the gospels, also exhibit the same characteristic of composite artistry. Let me give one instance, the Matthean pericope about the death of Judas (Matthew 27:3-10), which is a striking example of how the gospel writer fuses different texts in order to create a historical fiction. Herman Hendrickx writes:

> The context shows that the incident cannot possibly have taken place at the stage where it is inserted into the events by Matthew. The chief priests and elders, for instance, cannot be in the Temple, since they are on their way to Pilate! Also, the description of Judas' death is very different from that found in Acts (1:16-20). The pericope is a subtle composition built up with Old Testament allusions and passages. Judas is said to have hanged himself in circumstances which recall the story of Ahithophel who, having betrayed his friend and king David and seeing that his plans were not going wok out as he had hoped, "went off home...and hanged himself" (2 Samuel 17:23). The thirty silver pieces and the treasury remind us of the prophet Zechariah who was appointed by God as the *shepherd of Israel*, but who wanted to resign because of the people's stubbornness and asked them to pay him his wages. They paid him *thirty silver pieces* to get rid of him. Then God said: "Cast them in the treasury" (see Zech. 11:4-14; especially 12-13). This text is combined with the idea of the *purchase of the field* suggested by Jer. 32:6-15. Moreover, Jer. 18:2f. and 19:1, 10-12 speak of *potters*.[6]

---

[5] Alter, 132.

[6] Hendrickx, 6. I see in the Matthean pericope the use also of Buddhist sources, which make much of Devadatta, a cousin of Buddha, who tried to kill Buddha several times, betrayed him by creating a schism in the community, and finally met a death similar to the death of Judas described in the Acts.

In this book I have taken great pains to show the composite nature of the nativity narratives. My work in this regard is perfect agreement with what has been going in contemporary New Testament studies characterized by form criticism and redaction criticism. Of course, no serious New Testament critic today would argue that the evangelists are but collectors of traditions. On the contrary, the redaction critics point out against form critics that the narrow version of form criticism, when applied to the New Testament, undercuts the personality of the author, the uniqueness of his vision, and the originality of his message. No doubt, we find abundant creativity and fascinating originality in the juxtaposition and association of Indian subtexts with the Old Testament texts and in the integration of these two within the framework of the Christian theology. Norman Perrin once said that Bultmann spent so much time and effort in the Synoptic tradition that he failed to see clearly the special uses that Matthew and Luke made of that tradition.[7]

In fact, thanks to redaction criticism modern scholarship has rehabilitated the evangelists not by arguing that they have created literary works *de novo* but by emphasizing the vision and literary skills of the gospel writers and the later editors. Their originality and skill are obvious in the selection of their materials, their arrangement, their modification, and their editorial theologies. What redaction critics emphasize is each author's creative contribution to or his purpose in the editing of the received material. These critics have produced excellent works on the theologies of each book of the New Testament. What they have done is write books without taking into consideration some of the important sources of the gospels, which are Buddhist and Hindu religious traditions. Of course, I am being critaical here of parochialism; on the other hand, I admire their approach, effort, and accomplishments with one *caveat*: Since all scholarship is provisional and tentative in nature and scope, scholars of the past have not said the last word in biblical criticism. I have no intention of replicating the work of the redaction critics. What I have done in this book is to call the attention of scholars to the Indian sources of the New Testament and to identify once again the overriding concern (pretext) that the gospel writers had in their use of the Indian texts.

---

[7] Cited by Collins, 197-198.

The main concern of the gospel writers was to show that Jesus was not only the Messiah foretold in the Old Testament but also a God in human form who appeared on earth, died on the cross, and rose from the dead for the salvation of the whole human race. The gospels spell this idea out clearly: "Jesus did many other miraculous signs in the presence of his disciples, which are not recorded in this book. But these are written that you may believe that Jesus is the Christ, the Son of God, and that by believing you may have life in his name (John 20:30); "Go and make disciples of all nations." (Matthew 28:19).

This theological concern of the evangelists to portray Jesus as the divine savior was also their pretext to use all available literary sources to portray Jesus as such. As for the portrayal of the messianic dimensions attributed to Jesus in the gospels, the evangelists found abundant material and prooftexts in the Old Testament. They used their Old Testament sources very effectively to accomplish this purpose. But when the same writers had to present Jesus as a divine teacher-redeemer, they had recourse primarily to Indian sources which provide more material for this aspect of their work than Greek or Egyptian sources—I do not deny that Jesus is presented also as a Socrates-figure in the Synoptic gospels. Since there is no reason to believe that the evangelists had travelled all the way to India to gather their Indian material, it is more than likely that they found all this information in their own historical situation, the Gnostic milieu, in which they lived, taught, reflected, discussed, and debated. I am even inclined to believe that the gospels were composed not in Palestine but rather in Egypt—the hotbed of Gnostic ideologies—where, climatic considerations aside, we find all the earliest surviving fragments of the gospels .

The evangelists could use all their non-Jewish subtexts as a pretext to speak of God and Jesus since in their theology God had spoken through them all without exception. In fact, they argued that Jesus was the be-all and end-all of all salvation history for the final eon and that Jesus had superseded all the past messiahs, prophets, teachers, and redeemer-figures. The author of the Epistle to the Hebrews writes:

> In the past God spoke to our forefathers through the prophets at many times and in various ways, but in these last days he has spoken to us by his Son, whom he appointed heir of all things, and through whom he made the universe. The Son is the radiance of God's glory and the exact representation of his being, sustaining all things by his powerful word.

> After he had provided purification for sins, he sat down at the right hand of the Majesty in heaven. So he became as much superior to the angels as the name he has inherited is superior to theirs. For to which of the angels did God ever say, "You are my Son; today I have become your Father?"...And...God...says, "Let all God's angels worship him....The heavens...will perish, but you remain; they will all wear out like a garment....But you remain the same, and your years will never end....Sit at my right hand until I make your enemies a footstool for your feet" (1:1-13).

The gospel writers believed that this theological or Christological pretext gave them the licence to utilize not only the Old Testament but also Indian and other religious traditions as a means for glorifying the Jesus of the present eon as well as for denigrating the prophets of the past and many of their unacceptable their teachings as worn-out garments. The final triumph of Jesus would come soon, they suggested; it would be only a matter of time. As Paul says in his Epistle to the Romans, "I do not want you to be ignorant of this mystery, brothers, so that you may not be conceited: Israel has experienced a hardening in part until the full number of the Gentiles has come. And so all Israel will be saved" (11:25-26).

Though the evangelists might have pretended or presumed that the future-present or the eschatological age was what was really important, the past obviously refused to disappear into the black hole of the eschatological times. The past is too much with us. Jesus has not yet replaced Moses, nor has Muhammad replaced Jesus. It is not likely that they will ever, if the signs of the times are any indication. Judaism, Islam, Buddhism, and Hinduism are as strong as ever. The end of the world has not yet come; the day of the Anti-Christ seems to be still far, far away. From the literary perspective, the text of the New Testament has not yet supplanted its Jewish and Indian subtexts; rather we are discovering more and more new Eastern subtexts in the gospels. In view of these developments, we regard that textual history is very much a part of the text itself and that we have every reason to believe that no pretext can do away with the pre-text, which is as sacred as the text itself.

ABBREVIATIONS

A A	Acta Antiqua
A A O B	Association des amis de l'Orient, Bulletin
A M	Asia Minor
A N C L	Anti-Nicene Christian Library
A R W	Archiv für Religionswissenschaft
A W L M	Akademie der Wissenschaften und der Literatur, Mainz, Abhandlungen
B C O	Bibliotheca Classica Orientalis
B S O A S	Bulletin of the School of Oriental and African Studies
C B Q	Catholic Biblical Quarterly
C M	Classica et Mediaevalia
C Q	Classical Quarterly
C S C O	Corpus Scriptorum Christianorum Orientalium
D C B	Dictionary of Christian Bibliography
E R E	Encyclopedia of Religion and Ethics
E & W	East and West
F F C	Folklore Fellows Communications
F L	Folk-Lore
His	Historia
H O S	Harvard Oriental Series
H S C P	Harvard Studies in Classical Philology
I A	Indian Antiquary
J A	Journal asiatique
J A O S	Journal of the American Oriental Society
J B L	Journal of Biblical Literature
J G I S	Journal of the Greater India Society
J R A S	Journal of the Royal Asiatic Society
J T S	Journal of Theological Studies
Kai	Kairos
Kl	Klio
Loeb	Loeb Library Classics
M H S M B	Manichäische Handschriften der Staatlichen Museen Berlin
N T S	New Testament Studies
O G	Le Origini dello Gnosticismo
P B A	Proceedings of the British Academy
P G	Patrologia Graeca
P L	Patrologia Latina
P M L A	Publications of the Modern Language Association
R E	Real-Encyclopädie
R D M	Revue des deux mondes
R E L	Revue des études latines
R H	Revue historique
R H R	Revue de l'histoire des religions
R S P T	Revue des sciences philosophiques et théologiques
R S R	Recherches de science religieuse
S B A	Sitzungsberichte der Berliner Akademie der Wissenschaften
S B B	Sacred Books of the Buddhists
S B E	Sacred Books of the East
S H R	Studies in the History of Religions
S U K H	Skrifter Utgivna av Kungl. Humanistiska Vetenskaps-Samfundet i Uppsala

BIBLIOGRAPHY

Aiken, Charles Francis. *The Dhamma of Gotama the Buddha and the Gospel of Jesus the Christ.* Boston: 1900.
Alter, Robert. *The Art of Biblical Narrative.* New York: 1981.
Ammianus Marcellinus. Trans. John C. Rolfe. Loeb Classical Library, Cambridge, Mass: 1963. Vol. I.
Amore, Roy. *Two Masters, One Message.* Abingdon: 1978.
André, J. "Virgile et les Indiens," *REL,* 27 (1949), 157-63.
Anguttara Nikaya [of Sutta Pitaka]. Trans. Edmund R. J. Gooneratne. London: 1885.
Anonymous. "Charition," in D. L. Page, *Select Papyri,* III. Loeb Classical Library: 1970, 336-349.
Apocrypha [New Testament]. Trans. by Montague Rhodes James as *The Apocryphal New Testament.* Oxford: 1924.
Apocrypha [Old Testament]. Trans. Edgar J. Goodspeed as *The Apocrypha.* Chicago: 1938.
Archer, William George. *The Loves of Krishna in Indian Painting and Poetry.* London: 1957 & New York: n.d.
Armstrong, A. H. "Plotinus and India," *CQ,* 30 (1936), 22-28.
Arrian. *Anabasis Alexandri and Indica.* Trans. E. Iliff Robson. Loeb Library; London: 1954 & 1958. 2 vols.
Arya Sura. *Gatakamala.* Trans. J. S. Speyer. [Vol. I of *SBB.*] London: 1895.
Asoka. Edicts, in Vincent A. Smith, *Asoka, the Buddhist Emperor of India.* 3rd rev. ed. Oxford: 1920.
Asvaghosha. *Go-sho-hing-tsan-king, a Life of Buddha.* Trans. into Chinese by Dharmaraksha and into English by Samuel Beal. [Vol. XIX of *SBE*] Oxford: 1883.
Auerbach, Erich. *Mimesis.* New York: 1946.

Bailey, K. E. "The Manger and the Inn: The Cultural Background of Luke 2:7," *Near East School of Theology Theological Review* 2 (1979), 35-44.
——."The Song of Mary: Vision of a New Exodus (Luke 1:46-55)," *Near East School of Theology Theological Review* 2 (1979), 29-35.
Barnard, Mary E. "Garcilago's Poetics of Subversion and the Orpheus Tapestry," *PMLA* 102 (1987), 316.
Barthes, Roland. *S/Z.* Paris: 1974.
Basham, A. L. *The Wonder That Was India.* Rev. ed; London: 1954.
——, ed. *A Cultural History of India.* Oxford: 1975.
Beal, Samuel, trans. *Dhammapada with Accompanying Narratives.* Calcutta: 1952.
Beehert, Heinz and Gombrich Richard. *The World of Buddhism: Buddhist Monks and Nimo in Society and Culture.* New York: 1984.
Bell, Daniel. *The End of Ideologies.* Cambridge, Ma.: 1987.
Benfey, Theodor, trans. *Pantschatantra, fünf Bücher indischer Fabeln, Märchen und Erzählungen.* Leipzig: 1859.
Benveniste, Emile. "Édits d'Asoka en traduction grecque," *JA,* 252 (1964), 137-57.
Benz, Ernst. "Indische Einflüsse auf die frühchristliche Theologie," Abh. Nr. 3, *AWLM* (1951), 172-202.
Bergh van Eysinga, G. A. van den. *Indische Einflüsse auf evangelische Erzählungen.* Göttingen: 1904.
Bernard, Paul. "Ai Khanum on the Oxus: a Hellenistic City in Central Asia," *PBA,* 53 (1967), 71-95.

Bernstein, Richard. "Undermining Capitalism," *New York Times*, February 7, 1989, p. 14.
Bertholet, A. *Buddhismus und Christentum*. 2d ed. Tübingen: 1909.
Bhagavad Gita. Trans. Juan Mascaró. Harmondsworth: 1962.
Bharati, Agehananda. *The Ocre Robe*. Seattle: 1962.
Bianchi, Ugo. ed. *Le Origini dello Gnosticismo: colloquio di Messina 13-18 aprile 1966*. Leiden: 1970.
Bigg, Charles. *The Christian Platonists of Alexandria*. Oxford: 1913.
Bleeker, C. J. "The Egyptian Background of Gnosticism," *OG*, 229-37.
Bloom, Harold et al., eds. *Deconstruction and Criticism*. New York: 1979.
———. *Map of Misreading*. New York: 1975.
Bornkamm, Günther. *Mythos und Legende in den apokryphen Thomas-Akten*. Göttingen: 1933.
Boslooper, Thomas. *The Virgin Birth*. Philadelphia: 1962.
Bouyer, Louis. "Gnosis: le sens orthodoxe de l'expression jusqu'aux pères alexandrins," *JTS*, 4 (1953), 188-203.
Boyce, Mary. "The Indian Fables in the Letter of Tansar," *AM* (1954), 50-58.
———. *The Manichaean Hymn-Cycles in Parthian*. London: 1954.
Boyd, James W. *Satan and Mara: Christian and Buddhist Symbols of Evil*. Leiden: 1975.
Brown, Leslie Alfred. *The Indian Christians of St. Thomas: an Account of the Ancient Syrian Church of Malabar*. Cambridge: 1956.
Brown, Percy. *Indian Architecture (Buddhist and Hindu)*, 6th reprint. Bombay: 1971.
Brown, R. E. *Gospel According to John I-XII*. Garden City: 1966.
———. "Gospel Infancy Narrative Research From 1976 to 1986," *CBQ* 48 (1986): 468-483; 660-680.
Brown, R. E. "Luke's Description of the Virginal Conception," *Theological Studies* 35 (1974), 360-2.
———. *The Birth of the Messiah*. New York: 1977.
———. "The Meaning of the Magi; The Significance of the Star," *Worship* 49 (1975), 574-82.
———. "Significance of the Shepherds," *Worship* 50 (1976), 528-38.
———. "The Presentation of Jesus (Luke 2:22-40)," *Worship* 51 (1977), 2-11.
Brown, Truesdell S. *Onesicritus. A Study in Hellenistic Historiography*. [Vol. 39 of *University of California Publications in History*.] Berkeley: 1949.
Brown, William Norman. *The Indian and Christian Miracles of Walking on the Water*. Chicago: 1928.
Bruns, J. Edgar. "Ananda: The Fourth Evangelist's Model for 'the disciple whom Jesus loved'?" *Studies in Religion*, 1973-74, 236-43.
———. *The Art and Thought of John*. New York: 1969.
———. *The Christian Buddhism of St. John*. New York: 1971.
Bruns, J. Edgar. "The Magi Episode in Matthew 2," *The Catholic Biblical Quarterly* 22 (1961), 51-4.
Buchtal, H. "The Western Aspects of Gandhara Sculpture," *PBA*, XXXI (1945), 151-76.
Budge, E. A. Wallis. *Baralam and Yewasef: Being the Ethiopic Version of a Christianized Recension of the Buddhist Legend of the Buddha and the Bodhisattva*. 2 vols. Cambridge: 1923.
———. *Legends of Our Lady Mary the Perpetual Virgin and Her Mother Hanna*. London: 1933.
Bultmann, Rudolf. *Primitive Christianity*. Philadelphia: 1983.
———.*Theology of the New Testament*. Trans. Kendrick Grobel. New York: 1951.
Burkitt, Francis C. *Church and Gnosis*. Cambridge: 1932.
Burlingame, Eugene W. *Buddhist Legends, Translated from the Original Pali Text of the Dhammapada Commentary*. [Vols. 28-30 of *HOS*.] Cambridge, Mass.: 1921.
Burnouf, Emile. "Le Bouddhisme en Occident," *RDM* (1888).
Bødker, Laurits. "Indian Animal Tales: a Preliminary Survey," *FFC*, LXVIII, No. 170. Helsinki: 1957, 1-144.

Caldwell, Robert. *A Comparative Grammar of the Dravidian or South-Indian Family of Languages.* London: 1913.
Campbell, F. W. Groves. *Apollonius of Tyana.* Chicago: 1908.
Carrithers, Michael. *The Buddha.* New York: 1983.
Cave, C. H. "St. Matthew's Infancy Narrative," *New Testament Studies* 9 (1962-63), 382-90.
Cave, Terence. *The Cornucopian Text: Problems of Writing in the French Renaissance.* Oxford: 1979.
Cerfaux, Lucien. "La gnose Simonienne: culte et doctrines," *RSR* 16 (1926), 481-503.
——. "La gnose Simonienne: nos sources principales," *RSR,* 15 (1925), 489-511.
Chadwick, Henry. *The Early Church.* Grand Rapids, Mich.: 1967.
Chalmers, Lord. *Buddha's Teachings. Being the Sutta-Nipata or Discourse-Collection.* [Vol. 37 of *HOS.*] Cambridge, Mass.: 1932.
——. *Further Dialogues of the Buddha, Translated from the Pali of the Majjhima Nikaya.* [Vol. 6 of *SBB.*] London: 1927.
Charlesworth, Martin P. "Roman Trade with India: a Resurvey," *Studies in Roman Economic and Social History in Honor of Allan Chester Johnson.* Princeton: 1951.
——. "Some Notes on the *Periplus Maris Erythraei,*" *CQ* (1928), 92-100.
——. *Trade-Routes and Commerce of the Roman Empire.* 2nd ed. Cambridge: 1926.
Charpentier, Jarl. "The Indian Travels of Apollonius of Tyana," *SUKH,* Vol. 29. Uppsala: 1934.
Clark, S. L. "Said, Unsaid, Male and Female...," *Proceedings of the PMR Conference,*11 (Villanova, 1986), 51-70.
Clark, S. L. and J. M. Wasserman, "The Heart in *Troilus and Criseyde,*" *Chaucer Review,* 18 (1984), 316-328
Clemen, Carl. "Buddhistische Einflüsse im Neuen Testament," *ZNW,* 17 (1916), 128-38.
Clemen, Carl. *Primitive Christianity and Its Non-Jewish Sources.* Trans. Robert G. Nisbet. Edinburgh: 1912.
Clement of Alexandria. "Stromata," in *The Writings of Clement of Alexandria.* Trans. William Watson. 2 vols. [Vols. IV & XII of *ANCL.*] Edinburgh: 1871 & 1869.
Collins, John J. *Between Athens and Jerusalem.* New York: 1983.
——. *Apocalyptic Imagination: An Introduction to the Jewish Matrix of Christianity.*New York: 1987.
Collins, R. E. *Introduction to the New Testament.* New York: 1987.
Conybeare, F. C., Harris, J. Rendel, & Lewis, Agnes Smith. *The Story of Ahikar, from the Aramaic, Syriac, Arabic, Armenian, Ethiopic, Old Turkish, Greek and Slavonic Versions.* 2nd ed. Cambridge: 1913.
Conze, Edward. *A Short History of Buddhism.* London: 1981.
——. "Buddhism and Gnosis," in *OG,* 651-67. Leiden: 1970.
——. *Buddhism, Its Essence and Development.* New York: 1959.
Cosmas Indikipleustes. *The Christian Typography of Cosmas, an Egyptian Monk.* Trans. & ed. J. W. McCrindle. New York: 1897.
Cowley, A., ed. & trans. *Aramaic Papyri of the Fifth Century B. C.* Oxford: 1923.
Crossan, Dominic. *The Cross that Spoke.* New York: 1988.
Ctesias. *La Perse, l'Inde, les sommaires de Photius.* Ed. R. Henry. Brussels: 1947.
Culler, Jonathan. "Presupposition and Intertextuality," in *The Pursuit of Signs: Semiotics, Literature and Deconstruction.* Ithaca: 1981.
Cumont, Franz. *The Oriental Religions in Roman Paganism.* New York: 1956. [Originally published 1911.]
Cunningham, Alexander. *The Ancient Geography of India.* London: 1871.

Dahlquist, Allan. *Megasthenes and Indian Religion.* Stockholm: 1962.
Daniel, K. N. *The South Indian Apostolate of St. Thomas.* Serampore: 1952.

DasGupta, Surendranath. *A History of Indian Philosophy*. 5 vols. Cambridge: 1922-1955.
Davids, Caroline Rhys. *The Minor Anthologies of the Pali Canon*. Part I: *Dhammapada and Khuddaka-Patha*. [Vol. VII of SBB.] London: 1931.
Davids, Mrs. Rhys and F. L. Woodward, trans. *The Book of Kindred Sayings (Samyutta-Nikaya)* (London: Pali Text Society, 1919-), v. 208.
Davids, T. W. & C. A. F. Rhys. *Dialogues of the Buddha. Translated from the Pali of the Digha Nikaya*. 3 vols. London: 1899-1921.
——, trans. *Sacred Books of the Buddhists*, vol. III (London: Pali Text Society, 1899; 3rd ed., 1951).
Davids, T. W. Rhys & Oldenberg, Hermann. *Vinaya Texts*. Part III: *The Kullavagga, IV-XII*. [Vol. XX of SBE.] Oxford: 1885.
Davies, Stevan L. *The Gospel of Thomas and Christian Wisdom*. New York: 1983.
Davies, William David. *Christian Origins and Judaism*. London: 1962.
Davis, C. T. "Tradition and Redaction in Matthew 1:18-2:23," *Journal of Biblical Literature* 90 (1971), 404-21.
de Bunsen, Ernst. *The Angel-Messiah of Buddhists, Essenes and Christians*. London: 1880.
Dead Sea Scrolls. Trans. Geza Vermes. New York: 1962.
Deepavamsa. Trans. H. Oldenberg. London: 1879.
Demaitre, Edmond. *The Yogis of India*. London: 1937.
Derrett, J. Duncan M. "A Problem in the Book of Jubilees and an Indian Doctrine," *ZRGG*, 14 (1962), 247-62.
——. "Greece and India: the Milindapanha, the Alexander-romance and the Gospels," *ZRGG*, 19 (1967), 33-63.
——. "The History of 'Palladius on the Races of India and the Brahmans'," *CM*, XXI (1960), 64-84.
——. "The Theban Scholasticus and Malabar in c. 355-60," *JAOS*, 82 (1962), 21-31.
Deussen, Paul. *Allgemeine Geschichte der Philosophie, mit besonderer Berücksichtigung der Religionen*. Leipzig: 1907. Vol. I, Part II.
——. *The Philosophy of the Upanishads*. London: 1906.
Dhammapada. Trans. F. Max Müller. [Vol. X of SBE.] Oxford: 1881.
Dhammapada. Trans. S. Radhakrishnan. London: 1950.
Dibelius, Martin. *From Tradition to Gospel*. New York: 1965.
——. *Sermon on the Mount*. New York: 1948.
Digha Nikaya. Trans. T. W. & C. A. F. Rhys Davids as *Dialogues of the Buddha*. London: 1899-1921. 3 vols.
Dio Cassius. *Dio's Roman History*. Trans. Earnest Cary. Loeb Library; London: 1955.
Diogenes Laertius. *Lives of Eminent Philosophers*. Trans. R. D. Hicks. Loeb Library; London: 1925 & 1931. 2 vols.
——. *The Lives and Opinions of Eminent Philosophers*. Trans. C. D. Yonge. London: 1905.
Dion Chrysostom. Trans. J. W. Colson & H. Lamar Crosby. Loeb Library; London: 1932. 5 vols.
Drijvers, H. J. W. *Bardaisan of Edessa*. Assen: 1966.
Drower, E. S. *The Haran Gawaitha and the Baptism of Hibil Ziwa*. Città del Vaticano: 1953.

Edgerton, Franklin, trans. *The Panchatantra*. London: 1965.
Edmunds, Albert J. *Buddhist and Christian Gospels, Being 'Gospel Parallels from Pali Texts' Now Reprinted with Additions*. Ed. M. Anesaki. 4th ed. Philadelphia: 1908 & 1909. 2 vols.
——. *Buddhist and Christian Gospels: Being Gospel Parallels from Pali Texts*. Ed. M. Anesaki. 3rd ed. Tokyo: 1905.
Edwards, Richard A. *A Theology of Q*. Philadelphia: 1975.

Ehlers, Barbara. "Bardesanes von Edessa, ein syrischer Gnostiker," *ZKG*, 81 (1970), 334-51.
Eliade, Mircea. *Cosmos and History: the Myth of the Eternal Return.* Trans. Willard Trask. New York: 1954.
Eliot, Charles N. *Hinduism and Buddhism.* London: 1921. 3 vols.
———. *Collected Poems, 1909-1962.* New York: 1970.
Eli. *Selected Essays.* New York: 1950.
Ephraem Syrus. *Des Heiligen Ephraem des Syrers Hymen contra Haereses.* Trans. Edmund Beck. [Vol. 170 of *CSCO*.] Louvain: 1957.
———. Hymns, in A. E. Medlycott, *India and the Apostle Thomas.* London: 1905.
———. *S. Ephraim's Prose Refutations of Mani, Marcion, and Bardaisan.* Ed. C. W. Mitchell. London: 1912 & 1921. 2 vols.
Epiphanius. *Epiphanius' Treatise on Weights and Measures: the Syriac Version.* Ed. James Elmer Dean. [No. 11 of *SAOC*, Univ. of Chicago.] Chicago: 1935.
"Essenes," *The Interpreter's Dictionary of the Bible.* Nashville: 1962.
Eusebius. *Evangelicae Praeparationis.* Ed. E. H. Gifford. Oxford: 1903.
———. *The Ecclesiastical History.* Trans. Kirsopp Lake. Loeb Library; London: 1953. 2 vols.
———. "Treatises," in Philostratos, *The Life of Apollonius of Tyana.* Loeb Library; London: 1912. Vol. II.

Farquhar, J. N. "The Apostle Thomas in North India," *JRLB*, 10 (1926), 80-111.
Filliozat, Jean. *La Doctrine classique de la médécine indienne: ses origines et ses parallèles grecs.* Paris: 1949.
———. "La Doctrine des brahmanes d'après saint Hippolyte," *RHR*, CXXX (1945), 59-91.
———. "Les Echanges de l'Inde et de l'Empire romain aux premiers siècles de l'ère chrétienne," *RH* (1949), 1-29.
———. *Les Relations extérieures de l'Inde.* Pondichéry: 1956.
Fitzmyer, J. A. "The Virginal Conception of Jesus in the New Testament," *Theological Studies* 34 (1973), 541-75.
Foucher, A. *L'Art gréco-bouddhique du Gandhâra.* Paris: 1895. 2 vols.
France, R. T. "Herod and the Children of Bethlehem," *Novum Testamentum* 21 (1979), 98-120.
———. "The 'Massacre of the Innocents'—Fact or Fiction?" in *Studia Biblica 1978*, II: *Papers on the Gospels.* ed. E. A. Livingstone. Sheffield: 1980, 83-94.
———. "The Formula Quotations of Matthew 2 and the Problem of Communication," *New Testament Studies* 27 (1980-81), 233-51.
Francis, H. T. and Thomas, E. J. *Jataka Tales.* Bombay: 1970.

Gadamer, Hans-Georg. "The Eminent Text and Its Truth," *The Bulletin of the Midwest Modern Language Association* 13 (1980), 3-13.
———. *Truth and Method.* New York: 1989.
Gadd, C. J. "Seals of Ancient Indian Type Found at Ur," *PBA*, XVIII (1932).
Gandhi, Mohandas K. *An Autobiography; The Story of My Experiments with Truth.* Boston: 1957.
Garbe, Richard. *Indien und das Christentum, eine Untersuchung der religions-geschichtlichen Zusammenhänge.* Tübingen: 1914. Trans. by Lydia G. Robinson as *India and Christendom, the Historical Connections between Their Religions.* LaSalle, Illinois: 1959.
Geffré, Claude and Dhavamony, M., eds. *Buddhism and Christianity.* New York: 1979.
Geiger, Wilhelm, trans. *The Mahavamsa: or the Great Chronicle of Ceylon/* London: Pali Text Society, 1964.
Ghurye, Govind S. *Indian Sadhus.* Bombay: 1953.
Gibbs, J. M. "Purpose and Pattern in Matthew's Use of the Title 'Son of David'," *New Testament Studies* 10 (1963-64), 446-64; especially 447-8.

Giblin, C. H. "Reflections on the Sign of the Manger," *The Catholic Biblical Quarterly* 29 (1967), 87-101.
Gifford, Henry. *Comparative Literature*. London: 1969.
Glasenapp, Helmuth von. *Immortality and Salvation in Indian Religions*. Trans. E. J. J. Payne. Calcutta: 1963.
Goddard, Dwight. *Was Jesus Influenced by Buddhism?* Thetford, Vermont: 1927.
Gombrich, Richard F. "Ancient Indian Cosmology," in Blacker & Loewe, eds., *Ancient Cosmologies*, 110-39. London: 1975.
———. *Theravada Buddhism*. London: 1988.
Grant, Michael. *Jesus: An Historian's Review of the Gospels*. New York: 1977.
Grant, Robert M. "Gnostic Origins and the Basilidians of Irenaeus," *VC*, XIII (1959), 121-25.
———. *Gnosticism and Early Christianity*. 2nd ed. New York: 1966.
———. *Gnosticism, an Anthology*. London: 1961.
Greenblatt, Stephen. *The Form of Power and the Power of Forms in Renaissance Literature*. Norman: 1982.
Grierson, George A. "Modern Hinduism and Its Debt to the Nestorians," *JRAS* (1908), 337-62.
Guthrie, W. K. C. *A History of Greek Philosophy*. Cambridge: 1962. Vol. I.

Halbfass, Wilhelm. *India and Europe: An Essay in Understanding*. Albany: 1988.
Halliday, W. R. *Indo-European Folk-Tales and Greek Legend*. Cambridge: 1933.
———. "Notes upon Indo-European Folk-Tales and the Problem of Their Diffusion," *FL*, XXXIV (1923), 117-40.
Hardy, R. Spence. *Eastern Monachism*. London: 1850.
Hartman, Geoffrey and Buddick, Stanford, eds. *Literature and Midrash*. New Haven: 1986.
Hayles, D. J. "The Roman Census and Jesus' Birth. Was Luke Correct? Part I: The Roman Census System," *Buried History* 9 (1973), 113-32.
———. "The Roman Census and Jesus' Birth. Was Luke Correct? Part II: Quirinius' Career and a Census in Herod's Day," *Buried History* 10 (1974), 16-31.
Hegel, Wilhelm. *The History of Philosophy*. New York: 1955.
Hengel, Martin. *Judaism and Hellenism*. Philadelphia: 1974.
Henrichs, Albert. "Mani and the Babylonian Baptists: Historical Confrontation," *HSCP*, 77 (1973), 23-59.
Henry, Patrick J. and Swearer, Donald K. *For the Sake of the World: The Spirit of Buddhism and Christian Monasticism*. Minneapolis: 1989.
Herodotus. Trans. A. D. Godley, Loeb Library; London: 1960. 4 vols.
Hertel, Johannes. *The Panchatantra, a Collection of Indian Tales*. Ed. Charles Rockwell Lanman. [Vol. XI of *HOS*.] Cambridge: 1908.
Hesiod. *Theogony and Works and Days*. Trans. M. L. West. Oxford: 1988.
———. "Works and Days," in *The Homeric Hymns and Homerica*. Trans. H. G. Evelyn-White. London: 1959.
Hippolytus. *Philosophumena, or the Refutation of All Heresies*. Trans. F. Legge. London: 1921. 2 vols.
——— *The Refutation of All Heresies*. Trans. J. H. Macmillan [Vol. VI of *ANCL*.] Edinburgh: 1868.
Hirsch, E. D. *Validity in Interpretation*. New Haven: 1976.
Hopkins, E. Washburn. *India Old and New*. New York, London: 1901.
Horner, I. B., trans. *Milinda's Questions*. [Vol. XXII of *SBB*.] London: 1963.
Hort, F. J. A. "Bardaisan," in *DCB* (1877), I, 250-60.
———. "Basilides," in *DCB* (1877), I, 268-81.
Hourani, George Fadlo. *Arab Seafaring in the Indian Ocean in Ancient and Early Medieval Times*. Beirut: 1963.

Iamblichus. *De Vita Pythagorica*. Ed. Theophilus Kiessling. Leipzig: 1895.

―――. *The Life of Pythagoras* [abridged]. Trans. Thomas Taylor. Los Angeles: 1905.
Iersel, B. van. "The Finding of Jesus in the Temple. Some Observations on the Original Form of Luke II. 41-51a," *Novum Testamentum* 4 (1960), 161-73.
Irenaeus. *Against Heresies*. Trans. A. Roberts. [Vol. V of *ANCL*.] Edinburgh: 1868.
Iti-vuttaka. Sayings of Buddha. Trans. Justin H. Moore. [Vol. V of *CUIIS*.] New York: 1908.
Itivuttaka. Trans. F. L. Woodward in *The Minor Anthologies of the Pali Canon*, Part II. [Vol. VIII of *SBB*.] London: 1948.

Jack, Homer A. *The Gandhi Reader*. Bloomington: 1956.
Jacobs, Joseph, ed. *Barlaam and Josaphat*. London: 1896.
―――, ed. *The Fables of Aesop*. London: 1889.
―――. "Fable," in *ERE*, V, 676-78.
Jairazbhoy, R. A. *Foreign Influence in Ancient India*. Bombay: 1963.
James, Montague Rhodes, trans. *The Apocryphal New Testament*. Oxford: 1924.
Jatakas. Ed. E. B. Cowell as *The Jataka, or Stories or the Buddha's Former Births*. Cambridge: 1895-1907. 6 vols.
Jeremias, Joachim. *Unknown Sayings of Jesus*. London: 1964.
John of Damascus. *Barlaam and Ioasaph*. Trans. G. R. Woodward and H. Mattingly. Loeb Library; London: 1914.
Johnston, E. H. *The Buddacarita*. Delhi: 1984.
Jonas, Hans. "Delimitation of the Gnostic Phenomenon-Typological and Historical," in *OG*, 90-108. Leiden: 1970.
―――. *The Gnostic Religion*. Boston: 1958.
Jones, J. and Wake, William, eds. *The Lost Books of the Bible*. New York: 1979.
Jones, J. J. *The Mahavastu*. London: 1973. 3 vols.
―――, trans. *The Mahavastu. Sacred Books of the Buddhists*, vol. XVII. London: 1952.
Josephus, Flavius. *Jewish Antiquities*. Trans. H. St. Thackereay in *Josephus*. Loeb Library; Cambridge, Mass.: 1963-67. Vols. 4-9.
―――. *The Jewish War*. Trans. H. St. J. Thackeray in *Josephus*. Loeb Library; Cambridge, Mass.: 1927-28. Vols. 2-3.

Kale, M. R. *Hitopadesha*. Delhi: 1985.
Keay, Frank Ernest. *A History of the Syrian Church in India*. 2nd ed. Madras: 1951.
Kee, Howard Clark. *Jesus in History: An Approach to the Study of the Gospels*. New York: 1970.
―――. *Community of the New Age*. Philadelphia: 1977.
―――. *Jesus in History*. New York: 1970.
Keith, Arthur Berriedale. "Pythagoras and the Doctrine of Transmigration," *JRAS* (1909), 569-606.
Kennedy, J. "Buddhist Gnosticism, the System of Basilides," *JRAS* (1902), 377-415.
―――. "The Child Krishna, Christianity and the Gujars," in *JRAS*, 1907, 951-992.
―――. "The Child Krishna, Christianity, and the Gujars," *JRAS* (1907), 951-91.
―――. "The Early Commerce of Babylon with India—700-300 B.C.," *JRAS* (1898), 241-87.
Kephalaia. Trans. & ed. Hans J. Polotsky. [Vol. I, Part I of *MHSMB*.] Stuttgart: 1940.
Kern, H., trans. *Saddharm-Pundarika: or The Lotus of the True Law*. New York: 1963.
Kern, Heinrich (Hendrik). *Manual of Indian Buddhism* (Grundriss der indo-arischen Philologie und Altertumskunde, III, 8), 124. Strassburg: 1896.
King, Winston L. *Buddhism and Christianity: Some Bridges of Understanding*. Philadelphia: 1962.
Klimkeit, Hans J. "Christian-Buddhist Encounter in Medieval Central Asia," in G. W. Houston, ed., *The Cross and the Lotus*. Delhi: 1985.
Kristeva, Julia. *La Révolution de Language Poetique*. Paris: 1974.
―――. *Semeiotiké: Recherches pour une Semianalyse*. Paris: 1969.
Kugel, James L. and Greer, R. A. *Early Biblical Interpretation*. Philadelphia: 1986.

BIBLIOGRAPHY 285

Küng, Hans. *Justification: The Doctrine of Kari Barth and a Catholic Reflection.* New York: 1964.

Lachs, Samuel Tobias. *A Rabbinic Commentary on the New Testament.* Hoboken: 1987.
Lahiri, A. N. *Corpus of Indo-Greek Coins.* Calcutta: 1965.
Lang, D. M., trans. *The Balavariani: A Tale from the Christian East.* Berkeley: 1966.
——. "The Life of the Blessed Iodasaph: a New Oriental Christian Version of the Barlaam and Ioasaph Romance," *BSOAS,* XX (1957), 389-407.
——. *The Wisdom of Balahvar: a Christian Legend of the Buddha.* London: 1957.
Latourette, Kenneth Scott. *A History of the Expansion of Christianity.* Vol. I: *The First Five Centuries.* New York: 1937.
Laurentin, R. "Les Evangiles de l'enfance," *Lumière et Vie* 23 (no. 119, 1974), 84-105.
——. *Les évangiles de l'enfance du Christ: Vérité de Noël au-delà des mythes: Exégèse et sémiotique—historicité et théologie.* Paris: 1982.
——. *Structure de Luc I-II* (Etudes Bibliques; Paris: J. Gabalda et Cie, Editeurs, 1957).
——. *The Truth of Christmas.* Petersham: 1986.
Law, Bimala C. "Sakala: an Ancient Indian City," *E & W,* 19 (1969), 401-09.
Leaney, A. R. C. "The Birth Narratives of St. Luke and St. Matthew," *New Testament Studies* 8 (1961-62), 158-66.
Legge, Francis. *Forerunners and Rivals of Christianity.* Cambridge: 1915. 2 vols.
——. "Western Manichaeism and the Turfan Discoveries," *JRAS* (1913), 69-94.
Legrand, L. *The Biblical Doctrine of Virginity.* London: 1963).
Lester, Robert C. *Theravada Buddhism in Southeast Asia.* Ann Arbor: 1973.
Lévi, Sylvain. "Les 'Marchands de mer' et leur rôle dans le bouddhisme primitiv," *AAOB* (Oct. 1929), 19-39.
Lillie, Arthur. *Buddhism in Christendom.* London: 1887.
——. *The Influence of Buddhism on Primitive Christianity.* London: 1893.
Logan, A. H. B., and Wedderburn, A. J. M., eds. *The New Testament and Gnosis.* Edinburgh: 1983.
Loisy, Alfred. *The Birth of the Christian Religion.* Trans. L. P. Jacks. London: 1948.
Lubac, Henri de. "Buddhist Charity," in *Aspects of Buddhism.* Trans. George Lamb, 15-52. London: 1953.
——. *La Rencontre du Bouddhisme et de l'Occident.* Paris: 1952.
——. "Textes alexandrins et bouddhiques," *RSR,* 27 (1937), 336-51.
Lucian of Samosata. *Lucian* [Works]. Trans. A. M. Harmon. Loeb Library: London: 1925.
——. *The Works of Lucian of Samosata.* Trans. H. W. Fowler and F. G. Fowler. Oxford: 1905. 4 vols.

Mack, Burton. *The Myth of Innocence.* Philadelphia: 1987.
MacRae, George. "Gnosticism," *New Catholic Encyclopedia.*
Mahabharata. Trans. Pratap Chandra Roy as *The Mahabharata of Krishna-Dwaipayana Vyasa.* 2nd ed. Calcutta: n.d.
Mahavamsa. Trans. W. Geiger. London: 1980.
Majumdar, Bimanbehari. *Krsna in History and Legend.* Calcutta: 1969.
Majumdar, R. C., ed. *The History and Culture of the Indian People: The Age of Imperial Unity.* Bombay: 1968.
Marshall, John. *A Guide to Taxila.* 4th ed. Cambridge: 1960.
——. "Greeks and Sakas in India," *JRAS* (1947), 3-32.
McCrindle, J. W. *Ancient India as Described by Ktesias the Knidian.* Calcutta: 1882.
——. *Ancient India as Described by Megasthenes and Arrian.* London: 1877.
——. *Ancient India as Described in Classical Literature.* Westminster: 1901.
——. *The Invasion of India by Alexander the Great,* as Described by Arrian, Q. Curtius, Diodorus, Plutarch, and Justin. Westminster: 1893.
McGann, Jerome. *Textual Criticism and Literary Interpretation.* Chicago: 1985.

McHugh, J. "A New Approach to the Infancy Narratives," *Marianum* 40 (1978), 277-87.
McKenzie, John L. *Dictionary of the Bible.* Milwaukee: 1965.
McNamara, M. "Were the Magi Essenes?," *Irish Ecclesiastical Record* 110 (1968), 305-28.
Mead, G. R. S. *Apollonius of Tyana, the Philosopher-Reformer of the First Century A.D.* London: 1901.
Medlycott, A. E. *India and the Apostle Thomas.* London: 1905.
Memigliano, Arnaldo. *Alien Wisdom: the Limits of Hellenization.* Cambridge: 1976.
Messina, Giuseppe. *Cristianesimo, Buddhismo, Manicheismo nell'Asia antica.* Rome: 1947.
Milinda's Questions. Trans. I. B. Horner in Vol. XXII of SBB. London: 1963.
Miller, J. Innes. *The Spice Trade of the Roman Empire, 29 B.C. to A.D. 641.* Oxford: 1969.
Milton, H. "The Structure and the Prologue of Matthew's Gospel," *Journal of Biblical Literature* 81 (1962), 175-81.
Mingana, A. "The Early Spread of Christianity in India," *JRLB*, 10 (1926), 435-514.
Mitchell, Charles W., trans. *S. Ephraim's Prose Refutations of Mani, Marcion, and Bardaisan.* London: 1912 & 1921. 2 vols.
Mitra, Rajendralala. *The Lalitavistara.* Calcutta: 1987.
Mookerji, Radha Kumud. *Asoka.* Delhi: 1972.
——. *Indian Shipping: A History of the Sea-borne Trade and Maritime Activity of the Indians from the Earliest Times.* 2nd rev. ed. Bombay: 1957.
Müller, F. Max. *Last Essays,* 1st ser. London: 1901.
——. *The Science of Language.* New York: 1891. Vol. I.
——. *The Six Systems of Indian Philosophy.* London: 1919.
——. *The Upanishads.* [Vol. I of SBE.] Oxford: 1900.
——. *India, What Can It Teach Us?* London: 1882.

Nanamoli, Bhikku. *The Life of the Buddha* Kandy: 1972.
Narain, A. K. *The Indo-Greeks.* Oxford: 1957.
Neusner, Jacob, ed. *The Study of Ancient Judaism.* New York: 1981.
——. "Excursus," *History of Religions,* Nov., 1966, 176-77.
——. *From Testament to Torah.* Englewood Cliffs: 1988.
——. *Midrash and Literature: The Primacy of Documentary Discourse.* Lanham: 1987.
——. *Midrash in Context: Exegesis in Formative Judaism.* Atlanta: 1988.
——. *The Systemic Analysis of Judaism.* Atlanta: 1988.
——. "The Word and the World: Midrash Literature and Theology," *Religious Studies and Theology* 7 (1987), 48-58.
Northrop, F. S. C. *The Meeting of East and West.* New York: 1960.
Notovitch, Nicholas. *The Unknown Life of Christ,* trans. Alexina Loranger. Chicago: 1894.
Nyanatiloka. *Buddhist Dictionary.* Colombo: 1956.

Ojha, K. C. *The History of Foreign Rule in Ancient India.* Allahabad: 1968.
Oldenberg, H. *Buddha,* 6th ed.; English translation by William Hoey. London: 1882.
Oman, John Campbell. *The Mystics, Ascetics, and Saints of India.* 2d ed. London: 1905.
Origen. *Contra Celsum.* Introduction by Henry Chadwick. Cambridge: 1953.
——. *De Principiis.* Trans. G. W. Butterworth as Origen on First Principles. London: 1936.
Ort, L. J. R. "Jesus and Mani—a Comparison," *SHR* [suppl. to Num. XVIII]. Leiden: 1969.
Osborne, Arthur. *Buddhism and Christianity in the Light of Hinduism.* London: 1959.

Pagels, Elaine. *The Gnostic Gospels.* New York: 1981.
Palmer, J. A. JB. "Periplus Maris Erythraei: the Indian Evidence as to the Date," *CQ,* 41 (1947), 136-40.
Panchatantra. Trans. Franklin Edgerton. London: 1965.

Panchatantra. Trans. Johannes Hertel, ed. Charles R. Lanman. [Vol. XI of HOS.] Cambridge, Mass.: 1908.
Panchatantra. Trans. Theodor Benfey. Leipzig: 1859.
Parrinder, Geoffrey. *Avatar and Incarnation.* New York: 1982.
Pawlicki, Stephan. *Der Ursprung des Christentums.* Mainz: 1885.
Pearson, Lionel. "The Diary and the Letters of Alexander the Great," *His,* III (1954), 429-59.
Pearson, Lionel. *The Lost Histories of Alexander the Great.* New York: 1960.
Pelikan, Jaroslav. *The Christian Tradition: a History of the Development of Doctrine.* I: The Emergence of the Catholic Tradition (100-600). Chicago: 1971.
Periplus of the Erythraean Sea. Trans. Wilfred H. Schoff. New York: 1912.
Perry, Ben Edwin, ed. & trans. *Babrius and Phaedrus.* Loeb Library; Cambridge, Mass.: 1965.
Peters, F. E. *The Harvest of Hellenism.* New York: 1970.
Philipps, W. R. "The Connection of St. Thomas the Apostle with India," *IA,* XXXII (1903), 1-15.
Philo Judaeus. "The Contemplative Life," trans. F. H. Colson in *Philo.* Loeb Library; Cambridge, Mass.: 1960. Vol. IX.
Philostratus. *The Life of Apollonius of Tyana.* Trans. F. C. Conybeare. Loeb Library; London: 1912. 2 vols.
Pillai, V. Kanakasabhai. *The Tamils Eighteen Hundred Years Ago.* Madras: 1966. [Originally published 1904.]
Pischel. "Der Ursprung des christlichen Fischsymbols." in *SBA,* 1905, 506f.
Pischel. "Indische Religionen." in Brockhaus, *Konversations-Lexikon,* XVII, 594. 14th ed.
Pischel. *Leben und Lehre des Buddha;* 2d ed. by H. Lüders. Leipzig: 1910.
Pliny. *Natural History.* Trans. H. Rackham. Loeb Library; Cambridge, Mass.: 1947. 10 vols.
Plotinus. *Complete Works.* Trans. Kenneth S. Guthrie. London: 1918.
Plotinus. *The Essential Plotinus.* Trans. Elmer O'Brien. New York: 1964.
Plutarch. "Life of Alexander," in *Plutarch's Lives.* Trans. Bernadotte Perrin. Loeb Library; London: 1949. Vol. VII.
Plutarch. *The Lives of the Noble Grecians and Romans.* Trans. John Dryden & rev. Arthur H. Clough. Philadelphia: 1908-09.
Polotsky, Hans J., trans. *Kephalaia.* [Vol. I, Part I of *MHSMB.*] Stuttgart: 1940.
Porphyry. "Life of Plotinos," in K. S. Guthrie, *Plotinos. Complete Works.* London: 1918.
Porphyry. *On Abstinence from Animal Food.* Trans. Thomas Taylor, ed. Esme Wynne-Tyson. London: 1965.
Pothan, S. G. *The Syrian Christians of Kerala.* New York: 1963.
Poussin, Louis de la Vallée. "Adibuddha." In *ERE,* I, 93 f.
Poussin, Louis de la Vallée. "L'Histoire des religions de l'Inde et l'apologétique." In *Revue des sciences philosophiques et theologiques,* 1912.
Poussin, Louis de la Vallée. "Le Bouddhisme et les Evangiles canoniques à propos d'une publication récente." in *Revue biblique,* July 1906.
Przyluski, Jean. "Indian Influence on Western Thought before and during the Third Century A.D.," *JGIS,* I (1934), 1-10.
Puri, B. N. *India under the Kushans.* Bombay: 1965.

Quispel, Gilles. "Gnosticism and the New Testament," *VC,* 19 (1965), 65-85.

Radhakrishnan, Sarvepalli. *Eastern Religions and Western Thought.* Oxford: 1939.
Radhakrishnan, Sarvepalli. *Indian Philosophy.* London: 1923-27. 2 vols.
Radhakrishnan, Sarvepalli. trans. *The Principal Upanishads.* London: 1953.
Ramayana. Trans. H. P. Shastri. London: 1976.
Rawlinson, H. G. "India in European Literature and Thought," in G. T. Garratt, ed., *The Legacy of India,* 1-37. Oxford: 1937.

Reicke, Bo. "Traces of Gnosticism in the Dead Seas Scrolls?" *NTS*, I (1954-55), 137-41.
Reynolds, Frank E. *Guide to Buddhist Religion*. Boston: 1981.
Rig Veda. Trans. Ralph T. H. Griffith as *The Hymns of the Rigveda*. Benares: 1897.
Ringgren, Helmer. "Qumran and Gnosticism," *OG*, 379-88. Leiden: 1970.
Ringgren, Helmer. *The Faith of Qumran*. Trans. Emilie T. Sander. Philadelphia: 1963.
Roberts, Alexander, and Donaldson, James. Anti-Nicene Christian Library. Edinburgh: 1860's-1880's.
Robinson, Charles A., Jr. *The Ephemerides of Alexander's Expedition*. Providence: 1932.
Robinson, James M., ed. *The Nag-Hammadi Library*. San Francisco: 1977.
Röhr, Heinz. "Buddha und Jesus in ihren Gleischnissen," *Jeue Zeitschrift für Systematische Theologie und Religionsphilosophie*, 15.65-86.
Röhr, Heinz. "Buddhismus und Christentum: Untersuchung zur Typologie zweier Weltreligionen," *ZRGG*, 25 (1973), 289-303.
Rudolph, Kurt. "Gnosis und Gnostizismus, ein Forschungsbericht," *ThR*, 34 (1969), 121-75 & 181-231; 36 (1971), 89-124; 37 (1972), 289-360.
Rudolph, Kurt. *Gnosis: The Nature and History of Gnosticism*. New York: 1984.

Saeki, P. Y. *The Nestorian Documents and Relics in China*. Tokyo: 1951.
Sastri, K. A. Nilakanta. *Cultural Expansion of India*. Gauhati: 1959.
Schenke, Hans-Martin. "Das Problem der Beziehung zwischen Judentum und Gnosis," *Kai*, 7 (1965), 124-33.
Schoff, Wilfred H. "First Century Intercourse Between India and Rome." In *Monist*, XXII, Jan. 1912.
Schoff, Wilfred. H., trans. *The Periplus of the Erythraean Sea*. New York: 1912.
Scholem, Gershom G. *Jewish Gnosticism, Merkabah Mysticism and Talmudic Tradition*. New York: 1960.
Scholes, Robert. *Textual Power*. New Haven: 1985.
Schopenhauer, Arthur. *Sämmtliche Werke*. Ed. Wolfgang von Löhneysen. Stuttgart: 1960.
Schopenhauer, Arthur. *The Essential Schopenhauer*. London: 1962.
Schultz, H. J. *Jesus in His Time*. Philadelphia: 1971.
Schwarz, Franz F. "Arrian's *Indike* on India: Intention and Reality," *E & W*, 25 (1975), 181-200.
Schwarz, Franz F. "Candragupta-Sandrakottos; eine historische Legende in Ost und West," *Alt*, 18 (1972), 85-102.
Scott, Archibald. *Buddhism and Christianity, a Parallel and a Contrast*. Edinburgh: 1890.
Sedlar, Jean. *India and the Greek World*. Totowa: 1980.
Seydel, Rudolf. *Das Evangelium von Jesu in seinen Verhältnissen zu Buddha-Sage und Buddha-Lehre*. Leipzig: 1882.
Seydel, Rudolf. *Die Buddha-Legende und das Leben Jesu nach den Evangelien*. Leipzig: 1884.
Siegmund, Georg. *Buddhismus und Christentum*. Frankfurt: 1968.
Smith, K. F. "Ages of the World (Greek and Roman)," in *ERE*, I (1908).
Smith, Vincent A. *Asoka, the Buddhist Emperor of India*. Oxford: 1901, 1909, 1920.
Smith, Vincent A. "The Indian Travels of Apollonius of Tyana," *ZDMG* (1914), 329-44.
Smith, Vincent A. *The Oxford History of India*. Ed. Percival Spear. 3rd ed. Oxford: 1958.
Stallknecht, Newton P., and Frenz, Horst. *Comparative Literature: Method and Perspective*. Carbondale: 1971.
Staton, Shirley F. *Literary Theories in Praxis*. Philadelphia: 1987.
Stendahl, K. *The School of St. Matthew and Its Use of the Old Testament*. Philadelphia: 1968.
Sterling Berry, T. *Christianity and Buddhism: A Comparison and Contrast*. London: 1890.
Strabo. *Geography*. Trans. Horace L. Jones. Loeb Library; Cambridge, Mass. 8 vols.
Strack and Billerbeck, *Kommentar zum Neuen Testament aus Talmud und Midrasch*. Munich, 1922-26.

Sutta-Nipata, or Discourse Collection. Trans. Lord Chalmers. [Vol. 37 of *HOS.*] Cambridge, Mass.: 1932.
Sutta-Nipata. Trans. E. M. Hare as *Woven Cadences of Early Buddhists.* [Vol. XV of *SBB.*] London: 1945.
Suzuki, D. T. *Outlines of Mahayana Buddhism.* New York: 1963. [Originally published 1907.]

Tacitus. *The Annals of Imperial Rome.* Trans. Michael Grant. Baltimore: 1956.
Talbert, C. H. "The Birth of the Messiah: A Review Article," *Perspectives in Religious Studies* 5 (1978), 212-16.
Tarn, William W. "Alexander the Great and the Unity of Mankind," *PBA,* 19 (1933), 123-66.
Tarn, William W. *Alexander the Great. I: Narrative. II: Sources and Studies.* Cambridge: 1948 & 1950.
Tarn, William W. *The Greeks in Bactria and India.* Cambridge: 1951.
Tatum, W. B. "'The Origin of Jesus Messiah' (Matt. 1, 1.18a). Matthew's Use of the Infancy Traditions," *Journal of Biblical Literature* 96 (1977), 523-35.
Tessitori, L. P. "Two Jaina Versions of the Story of Solomon's Judgment." In *Indian Antiquary,* 1913.
Thapar, Romila. *Asoka and the Decline of the Mauryas.* Oxford: 1961.
Theissen, Gerd. *Sociology of Early Palestinian Christianity.* Philadelphia: 1985.
Theodoret. *Ecclesiastical History.* London: 1843.
Thomas, Edward J. *The History of Buddhist Thought.* London: 1933.
Thomas, Edward J. *The Life of Buddha as Legend and History.* London: 1927.
Thompson, Stith. *The Folktale.* New York: 1946.
Thomson, James Oliver. *History of Ancient Geography.* New York: 1965.
Thucydides. *The History of Peloponnesian War.* Oxford: 1960.
Thundy, Zacharias. "The Egyptian Osiris-Myth and the Tamil *Cilappadikaram,*" *Tamil Civilization* 1 (1983), 83-90.
Thundy, Zacharias P. "Intertextuality Buddhism and the Infancy Gospels," in *Religious Writings and Religious Systems.* ed., Jacob Neusner et al. Vol. 1. Atlanta: 1989, 17-73.
Tisserant, Eugène. *Eastern Christianity in India.* Trans. E. R. Hambye. Bombay: 1957.
Tracy, David. *The Analogical Imagination: Christian Theology and the Culture of Pluralism.* New York: 1981.
———. "Creativity in the Interpretation of Religion," *New Literary History* 15 (1983-84): 289-309.

Upanishads. Trans. S. Radhakrishnan as *The Principal Upanishads.* London: 1953.

Van den Bergh van Eysinga, G. A. *Die holländische radikale Kritik des Neuen Testaments.* Jena: 1912.
Van den Bergh van Eysinga, G. A. *Indische Einflüsse auf evangelische Erzählungen,* 2d ed. Göttingen: 1909.
Vermes, Geza, trans. *The Dead Sea Scrolls in English.* New York: 1962.

Waley, Arthur, trans. "Hymn of the Soul" ["Hymn of the Pearl"], in *The Secret History of the Mongols.* London: 1963.
Warder, A. K. *Indian Buddhism.* Delhi: 1980.
Warmington, Eric H. *The Commerce between the Roman Empire and India.* Cambridge: 1928.
Warren, Henry Clarke. *Buddhism in Translations.* Cambridge, Mass.: 1896.
Watters, Thomas. *On Yuan Chwang's Travels in India.* London: 1904-05. 2 vols.
Weber, Albrecht. "Die Griechen in Indien." In *SBA,* 1890, 832.
Wecker, O. *Christus und Buddha.* 3d ed. Münster i. Westf., 1910.
Wecker, O. *Lamaismus und Katholizismus;* ein Vortrag. Rottenburg a. N., 1910.

Welles, Charles Bradford. *Alexander and the Hellenistic World.* Toronto: 1970.
Wenzel, H. "Coincidences in Buddhist Literature and the Gospels." In *Academy,* Jan. 12, 1889.
Wheeler, Mortimer. *Civilizations of the Indus Valley and Beyond.* New York: 1966.
Wheeler, Mortimer. *Flames over Persepolis.* New York: 1968.
Wheeler, Mortimer. "Roman Contact with India, Pakistan and Afghanistan," *Aspects of Archaeology, Essays Presented to O. G. S. Crawford,* 345-73. London: 1951.
Wheeler, Mortimer. *Rome Beyond the Imperial Frontiers.* London: 1954.
Wilson, R. McL. *Gnosis and the New Testament.* Oxford: 1968.
Wilson, R. McL. "Gnostic Origins Again," *VC,* XI (1957), 93-110.
Wilson, R. McL. "Gnostic Origins," in *VC,* IX (1955), 193-211.
Wilson, R. McL. "Simon, Dositheus and the Dead Sea Scrolls," *ZRGG,* IX (1957), 21-30.
Wilson, R. McL. *The Gnostic Problem: a Study of the Relations between Hellenistic Judaism and the Gnostic Heresy.* London: 1958.
Windisch, Ernst. *Buddhas Geburt und die Lehre von der Seelenwanderung,* 195-222. Leipzig, 1908.
Windisch, Ernst. *Mara und Buddha.* Leipzig: 1895.
Winston, David. "The Iranian Component in the Bible, Apocrypha, and Qumran: A Review of the Evidence," *History of Religions,* Feb., 1966, 183-216.
Winter, P. "'Nazareth' and 'Jerusalem' in Luke chs I and II," *New Testament Studies* 3 (1956-57), 136-42.
Winter, P. "Some Observations on the Language in the Birth and Infancy Stories of the Third Gospel," *New Testament Studies* 1 (1954-55), 111-21.
Winternitz, M. *Geschichte der indischen Litteratur,* I, II. Leipzig: 1913.
Woodcock, George. *The Greeks in India.* London: 1966.
Wright, A. G. *The Literary Genre of Midrash.* Staten Island: 1967.

Yuan Chwang. *On Yuan Chwang's Travels in India.* Trans. Thomas Watters. London: 1904-05. 2 vols.

Zeller, Eduard. *A History of Greek Philosophy from the Earliest Period to the Time of Socrates.* Trans. S. F. Alleyne. London: 1881. 2 vols.
Zimmer, Heinrich. *Philosopies of India.* Ed. Joseph Campbell. London: 1951.

INDEX

Abhidharma 59
Abhinishkramanasutra 61, 81, 96
Acchariyabhutadhammasutta 85
Acts of Judas Thomas 253
Aeneid 19, 48
Aeons 203
Aesop's Fables 259
agaru 213
Agatharchides of Alexandria 237
ahalim 213
Ahasuerus 212
Ai Khanum 227
Ajivakas 231
Akkenapalli 240
Aleph 121
Alexander 218, 223, 242
alien soul 177
Allogenes 190
Alpha 121
Amore, Roy C. 8
Angels and Others at Birth 100-101
Angels at Conception 135
Anna 146
Annunciation of Birth by a Woman 113-114
Annunciation to the Husband 89-90
anti-Semitism 158
apes 213
Apocalypse of Adam 190
Apocalypse of Peter 189
Apocryphal Traditions 147
Apocryphon of John 203
Apollonius of Tyana 243, 250
Appellation of King 123
Apuleius 251
arché 219
Archons 192
Arimaspea, 218
Aristoxenos 219
Arrian 221
Artaxerxes Memnon 218
asamkheyas 220
Asita 107, 108, 116
Asita and Simeon 115-116
Askew Codex 176
Asoka 62, 242, 245
Assumption to Heaven 116-117
Asvaghosha 14, 90, 134
Augustine 67
Augustus 238, 248
avadanas 54
Avici 102

avidya 200
Babrius 259
Baby in Swaddling Clothes 108-109
Bactria 225, 227-229, 233
Baldensperger, Fernand 19
Bardaisanes 255
Barthes, Roland 29
Barygaza 239
Basham, A. L. 231
Basilides 76, 255
Baveru 217
Beal Samuel 16, 247
Bending Tree 110-111
Berlin Codex 176
Betaillon, Marcel 19
Bhagavadgita 199, 203
Bhagavat 58
bhakti 200
Bhiskshuni 55
Biographical Theory 151-154
Bodhisatva 235
Bødker, Laurits 261
Book of Kings 217
Book of the Laws 253
brahmavidya 204
Brhadaranyaka Upanishad 196, 220
Brown, W. Norman 153
Bruce Codex 176
Buddha 53 (passim)
Buddha of faith 53
Buddha of history 53
Buddhacarita 62, 90
Buddhavacana 59
Buddhavamsa 80
Buddhism 53
Burnouf, Émile 2
Callisthenes of Olynthus 223
camphor 239
Canonical Gospels 147
Carpocrates 176
Carré, Jean-Marie 19
Cave, Terence 31
chandana 213
Chandragupta 225
Christ of faith 56
Christ of history 56
Chronicles of Ceylon 64
Chronology of Buddhist Scriptures 53
Chronology of Christian Scriptures 56
Cicero 232
Cilappadikaram 239
Cinnamon 242

Clearchos 232
Cleitarchus of Colophon 224
Clement of Alexandria 67, 176, 243
Clement of Rome 254
clover 239
cloves 239
Collins, Raymond 66
Comparative literature 18-20
Conze, Edward 15, 76, 234
Ctesias 218
Daimachos 225
Daniélou, Jean 177
Davids, Rhys 261
de Bunsen, Ernst 2
De la Vallée Poussin, Louis 4
Deconstructionism 20-26
Demetrius of Phaleron 259
Derrett, Duncan 75
Descent into Hell 149-151
Devadaha 92
Devatideva 111
Dhammapada 235
dharma 58, 83
Dharma 242
Dibelius, Martin 151
Didache 68
Dighabhanakas 59
Dighanikaya 81
Dio Chrysostom 247
Diogenes Laërtius 233, 252
Dipavamsa 54, 60
Discourse on the Eighth and the Nineth 195
Dream Vision 87, 135
Dvapara 220
Earthquakes and the Redemption of the Dead from Hell 101
Edmunds, Albert J. 3
Eightfold Path 55
Emperor Kanishka 63
Ephrem 176
Epiphanius 176
Eratosthenes 226, 237
ethics 163
ethnos 162
ethos 163
Eurocentrism 10
Eusebius 67, 176, 219
Fables 258
Fall of Idols 111-112
First Council 59
Flavius Josephus 233
Gandhara 229, 235
gandharva 58
Gandhi, Mahatma 11
Garbe, Richard 4

Gargi Samhita 256
Gaudapada 197
Gautama Buddha 220, (passim)
Genealogy and Royal Origin 132
Geographica 226
Ghata Jataka 97
Gibbon, Edward 41
Girnar Edict 245
Gita 200
Giving of Gifts 114
Gnosis 195
Gnostic 176
Gnosticism 175-211
Goddard, Dwight 6
Gordianus III 251
Gospel of Thomas 194
Great Council 60
Growing Up 126-127
gunas 199
Guyard, M. F. 19
gymnosophists 230, 232, 244, 251
Halbfass, Wilhelm 252
Harrowing of Hell 101-105
Hazard, Paul 19
Healing Miracles 112-113
Hecateus of Miletus 218
Hegel 10
Hegesippus 176
Heidegger, Martin 156
Hellenism 173, 175, 224
Herakleites of Ephesus 219
Hereford, R. T. 167
Hesiod 45
Hinayana 78, 79
Hipparchus 226
Hippokleides 258
Hippolytus 176, 207, 255, 265
Historical School 18
History 218
Hsüan-tsang 233
Ignatius of Antioch 67
Illumination of Hearts 116
infancy gospels 75
Infant Prodigy 120-122
Intertextuality 29-44
Ireneus of Lyons 176
Isvara 198
jamitra 257
Jatakas 81
Jesus Christ 56
Jesus movement 161
jnana 200
Jong, Erica 43
Kalanos 232
Kali 220
Kalinga 242

INDEX

Kaliyuga 220
Kanishka 234
Kapila 198
karma 200
Klimkeit, Hans J. 234
Knox, John 69
Koester, Helmut 185
Krishna 96, 97, (passim)
Kristeva, Julia 29
Krta 220
Kushanas 228, 234
Lalitavistara 2, 86, 89, 105, 133, 159, 202, (passim)
Levitation 148
Libyan fables 263
Lillie, Arthur 2
Literary Relationship 44-52
Lost and Found 118-119
Lotus Sutra 204
Lucan Annunciation 140
MacGregor, Geddes 175
Magis' Visit 122-123
Mahabharata 247
mahakalpa 220
Mahamangala Sutta 64
Mahaniddesa 248
Mahapadana Suttanta 79, 80
Mahaprajapati and Mary 124-125
Mahapurusha 58
Mahasanghika school 60
Mahasanghikas 77
Mahavamsa 54, 60, 65, 246
Mahavastu 80, 136
Mahayana 79
Mahayana movement 77
Mahayana texts 75
Mahayana Traditions 75
mahayuga 220
Mahosadha Jataka 216
Maitreya 235
Maitri Upanishad 255
Majjhimabhanakas 59
Majjhimanikaya 107
Malabar coast 253
Manger, Taxes, Holy Innocents, and Exile 96-100
Mani 235
Marcion 176
Marsanes 190
Martyr, Justin 67
Marvelous Light/Star 106-108
Massacre of the Innocents 138-140
Masters in Mothers' Wombs 91-92
Mauryas 233
McGann, Jerome 17
Megasthenes 225, 232

metempsychosis 219
midrash 32, 167
Midrash Rabbah 261
Milindapanha 76, 225, 248
Mill, John 67
Mother-Son Dialogue 119-120
Mulasarvastivada 235
Müller, Max 6, 154
Nag-Hammadi 176
Naming Ceremony 109
Nature Miracle 105-106
New Covenant 129
new historicism 26-29
New School 20
New Testament 129, 156
Nidanakatha 61, 87
nirvana 61, 230
Odes of Solomon 103
Old Covenant 129
Old Testament 129, 156
Old Wisdom School 78
Old Women 117-118
Onesikritos 231
Ophir 213
Orientalism 156-160
Origen 67, 176
Oxyrhyncus 211, 246, 265
Pagels Elaine 179, 210
Pancha Siddhantika 257
Panchatantra 216
Papias 67
Parable of the Sower 159
paramatman 198
Paraphrase of Shem 190
paribhajakas 243
Parinirvana 77
Patrocles 237
Paulika siddhanta 257
pax romana 238
Periplus of the Erithraean Sea 238
Persian Empire 212
Peutinger Table 239
Pfeiderer, Otto 2
Phaedrus 259
Philo 251
Philo Judaeus 244
Philostratos 244, 250
Piercing of Heart 116
plagiarism 18
Pliny 218, 238, 240, 241, 249
Pliny the Younger 56
Plotinus 251
Plutarch 231
Polycarp 67
Pomponius Mela 238
prakrti 199

Pre-existence 79-81, 130
Preparing the Way 125-126
Presentation in the Temple 114-115, 143
Prudentius 255
Pseudo-Callisthenes 224
Ptolemy II 237
Ptolemy IV 237
Purusha 199
Puteoli 241
Pyrrhon of Ellis 233
Pythagoras 222, 244
Pythagorean Brotherhood 221
Q-source 8
Rabbi Gamaliel 164
Radhakrishnan 8, 200
MacRae 177
rajas 199
Ramayana 247, 248, 259
Rawlinson 229
Reference to signs 127-128
religious endogamy 13
religious narcissism 13
Righteous Fosterfather 96
Rock Edict XIII 83
Roddier, Henri 19
Romaka siddhanta 257
Royal origin and geneaology 81-83
Rudolph, Kurt 187
Rutherford, W. G. 266
Sakyamunibuddhacarita 61
samanaioi 233
Samkhya system 198
sandalon 213
sangha 55, 58
sannyasi 247
sannyasins 230
Sarvastivada School 63
sati 232
satkaryavada 199
sattva 199
Schenke, Hans Martin 186
Schopenhauer, Arthur 1
Second Council 59
Sedlar, Jean 229, 236, 240, 264
Seleucus Nicator 224
Seven Steps 106
Seydel, Rudolf 2
siddhantas 257
Sigalovada Suttanta 64
Simon Magus 180, 194
skandhas 255
Socrates 219, 237
Solomon 214
sramana 55
sramanacharya 249

sramanas 230
sravaka 55
Stein, Sir Aurel 235
Strabo 232, 238, 248
Sudhodana 53
sutradharas 59
Sutta Nipata 64, 143
Svetasvatara 198
Tacitus 56
Talmud 167, 261
tamas 199
Taming of Wild Animals 109-110
Tatian 67
Tertullian 176, 254
Therapeutae of Alexandria 244-250
Third Council 60
Thomas, Edward J. 6
Thucydides 16
Tiberius 240
Torah 129, 156
Toy Cart 257
Tracy, David 22
Treta 220
Tripitaka 59, 60, 64, 71
Turmoil at Birth 90-91
Universal Salvation 83-84, 132
upasaka 55
Vajrapani 235
Valentinus 176
van Baaren, T. P. 178
van den Bergh van Eysinga, G.A. 2
Van Tieghten, Paul 19
Vinaya 237
Virginal Conception 132
virginitas ante partum 84
virginitas in partu 92-95, 134
Virginitas post partum 135
Virginity —post partum 95
Visitation 141
von Campenhausen, Hans 69
white elephant 87
white lotus 87
Wilson, Robert McL. 180
Windisch, Ernst 3
Winternitz 258
Works and Days 220
Yaksha 58
Yasodhara 54
yavanika 257
Zarmanochegas 249, 264
Zeller 222
Zostrianos, 190

STUDIES IN THE HISTORY OF RELIGIONS
NUMEN BOOKSERIES

4 *The Sacral Kingship/La Regalità Sacra.* Contributions to the Central Theme of the VIIIth International Congress for the History of Religions, Rome 1955. 1959. ISBN 90 04 01609 0

8 K.W. Bolle. *The Persistence of Religion.* An Essay on Tantrism and Sri Aurobindo's Philosophy. Repr. 1971. ISBN 90 04 03307 6

11 E.O. James. *The Tree of Life.* An Archaeological Study. 1966.
ISBN 90 04 01612 0

12 U. Bianchi (ed.). *The Origins of Gnosticism.* Colloquium Messina 13-18 April 1966. Texts and Discussions. Reprint of the first (1967) ed. 1970.
ISBN 90 04 01613 9

14 J. Neusner (ed.). *Religions in Antiquity.* Essays in Memory of Erwin Ramsdell Goodenough. Reprint of the first (1968) ed. 1970. ISBN 90 04 01615 5

16 E.O. James. *Creation and Cosmology.* A Historical and Comparative Inquiry. 1969. ISBN 90 04 01617 1

17 *Liber Amicorum.* Studies in honour of Professor Dr. C.J. Bleeker. Published on the occasion of his retirement from the Chair of the History of Religions and the Phenomenology of Religion at the University of Amsterdam. 1969.
ISBN 90 04 03092 1

18 R.J.Z. Werblowsky & C.J. Bleeker (eds.). *Types of Redemption.* Contributions to the Theme of the Study-Conference held at Jerusalem, 14th to 19th July 1968. 1970. ISBN 90 04 01619 8

19 U. Bianchi, C.J. Bleeker & A. Bausani (eds.). *Problems and Methods of the History of Religions.* Proceedings of the Study Conference organized by the Italian Society for the History of Religions on the Occasion of the Tenth Anniversary of the Death of Raffaele Pettazzoni, Rome 6th to 8th December 1969. Papers and discussions. 1972. ISBN 90 04 02640 1

20 K. Kerényi. *Zeus und Hera.* Urbild des Vaters, des Gatten und der Frau. 1972.
ISBN 90 04 03428 5

21 *Ex Orbe Religionum.* Studia G. Widengren. Pars prior. 1972.
ISBN 90 04 03498 6

22 *Ex Orbe Religionum.* Studia G. Widengren. Pars altera. 1972.
ISBN 90 04 03499 4

23 J.A. Ramsaran. *English and Hindi Religious Poetry.* An Analogical Study. 1973.
ISBN 90 04 03648 2

25 L. Sabourin. *Priesthood.* A Comparative Study. 1973. ISBN 90 04 03656 3

26 C.J. Bleeker. *Hathor and Thoth.* Two Key Figures of the Ancient Egyptian Religion. 1973. ISBN 9004 03734 9
27 J.W. Boyd. *Satan and Māra.* Christian and Buddhist Symbols of Evil. 1975. ISBN 9004 04173 7
28 R.A. Johnson. *The Origins of Demythologizing.* Philosophy and Historiography in the Theology of R. Bultmann. 1974. ISBN 9004 03903 1
29 E. Berggren. *The Psychology of Confession.* 1975. ISBN 9004 04212 1
30 C.J. Bleeker. *The Rainbow.* A Collection of Studies in the Science of Religion. 1975. ISBN 9004 04222 9
31 C.J. Bleeker, G. Widengren & E.J. Sharpe (eds.). *Proceedings of the 12th International Congress, Stockholm 1970.* 1975. ISBN 9004 04318 7
32 A.-Th. Khoury (ed.), M. Wiegels. *Weg in die Zukunft.* Festschrift für Prof. Dr. Anton Antweiler zu seinem 75. Geburtstag. 1975. ISBN 9004 05069 8
33 B.L. Smith (ed.). *Hinduism.* New Essays in the History of Religions. Repr. 1982. ISBN 9004 06788 4
34 V.L. Oliver, *Caodai Spiritism.* A Study of Religion in Vietnamese Society. With a preface by P. Rondot. 1976. ISBN 9004 04547 3
35 G.R. Thursby. *Hindu-Muslim Relations in British India.* A Study of Controversy, Conflict and Communal Movements in Northern India, 1923-1928. 1975. ISBN 9004 04380 2
36 A. Schimmel. *Pain and Grace.* A Study of Two Mystical Writers of Eighteenth-century Muslim India. 1976. ISBN 9004 04771 9
37 J.T. Ergardt. *Faith and Knowledge in Early Buddhism.* An Analysis of the Contextual Structures of an Arahant-formula in the Majjhima-Nikāya. 1977. ISBN 9004 04841 3
38 U. Bianchi. *Selected Essays on Gnosticism, Dualism, and Mysteriosophy.* 1978. ISBN 9004 05432 4
39 F.E. Reynolds & Th. M. Ludwig (eds.). *Transitions and Transformations in the History of Religions.* Essays in Honor of Joseph M. Kitagawa. 1980. ISBN 9004 06112 6
40 J.G. Griffiths. *The Origins of Osiris and his Cult.* 1980. ISBN 9004 06096 0
41 B. Layton (ed.). *The Rediscovery of Gnosticism.* Proceedings of the International Conference on Gnosticism at Yale, New Haven, Conn., March 28-31, 1978. Two vols.
   1. *The School of Valentinus.* 1980. ISBN 9004 06177 0
   2. *Sethian Gnosticism.* 1981. ISBN 9004 06178 9
42 H. Lazarus-Yafeh. *Some Religious Aspects of Islam.* A Collection of Articles. 1980. ISBN 9004 06329 3
43 M. Heerma van Voss, D.J. Hoens, G. Mussies, D. van der Plas & H. te Velde (eds.). *Studies in Egyptian Religion, dedicated to Professor Jan Zandee.* 1982. ISBN 9004 06728 0
44 P.J. Awn. *Satan's Tragedy and Redemption.* Iblīs in Sufi Psychology. With a foreword by A. Schimmel. 1983. ISBN 9004 06906 2

45 R. Kloppenborg (ed.). *Selected Studies on Ritual in the Indian Religions.* Essays to D.J. Hoens. 1983. ISBN 9004071296
46 D.J. Davies. *Meaning and Salvation in Religious Studies.* 1984. ISBN 9004070532
47 J. H. Grayson. *Early Buddhism and Christianity in Korea.* A Study in the Implantation of Religion. 1985. ISBN 9004074821
48 J. M. S. Baljon. *Religion and Thought of Shāh Walī Allāh Dihlawī, 1703-1762.* 1986. ISBN 9004076840
50 S. Shaked, D. Shulman & G. G. Stroumsa (eds.). *Gilgul.* Essays on Transformation, Revolution and Permanence in the History of Religions, dedicated to R.J. Zwi Werblowsky. 1987. ISBN 9004085092
51 D. van der Plas (ed.). *Effigies Dei.* Essays on the History of Religions. 1987. ISBN 9004086552
52 J. G. Griffiths. *The Divine Verdict.* A Study of Divine Judgement in the Ancient Religions. 1991. ISBN 9004092315
53 K. Rudolph. *Geschichte und Probleme der Religionswissenschaft.* 1991. ISBN 9004095039
54 A. N. Balslev & J. N. Mohanty (eds.). *Religion and Time.* 1993. ISBN 9004095837
55 E. Jacobson. *The Deer Goddess of Ancient Siberia.* A Study in the Ecology of Belief. 1993. ISBN 9004096280
56 B. Saler. *Conceptualizing Religion.* Immanent Anthropologists, Transcendent Natives, and Unbounded Categories. 1993. ISBN 9004095853
57 C. Knox. *Changing Christian Paradigms.* And their Implications for Modern Thought. 1993. ISBN 9004096701
58 J. Cohen. *The Origins and Evolution of the Moses Nativity Story.* 1993. ISBN 9004096523
59 S. Benko. *The Virgin Goddess.* Studies in the Pagan and Christian Roots of Mariology. 1993. ISBN 9004097473
60 Z. P. Thundy. *Buddha and Christ.* Nativity Stories and Indian Traditions. 1993. ISBN 9004097414

ISSN 0169-8834